8080/8085

Software Design

Book 1

by
**Christopher A. Titus, Peter R. Rony,
David G. Larsen, and Jonathan A. Titus**

Also published as

**8080/8085 Software Design
by E & L Instruments, Inc.**

Howard W. Sams & Co., Inc.
4300 WEST 62ND ST. INDIANAPOLIS, INDIANA 46268 USA

International Standard Book Number: 0-672-21541-1
Library of Congress Catalog Card Number: 78-57207

Printed in the United States of America.

Preface

Although it did not look like a revolution at the time, the Intel Corporation introduced the world to the concept of microprocessors and microcomputers with its four-bit 4004 microprocessor "chip." The microcomputer revolution gained momentum as improvements were made in earlier integrated circuits, and more and more manufacturers began to produce microprocessor integrated circuits and microcomputers. Now these devices, made from one of the chemical components of purified *sand*, have begun to truly change the way in which we live.

In the supermarket, the electronic cash register not only performs all of the tasks of its mechanical predecessor, but it can also perform inventory control. Some sewing machines no longer require complex gears and cams to do special stitches. Instead, a microcomputer controls the position of the needle when a particular stitch is used. In the near future, you will probably be able to even "teach" your sewing machine the latest stitch.

Instead of using a slide rule to perform complex calculations, calculators can be used that have more "power" than state-of-the-art computers produced 10 or 20 years ago. Watches no longer have to be wound, and, in fact, the terms *clockwise* and *counterclockwise* may soon be archaic. Today, you can even use a checkbook that electronically keeps track of how much money you have in your checking account. No longer do you have to balance your checkbook every month. In the not-too-distant future, microwave ovens may "know" more about cooking than you do.

Of course, to use a microcomputer to solve a problem requires both *hardware* and *software*. The hardware consists of the microprocessor integrated circuit(s) and possibly some memory integrated circuits, light-emitting diodes, and *interface* electronics so that the microcomputer can control *peripheral devices* (lights, motors, valves, solenoids, or gauges). The software consists of the sequence of instructions that the microcomputer executes so that it can process data or control peripheral devices. Unfortunately, the design and implementation of software is not as well defined as the design and implementation of hardware.

Some current microcomputer users program their microcomputers in the BASIC* programming language. To do this, a BASIC interpreter, an assembly language program, must be stored in from 5000 to 8000 memory locations. This assembly language program enables you to enter a BASIC program into the microcomputer and actually execute it. Like everything else in the world, there are advantages and disadvantages to programming a microcomputer in the BASIC language. Due to the disadvantages of using the BASIC language, *assembly language* is often used when programming microcomputers. This is the type of programming language that we will discuss in this book.

There is no doubt in our minds that assembly language is the more difficult of the two to teach and to learn. You cannot write an assembly language program in 10 or 15 minutes that will calculate the cube roots of all numbers between 1 and 1000 to six significant digits. Using the BASIC language, you probably could. However, there are advantages in using assembly language. In fact, many tasks can be performed using assembly language that cannot be performed using the BASIC language, particularly in the areas of process control, peripheral control, high-speed calculations, and real-time data acquisition. In fact, most consumer products that incorporate microcomputers are programmed in assembly language; video (television) games, microwave ovens, sewing machines, electronic cash registers (point-of-sale terminals), gasoline pumps, and blood-pressure monitors. Therefore, assembly language is a very powerful and useful language to learn.

In the first chapter of this book, we do not discuss any assembly language programming, but rather the characteristics of the 8080 and 8085 microprocessor integrated circuits. This includes a discussion of the various *registers* contained within these two integrated circuits. These registers are important because you will use them time and time again in your assembly language programs. The next three chapters deal with the assembly language instructions that the 8080 and 8085 can actually execute. You will not find long, detailed programs in these first few chapters, since you will not have enough familiarity with all of the important instructions to understand long,

---

* BASIC is a registered trademark of the trustees of Dartmouth College.

complex programs. When these instructions are understood, you can begin to program the microcomputer in assembly language so that it performs useful tasks. The remaining chapters of the book deal with the application of the 8080's assembly language instructions to mathematical operations, number-base conversions, and input/output device (peripheral device) control.

There are some unusual features of this book which we believe that you will appreciate. We have not included a chapter on binary, octal, hexadecimal, and decimal numbering systems. In some of the chapters, we do show you how some of these operations are performed using paper and pencil. However, we are personally more interested in the instruction sequence that the microcomputer must execute to perform these same operations. If you need more information on basic mathematical operations, you can find it in just about any other book on computer programming. You will also find that the programs in this book can be executed on just about any 8080-based microcomputer. We do not have hardware or software examples that feature one or another manufacturer's hardware. The program examples will execute equally well on a MITS, Processor Technology, Intel Corporation, National Semiconductor Corporation, Digital Group, Control Logic, IMS Associates, or E & L Instruments 8080-based microcomputer. Of course, peripheral devices may vary from system to system just as device addresses may vary from system to system.

In the Input/Output chapter (Chapter 7), we have included the electrical schematic diagrams for the devices that we are controlling with software. A software listing of a program that controls a peripheral device is *worthless* unless you can see how the peripheral device is actually wired (interfaced) to the microcomputer. Also, if you want to use a particular program on your own microcomputer, you will probably need the schematic diagram of the peripheral device in order to duplicate the hardware.

In the first three chapters of the book, we have included both octal and hexadecimal op codes for the instructions being discussed. We prefer the octal numbering system. We feel strongly that the op codes for the 8080's assembly language instructions are easier to remember in octal, and when you examine an octal op code, it is easy to determine the registers or memory locations that are af-ected by the instruction. If the hexadecimal numbering system is used, this process is very difficult. On the other hand, many programmers prefer the hexadecimal numbering system because they only have to remember a two-digit op code rather than a three-digit octal op code. The only conclusion that we could reach was to use both numbering systems in our examples. We recommend that a beginning 8080 or 8085 programmer use octal, simply because it is easier to remember. At a later time, it may be more convenient to use hexadecimal. If you are unsure of which numbering system to use, try both and stay with the numbering system that you are the most comfortable with. Hexadecimal numbers are usually found in the text bracketed with parentheses; e.g., (5F).

Another goal that we had was to provide detailed descriptive explanations of how the program examples operate. We do not say, "Here it is, you figure out how it works." You would learn very little if this approach were used. Instead, we *develop* programs, starting with the simplest sequence of instructions that can accomplish a particular task. These programs often have limitations, and if they do, we add instructions so that the microcomputer can better perform either a more general-purpose task or a specific task. Therefore, we *design* the best solution to a problem, learning from previous examples.

As you go through this book, you may notice that the computer printouts in the program examples are in a format that is different than the formats used by other authors. The reason that we have chosen the format that we have is so that newcomers to assembly language programming can grasp the *concepts* of assembly language programming. One of the most important concepts is the fact that multibyte instructions *must* be stored in consecutive memory locations. This concept is difficult to grasp if you look at the computer printouts used as examples in other books. For this reason, we have written a coresident editor/assembler (TEA) that produces the listings that we felt would be most appropriate to a book on assembly language programming. It is important to emphasize that once you learn the principles of good assembly language programming, it really does not matter what editor/assembler software package you use for assembly language program development. Remember, editors and assemblers are only the means to the end. They are just tools that are used to aid you in the development of a properly operating assembly language program.

One of the nice features of software is that it is easy to print and distribute. Because of this, a number of professional and hobbyist computer magazines provide listings and source and object paper tapes or audio cassettes for the programs in their software libraries. Software listings often appear in *Electronic Design, Computer Design,* and *Electronics.* The hobbyist magazines, *Interface Age* (McPheters, Wolfe & Jones, Cerritos, CA 90701), *SCCS Interface* (SCCS, Santa Monica, CA 90405), *Kilobaud* and *Byte* (both of Peterborough, NH 03458), and *Dr. Dobbs Journal of Computer Calisthenics and Orthodontia* (Menlo Park, CA 94025) also have numerous program listings. There are also a number of software libraries, including the Intel User's Library, 3065 Bowers Ave., Santa Clara, CA

95051, and the Microcomputer Software Depository, 2361 E. Foothill Blvd., Pasadena, CA 91107. Entries in the Depository are listed in *Interface Age* every month.

Tychon, Inc., is dedicated to educating the scientist, engineer, and electronics/computer hobbyist in the areas of digital electronics, microcomputer hardware, and microcomputer software. We currently have monthly columns that appear in *American Laboratory* (International Scientific Communications, Inc., 808 Kings Highway, Fairfield, CT 06430), the Thai publication, *Semiconductor Electronics Journal* (Science, Engineering and Education Co., Ltd., Bangkok, Thailand), and the German publication, *Elektroniker* (Burgdorf, Switzerland). Our columns also appear in *Electronic News* (IPC Business Press Pty. Ltd., Sydney, Australia), *Ham Radio* (Greenville, NH), *Computer Design* (Concord, MA), and *Radio-Electronics* (New York City, NY). Our books are currently being translated into Italian, German, French, Spanish, and Thai.

If you are interested in learning basic digital electronics, a two-volume set of books in the *Blacksburg Continuing Education Series*™, entitled *Logic & Memory Experiments Using TTL Integrated Circuits*, will introduce you to the subject and give you the ability to try student-proven experiments. Another book in the series, *Interfacing and Scientific Data Communications Experiments*, has been specifically written for those engineers, scientists, and hobbyists interested in asynchronous communications techniques using UARTs. This book includes experiments that will permit you to use asynchronous communications techniques to interface instrumentation to computers or other UART-based devices. Three books in the series have been written about the 8080 microprocessor/microcomputer: *The 8080A Bugbook®: Microcomputer Interfacing and Programming*, and a two-volume set, *Introductory Experiments in Digital Electronics and 8080A Microcomputer Programming and Interfacing*. These self-teaching texts describe the design of elementary interface hardware and software and how they are applied to probblems, the substitution of software for hardware, and many other interesting topics. One of our latest books, *Microcomputer—Analog Converter Software and Hardware Interfacing*, deals entirely with interfacing digital-to-analog and analog-to-digital converters to microcomputers. The number of titles in the *Blacksburg Continuing Education Series*™ grows constantly. They are listed on the inside front cover.

Many of the programming concepts that are presented in this book have been incorporated into the material taught at seminars

---

Bugbook is a registered trademark of E & L Instruments, Inc., Derby, CT 06418.

presented by Tychon, Inc., here in Blacksburg. Three courses are currently being taught: *Designing with Microcomputers (626)*, *Microprocessor Interfacing (628), and Software Design for the 8080/8085 Processors (690)*. If you are interested in these courses, write to The Course Director, Tychon, Inc., P.O. Box 242, Blacksburg, VA 24060. Courses are also provided through the Center for Continuing Education and the Extension Division at Virginia Polytechnic Institute and State University, Blacksburg, VA 24061. Call Dr. Linda Leffel at (703) 961-5241 for further information.

Again, we would like to thank Mr. Murray Gallant of E & L Instruments, Inc., for his continued support of our educational efforts.

CHRISTOPHER A. TITUS
PETER R. RONY
DAVID G. LARSEN
JONATHAN A. TITUS

Contents

CHAPTER 4

CHAPTER 5

CHAPTER 6

CHAPTER 7

List of Program Examples

° Not an executable example.

CHAPTER 3

---

* Not an executable example.

CHAPTER 4

CHAPTER 5

CHAPTER 6

° Not an executable example.

CHAPTER 7

1

An Introduction to the 8080/8085 Microprocessors

The purpose of this chapter is to introduce the 8080 and 8085 microprocessors and 8080- and 8085-based microcomputers to those readers who are unfamiliar with their operation. This introduction is detailed enough so that you will achieve an understanding of the operation of both the 8080 and the 8085 microprocessor integrated circuits and how each functions in a small computer system. However, do not expect to become an expert on these integrated circuits just by reading this chapter alone. For further information on the circuitry required to actually build a microcomputer using either the 8080 or 8085, please refer to the references at the end of this chapter.[1, 2, 3]

The 8080 microprocessor integrated circuit was introduced by the Intel Corporation in 1973. It evolved from an earlier microprocessor, also produced by Intel, the eight-bit 8008. Because the 8080 is now so popular, it is manufactured by a number of "second sources," including Advanced Micro Devices, Inc. (AMD), NEC Microcomputers, Inc. (NEC), Texas Instruments Inc. (TI), and National Semiconductor Corporation, among others. It is interesting to note that in just five years, the price of a single 8080 integrated circuit has dropped from $360 to only $10.

THE 8080 MICROPROCESSOR

The 8080 microprocessor integrated circuit may be used as the "heart" of a microcomputer system that can execute 72 different *types* of instructions. The total number of different instructions that the 8080 can execute is 244. The 8080 integrated circuit contains most of the control and decision-making logic, so only a few additional integrated circuits are required to configure a small microcomputer system. One of the functions of this additional control logic is to provide the 8080 with a two-phase, nonoverlapping clock with a voltage swing of from 0 to +12 volts. The 8080 also requires power supplies of +12, +5, and −5 volts. The other inputs to, and all the outputs from, the integrated circuit, aside from the two clock inputs, are compatible with standard transistor-transistor-logic (TTL) voltage levels.

Therefore, a small 8080 microcomputer is composed of a single 8080 integrated circuit and several supporting integrated circuits that provide not only the two-phase clock, but additional control signals. The control signals permit the 8080 to access memory integrated circuits, which contain instructions or data values; and input/output (I/O) devices, which the 8080 uses to communicate with the "outside world." The 8080 addresses memory with the aid of 16 address lines, which is equivalent to an addressing capability of 2^{16}, or 65,536 memory locations (64K). Each memory location can store a single eight-bit byte.

Data are transferred between the 8080 and either memory or I/O devices by means of an eight-bit bidirectional data bus. The actual flow of data between the 8080 and memory is controlled by two signals that are generated by the 8080. These signals are often called $\overline{\text{MEMORY}}$ $\overline{\text{READ}}$ ($\overline{\text{MR}}$ or $\overline{\text{MEMR}}$) and $\overline{\text{MEMORY}}$ $\overline{\text{WRITE}}$ ($\overline{\text{MW}}$ or $\overline{\text{MEMW}}$). When the 8080 reads instructions or data values from memory, it must provide both a 16-bit address on the *address bus* and also pulse the memory read line. The memory then transfers an eight-bit value to the 8080 over the bidirectional data bus. When the 8080 writes data to memory, the 8080 again provides a 16-bit address, but this time it places an eight-bit data byte on the bidirectional data bus and pulses the memory write line.

There are two basic types of memory integrated circuits that are used in most microcomputer systems. These are read/write (R/W) memory and read-only memory (ROM). If information must be stored in memory, but must at a later time be changed by the program, the information must be stored in R/W memory. In general, ROM is used to store program steps (instructions) and data values that will not be changed.

The 8080 also contains some internal R/W memory-like devices called *registers*. There are seven general-purpose registers. This means that the programmer can program the 8080 so that temporary data values, results from some computer operation, or even address information can be saved in these registers. Each register can contain eight bits of information. To make programming the 8080 easier, each register is assigned a single letter name: A, B, C, D, E, H, and L. The A register is also called the *accumulator*, since it can be used to "accumulate" the results of a mathematical or logical operation performed by the 8080. If an eight-bit value is contained in register A, it can be rotated to the left or right; this is not possible if the data value is contained in any of the other general-purpose registers. The A register is generally used to accept data from input devices such as keyboards, sensors, switches, or analog-to-digital converters. The content of the A register can also be output, under program control, to devices such as digital-to-analog converters, lamps, controllers, and printers.

There are five *flags* associated with the A register. These flags are set or cleared when one of the 8080's logical or mathematical instructions is executed. Three flags indicate the parity and the sign of the result and whether or not the result is zero. There are also two carry flags, the carry and auxiliary carry. Quite often, programmers refer to the eight-bit flag word (which really only contains five flags) and the A register together as the *processor status word*, or *PSW*. Perhaps the most important feature of the flags is the fact that the 8080 can be programmed to test the condition, or state, of one or more of these flags. Based on the results of these tests, the 8080 can decide whether or not to execute one or another sequence of instructions. The flags remain set or cleared until another mathematical or logical operation alters them.

There are three other important registers contained within the 8080 integrated circuit that deserve our attention. These are the *stack pointer* (SP), the *instruction register* (IR), and the *program counter* (PC). These registers are not general-purpose registers because they can only be used to perform specific tasks, and they cannot be used for the temporary storage of data.

The stack-pointer (SP) register is a 16-bit register that is used to store a 16-bit address generally associated with R/W memory. Instructions can be executed that cause the content of the general-purpose registers to be stored on the "stack." When this is done, the stack pointer provides the 8080 with an address so that the registers can be stored in R/W memory. Therefore, the stack, or stack area, is simply a section of R/W memory that is set aside for temporary storage. Address information can also be saved on the stack. For the stack to be useful, the stack pointer must be loaded with an address associated with R/W memory. The stack is particularly useful for storing *return*, or *linking*, addresses when subroutines are called within a program.

The 16-bit program counter (PC) and the eight-bit instruction register (IR) are closely related, since they actually control the sequential execution of a program. When instructions are executed, the instruction register actually determines what actions will take place and where data will flow from and to, both internally in the 8080 integrated circuit, and externally between memory and the 8080 and between peripheral devices and the 8080. The program counter is used to provide the memory address of the location in which the next instruction to be executed is stored. All of the registers that we have discussed, and many registers that we have not discussed, are shown in Fig. 1-1.

When the 8080 integrated circuit is *reset*, which is caused by grounding the RESET pin of the 8080 integrated circuit, the PC is cleared to all zeros. Since the PC always points to the memory location that contains the next instruction to be executed, the first instruction that the 8080 executes, after it is reset, must be in memory location zero. Therefore, after the 8080 is reset, the 16-bit content of the PC is placed on the 16-bit address bus, and the instruction that is contained in this memory location is fetched from memory and written into the eight-bit IR. The logic associated with the IR then decodes the instruction and decides what actions are required for the instruction to be executed. When the instruction is decoded, the 8080 may transfer data from one register to another, it may output data to a peripheral device, or it may test the condition of one of the flags contained in the flag word.

As instructions are fetched and executed, the PC is incremented so that it points to the memory location that contains the *next* instruction that is to be fetched from memory and executed. Not only can the PC be reset to all zeros and incremented, but it can also be loaded with a nonsequential 16-bit address. This loading operation is generally performed when the 8080 branches, or jumps, to instructions stored in another section of memory.

For more information about the circuitry required to generate the control signals that we have mentioned, and for more information concerning how a small microcomputer is actually built using an 8080 integrated circuit, please refer to *The 8080A Bugbook®: Microcomputer Interfacing and Programming*.[1]

How fast can the 8080 process data or communicate with peripheral devices? This will depend on the instructions that are executed. All instructions require a known amount of time to be executed, and not all instructions can be executed in the same amount of time. The speed at which the instructions are executed is determined by the frequency of the two-phase clock. The frequency of this clock may be between 2 MHz and 500 kHz. At a frequency of 2 MHz, the simplest instruction will be executed in two microseconds (2 μs), and the most complex instruction will require 9 μs. In general, most instructions require about 4 or 5 μs to be executed. The time re-

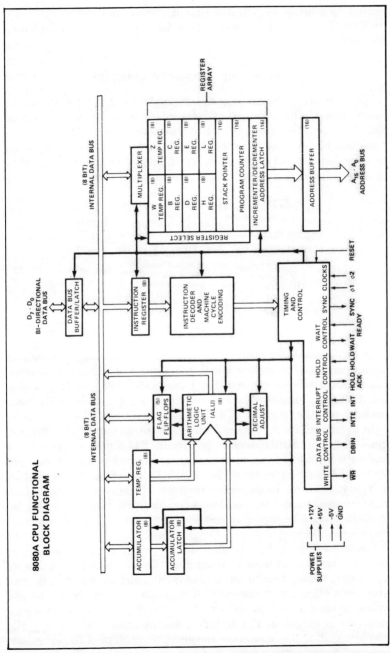

8080A CPU FUNCTIONAL BLOCK DIAGRAM

Courtesy Intel Corp.

Fig. 1-1. Block diagram of the 8080 microprocessor integrated circuit.

21

quired to execute each instruction is known, and these times are published in most of the 8080 manufacturers' literature concerning the 8080.

MACHINE AND ASSEMBLY LANGUAGE

To cause the 8080 to perform a specific task, the 8080 must be programmed. This means that a sequence of instructions must be stored in the 8080's memory, starting at address zero. These instructions can be saved in ROM or in R/W memory; it does not matter to the 8080 which type of memory is used. For example, an 8080 program stored in memory might appear as follows:

Example 1-1: A Typical 8080 Program

BINARY	OCTAL	HEXADECIMAL
00111100	074	3C
11111110	376	FE
10000000	200	80
11000010	302	C2
00101101	055	2D
00111000	070	38

In this example, the contents of six consecutive memory locations have been listed using the binary, octal, and hexadecimal numbering systems. This means that the numbers 00111100_2, 074_8, and $3C_{16}$ are all equal. Sometimes, an H subscript is used to denote a hexadecimal number, such as $3C_H$.

In its present form, it is very difficult to understand what this program does. The 8080 can actually execute 244 different instructions, and each instruction is represented by a different operation code, or *op code*. The op codes for all 244 instructions can be represented by a binary, octal, or hexadecimal number. It does not matter which numbering system you use. However, the proper sequence of instructions must be stored in memory so that the program executes correctly.

Unfortunately, it is very difficult to program the 8080 in this manner. You would have to remember the op codes for all 244 instructions. Rather than program the 8080 using such numbers, programmers often use *mnemonics*. A mnemonic is simply a symbolic abbreviation for an operation that the 8080 performs when an instruction is executed. For instance, the mnemonic INRA is really an abbreviation for "increment the eight-bit content of the A register by one." Several mnemonics, and the corresponding operations that the 8080 performs, are shown in Table 1-1.

Table 1-1. Some Typical Mnemonics and Operations

MNEMONIC	OPERATION(S)
DCRA	Decrement the eight-bit content of the A register.
JMP	Jump to another memory location and continue program execution at that memory location.
PUSHB	Save (push) register pair B on the stack.
XCHG	Exchange register pairs D and H.
OUT	Output the content of the A register to the specified peripheral device.

What are mnemonics used for? By looking at a mnemonic, it is easy for a programmer to visualize the operation that the 8080 is to perform. In Example 1-2, some 8080 mnemonics are listed along with the corresponding binary, octal, and hexadecimal op codes.

Example 1-2: Mnemonics and Op Codes for Several 8080 Instructions

BINARY	OCTAL	HEXADECIMAL	MNEMONIC
00111100	074	3C	INRA
11111110	376	FE	CPI
10000000	200	80	<DATA>
11000010	302	C2	JNZ
00101101	055	2D	<LO>
00111000	070	38	<HI>

Even though you may not know what these mnemonics mean, you probably now realize that it will be easier to "understand" a list of mnemonics than a list of binary, octal, or hexadecimal numbers.

Can you program an 8080 by saving mnemonics in memory? No. Only the binary op codes corresponding to the mnemonics may be stored in memory. Even octal and hexadecimal notations are "shorthand" for these binary codes. In reality, mnemonics are a programmer's "crutch." By writing a program in mnemonic form, it is easier to understand the sequence in which the instructions are executed and what their overall effect will be. However, the binary op codes for the instructions must still be stored in memory. Therefore, the programmer must translate the mnemonics into the proper op codes. There are a number of methods that can be used to perform this translation.

Although you may not realize it, you now know the difference between *machine language* and *assembly language*. In machine language, a programmer works with binary, octal, or hexadecimal op codes for the instructions. Programs that contain a sequence of op codes can be stored directly in the 8080's memory and then executed. With assembly language, the programmer creates a program by writing down a sequence of mnemonics for the instructions that are to be executed. The proper binary codes for the mnemonics are determined, these op codes are saved in memory, and the program is then executed. Because it is easier to understand and remember mnemonics rather than binary, octal, or hexadecimal op codes, all of the programs in the remainder of this book will be in mnemonic form. This means that all programs will be in assembly language.

THE 8085 MICROPROCESSOR

The 8085 integrated circuit is an improved version of the 8080 (see Fig. 1-2). Most of the improvements affect the hardware design of the microcomputer based on the 8085. The 8085 requires only a single +5-volt power supply, whereas the 8080 requires power supplies of +12, +5, and −5 volts. This is a nice feature, but many memory and interface devices require other power supplies in addition to +5 volts.

The clock input requirement of the 8085 has also been simplified, so that a two-phase, nonoverlapping, 0- to +12-volt clock is no longer required. Instead, a crystal or resistor-capacitor combination can be wired directly to the 8085. This is similar in function to the 6502, manufactured by MOS Technology, Inc.

A large part of the control logic required by the 8080 can be eliminated in 8085 designs. However, one or two integrated circuits are still required to gate some of the signals produced by the 8085 in order to generate control signals.

The 8085 has only eight address output pins, whereas the 8080 has 16 address pins. However, both microprocessors can directly address 65,536 (64K) memory locations. The 8085 can do this because the 16-bit address is multiplexed. The eight address pins on the 8085 are dedicated to the eight high address bits (A_{15} through A_8), and the eight low address bits are multiplexed with the eight data bits on the multiplexed address/data bus (AD_7 through AD_0). It is very easy to latch the eight low address bits from the address/data bus, because there is a positive-going *address latch enable* (*ALE*) pulse, generated by the 8085 just for this purpose.

Some of the pins on the integrated circuit that were saved by multiplexing the address and data signals on one set of eight bus lines are used for the expanded interrupt capability of the 8085. This will be discussed in detail in a later chapter on interrupts.

The last significant changes in the 8085 are two pins that are dedicated to transferring information between the 8085 and external I/O

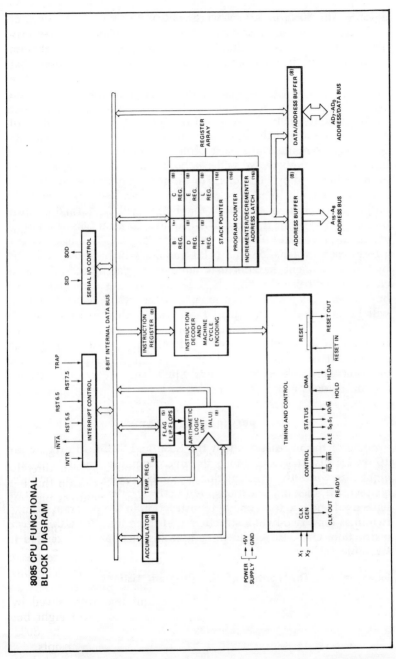

8085 CPU FUNCTIONAL BLOCK DIAGRAM

Courtesy Intel Corp.

Fig. 1-2. Block diagram of the 8085 microprocessor integrated circuit.

devices. The 8085, under software control, can set one of the pins, SOD, to either a logic 1 or logic 0 level (TTL compatible). The 8085 can also read the state of another pin, SID. These two pins are particularly useful in serial communications.

CONVENTIONS USED IN THIS BOOK

Throughout this book, we will use octal (base 8), decimal (base 10), and hexadecimal (base 16) numbers. Because the 8080 and 8085 microcomputers are most often programmed with octal and hexadecimal numbers, we will use both numbering systems in program listings and explanations. For example, a typical sentence from one chapter might be: "If register A contains 360 (F0) when this output instruction is executed, the LEDs will be turned off and then . . ." The point is, register A contains an octal 360 or its equivalent, hexadecimal F0. Rather than write "octal *XXX* or hexadecimal *YY*" in each explanation, the octal number will be listed, followed by the equivalent hexadecimal number in parentheses. In some cases, we will use the term hexadecimal, or the equivalent term, hex, in an explanation. Occasionally, a binary or decimal number will be included in an explanation, with both the octal and hex equivalents in parentheses. For example, ". . . when register B contains 11001010 (octal 312, hex CA), the jump . . ." In this particular example, it is important to observe the binary bit pattern of the eight-bit word. The octal and hex equivalents are simply included for the reader's convenience.

PROGRAM FORMAT

Some of the instructions that the 8080 and 8085 can execute are 16 or 24 bits in length. Since the microcomputer memory is only eight bits wide, these instructions *must* be stored in two or three consecutive memory locations, respectively. Because of this, we have used one line for a one-byte instruction in the program listings, two lines for a two-byte instruction, and three lines for a three-byte instruction. One-, two-, and three-byte instructions are included in Example 1-3.

Example 1-3: The Format of the Program Listings

```
        ADDB

        MVIA
        103

        JMP
        314
        023
```

Regardless of what these mnemonics stand for or what this program does, ADDB is a one-byte instruction, MVIA is a two-byte instruction, and JMP is a three-byte instruction. This means that 103 (43) is really the second byte of the MVIA instruction, and that 314 (CC) and 023 (13) are really parts of the JMP instruction. Note the listing of the octal numbers, with the hex equivalents in parentheses, in the previous sentence. In other books on assembly language programming, the same program might be listed as given in Example 1-4.

Example 1-4: Another Possible Program-Listing Format

```
ADDB
MVIA, 103
JMP, 314 023
```

It may be difficult for some readers to relate this listing to how the one-, two-, and three-byte instructions are actually stored in memory. It is important to note, however, that no matter how a program is listed on paper, the appropriate binary numbers must still be stored in consecutive memory locations. Only then can the program be executed.

SIMILARITIES BETWEEN THE 8080 AND 8085

As you observed in another section of this chapter, the 8085 is very similar to the 8080. In fact, most of the programs and circuits described in this book can be used with either the 8080 or 8085. At one time, we thought about using the notation "8080/8085" to represent the fact that the hardware or software being explained could be used with both microprocessors. However, this is cumbersome to read. *Therefore, unless stated otherwise, programs and interface electronics can be used with either the 8080 or 8085. If a program or interface can only be used with the 8080 or 8085, we will state with which processor it can be used.*

With this brief introduction to the 8080 and 8085 microprocessor integrated circuits, let us now examine the instructions that these two microprocessors can execute. Once this is done, we can put together sequences of instructions that cause the 8080 or 8085 to perform useful tasks.

REFERENCES

1. Rony, P. R., Larsen, D. G., and Titus, J. A. *The 8080A Bugbook®: Microcomputer Interfacing and Programming.* Howard W. Sams & Co., Inc., Indianapolis, IN, 1977.
2. *The 8080 Microcomputer System User's Manual.* Intel Corporation, Santa Clara, CA, 1975.
3. *The 8085 Microcomputer System User's Manual.* Intel Corporation, Santa Clara, CA, 1977.

Bugbook is a registered trademark of E & L Instruments, Inc., Derby, CT 06418.

2

The Basic 8080/8085 Instructions

The 8080 can execute 244 different instructions. Rather than discuss each instruction in a piecemeal fashion, we have arranged the instructions in the following groups of functionally similar instructions:

1. Data-Movement Instructions
2. Input/Output (I/O) Instructions
3. Logical and Mathematical Instructions
4. Branch and Decision-Making Instructions
5. Interrupt Related Instructions

As you already know, there are seven general-purpose registers within the 8080 integrated circuit, each of which we can access using software instructions. By discussing the instructions that the 8080 can execute, we will be able to determine what happens to the content of these registers, how the flags are affected by each instruction, and how we can test the state of these flags with instructions so that the 8080 can be programmed to make decisions based on the data with which it is operating. Also, by discussing the input/output (I/O) and interrupt instructions, we can learn how to program the 8080 so that it can communicate with the "outside world."

As you will see, the 8080 is really an eight-bit *microprocessor* that is used in eight-bit *microcomputers*. This means that the transfer of data, or the use of data by mathematical and logical instructions, usually involves eight bits at a time. We have already mentioned that the 8080 has a bidirectional data bus; this means that data can flow in both directions, one direction at a time. The 8080 uses the data bus to communicate with memory and I/O devices.

THE DATA-MOVEMENT INSTRUCTIONS

Probably the simplest instructions to understand are the 8080's data-movement instructions. These instructions are used to transfer eight-bit data words between the internal general-purpose registers, (A, B, C, D, E, H, and L), and also between these registers and memory. Assuming that we already have some data stored in some of these registers, we can easily program the 8080 to move or transfer this data to any of the other general-purpose registers with a move instruction, which has the mnemonic, MOV. This single-byte instruction requires only one memory location for storage. How do we know which register is to receive the data and which register is to send the data? The MOV instruction must specify the *source register*, which contains the data to be moved, and the *destination register*, where the data is to be moved to. For example, to move the eight-bit data word contained in the E register to the B register, we would use the instruction MOVBE. This instruction *moves to the B register the eight-bit data word contained in the E register*. To execute this instruction, the proper binary *operation code*, or *op code*, for the instruction, MOVBE, must be stored in the micro-computer's memory. Within this eight-bit op code, there has to be a method of distinguishing between the source and destination registers. There also has to be a method of distinguishing between *all* of the general-purpose registers. In this case, a binary code has been assigned to each register by the Intel Corporation, the creators of the 8080, as is shown in Table 2-1.

Table 2-1. The Binary Codes Assigned to the Eight-Bit Registers

Register	Assigned Binary Code	Equivalent Octal Code
A	111	7
B	000	0
C	001	1
D	010	2
E	011	3
H	100	4
L	101	5

As you can see, the binary code 110 (octal 6) has been excluded from Table 2-1. This code has a special use, which we will discuss shortly. Now that we can distinguish one register from another, there still has to be a way of specifying the class of move instructions. To do this, you need to remember a very simple rule: *All register-to-register move instructions start with an octal 1.* This means that all of the move instructions that we have been discussing have octal op codes between 100 and 177 (hexadecimal 40 through 7F). To specify the destination and source registers, you need to remember MOV*DS* = 1*DS*. The *D* represents the octal code for the destination register, and the *S* represents the octal code for the source register. Therefore, the MOVBE instruction has an octal op code of 103 (hexadecimal 43). When this op code is stored in the microcomputer's memory and executed, the content of the E register is moved to the B register.

Data may be moved from any one register to any other register. Table 2-2 contains several MOV instructions and the appropriate octal and hexadecimal op codes for these instructions. Whenever any of these move instructions are executed, the data is *copied* from the source register to the destination register. *The content of the source register remains unchanged when a move instruction is executed.*

Table 2-2. Some MOV Instructions and Their Octal and Hexadecimal Op Codes

Mnemonic	Octal	Hexadecimal	Function
MOVAH	174	7C	MOVE TO A THE CONTENT OF H
MOVCB	110	48	MOVE TO C THE CONTENT OF B
MOVLD	152	6A	MOVE TO L THE CONTENT OF D
MOVDL	125	55	MOVE TO D THE CONTENT OF L
MOVEE	133	5B	MOVE TO E THE CONTENT OF E

Suppose that you have used a MOVLD instruction in a program. What does this instruction do? It moves the content of the D register to the L register. The op code that is stored in memory for this instruction is really binary 01101010, but it may be expressed as octal 152 or hexadecimal 6A. However, let us assume that for the program to operate properly, we instead require a MOVDL instruction. To change the program, we simply need to replace the previous instruction in memory by an octal 125 or hexadecimal 55. Note that the only difference between these two instructions is the fact that the destination and source register codes are reversed. As you can see, reversing the register codes is particularly easy when the octal numbers, 152 and 125, are used to represent the instructions, instead of the hexadecimal numbers, 6A and 55. For this reason, many programmers prefer octal codes when programming the 8080.

You should also notice the MOVEE instruction in Table 2-2. The net result of this instruction, when it is executed, is to leave the content of the E register unchanged. This is a valid 8080 instruction, but it has no visible effect and can be called a "do-nothing" instruction. This type of instruction also exists for the six other general-purpose registers, MOVAA, MOVBB, MOVCC, MOVDD, MOVHH, and MOVLL.

How many bits of information can the 8080 store in the general-purpose registers? There are seven general-purpose registers, so 56 bits of information or seven eight-bit words can be stored in these registers. What happens if we need to store more information than this? To solve this problem, data values can also be stored and retrieved from memory.

USING R/W MEMORY FOR DATA STORAGE

It is more difficult to move data between one of the 8080's general-purpose registers and memory than to move data between the 8080's general-purpose registers. Can you guess why? When a data word is moved between the internal 8080 registers, the source and destination of the data word must be specified. The same is true when a data word is moved between memory and the 8080. However, there are 65,536 possible memory locations to or from which you can move data. This means that you must uniquely specify which memory location to or from which you wish the 8080 to move data.

Surprisingly enough, a single-byte instruction can be used to move a data word between any of the 65,536 memory locations and the internal registers of the 8080. How is this possible? Before this single-byte instruction is executed, a 16-bit memory address must be stored in registers H and L. The H register is used to hold the high byte, or most-significant eight bits of the address, and the L register is used to hold the low byte, or least-significant eight bits of address. Once these two address bytes have been loaded into registers H and L, a single-byte instruction can be used to transfer a single eight-bit byte of data between *the memory location specified by the address in registers H and L, and the A, B, C, D, or E register in the 8080*. There are a number of single-byte instructions that can be used to perform this transfer of data. All of these instructions follow the format already established for the register-to-register data-movement instructions; that is, MOVDS = 1DS, where octal codes for the destination and source registers are used. When an external memory location is to be addressed by the content of registers H and L, it is assigned the octal code 6. This code must be used when we wish to specify a memory location addressed by registers H and L as either the destination or source of data.

For example, to move the content of memory location 030 123 (1853) to the D register, a MOVDM instruction can be used. However, before this instruction is executed, a 16-bit address must be loaded into the H and L registers. The high address, octal 030 (18), must be loaded into register H, *and* the low address, octal 123 (53), must be loaded into the L register before the MOVDM instruction is executed. Can you think of all the move instructions that use a memory location addressed by registers H and L as either the source or destination of data? These instructions are summarized in Table 2-3.

Table 2-3. The Memory Reference MOV Instructions

Memory Is the Source		Memory Is the Destination
MOVAM		MOVMA
MOVBM		MOVMB
MOVCM		MOVMC
MOVDM		MOVMD
MOVEM		MOVME
MOVHM *		MOVMH $
MOVLM *		MOVML $
	MOVMM	

Unlike some of the other move instructions, such as MOVEE and MOVBB, the MOVMM instruction (octal 166, hexadecimal 76) is *not* a "do-nothing" instruction. Instead, it is the halt, or HLT, instruction for the 8080. If this instruction is executed, the 8080 will cease executing a program. We have placed asterisks by the instructions MOVHM and MOVLM. Why do you think these instructions are marked? Depending on which one of these instructions is executed, the eight-bit address byte in register H or L will change. If the MOVHM instruction is executed, the content of memory addressed by registers H and L is loaded into register H, which previously contained the high byte of the memory address. If the MOVLM instruction is executed, the content of the memory location addressed by registers H and L is loaded into the L register.

The MOVMH and MOVML instructions can also cause some problems if you do not use them carefully. These instructions save the address in register H or L in the memory location addressed by registers H and L. If register H contains 001 (01) and register L contains 100 (40), the MOVMH instruction will save a 001 (01) in memory location 001 100 (0140). If the MOVML instruction is executed with the address 001 100 (0140) in registers H and L, a 100 (40) will be saved in memory location 001 100 (0140).

The 8080 can execute a number of instructions to store data in or retrieve data from memory. We have just discussed the *memory reference instructions* that are of the MOV*DS* format. These instructions operate by moving an eight-bit data word between a register and a uniquely addressed memory location. Other memory reference instructions will be discussed in another chapter.

One of the problems that we have not discussed involves the loading of a data value into a register or the loading of an address value into registers H and L. How is this done? We already know how to move a data value once it is in a register, but how do we get the value into the register initially? The answer will be discussed in the following section.

THE MOVE-IMMEDIATE INSTRUCTIONS

How does one initially get data values into any of the 8080's general-purpose registers? One of the methods for loading a data value into a register is to execute an instruction that contains a data byte. How can an instruction contain not only the instruction op code, but also a data byte? It is very easy for the 8080, because there are *two-byte instructions* in the instruction set. Two-byte instructions require two *consecutive* memory locations for storage, where the first memory location is used to store the eight-bit op code for the instruction, and the second memory location is used to store the *immediate data byte*. The move-immediate instructions are, in fact, two-byte instructions. These instructions load the data byte contained in the second byte of the instruction into the specified register. Any of the 8080's general-purpose registers can be loaded with an eight-bit data value by executing one of these instructions. The move-immediate instructions have the following format: MVID $<B_2>$. The D in the MVID instruction represents the destination register for the data byte. You can substitute any of the registers that we have discussed, A, B, C, D, E, H, or L, for the D. The notation, $<B_2>$, means that the next successive memory location has been reserved for the storage of an eight-bit data byte (word) that will be loaded into the register specified in the move-immediate instruction.

Suppose that you need to load registers B, C, D, and E with the value 246 (A6). This can be accomplished by using the program in Example 2-1.

Example 2-1: Loading Registers B, C, D, and E With the Same Value

Octal	Mnemonic	Hexadecimal	Comments
006	MVIB	06	MOVE THE IMMEDIATE
246	$<B_2>$	A6	DATA BYTE TO REGISTER B
110	MOVCB	48	MOVE IT TO C FROM B
120	MOVDB	50	MOVE IT TO D FROM B
130	MOVEB	58	MOVE IT TO E FROM B

Why were the MVIC, MVID, and MVIE instructions not used in Example 2-1? These instructions were not used because the program would require eight memory locations for storage, whereas the instructions listed in Example 2-1 require five memory locations for storage. If you can write two versions of a program, both of which perform the same function, and one of the programs requires fewer memory locations for storage, which program would you use? You would probably use the program that requires the least amount of memory for storage. This point is illustrated in Example 2-2.

Example 2-2: Two Methods of Duplicating a Data Byte in Four Registers

Method 1	Method 2
MVIB	MVIB
$<B_2>$	$<B_2>$
MOVCB	MVIC
MOVDB	$<B_2>$
MOVEB	MVID
	$<B_2>$
	MVIE
	$<B_2>$

Which op codes must actually be stored in memory for the move-immediate instructions to be executed? Some examples of the move-immediate instruction op codes are listed in Table 2-4.

Table 2-4. Op Codes for Some of the Move-Immediate Instructions

Octal	Mnemonic	Hexadecimal
006	MVIB	06
016	MVIC	0E
026	MVID	16
036	MVIE	1E
076	MVIA	3E

In Table 2-4, the data bytes for the move-immediate instructions are not shown. From your examination of this table, can you determine the op codes for the MVIH, MVIL, and MVIM instructions? All of the op codes for the move-immediate instructions can be derived from the generalized move-immediate instruction op code, 0D6. In this generalized op code, the D represents the octal register code for the register that is to be loaded with the immediate data byte. Knowing this, and by referring to the octal register codes listed in Table 2-1, you should be able to determine the op codes for the MVIH, MVIL, and MVIM instructions. The octal and hexadecimal op codes for these instructions are shown in Table 2-5. Like the other move-immediate instructions, these move-immediate instructions are all two bytes long. This means that where these instructions are used, the op code for the instruction must be stored in memory, immediately followed by the eight-bit data byte that is to be loaded into the specified register or memory.

**Table 2-5. The Octal and Hexadecimal Op Codes for
All of the Move-Immediate Instructions**

Octal	Mnemonic	Hexadecimal
006	MVIB	06
016	MVIC	0E
026	MVID	16
036	MVIE	1E
046	MVIH	26
056	MVIL	2E
066	MVIM	36
076	MVIA	3E

The MVIM instruction is particularly interesting. Do you know what the 8080 does when this instruction is executed? The MVIM instruction can be used to *load an immediate data byte into the memory location addressed by registers H and L.* Like the other memory reference instructions, which moved eight-bit bytes between memory and one of the general-purpose 8080 registers, an address must be contained in registers H and L before this instruction is executed.

Now we can write a program that loads an address into registers H and L, and then transfers an eight-bit byte between memory and a general-purpose register. For example, we can move the content of memory location 030 123 (1853) to the D register. To do this, we must load the address 030 123 (1853) into registers H and L before the actual MOVDM instruction is executed. The sequence of instructions in Example 2-3 actually performs this movement of data.

**Example 2-3: Moving the Content of Memory Location 030 123
(1853) to the D Register**

Octal	Mnemonic	Hexadecimal
056	MVIL	2E
123	$<B_2>$	53
046	MVIH	26
030	$<B_2>$	18
126	MOVDM	56

In Example 2-3, the L register is loaded with a data byte of 123 (53) by the MVIL instruction. The H register is then loaded with the data byte, 030 (18). Once this is done, the content of the memory location addressed by registers H and L is copied into the D register. Is there any reason why the L register is loaded before the H register? No, the H register could be loaded with an immediate data byte first. The important point to remember is that both the H and L registers must contain the complete 16-bit address before any of the memory reference instructions that we have discussed are executed. Note that there is nothing to indicate that registers H and L can only contain a memory address. These registers are general-purpose registers too, so they can also contain eight-bit data values. It is your responsibility to ensure that an address is contained in registers H and L *before* one of the memory reference instructions that we have discussed is executed. The 8080 does not know whether a data value or whether an address is contained in either of these two registers. However, as we have mentioned before, the high-address byte must be contained in the H register, and the low-address byte must be contained in the L register, when the registers are used to specify a 16-bit address.

What would the instruction sequence be to write the data byte, 042 (22), into a memory location with an address of 102 341 (42E1)? The program listed in Example 2-4 can be used.

Example 2-4: Saving an Immediate Data Byte in Memory

Octal	Mnemonic	Hexadecimal
046	MVIH	26
102	$<B_2>$	42
056	MVIL	2E
341	$<B_2>$	E1
066	MVIM	36
042	$<B_2>$	22

In this program, register H is loaded with an immediate data byte before the L register is loaded. Remember, even though the registers are loaded with these immediate *data* bytes, the two data bytes will be the *address* used when a memory reference instruction is executed. After the H and L registers are loaded, the actual transfer of the data, 042 (22), to memory is performed when the MVIM instruction is executed.

SIMPLE REGISTER PAIR INSTRUCTIONS

As you have just seen, a 16-bit address must be contained in the H and L registers before a memory reference instruction, such as MOVBM, is executed. For this reason, registers H and L are often called *register pair H*. Instructions that use or change register pair H always treat the content of registers H and L as a 16-bit value.

In previous examples, the two, two-byte instructions, MVIL and MVIH, were used to load eight-bit values into the individual L and H registers. There is also a three-byte instruction that can be used to load 16 bits of data (or address) into register pair H (registers

H and L). This instruction is LXIH $<B_2>$ $<B_3>$, and the op code for this instruction is 041 (21).

In Example 2-5, the LXIH instruction loads register pair H with 005 341 (05E1). As you can see, this instruction accomplishes the same task as executing either an MVIL and MVIH instruction or an MVIH and MVIL instruction. The only advantage in using the LXIH instruction is the fact that it only requires three memory locations for storage (the two equivalent MVI instructions, MVIH and MVIL, require four memory locations).

Example 2-5: The LXIH and Equivalent MVI Instructions

MVIL	LXIH	MVIH
341	341	005
MVIH	005	MVIL
005		341

When the LXIH instruction is executed, which of the data bytes is loaded into H, and which data byte is loaded into L? *The second byte of the three-byte instruction (341 or E1 in Example 2-5) is loaded into register L, and the third byte of the instruction (005 or 05) is loaded into register H.*

The H and L registers are general-purpose registers, so the LXIH instruction may be used to load 16-bit data values or 16-bit address values into register pair H. Since a complete 16-bit value may be contained in two eight-bit registers (a register pair), we will often use the terms MSBY (most-significant eight-bit byte) and LSBY (least-significant eight-bit byte) to describe the eight-bit bytes contained therein.

Registers H and L are not the only 8080 general-purpose registers that can be grouped together to form a register pair. Registers B and C, and registers D and E, can also be used as register pairs. These new register pairs and the MSBY and LSBY designations are summarized in Table 2-6.

Table 2-6. The Register Pairs and Their MSBY and LSBY Designations

In register pair B, register B contains the MSBY and register C contains the LSBY.
In register pair D, register D contains the MSBY and register E contains the LSBY.
In register pair H, register H contains the MSBY and register L contains the LSBY.

There are also LXI-type instructions that can be used to load 16-bit values into register pairs B and D. These additional 8080 instructions are listed in Table 2-7, along with their corresponding octal and hexadecimal op codes.

These LXI instructions are all three bytes long. When the op codes for these instructions are stored in memory, the two data

Octal	Mnemonic	Hexadecimal
001	LXIB	01
021	LXID	11
041	LXIH	21

bytes must be stored in the next two consecutive memory locations, with the LSBY first and then the MSBY.

When the program listed in Example 2-6 is executed, what will be contained in the individual eight-bit registers?

Example 2-6: Using the LXIB, LXID, and LXIH Instructions

Octal	Mnemonic	Hexadecimal
001	LXIB	01
100	$<B_2>$	40
002	$<B_3>$	02
041	LXIH	21
005	$<B_2>$	05
341	$<B_3>$	E1
021	LXID	11
275	$<B_2>$	BD
300	$<B_3>$	C0

After these three, three-byte instructions are executed, the 8080's general-purpose registers will contain the values listed in Table 2-8.

Table 2-8. The Content of the Registers After Executing
the LXI Instructions Listed in Example 2-6

Octal	Register	Hexadecimal
002	B	02
100	C	40
300	D	C0
275	E	BD
341	H	E1
005	L	05

Remember that the second byte of the instruction is the LSBY, and it is loaded into either the C, E, or L register, depending on which one of the LXI instructions is executed. The third and thus the last byte of the instruction is the MSBY, and it is loaded into either the B, D, or H register, depending on which one of the LXI instructions is executed. Finally, these instructions can be used to load either a 16-bit address or data value into the register pair. There is no way for the 8080 to distinguish between data and address information that is stored in a register pair. Only in the

MOVMS- and MOVDM-type instruction does the 8080 assume that there is an address stored in register pair H.

Since you cannot pair the 8080 registers at will (register B can only be paired with register C, D with E, and H with L), you must carefully plan your software to make effective use of the register pair instructions. For example, if you wish to load registers C and D with data values for some operation, you could not use a single LXI-type instruction to load them, because there is no instruction that loads registers C and D as a register pair. Instead, two, two-byte MVI-type instructions would have to be used. If you had instead chosen to use registers B and C, or D and E, a single LXI-type instruction could be used to load data values into these registers.

When using two- and three-byte instructions, remember to leave room (one or two *additional* memory locations, respectively) in the software (program) for the additional data or address bytes. A two- or three-byte instruction must be stored in two or three *consecutive* memory locations, respectively.

INPUT AND OUTPUT INSTRUCTIONS

The input (IN) and output (OUT) instructions are used so that data may be transferred between peripheral devices, often called input/output (I/O) devices, and the 8080 microcomputer. If there is a teletypewriter, cathode-ray terminal (crt), floppy disk, cassette, digital-to-analog or analog-to-digital converter connected to the microcomputer, the 8080 probably uses IN and OUT instructions to communicate with these devices. The octal and hexadecimal op codes for these two, two-byte instructions are listed in Table 2-9.

Table 2-9. The Octal and Hexadecimal Op Codes for the IN and OUT Instructions

Octal	Mnemonic	Hexadecimal
333	IN	DB
027	$<B_2>$	17
323	OUT	D3
171	$<B_2>$	79

Of course, there has to be some way in which the 8080 can specify which one of the many input devices may send data to the 8080 over the data bus, and which one of the output devices may receive the data that the 8080 outputs, also over the data bus. Therefore, the instructions, IN and OUT, are two-byte instructions, where the second byte is the eight-bit address of the device that will send or receive the data. This address is similar in function to a memory address that is generated by the 8080. However, the I/O *device address* may only be within the range of 000 to 377 (hexadecimal 00 to FF). This means that there can be up to 256 input devices and 256 output devices, each of which may be individually addressed. Both the IN and OUT instructions cause an eight-bit data byte to be transferred between the I/O device that is addressed, and the 8080's A register.

To output data to a device, also called an *output port*, the data must first be present in the 8080's A register. There are a number of instructions that can be used to load an eight-bit data byte into the A register, some of which include the following:

MVIA   MOVAM   MOVAE
<B₂>

When the data is available in the A register, it can then be output to the selected output port, as Example 2-7 demonstrates.

Example 2-7: Sending an Eight-Bit Value to Device 015 (0D)

Octal	Mnemonic	Hexadecimal
076	MVIA	3E
101	<B₂>	41
323	OUT	D3
015	<ADDR>	0D

This program loads the A register with the data value, 101 (41), and then transfers the data word in A to output port 015 (0D). After the OUT instruction has been executed, the A register will still contain the data value, 101 (41).

It is just as easy to input data, as Example 2-8 demonstrates.

Example 2-8: Receiving an Eight-Bit Value From Device 103 (43)

Octal	Mnemonic	Hexadecimal
333	IN	DB
103	<ADDR>	43
107	MOVBA	47

In Example 2-8, the eight-bit data word from the input port with the address, 103 (43), is loaded into the A register when the IN instruction is executed. The data word is then moved into the B register by the MOVBA instruction. After the MOVBA instruction has been executed, both the A and B registers contain the same input data values. *Data can only be input or output between the I/O devices and the 8080's A register, when using the IN and OUT instructions.* There are no instructions that can be used to input data directly into any of the other registers or memory. In another section of this book, a more powerful technique of communicating with I/O devices, called *memory-mapped I/O*, will be discussed.

How do I/O devices actually receive the I/O address that is contained in the second byte of the IN and OUT instructions, and how do the I/O devices know whether to send data to the 8080 or receive data from the 8080? When the 8080 executes an IN or an OUT instruction, the second byte of the instruction, the I/O device address, is placed on the 8080's 16-bit address bus. The device address can be found on address lines A_{15} through A_8, and also on address lines A_7 through A_0. These signals originate at the 16 address pins on the 8080 integrated circuit. If you look at the memory-address bus during the execution of either an IN or an OUT instruction, it might appear as follows:

A_{15}	A_{14}	A_{13}	A_{12}	A_{11}	A_{10}	A_9	A_8		A_7	A_6	A_5	A_4	A_3	A_2	A_1	A_0
0	1	1	0	1	0	0	1		0	1	1	0	1	0	0	1

By examining the address bus, there is no way to determine whether an IN or an OUT instruction is being executed. However, the device address used as the second byte in either of these instructions can be determined. What is the device address in the preceding diagram? The device address is 151 (69). Notice that the 151 (69) is present on address lines A_{15} through A_8, and also on address lines A_7 through A_0. These address lines are also called the HI address bus (A_{15} through A_8) and the LO address bus (A_7 through A_0).

Either set of address lines may be used for device address decoding. Device address decoding is an action that must be performed by every peripheral device. The peripheral device decodes the I/O address on A_{15} through A_8 or A_7 through A_0, and from this, decides whether or not it will be involved in the transfer of data to or from the 8080.

While an IN or an OUT instruction is being executed by the 8080, how does the I/O device know whether it is to send or receive data? There are two "control" pulses that the 8080 generates with the aid of some external gates that signal the I/O devices which way the data is traveling on the eight-bit bidirectional data bus. These pulses are called $\overline{I/O\ R}$ ($\overline{I/O\ Read}$) for input, and $\overline{I/O\ W}$ ($\overline{I/O\ Write}$) for output. Sometimes, the pulses are simply called $\overline{IN}$ and $\overline{OUT}$. The $\overline{I/O\ R}$ (or $\overline{IN}$) pulse can be used to gate the data from a selected input device onto the data bus so that it can be loaded into the A register by the 8080 as the IN instruction is being executed. The $\overline{I/O\ W}$ (or $\overline{OUT}$) pulse can be used by the selected output device to latch the content of the A register, which is placed

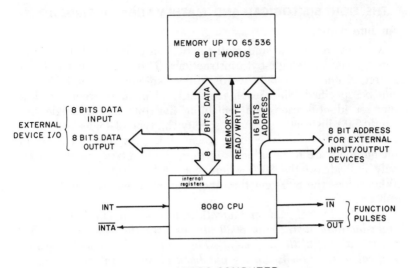

MICRO COMPUTER

Fig. 2-1. Block diagram of a typical 8080 microcomputer system.

on the data bus by the 8080, while the OUT instruction is being executed. These concepts are summarized in Figs. 2-1 and 2-2. For further information on device addressing and device address decoding, please refer to the references at the end of this chapter.[1,2]

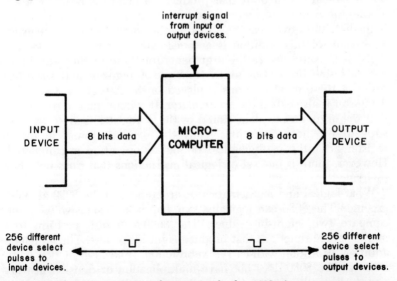

Fig. 2-2. The important input and output signals of an 8080 microcomputer system.

THE EIGHT-BIT LOGICAL AND MATHEMATICAL INSTRUCTIONS

An Introduction

Most of the logical and mathematical instructions that the 8080 can execute are single-byte instructions. This means that only the source of *one* of the data words to be manipulated, *one argument,* can be specified. Since each register, and memory, requires three bits for identification, the remaining five bits in the single byte (eight-bit) instruction actually specify the type of logical or mathematical instruction that is to be executed. For instance, if two, eight-bit numbers are to be added together, the addition instruction can only indicate to the 8080 where one of the arguments is stored. Where does the 8080 get the other argument and where is the result stored?

For the logical and mathematical instructions that operate on eight-bit data words, the 8080 always uses the content of the A register as one of the arguments. The result of the logical or mathematical instruction is always put back or saved in the A register. This means that the 8080 can "add B to A and save the result in A" or "subtract D from A and save the result in A."

When the move instructions were discussed, you saw that there were basically three sources of data: the content of one of the general-purpose registers, the content of memory addressed by register pair H, or an immediate data byte. These same three sources of data can also be used to provide one of the arguments for the logical and mathematical instructions that produce an eight-bit result. For example, the content of memory addressed by register pair H, or an immediate data byte, can be added to the content of the A register. The result of this addition is automatically saved in the 8080's A register. Because one of the arguments for these mathematical and logical instructions is obtained from the A register, and since the result of these manipulations is placed in the A register, the 8080's A register is also called the *accumulator.* It is important to remember that the argument or data stored in the A register is "lost" or "destroyed" by these operations. Only the *result* is found in the A register after the mathematical or logical operation is completed. However, there is one set of logical instructions that does not obey this rule.

What logical and mathematical instructions can the 8080 actually execute? The 8080 can logically AND, OR, EXOR (exclusive-OR), and compare two, eight-bit values. The 8080 can also perform four mathematical functions that produce eight-bit results. These include addition, addition-with-carry, subtraction, and subtraction-with-borrow. The 8080 does not have multiplication or division instructions. Although not strictly a logical or mathematical instruction, the 8080 can also increment or decrement the content of any of the general-purpose registers, the content of memory addressed by register pair H, or the content of a register pair (a 16-bit number). The 8080 can also rotate the content of the A register one bit position to the left or to the right.

The 8080 Flags

After executing one of these logical or mathematical instructions, the 8080 can test the result of the operation that has been performed. The 8080 can do this by testing the state (logic 1 or logic 0) of four *internal condition flags*. These flags and what they indicate are listed in Table 2-10.

Table 2-10. The Four Condition Flags and What They Indicate

1. CARRY flag	The carry flag indicates whether a carry or a borrow has occurred as a result of a logical or mathematical instruction.
2. SIGN flag	The sign flag indicates whether the sign of the result of a logical or mathematical instruction is positive or negative.
3. PARITY flag	The parity flag indicates whether the parity of the result of a logical or mathematical instruction is even or odd.
4. ZERO flag	The zero flag indicates whether the result of a logical or mathematical instruction is zero or nonzero.

In most of our examples, the condition of the carry and zero flags will be tested. The sign and parity flags are not as general purpose as these other two flags. The sign flag is generally tested after operations that involve signed mathematical numbers (such as the addition of 5 and −7), and the parity flag is useful in communications applications.

You can think of the flags as being individual *flip-flops* within the 8080 integrated circuit. As such, they have two possible states, which are summarized in Table 2-11.

Table 2-11. The State and Meaning of the Condition Flags

CARRY = 0	A carry or borrow did not occur.
= 1	A carry or borrow did occur.
ZERO = 0	The result is not zero.
= 1	The result is zero.
SIGN = 0	The sign of the result is positive.
= 1	The sign of the result is negative.
PARITY = 0	The parity of the result is odd.
= 1	The parity of the result is even.

LOGICAL INSTRUCTIONS

The logical operations enable software instructions to imitate hardware logic devices. The contents of the A register can be ANDed, ORed, exclusive-ORed, compared, and rotated under software control. Most of these instructions operate on two data bytes. Only the rotate instructions operate on a single byte. One of the data bytes involved in these logical operations must be contained in the A register. Some examples that use these instructions are useful so that you can see how they are applied.

The AND operation is particularly useful when it is desirable to *clear, filter*, or *mask-out* particular bits within an eight-bit byte. For example, in the American Standard Code for Information Interchange (ASCII), the characters 0 through 9 are assigned the values that are listed in Table 2-12. Assume that the most-significant bit (MSB) or the *parity bit*, is always a logic 1.

Table 2-12. The ASCII Values for the Characters 0 Through 9

Character	ASCII		Binary	BCD
	Octal	Hex		
0	260	B0	10110000	0000
1	261	B1	10110001	0001
2	262	B2	10110010	0010
3	263	B3	10110011	0011
4	264	B4	10110100	0100
5	265	B5	10110101	0101
6	266	B6	10110110	0110
7	267	B7	10110111	0111
8	270	B8	10111000	1000
9	271	B9	10111001	1001

If the four most-significant bits are *stripped* or *masked-out* of the ASCII values so that they become zero, then the *binary-coded-decimal (BCD)* value for each character will remain in the four least-significant bits (the four LSBs).

$$5_{10} = \text{ASCII } 5 = 10110101_2 \quad and \quad 00000101_2 = 5 \text{ (BCD)}$$

The character "5" is represented by the ASCII value 265 (B5). How are the four most-significant bits set to zero (i.e., *masked out*)? The truth table for the logical AND operation between two binary bits is shown in Table 2-13.

As you can see, the two binary bits can assume two different states; therefore, there are four different combinations of logic 1s and 0s that can be ANDed together. Note that only when A is a logic

**Table 2-13. A Logical AND
Operation Between Two
Binary Bits, A and B**

A	B	Result
0	0	0
0	1	0
1	0	0
1	1	1

1 AND B is a logic 1 is the result a logic 1. Column A could have also been labeled "Mask" and column B, "Data."

**Table 2-14. A Logical AND
Operation Between a
Mask and Data**

Mask	Data	Result
0	0	0
0	1	0
1	0	0
1	1	1

So far, we have only discussed 8080 instructions that operate on eight-bit data words (bytes). The AND instructions also fall into this category. Therefore, the "mask" in Table 2-14 only represents a single bit within an eight-bit word that is being ANDed with a corresponding bit in the eight-bit word contained in the A register. This means that if a byte is ANDed with the byte in the A register, bit D_0 in register A is ANDed with bit D_0 in the other byte. The result of this logical operation is then saved in bit D_0 of the A register. Likewise, the D_1 bits of each byte are ANDed and the result is saved in bit D_1 of the A register. This is shown in Table 2-15.

**Table 2-15. The Logical AND Operation
Between Two, Eight-Bit Bytes**

Data Byte		Contents of A	Results in A
D_0	AND	D_0	D_0
D_1	AND	D_1	D_1
D_2	AND	D_2	D_2
D_3	AND	D_3	D_3
D_4	AND	D_4	D_4
D_5	AND	D_5	D_5
D_6	AND	D_6	D_6
D_7	AND	D_7	D_7

The two, eight-bit bytes are ANDed together simultaneously, and the eight-bit result is saved in register A. For this reason, the 8080 is called a *parallel* microprocessor, as opposed to a *serial* micro-processor, which would operate on each bit position, one after the next.

After the AND operation shown in Examples 2-9 and 2-10 is per-formed, the four LSBs of register A contain the BCD number for the key that is pressed on the ASCII keyboard. We have assumed that only the numeric keys, 0 through 9, of the keyboard will be pressed. The remaining four bits in register A could be used to store another four-bit BCD number. However, additional software instructions would be required to position a second BCD digit in these bit posi-tions. In fact, 50% of the microcomputer's memory, which is used to store BCD numbers, will be wasted if these additional four bits of storage space are not used. The technique of storing two or more pieces of information within one word is often called *packing*.

At this point in the discussion, it is not important to know how the ASCII keyboard is interfaced to the microcomputer, or how the microcomputer actually inputs the data from the keyboard. We have only used an ASCII keyboard as an example to demonstrate the application of the logical instructions to a software problem.

Two other logical instructions will be used to perform the packing operation, thus permitting the microcomputer's memory (storage space) to be used efficiently. After masking the ASCII characters with the mask value of 017 (0F), to remove the four MSBs (the un-wanted bits of information), the four LSBs containing the BCD data have to be moved into the four MSB positions in the eight-bit word. To move these bits into the four MSBs, rotate instructions will be used. There are four of these rotate instructions that the 8080 can execute. The effect that these four instructions have on the contents of the A register is shown in Fig. 2-3.

Note that there is a *carry bit* associated with the A register (accu-mulator). The *carry flag* indicates the state of this carry bit. *The A register is the only register the contents of which can be rotated by these instructions.* The contents of the other registers can be rotated simply by moving them to the A register, rotating the con-tents of the A register, and then by moving the rotated data back to the original register. The rotate instructions will also be encoun-tered when we discuss decision-making operations that the 8080 can perform.

Note the differences between the RAR (*Rotate All Right*) and RAL (*Rotate All Left*) instructions, and the RRC (*Rotate Right into the Carry*) and RLC (*Rotate Left into the Carry*) instructions. The RAR instruction causes the LSB of the A register to be rotated into the carry, the carry to be rotated into the MSB, etc. The RAL

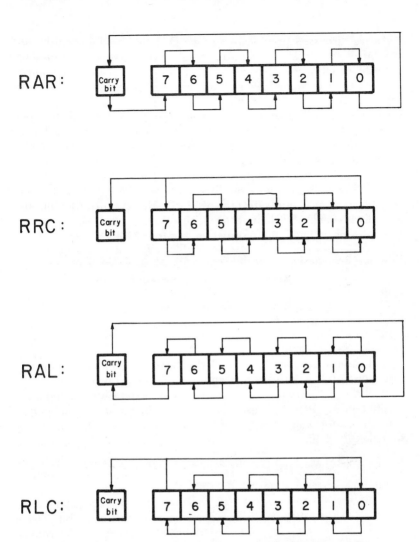

Fig. 2-3. The effect of the rotate instructions on register A and the carry bit.

instruction operates in the same manner, except the direction of rotation is reversed; bit D_7 is rotated into the carry, the carry into D_0, etc. When the other two rotate instructions, RRC and RLC, are executed, bit D_7 or D_0 is duplicated in the carry. The RRC instruction causes bit D_0 to be rotated into bit D_7 and the carry. After this instruction is executed, both D_7 and the carry will be the same. With the RLC instruction, the content of bit D_7 is rotated into bit D_0 and the carry. After this instruction is executed, both D_0 and the carry will be the same.

As we discussed previously, two BCD digits can be rotated and combined to "pack" them into a single byte. Assume that one of the ASCII characters has been input, ANDed with 017 (0F), and rotated into the four MSBs of the A register by executing four consecutive RLC instructions. The rotated BCD digit is then stored in register B. Also assume that the second ASCII character has already been input and ANDed with 017 (0F). To combine the two digits, one in the four LSBs of register A and the other in the four MSBs of register B, a logical OR instruction can be executed. The truth table for ORing two binary bits is shown in Table 2-16.

To allow us to save only the four LSBs of an ASCII character in register A, a *mask* of 00001111₂ (octal 017, hexadecimal 0F) can be ANDed with each ASCII character. If this is done, only the four LSBs of the result will contain information, the four MSBs being 0s.

Example 2-9: Masking-Out the Four MSBs of an ASCII Character

Mnemonic	Content of Register A
IN	
<ADDR>	10110101
ANI	
<B₂>	00000101

In Example 2-9, we have used the two-byte AND immediate instruction, ANI. Like all other immediate instructions, the second byte of the instruction is the immediate data byte. Can you think of a different sequence of instructions that will perform exactly the same function? There are numerous methods, one of which is listed in Example 2-10.

Example 2-10: Masking-Out the Four MSBs With an ANDC Instruction

Mnemonic
MVIC
<B₂>
IN
<ADDR>
ANDC

There is no particular (specific) reason why the C register is used to contain the mask in Example 2-10. No matter which register is used, what must the value of the data byte for the move-immediate instruction be? The value of the immediate data byte must be that of the mask, 017 (0F).

After the IN instruction is executed, the contents of register A are ANDed with the contents of register C, and the results of this operation are saved in register A. As you have seen, the ANDC and ANI instructions can be used to mask-out the four MSBs when the mask of 00001111$_2$ is used. The ANDM instruction could also be used, but what must be done before this instruction can be properly executed? Before executing an ANDM instruction, a 16-bit memory address must be loaded into register pair H (registers H and L). Once this is done, the ANDM instruction can be executed. You must remember to actually store the mask in the referenced memory location, too.

As you have seen, these logical instructions require two arguments. One of the arguments is contained in the A register, and the other argument may be an immediate data byte, the content of another register, or the content of a memory location addressed by the content of register pair H.

Table 2-16. The Logical
OR Operation

A	B	Result
0	0	0
0	1	1
1	0	1
1	1	1

When a logical OR instruction is executed, the data word containing the four MSBs can be combined with the data word containing the four LSBs, without either group affecting the other bits. The result will be a single packed byte containing both four-bit BCD digits, as shown in Table 2-17.

Table 2-17. The Combination of Two BCD Digits
With an OR Instruction

0000 0111	register A
0101 0000	ORed with register B
0101 0111	the ORed result in register A

The software required to input two ASCII characters, mask-out the unwanted bits, and combine the two data words is listed in Example 2-11.

In Example 2-11, the op codes for the instructions have not been listed. The contents of the A register have been listed to show the results of the execution of the various instructions in the program. After these instructions have been executed, the BCD values from two, eight-bit ASCII characters will be combined to form a single "packed" data byte. The result has been left in the A register for subsequent use. It could also be stored in a memory location or another register.

Example 2-11: Input, Mask, Rotate, and Combine Two ASCII Characters

Contents of A	Mnemonic	Comments
	IN	/INPUT ONE OF THE ASCII CHARACERS
10110101	015	/FROM INPUT PORT 015 (0D).
	ANI	/SET THE FOUR MSB'S TO ZERO
00000101	017	/BY MASKING WITH 017 (0F).
00001010	RLC	/ROTATE THE FOUR LSB'S TO
00010100	RLC	/THE LEFT FOUR TIMES.
00101000	RLC	
01010000	RLC	
01010000	MOVBA	/SAVE THE BCD DIGIT IN B.
	IN	/INPUT THE SECOND ASCII CHAR-
10110111	015	/ACTER FROM INPUT PORT 015 (0D).
	ANI	/SET THE FOUR MSB'S TO ZERO
00000111	017	/BY MASKING WITH 017 (0F).
01010111	ORAB	/OR THE CONTENT OF B WITH A.
		/THE TWO BCD DIGITS ARE NOW PACKED.

In Example 2-11, we have included a *comments* column. All the comments in future program examples will be listed in this manner and they will all be "set off" from the instruction mnemonics by the slash character (/).

The content of the A register can also be *compared* with the content of other registers, the content of a memory location addressed by register pair H, or an immediate data byte. This last type of compare instruction is particularly useful if you want the microcomputer to test or wait for a particular data word from a peripheral device. You can also use it to permit the microcomputer to make decisions based on whether a data value is less than, equal to, or greater than another data value.

There are also many applications where you might like to know whether a data value is within a preset upper and lower limit. Using special internal registers, which are not directly accessible to you, the 8080 performs the compare instructions by *invisibly subtracting* the content of the specified register, the specified memory location, or the immediate data byte from the content of the A register. The result of the subtraction is only reflected in the state of the four condition flags. *The content of the general-purpose register, the memory location addressed by register pair H, or the immediate data byte and the content of the A register, which it is being compared to, is unaffected by the compare instructions. The subtraction that takes place only affects the four condition flags.*

Here are some examples in which the content of the A register is compared to an immediate data byte by means of the two-byte compare-immediate instruction, CPI.

Assume that the content of the A register is 127 (57). After executing a:

$$\begin{array}{ccc} \text{CPI} & \text{or} & \text{CPI} \\ 126_8 & & 56_{16} \end{array}$$

the *carry flag* will be a logic *0*, and the *zero flag* will be a logic *0*. This indicates that the content of the A register is *greater than* the data byte. The state of the sign and parity flags is unimportant.

After executing a:

$$\begin{array}{ccc} \text{CPI} & \text{or} & \text{CPI} \\ 127_8 & & 57_{16} \end{array}$$

the *carry flag* will be a logic *0*, and the *zero flag* will be a logic *1*. This indicates that the content of the A register is *equal to* the data byte. The state of the sign and parity flags is unimportant.

After executing a:

$$\begin{array}{ccc} \text{CPI} & \text{or} & \text{CPI} \\ 130_8 & & 58_{16} \end{array}$$

the *carry flag* will be a logic *1*, and the *zero flag* will be a logic *0*. This indicates that the content of the A register is *smaller than* the data byte. The state of the sign and parity flags is unimportant.

These examples show the state of the carry and zero flags as a result of executing the two-byte compare-immediate instruction, CPI. *The content of the A register is still 127 (57) after the CPI instruction is executed.* Note that the flags do not have to be cleared before a mathematical or logical instruction is executed, just as registers do not have to be cleared before they are loaded with data. The flags are set or cleared to reflect the results of the current mathematical or logical instruction. They will remain set or cleared until another instruction is executed that has the ability to change them.

As you have seen, the logical instructions can be either one or two bytes long. The logical instructions are summarized in Table 2-18.

Table 2-18. A Summary of the 8080's Logical Instructions

Source Register	AND	OR	exOR	Compare
A	ANAA	ORAA	XRAA	CMPA
B	ANAB	ORAB	XRAB	CMPB
C	ANAC	ORAC	XRAC	CMPC
D	ANAD	ORAD	XRAD	CMPD
E	ANAE	ORAE	XRAE	CMPE
H	ANAH	ORAH	XRAH	CMPH
L	ANAL	ORAL	XRAL	CMPL
Memory	ANAM	ORAM	XRAM	CMPM
Immediate	ANI	ORI	XRI	CPI
	$\langle B_2 \rangle$	$\langle B_2 \rangle$	$\langle B_2 \rangle$	$\langle B_2 \rangle$
Rotate Instructions—RLC, RRC, RAL, RAR				

Remember that memory, in an instruction such as ANAM, is the memory location addressed by register pair H. Also note that the immediate instructions are *always* two-byte instructions. Although we have not shown any examples that use the exclusive-OR instructions, such as XRAA, XRAE, or XRI, they will be discussed in another chapter.

MATHEMATICAL INSTRUCTIONS

The 8080 can only execute addition and subtraction instructions. More complex functions such as multiplication and division can be performed, but these functions must be accomplished by means of multiple additions or subtractions.

The mathematical instructions that will be discussed in this chapter all operate on eight-bit, unsigned, binary numbers. However, *2s-complement* mathematical operations can be performed. The 8080 also has the capability of operating on BCD numbers and adding 16-bit binary numbers. The instructions that perform these operations will be discussed in another chapter.

The mathematical instructions that operate on eight-bit binary words, like the logical instructions, always use the content of the A register as one of the arguments being added or subtracted. The condition flags are all affected by any of these instructions. These instructions are used in the following examples and they are fairly straightforward.

Addition

The 8080 can execute two types of addition instructions, add (ADD) and add-with-carry (ADC). Both add instructions can be used to add the content of the A register to the content of one of the general-purpose registers, the content of memory addressed by register pair H, or an immediate data byte. No matter which one of the ADD instructions is executed, the result will always be left in the A register. Also, the carry flag will be set or cleared to indicate the state of the carry bit. If a carry occurs, the carry flag will be true, or a logic 1.

There are eight different single-byte add (ADD) instructions and one add-immediate (ADI) instruction. Like the other immediate instructions, the ADI instruction is a two-byte instruction. Some of the addition instructions are:

ADDB   ADDM   ADDE   ADDA   ADDH   ADI
$<B_2>$

Note that any of the general-purpose registers, including the A register, can be used as the *addend*. As is true with all of the immediate instructions, there must be a data byte stored in the next consecutive memory location after the op code for the add-immediate instruction, ADI.

To add the content of the B register to the A register, the single-byte instruction, ADDB (octal 200, hex 80), would have to be included in your program. Example 2-12 shows the results of executing an ADDB instruction.

Example 2-12: Adding the Content of B to A Using the ADDB Instruction

Register A	10110101
+ Register B	+ 00101111
Register A	11100100

After the ADDB instruction has been executed, the content of the A register is 11100100_2. No carry was generated; therefore, the carry flag is a logic 0 after the ADDB instruction is executed. The program in Example 2-13 loads eight-bit numbers into both the A and B registers and then adds them by executing an ADDB instruction.

Example 2-13: A Program That Adds the Content of the A and B Registers

```
/THIS PROGRAM ADDS THE CONTENT OF REGISTER B
/TO REGISTER A. THE RESULT IS LEFT IN
/REGISTER A.

ADD,  MVIA   /LOAD A VALUE INTO REGISTER A.
      265    /(OCTAL 265, HEX B5).
      MVIB   /LOAD A VALUE INTO REGISTER B.
      057    /(OCTAL 057, HEX 2F).
      ADDB   /ADD A TO B, LEAVE THE RESULT IN
      •      /A. THE REMAINDER OF THE PRO-
      •      /GRAM IS STORED HERE.
```

Example 2-14 shows what happens to the carry when two numbers are added together and the result is greater than 255_{10}, or 11111111_2.

Example 2-14: Adding the Content of the A and B Registers and Generating a Carry

Register A	11110111_2	247_{10}
+ Register B	+ 00101111_2	+ 47_{10}
Register A	00100110_2	38_{10}
Carry =	1	

Notice in Example 2-14 that the carry is set to a logic 1 when the content of the B register is added to the content of the A register.

The carry flag is also set to a logic 1 to indicate that the carry is set to a logic 1.

You probably know that the addition of 47_{10} to 247_{10} is not 38_{10}. To determine the proper result, you can assign a decimal value of 256_{10} to the carry. In the first example that used the ADDB instruction (Example 2-12), there was no carry, since the result of the addition did not exceed 255_{10}. However, when 47_{10} is added to 247_{10}, a carry is generated. Therefore, the proper result is 256_{10} (carry bit position) $+ 38_{10} = 294_{10}$. This is what you would expect when you add 47_{10} to 247_{10}.

The program listed in Example 2-15 adds the content of the B register to the A register. The result is left in the A register and the carry is set to a logic 1 as a result of the addition. The carry flag will also be a logic 1 to indicate the state of the carry.

If an add-with-carry (ADC) instruction is used in a following addition process, the carry, along with an eight-bit value contained in memory, a general-purpose register, or an immediate data byte, can be added to the content of the A register. This feature permits the 8080 to operate on data words that are longer than eight bits. If two 16-bit numbers are to be added together, the two LSBYs

Example 2-15: A Program That Adds Two Numbers and Sets the Carry to a Logic 1

```
/THIS PROGRAM ADDS TWO NUMBERS THAT PRODUCE
/AN EIGHT-BIT RESULT AND A CARRY.

ADD1,   MVIA    /LOAD A VALUE INTO REGISTER A.
        367     /(OCTAL 367, HEX F7).
        MVIB    /LOAD A VALUE INTO REGISTER B.
        057     /(OCTAL 057, HEX 2F).
        ADDB    /ADD B TO A AND THE RESULT IS LEFT
        •       /IN A. THE REMAINDER OF THE PRO-
        •       /GRAM IS STORED HERE.
```

would be added together first with an ADD instruction. After the result of the addition is saved, the two MSBYs would then be added together with an ADC instruction. The ADC instruction adds the carry from the addition of the two LSBYs to the result of the addition of the two MSBYs.

With eight binary bits, data can be represented by any decimal number between 0 and 255:

128	64	32	16	8	4	2	1	Decimal Weighting
0	0	0	0	0	0	0	0	= 0 Smallest Word
1	1	1	1	1	1	1	1	= 255 Largest Word

Obviously, many problems require numbers larger than 255_{10}. Therefore, two-, three-, and four-byte words (16, 24, and 32 bits) are often used.

32,768	16,384	8192	4096	2048	1024	512	256	128	64	32	16	8	4	2	1	Decimal Weighting	
0	0	0	0	0	0	0	0	0	0	0	0	0	0	0	0	= 0	Smallest Word
1	1	1	1	1	1	1	1	1	1	1	1	1	1	1	1	= 65,535	Largest Word

The smallest word that can be represented by a 16-bit word is still 0, but the largest word that can be represented by a 16-bit word is 65,535. By using more and more bytes, larger and larger numbers can be manipulated. If the two numbers that were added together in the previous example (Example 2-15) were only the two LSBYs of two 16-bit numbers, then the addition of the two MSBYs can be performed with an add-with-carry instruction (Example 2-16).

As you can see, the carry resulting from the addition of the two LSBYs must be added to the result of the addition of the two MSBYs. The add-with-carry (ADC) instruction permits the 8080 to do this. In Example 2-16, the carry from the addition of the two

Example 2-16: The Addition of Two 16-Bit Numbers

MSBYs

```
  10101010 from register D
+ 01000100 from register B
  ────────
  11101110
+        1  ← ← ← ← ← ← ← Carry
  ────────
  11101111 in register H
```

LSBYs

```
  11110111 from register E
  00101111 from register C
1 00100110 in register L
```

LSBYs is added to the MSBYs. Now the state of the carry reflects the result of adding the MSBYs and the previous carry bit together. This add-with-carry (ADC) instruction may be used to add together two binary numbers having almost any number of eight-bit bytes. The program listed in Example 2-17 shows the addition of the 16-bit number in register pair B to the 16-bit number in register pair D. The 16-bit result is saved in register pair H. Note the use of the ADCB (add-with-carry register B) instruction.

The purpose of these mathematical programs is to demonstrate how the mathematical instructions are used. We have not included any instructions that save the *final* carry, generated by the addition of the two MSBYs. If the ADD16 program is used to add 377 377 (FFFF) to 377 377 (FFFF), the result stored in register pair H would be 377 376 (FFFE). The carry will be set to a logic 1, but there are no instructions in the ADD16 program that save this final carry. Therefore, the 16-bit result, 377 376 (FFFE), is incorrect. If these program examples are used to perform addition operations,

Example 2-17: Using an ADC-Type Instruction in a 16-Bit Addition

/THIS PROGRAM ADDS THE 16-BIT NUMBER IN REGISTER
/PAIR B TO THE 16-BIT NUMBER IN REGISTER PAIR D.
/THE RESULT IS SAVED IN REGISTER PAIR H.

ADD16,	LXIB	/LOAD REGISTER PAIR B WITH ONE
	057	/OF THE 16-BIT NUMBERS.
	104	/(OCTAL 104 057 = HEX 442F).
	LXID	/LOAD REGISTER PAIR D WITH THE
	367	/OTHER 16-BIT NUMBER.
	252	/(OCTAL 252 367 = HEX AAF7).
	MOVAE	/MOVE THE LSBY OF REGISTER PAIR D TO A.
	ADDC	/ADD THE LSBY OF REGISTER PAIR B.
	MOVLA	/SAVE THE RESULT'S LSBY IN L.
	MOVAD	/MOVE THE MSBY OF REGISTER PAIR D TO A.
	ADCB	/ADD-WITH-CARRY THE MSBY OF REGISTER PAIR B.
	MOVHA	/SAVE THE RESULT'S MSBY IN H.
	•	/NOW EXECUTE THE REMAINING INSTRUC-
	•	/TIONS IN THE PROGRAM.

it is your responsibility to ensure that the sum of any two numbers never exceeds 377 377 (FFFF).

It is extremely important to realize that if numbers larger than eight bits are added together, the LSBYs must always be added together first, then the next more-significant LSBYs, and so on, in sequence up to the MSBYs.

Subtraction

There are two types of subtraction instructions. These are subtract (SUB) and subtract-with-borrow (SBB). Like the addition instructions, the content of memory addressed by register pair H, an immediate data byte, or the content of one of the general-purpose registers, can be subtracted from the content of the A register. The result of the subtraction is then left in the A register.

Example 2-18: Subtracting the Content of Register E From Register A

Register A	00110111
− Register E	− 00010100
Register A	00100011

The program listed in Example 2-19 subtracts the content of the E register from the B register. The content of the B register is moved to the A register before the subtraction is performed.

If the subtraction of a larger number from a smaller number is performed, the carry will be set to a logic 1, indicating that a borrow has occurred. In Example 2-20, the larger number, which is contained in the B register, is subtracted from the smaller number, which is contained in the A register.

Example 2-19: Subtracting Register E From Register B

```
/THIS PROGRAM SUBTRACTS THE CONTENT OF THE E
/REGISTER FROM THE CONTENT OF THE B REGISTER
/AND SAVES THE RESULT IN THE D REGISTER.

SUB1,   MVIB    /LOAD THE B REGISTER WITH THE
        067     /MINUEND (OCTAL 067 = HEX 37).
        MVIE    /LOAD THE SUBTRAHEND INTO THE E
        024     /REGISTER (OCTAL 024 = HEX 14).
        MOVAB   /MOVE THE MINUEND TO A.
        SUBE    /SUBTRACT THE SUBTRAHEND
        MOVDA   /AND SAVE THE RESULT IN D.
          •     /THE REMAINDER OF THE PROGRAM IS
          •     /STORED STARTING HERE.
```

The program listed in Example 2-21 contains the instruction mnemonics required to load immediate data bytes into both the A and B registers. The content of the B register is then subtracted from the A register.

Example 2-20: Generating a Borrow During a Subtraction

$$\begin{array}{r} \text{Register A} \\ -\text{Register B} \\ \hline \text{Register A} \\ Carry \quad = \end{array} \quad \begin{array}{r} 01010110 \\ -10001011 \\ \hline 11001011 \\ 1 \end{array}$$

Example 2-21: Subtracting a Larger Number From a Smaller Number

```
/THIS PROGRAM SUBTRACTS THE CONTENT OF THE B
/REGISTER FROM THE A REGISTER AND SAVES THE RESULT
/IN THE L REGISTER. THE NUMBER IN B IS LARGER
/THAN THE NUMBER IN A.

SUB2,   MVIA    /LOAD THE MINUEND INTO THE A
        126     /REGISTER (OCTAL 126 = HEX 56).
        MVIB    /LOAD THE SUBTRAHEND INTO THE
        213     /B REGISTER (OCTAL 213 = HEX 8B).
        SUBB    /SUBTRACT THE CONTENT OF B FROM A.
        MOVLA   /SAVE THE RESULT IN THE L REGISTER
          •     /THEN EXECUTE THE REMAINING INSTRUC-
          •     /TIONS IN THE PROGRAM.
```

The fact that the carry contains a logic 1 enables us to subtract two very large binary numbers, as long as the numbers are separated into bytes. In the subtraction of two 16-bit numbers, the LSBYs are subtracted first. In the addition of two 16-bit numbers, the LSBYs were added first.

If the carry is set to a logic 1 after the subtraction is performed, a borrow has really occurred. This means that 1 must be subtracted from the result of the subtraction of the two MSBYs.

Example 2-22: Subtracting Two 16-Bit Numbers

```
  01110101 from register D        11010000 from register E
- 00101011 from register B        10111001 from register C
  ─────────                       ─────────
  01001010 in register H          00010111 in register L
```

In Example 2-22, a borrow is not generated because the 10111001 in register C is smaller than the 11010000 in the E register. The software instructions that perform this 16-bit subtraction are listed in Example 2-23.

In the next 16-bit subtraction example (Example 2-24), a borrow does occur when the two LSBYs are subtracted. This occurs because the 11000101 in the C register is larger than the 01011100 in the E register.

Example 2-23: Subtracting Register Pair B From Register Pair D

```
/THIS PROGRAM SUBTRACTS THE 16-BIT CONTENT OF REGISTER
/PAIR B FROM THE 16-BIT CONTENT OF REGISTER PAIR D.
/THE 16-BIT RESULT IS SAVED IN REGISTER PAIR H.

SUB16,  LXID     /LOAD REGISTER PAIR D WITH THE
        320      /MINUEND.
        165      /(OCTAL 165 320 = HEX 75D0).
        LXIB     /LOAD REGISTER PAIR B WITH THE
        271      /SUBTRAHEND.
        053      /(OCTAL 053 271 = HEX 2BB9).
        MOVAE    /MOVE THE LSBY OF THE MINUEND TO A.
        SUBC     /SUBTRACT THE LSBY OF THE SUBTRAHEND.
        MOVLA    /SAVE THE RESULT'S LSBY IN L.
        MOVAD    /MOVE THE MSBY OF THE MINUEND TO A.
        SBBB     /SUBTRACT-WITH-BORROW THE SUBTRAHEND'S MSBY.
        MOVHA    /SAVE THE RESULT'S MSBY IN H
          •      /THEN EXECUTE ANY REMAINING
          •      /PROGRAM STEPS.
```

Example 2-24: Generating a Borrow by Subtracting Register Pair B From Register Pair D

```
        MSBYs                              LSBYs
  01101111 from register D        01011100 from register E
- 00010011 from register B        11000101 from register C
  ─────────                       ───────────
  01011100                        1 10010111 in register E
-        1  ← ← ← ← ← ← ←  Borrow
  ─────────
  01011011 in register D
```

In Example 2-24, a borrow is generated and the carry is set to a logic 1, because 11000101 is subtracted from 01011100, a smaller number. A program that can actually perform this 16-bit subtraction is listed in Example 2-25.

Example 2-25 performs the same subtraction operations as the program listed in Example 2-23. You should note that the program operates effectively with or without the generation of a borrow. We have kept the program general-purpose, since the "borrows" may or may not occur.

There are also two-byte immediate mathematical instructions, such as add-immediate (ADI), add-with-carry-immediate (ACI), subtract-immediate (SUI), and subtract-with-borrow-immediate (SBI). These instructions, as well as the other add and subtract instructions, are summarized in Table 2-19.

Example 2-25: Subtracting Register Pair B From Register Pair D

```
/THIS PROGRAM SUBTRACTS THE 16-BIT CONTENT OF REGISTER
/PAIR B FROM THE 16-BIT CONTENT OF REGISTER PAIR D AND
/SAVES THE RESULT IN REGISTER PAIR D.

SUB16,   LXIB      /LOAD REGISTER PAIR B WITH THE
         305       /SUBTRAHEND.
         023       /(OCTAL 023 305 = HEX 13C5).
         LXID      /LOAD REGISTER PAIR D WITH THE
         134       /MINUEND.
         157       /(OCTAL 157 134 = 6F5C).
         MOVAE     /MOVE THE LSBY OF THE MINUEND TO A.
         SUBC      /SUBTRACT THE LSBY OF THE SUBTRAHEND.
         MOVEA     /SAVE THE RESULT'S LSBY IN E.
         MOVAD     /MOVE THE MSBY OF THE MINUEND TO A.
         SBBB      /SUBTRACT-WITH-BORROW THE MSBY OF THE
         MOVDA     /SUBTRAHEND AND SAVE THE MSBY'S RESULT
          •        /IN D. THEN EXECUTE ANY REMAINING
          •        /PROGRAM STEPS.
```

Table 2-19. A Summary of the 8080's Instructions for Eight-Bit Addition and Subtraction

Source Register	Add	Add-With-Carry	Subtract	Subtract-With-Borrow
A	ADDA	ADCA	SUBA	SBBA
B	ADDB	ADCB	SUBB	SBBB
C	ADDC	ADCC	SUBC	SBBC
D	ADDD	ADCD	SUBD	SBBD
E	ADDE	ADCE	SUBE	SBBE
H	ADDH	ADCH	SUBH	SBBH
L	ADDL	ADCL	SUBL	SBBL
Memory	ADDM	ADCM	SUBM	SBBM
Immediate	ADI $<B_2>$	ACI $<B_2>$	SUI $<B_2>$	SBI $<B_2>$

Increment and Decrement Instructions

There are two special mathematical instructions, increment (INR) and decrement (DCR). Each instruction enables the 8080 to add or subtract 1 from a general-purpose register or the memory location addressed by register pair H. These instructions are summarized in Table 2-20.

Table 2-20. The Increment and Decrement Instructions

INRS = 0S4	Increment register S by 1
DCRS = 0S5	Decrement register S by 1

You can use any of the octal register codes, which were used in the section of this chapter that described MOV instructions, for the source register, S. The increment and decrement instructions (INR and DCR) do not affect the carry flag, but when a register is incremented or decremented to equal zero, the zero flag is set to a logic 1.

These instructions are particularly useful when you want a program to count events. These events could be external to the microcomputer system, such as the number of cars going through an intersection, or internal events, such as the number of times a particular mathematical program is executed.

Each of these increment and decrement (INR and DCR) instructions operates on a single data byte. To see how one of the increment instructions affects the content of a register and the zero flag, we have assumed in Example 2-26 that the B register has been loaded with 374 (FC).

Example 2-26: Incrementing the Content of the B Register With INRB

Content of B				Zero Flag Condition After
Binary	Octal	Hex	Mnemonic	Instruction Execution
11111100	374	FC	MVIB $<B_2>$	Unknown
11111101	375	FD	INRB	Logic 0
11111110	376	FE	INRB	Logic 0
11111111	377	FF	INRB	Logic 0
00000000	000	00	INRB	Logic 1
00000001	001	01	INRB	Logic 0
00000010	002	02	INRB	Logic 0

Note that only when the content of the B register is incremented from 377 (FF) to 000 (00) is the zero flag set to a logic 1 condition. The next increment instruction clears this condition, since the incremented content of register B is no longer zero.

The decrement operation can be illustrated in a similar manner as shown in Example 2-27.

Note that only when the content of the E register has been decremented to 000 (00) will the zero flag be a logic 1. The next decre-

Example 2-27: Decrementing the Content of the E Register With DCRE

Content of E				Zero Flag Condition After
Binary	Octal	Hex	Mnemonic	Instruction Execution
00000100	004	04	MVIE	Unknown
			$<B_2>$	
00000011	003	03	DCRE	Logic 0
00000010	002	02	DCRE	Logic 0
00000001	001	01	DCRE	Logic 0
00000000	000	00	DCRE	Logic 1
11111111	377	FF	DCRE	Logic 0
11111110	376	FE	DCRE	Logic 0

ment instruction (DCRE) after that causes the E register to be decremented to 377 (FF) and the zero flag to be cleared to zero.

The Register Pair Increment and Decrement Instructions

There is also a special class of increment and decrement instructions (INX and DCX) that operate on the content of register pairs B, D, and H. These increment and decrement instructions increment and decrement the 16-bit content of these register pairs. For example, to increment the 16-bit content of register pair H, you would use an INXH instruction. In Example 2-28, we will assume that register pair H already contains 00001000 11111110 (octal 010 376, hexadecimal 08FE).

Example 2-28: The Use of the INXH Instruction

Content of Register Pair H After Instruction Execution				Mnemonic
Binary		Octal	Hex	
Register H	Register L			
00001000	11111110	010 376	08FE	INXH
00001000	11111111	010 377	08FF	INXH
00001001	00000000	011 000	0900	INXH
00001001	00000001	011 001	0901	INXH

In Example 2-3, we demonstrated how register pair H could be used to point to a memory location when the content of that memory location is required for another microcomputer operation. Recalling that example, suppose you need to move the content of memory location 030 123 (1853) to register D, and the content of memory location 030 124 (1854) to register E. Your first attempt might appear like Example 2-29.

Of course, this program will work quite well; but, with one of the instructions that we just introduced, this program can be simplified.

In both Examples 2-29 and 2-30, an LXIH instruction is used to load the initial memory address into register pair H. In Example

Example 2-29: Loading the Content of Memory into Registers D and E

```
LXIH      /LOAD REGISTER PAIR H WITH A 16-BIT
123       /MEMORY ADDRESS.
030       /(OCTAL 030 123 = HEX 1853).
MOVDM     /MOVE THE CONTENT OF MEMORY TO D.
LXIH      /LOAD REGISTER PAIR H WITH THE 16-BIT
124       /MEMORY ADDRESS FOR THE NEXT CONSECUTIVE
030       /MEMORY LOCATION. (OCTAL 030 124 = HEX 1854).
MOVEM     /MOVE THE CONTENT OF MEMORY TO E.
```

2-29, the content of the memory location addressed by register pair H is loaded into register D. Register pair H is then loaded with the next memory address, and the content of memory at that address is loaded into register E.

Example 2-30: An Improved Program for Loading Registers D and E With the Content of Memory

```
LXIH      /LOAD REGISTER PAIR H WITH A 16-BIT
123       /MEMORY ADDRESS.
030       /(OCTAL 030  123 = HEX 1853).
MOVDM     /MOVE THE CONTENT OF MEMORY TO D.
INXH      /INCREMENT THE ADDRESS (OCTAL 030 124 = HEX 1854).
MOVEM     /MOVE THE CONTENT OF MEMORY TO E.
```

By storing the two data values in consecutive memory locations, we do not have to perform the second LXIH instruction, as demonstrated in the second example, Example 2-30. Instead, after the first data value is loaded into register D, the content of register pair H is incremented by 1 when the INXH instruction is executed. The content of register pair H now points to the next consecutive memory location which contains the data value that is to be moved into register E. After the INXH instruction is executed, the content of memory addressed by register pair H is then loaded into register E.

After the MOVEM instruction is executed, what is contained in register pair H? Register pair H contains the value 030 124 (1854). If data values are stored in consecutive memory locations, programs such as the one in Example 2-30 can be very useful in storing or retrieving data in continuous sections of memory.

The DCXH instruction is also very useful in that it gives you the ability to examine or move the content of memory, starting from the highest address and moving to the lowest. Example 2-31 demonstrates the effect that the DCXH instruction has on the content of register pair H.

As you can see in Example 2-31, the DCXH instruction performs a 16-bit decrement operation on the content of register pair H.

Example 2-31: A Demonstration of the DCXH Instruction

Content of Register Pair H After Instruction Execution				Mnemonic
Binary		Octal	Hex	
Register H	Register L			
00101011	00000011	053 003	2B03	DCXH
00101011	00000010	053 002	2B02	DCXH
00101011	00000001	053 001	2B01	DCXH
00101011	00000000	053 000	2B00	DCXH
00101010	11111111	052 377	2AFF	DCXH
00101010	11111110	052 376	2AFE	DCXH
00101010	11111101	052 375	2AFD	DCXH

We mentioned that it is possible to increment and decrement the content of register pairs B, D, and H. The instructions that perform these operations are summarized in Table 2-21 along with their octal and hexadecimal op codes.

Table 2-21. The Register Pair Increment and Decrement Instructions

Octal	Mnemonic	Hexadecimal
003	INXB	03
013	DCXB	0B
023	INXD	13
033	DCXD	1B
043	INXH	23
053	DCXH	2B

Unlike the INR and DCR instructions that increment and decrement the eight-bit content of a register, *none of the instructions in Table 2-21 affect any of the condition flags. Therefore, we cannot "directly" test the incremented or decremented 16-bit value for the "equal-to-zero" condition.*

We have now introduced you to the "basic" register pair instructions. Other register pair instructions exist and will be discussed later. The register pairs that have been discussed are register pairs B, D, and H. The instructions that affect these register pairs include LXI, INX, and DCX.

The Halt and No-Operation Instructions

Of the many instructions that have not been discussed, there are two simple single-byte instructions, HLT and NOP. The op codes for these instructions are listed in Table 2-22.

The HLT, or halt, instruction causes the microcomputer to stop any program that it is executing. If you have a small program that

**Table 2-22. The Op Codes for the HLT
and NOP Instructions**

Octal	Mnemonic	Hexadecimal
166	HLT	76
000	NOP	00

you want to execute only once, a HLT instruction might be placed at the end of the program. A typical program sequence is shown in Example 2-32.

Example 2-32: Using a HLT Instruction

```
MVIA    /LOAD THE A REGISTER WITH
001     /(OCTAL 001 =. HEX 01).
OUT     /OUTPUT THE VALUE TO OUTPUT
053     /PORT 053 (HEX 2B).
INRA    /INCREMENT THE CONTENTS OF A.
OUT     /OUTPUT THE VALUE TO OUTPUT
054     /PORT 054 (HEX 2C).
HLT     /THEN HALT.
```

This program causes action to take place at two output ports; then the microcomputer halts. There is no easy way to cause the microcomputer to resume normal program execution after a HLT instruction has been executed. To get the microcomputer running again, you could generate a hardware interrupt (we will discuss this in another chapter) or you could reset the 8080 microcomputer and begin executing the program stored in memory location 000 000 (0000).

The NOP instruction is generally used when you are programming the 8080 microcomputer with a simple debugger or monitor program. NOPs are generally inserted into a section of a program to "leave room" for additional instructions, if they may be required. If you discover, while debugging a program, that instructions have been mistakenly omitted, the additional instructions can generally

Example 2-33: Using NOP Instructions to "Leave Room" in a Program

```
MVIA    MVIA    /LOAD THE A REGISTER
075     075     /WITH 075 (HEX 3D).
ADDB    MVIB
NOP     051
NOP     INRC
NOP     NOP
OUT     OUT     /OUTPUT A TO DEVICE 120
120     120     /(HEX 50).
INRA    INRA
OUT     OUT     /OUTPUT A TO DEVICE 121
121     121     /(HEX 51).
HLT     HLT     /THEN HALT.
```

be stored in the memory locations where the NOPs were stored. Example 2-33 shows how the NOP instructions are replaced by other instructions.

It really does not matter what this program does. What is important is that by leaving some NOPs in the program, the instructions MVIB 051 and INRC can be added to the program, while the incorrect instruction, ADDB, can be eliminated.

BRANCHING, TRANSFER-OF-CONTROL, AND DECISION-MAKING INSTRUCTIONS

Up to this point, all of the program examples have been straight line programs, often termed *pipeline* programs. Control has not been transferred to another section of a program based on the results of executing an instruction or a series of instructions. The next class of instructions that we will discuss shows how program execution can be transferred from one section of a program to another and why this is useful to you.

Jump Instructions

Jump instructions are used to transfer control (program execution) to a new program, a different section of the program currently being executed, or perhaps to a special test program. The jump instruction can be thought of as an instruction in the program that breaks the normal execution of the program and causes the 8080 to continue execution of the program at some other point. If you were working with a set of step-by-step instructions to fix an automobile, one of the instructions might state: "Go back to Step 5." This is a jump, because it has caused you to transfer your attention (program execution) back to Step 5. Notice that the instruction specified *exactly* where you were to jump. You already know that to uniquely specify a single memory location, a 16-bit address is required. This is also true of the jump instructions, since the computer must know exactly where it is going.

All of the 8080 jump instructions are three-byte instructions. The first byte contains the op code for the jump instruction, the second byte contains the low address, and the third byte contains the high address. This is shown in Example 2-34.

In this instruction, and in all other instructions that specify a memory address, the second byte contains the low address or the eight

Example 2-34. The Format of the Jump Instructions

Octal	Mnemonic	Hexadecimal
303	JMP	C3
034	$<B_2>$	1C
005	$<B_3>$	05

least-significant bits (the LSBY), and the third byte contains the high address or the eight most-significant bits (the MSBY). In Example 2-34, the 8080 would jump to memory location 005 034 (051C) when the JMP instruction is executed. At that address, you would have stored some additional program instructions.

Can you guess how this instruction is executed? When the 8080 fetches the JMP instruction's op code from memory, the 8080 realizes that it is a jump instruction. Therefore, the next two bytes stored in memory after the JMP instruction are fetched and loaded directly into the program counter (PC). Since the PC always points to the memory location that contains the next instruction to be executed, the next instruction will be located in the memory location specified by the second and third bytes of the jump instruction.

We have specified *exactly* where the 8080 is to jump to. Perhaps at the end of a program you may want the 8080 to jump back to the start of the program and execute it again. If the starting address of the program is 000 000 (0000), you could use the JMP instruction listed in Example 2-35.

Example 2-35: Jumping Back to the Beginning of a Program

Octal	Mnemonic	Hexadecimal
303	JMP	C3
000	$<B_2>$	00
000	$<B_3>$	00

After the 8080 executes this instruction, the next instruction that it will execute will be found in memory location 000 000 (0000).

Whenever the 8080 reaches a JMP instruction in a program, it will *always* be executed. Therefore, the JMP instruction is called an *unconditional* instruction. There are *no software or flag conditions* that can prevent the JMP instruction from being executed.

However, there are many programs where you might want the 8080 to execute a jump instruction only when certain conditions are met. In Example 2-11, where numeric ASCII characters were packed into a single byte, the assumption was made that all characters that were input were numeric characters. Actually, you might accidentally input a nonnumeric character. The software would then have to be written so that this character is ignored. However, let us assume that when a question mark (?) is entered (ASCII value of octal 277 or hexadecimal BF), the BCD packing routine must be ended and control transferred to a different section of the program. This would be a good application for a *conditional* jump instruction.

Conditional Jump Instructions

The 8080's conditional jump instructions allow us to attach a condition to the jump instruction so that the jump instruction is only executed if the specified condition is met. The conditions that may be tested in this way are the states of one of the internal 8080 flags; carry, sign, zero, and parity. We will concentrate our program examples on the use of the carry and zero flags.

As you might guess, all of the *conditional jump instructions* are three-byte instructions, where the 16-bit address is specified in the second and third bytes. Remember that the flags are set and cleared as the result of a logical or mathematical instruction. *Regardless of whether or not the conditional instruction is executed, the state of the flags does not change.* The 8080 conditional jump instructions are listed in Table 2-23.

Table 2-23. The 8080 Conditional Jump Instructions

Operation	Mnemonic	Octal	Hexadecimal
Jump if the result of an instruction[1] is not zero.	JNZ	302	C2
Jump if the result of an instruction is zero.	JZ	312	CA
Jump if the result of an instruction has no carry (borrow).	JNC	322	D2
Jump if the result of an instruction has a carry (borrow).	JC	332	DA
Jump if the result of an instruction has odd parity.	JPO	342	E2
Jump if the result of an instruction has even parity.	JPE	352	EA
Jump if the result of an instruction is positive.	JP	362	F2
Jump if the result of an instruction is minus (negative).	JM	372	FA

[1] Mathematical or logical.

Note that all four of the flags can be tested separately with conditional jump instructions. Also, the conditional jump instructions can test for both the true and the false condition of each flag, which means that there are eight conditional jump instructions that the 8080 can execute.

In the ASCII character input-and-pack program that was previously discussed (Example 2-11), there was no way to exit from the program and continue with another section of the program. Therefore, some instructions must be added so that when a particular key on the keyboard is pressed, the 8080 will begin execution of another section of the program. The question mark (?) was arbitrarily chosen as the character to be used to terminate the input section of the program. The number sign (#), exclamation mark (!), or percent sign (%) could have just as easily been used. The

ASCII representation for the question mark is 277 (BF), assuming that the MSB (the parity bit) is a logic 1.

In the ASCII character input program, all of the input characters must be compared to the value, 277 (BF). If the zero flag is set to a logic 1 by the comparison operation, then the eight-bit character contained in the A register must have been produced by pressing the question-mark key on the keyboard. The 8080 can then conditionally jump to another section of the program. These additional program steps are included in Example 2-36.

Example 2-36: Terminating the Input Program With a Question Mark

```
IN        /INPUT AN ASCII CHARACTER FROM
015       /INPUT DEVICE 015 (HEX 0D).
CPI       /COMPARE THE CHARACTER TO THE
277       /DATA BYTE 277 (AN ASCII QUESTION MARK).
JZ        /IF THE CHARACTER IS A QUESTION MARK,
<LO>      /THE JZ TO THE SPECIFIED ADDRESS WILL
<HI>      /BE EXECUTED.
ANI       /THE CHARACTER IS NOT A QUESTION MARK, SO
017       /AND THE CHARACTER WITH 017 (HEX 0F).
  •       /THE REMAINDER OF THE PROGRAM IS
  •       /STORED HERE.
```

Two new instructions have been added to program Example 2-11, and they require five memory locations for storage. The compare-immediate (CPI) and the jump-on-zero (JZ) instructions have been added. Initially, the A register contains the data word from input port (device) 015 (0D). The compare instruction then *invisibly subtracts* the immediate data byte 277 (BF) from the content of the A register. The result of the comparison (subtraction) then sets or clears the flags, as appropriate.

The compare instruction *does not* change the content of the A register. Therefore, if the A register does not contain a 277 (BF), the JZ instruction is not executed because the zero condition specified by the instruction is not met. Only if the zero flag is set, or true, meaning that the A register does contain a 277 (BF) when the CPI instruction is executed, will the JZ instruction be executed. If the jump is not executed, the 8080 will execute the instruction stored in the next consecutive memory location, the ANI instruction. The address bytes of the jump instruction are ignored if the jump is not executed. This is because the 8080 microprocessor integrated circuit knows exactly how many bytes (one, two, or three) are required by each instruction. Therefore, the 8080 knows the 16-bit address of the *next instruction* after the JZ instruction. For this reason, the 8080 will never attempt to execute the address or data bytes of the two- or three-byte instructions as op codes, provided that your program is correctly written.

Could you use the decision-making instructions in other ways? You could test all of the ASCII input characters so that only the numeric characters, 0 through 9, are "packed." All other characters, with the exception of the question mark, are ignored. The numeric representation for the ASCII characters, 0 through 9, is 260 through 271 (B0 through B9). How can all of the ASCII characters with values less than 260 (B0) and greater than 271 (B9) be ignored? There are numerous methods that can be used to screen-out the other ASCII characters. However, CPI instructions can be used to make this software very simple.

Example 2-37: Ignoring All ASCII Characters Other Than 0–9 and ?

```
START,  IN      /INPUT AN ASCII CHARACTER
        015     /FROM INPUT PORT 015 (HEX 0D).
        CPI     /IS THE CHARACTER A QUESTION MARK ?
        277
        JZ      /YES, TERMINATE THE INPUT
        TERMIT  /BY JUMPING TO THE ADDRESS THAT IS
        0       /ASSIGNED THE SYMBOLIC ADDRESS "TERMIT."
        CPI     /IT WAS NOT A QUESTION MARK, COMPARE THE
        260     /DATA TO AN ASCII 0.
        JC      /IF THE CARRY IS SET, THEN
        START   /260 IS GREATER THAN THE CHARACTER TYPED
        0       /IN. THEREFORE, JUMP TO "START."
        CPI     /NOW SEE IF IT IS GREATER THAN 271.
        272     /COMPARE THE CHARACTER TO 1 GREATER
        JNC     /THAN ASCII 9. IS THE CHARACTER
        START   /272 OR GREATER ? IF SO, JUMP BACK
        0       /TO THE BEGINNING ("START").
        ANI     /IT WAS ONE OF THE ASCII CHARACTERS
        017     /BETWEEN 0 AND 9. MASK OUT THE
         •      /4 MOST SIGNIFICANT BITS.
         •
         •

        ETC
```

In this program, we have used two *symbolic addresses*. Do you know what these symbolic addresses are? One of the symbolic addresses is the word START, and the other symbolic address is TERMIT. The START symbolic address is used three times in Example 2-37, and the TERMIT symbolic address is used only once. Using a symbolic address is one method of indicating that a memory location contains an instruction or data value that the program may have to reference. In this program, we know that if the question-mark key is pressed, the 8080 should not execute any of the instructions in the ASCII-packing section of the program. If the question-mark key is not pressed, then the 8080 must determine if one of the numeric keys, 0 through 9, is pressed. If a nonnumeric key is pressed at this point in the program, the 8080 must ignore it by jumping back to the IN instruction.

If this program is loaded into memory, we would have to remember the address of the memory location in which the IN instruction is stored. This address would then be used as the 16-bit address for the JC and JNC instructions. The address where the 8080 is to jump to, if the question-mark key is pressed, must also be determined and stored after the JZ instruction. By *defining* or *associating* the symbolic address, START, with the IN instruction, we can easily remember where the 8080 should jump to if the character entered has a value less than 260 (B0) or greater than 271 (B9). Once a symbolic address has been defined, it can be used with the JC and JNC instructions. In fact, as you will see in other software examples, symbolic addresses can be used with all three-byte instructions.

Of course, when this program is loaded into memory, we will still have to determine the 16-bit address for the JZ, JC, and JNC instructions. However, it is easier to use symbolic addresses than to write $<B_2>$ and $<B_3>$ after the jump instructions. If we did use the $<B_2>$ and $<B_3>$ address notation, then it would be difficult to remember exactly where we want the 8080 to jump to. As you can see, we also leave a zero (0) after the symbolic addresses used in the JZ, JC, and JNC instructions. This permits us to remember to leave room for the $<B_3>$ or the high address byte of the instruction. Remember, no matter what notation or symbolic address that we use, when a jump instruction is loaded into memory, it requires *three* memory locations for storage.

Four instructions have been added to Example 2-37, and they require an additional ten memory locations for storage. The first compare instruction determines whether or not a question mark has been entered. If it has been, the JZ instruction is executed and the 8080 transfers control elsewhere. If the character entered is not a question mark, then it is compared to 260 (B0). If the value entered is less than 260 (B0), the carry flag will be set to a logic 1. If the value is equal to or greater than 260 (B0), the carry flag will be cleared to a logic 0.

Note that the carry flag is only a logic 1 when data values less than 260 (B0) are input from the keyboard. So far, this software

Table 2-24. Three Different Comparison Situations

Content of Register A	Comparison Byte	Carry Flag
257 (AF) or less	260 (B0)	logic 1
260 (B0)	260 (B0)	logic 0
261 (B1) or greater	260 (B0)	logic 0

ignores all characters less than ASCII 0 (260, B0). Only if the carry flag is a logic 1 will the JC to START be executed.

The third CPI instruction determines if the ASCII character entered has a value less than 272 (BA), which are the ASCII characters 0 through 9 (260 through 271, B0 through B9), which are the values to be packed. If one of the numeric keys is pressed, the carry flag will be a logic 1 after the third CPI instruction, because the values for the ASCII characters 0 through 9 (260 through 271, B0 through B9) are less than the immediate data byte of the CPI instruction. Therefore, the JNC will not be executed. If a nonnumeric key is pressed, the comparison will cause the carry flag to be cleared to a logic 0, and the JNC to START is executed.

Why did we test for the question mark as the input character, rather than first testing for one of the ASCII numeric characters (0

Table 2-25. Comparing the ASCII Character to 272 (B9)

Content of Register A	Comparison Byte	Carry Flag
271 (B9) or less	272 (BA)	logic 1
272 (BA)	272 (BA)	logic 0
273 (BB) or greater	272 (BA)	logic 0

Example 2-38: Testing for the ASCII Numeric Characters First

```
START,  IN      /INPUT AN ASCII CHARACTER
        015     /FROM INPUT PORT 015 (HEX 0D).
        CPI     /IS THE CHARACTER LESS THAN 260
        260     /(HEX B0), AN ASCII 0 ?
        JC      /YES, THE CARRY IS SET, THEN IGNORE
        START   /THE CHARACTER AND JUMP BACK
        0       /TO "START."
        CPI     /IS THE CHARACTER LESS THAN 272
        272     /(HEX BA), AN ASCII : ?
        JC      /YES, THE CARRY IS SET, SO THIS IS
        CHROK   /A VALID CHARACTER (0-9). THEREFORE,
        0       /JUMP TO "CHROK" (CHARACTER OK).
        CPI     /IT WAS NOT ONE OF THE CHARACTERS 0-9.
        277     /IS IT A QUESTION MARK ?
        JNZ     /NO, IT IS NOT A QUESTION MARK
        START   /SO JUMP BACK TO THE "START"
        0       /OF THE PROGRAM.
          •     /THE 8080 WILL EXECUTE THE INSTRUCTION STORED
          •     /HERE IF THE CHARACTER WAS A QUESTION MARK.
          •

CHROK,  ANI     /THE 8080 WILL EXECUTE THIS INSTRUCTION IF
        017     /THE CHARACTER ENTERED WAS 0-9.
          •
          •
          •
        ETC
```

through 9)? The test for the question mark can be performed either before or after the test for the ASCII numeric characters. This is shown in Example 2-38.

Bit-Oriented Operations

Besides testing complete eight-bit words, individual bits in a data word can also be tested to determine if they are a logic 1 or 0. As with most other software tasks, there are a number of methods that can be used to test individual bits within an eight-bit word. We will assume that you wish to check bit D_3 of the A register when an eight-bit data word is input from device 125 (55).

Example 2-39: Using Rotate Instructions and the Carry Flag to Test a Selected Bit

```
IN       /INPUT THE EIGHT-BIT DATA WORD
125      /FROM INPUT PORT 125 (HEX 55).
RRC      /ROTATE THE CONTENTS OF THE A REGISTER
RRC      /FOUR TIMES TO THE RIGHT.
RRC
RRC
JC       /IF THE CARRY (THE BIT ROTATED INTO IT) IS
BITOK    /A LOGIC 1, JUMP TO "BITOK"
0        /(THE BIT IS OK).
   •     /OTHERWISE, THE INSTRUCTIONS STORED HERE
   •     /WILL BE EXECUTED.
```

In Example 2-39, the data word is input from input port 125 (55) into the A register. The bits in the A register are then rotated one bit position to the right, four times, until bit D_3 is rotated into the carry. The state of the carry flag, which indicates the state of the carry, is then tested with a conditional jump instruction. The JC (Jump-on-Carry) will only be executed if the carry flag is a logic 1, caused by rotating a logic 1 into the carry. If bit D_3 is a logic 0, the JC instruction is not executed following the rotate instructions.

What would have to be changed in this program if, instead of jumping when bit D_3 is a logic 1, you wanted the 8080 to jump only when bit D_3 is a logic 0? This may appear to be more difficult than it really is. The zero condition can be tested just as easily by substituting a JNC (Jump-on-No-Carry) instruction for the JC (Jump-on-Carry) instruction.

The bit-testing operation can also be accomplished by using AND instructions, as Example 2-40 demonstrates. In Example 2-40, a *mask* of 010 (08) is used. Only if bit D_3 is a logic 1 will the contents of the A register be nonzero after the ANI instruction is executed. If bit D_3 is a logic 1, the JNZ (Jump-on-a-NonZero) instruction will be executed. If this occurs, the next instruction to be executed will be at the address specified by the second and third bytes of the

JNZ instruction. If bit D_3 is a logic 0, the JNZ will not be executed. Instead, the next instruction to be executed will be the instruction stored after the three-byte JNZ instruction in memory. Suppose you want the 8080 to jump only when bit D_3 is a logic 0. How would this be done?

Example 2-40: Using an ANI Instruction and the Zero Flag to Test a Selected Bit in the A Register

```
IN      /INPUT THE EIGHT-BIT DATA WORD FROM INPUT
125     /PORT 125 (HEX 55).
ANI     /MASK OUT ALL THE BITS EXCEPT BIT D3
010     /WITH A 010 (HEX 08).
JNZ     /IF THE CONTENT OF THE A REGISTER IS
D3IS1   /NONZERO (00001000) THE JNZ TO "D3IS1"
0       /IS EXECUTED (BIT D3 IS A 1).
 •      /ONLY WHEN BIT D3 IS A LOGIC 0 WILL THE
 •      /8080 EXECUTE THE INSTRUCTIONS STORED HERE.
```

The simplest solution would be to change the JNZ instruction to a JZ instruction. This would be done by storing the op code for the JZ instruction in the memory location where the op code for the JNZ instruction was originally stored. After this is done, the JZ will only be executed when bit D_3 of the A register is a logic 0. If bit D_3 is a logic 1, the JZ will not be executed. Instead of changing the JNZ to a JZ instruction, the input port hardware could have been changed. You would simply invert bit D_3. However, as you have just seen, it is very easy to change the instruction in order to change the condition upon which the decision to jump is based.

This is one of the many examples of a *hardware/software tradeoff*, which means that it may be easier to change the software than the hardware, or *vice versa*, depending on the particular problem being tackled. In this example, we will assume that it is easier to change the software than the hardware.

After using rotate instructions, the entire eight-bit word is still contained in the A register, even though the bit positions have changed. When the ANI instruction is used, some of the data is destroyed. If AND instructions were to be used to check the other bit positions for logic 1s and 0s, the data word would have to be temporarily stored. This temporary storage of the word to be tested would not be necessary if rotate instructions are used.

Multibit Testing Operations

You have seen how to test individual bits within an eight-bit word by using both rotate and AND instructions. How are a number of bits within the same word tested? To test a number of bits within the same eight-bit word, one at a time, rotate instructions can again be used (Example 2-41).

In Example 2-41, we have inadvertantly assigned a *priority* to each bit within the eight-bit word undergoing the testing. The priority that has been established is that the state of data bit D_3 is more

Example 2-41: Testing More Than One Bit in a Word With Rotate Instructions

```
IN
125        /INPUT THE STATUS WORD.
RRC
RRC        /ROTATE D3 INTO THE CARRY.
RRC
RRC
JC         /IF D3=1, EXECUTE THE JUMP
D3ISI
0
RRC        /OTHERWISE, WE COME HERE.
JNC        /NOW ROTATE AND TEST D4. IF D4= 0
D4ISO      /THE JUMP IS EXECUTED.
0
RRC        /NOW TEST D6.
RRC
JC         /IF D6= 1, EXECUTE THE JUMP.
D6ISO
0
    •
    •
    •
```

important than the state of bit D_4, and the state of bit D_4 is more important than the state of data bit D_6. This has happened because data bit D_3 is tested first for a logic 1 or logic 0. If bit D_3 is a logic 1, the JC instruction is executed. If this JC instruction is executed, then data bits D_4 and D_6 will not be tested, since the computer will jump to some other portion of the program. If data bit D_4 is a logic 0, the JNC is executed and data bit D_6 is not tested. Only if data bit D_3 is a logic 0, and data bit D_4 is a logic 1, will data bit D_6 be tested. Suppose that the priority, or the order in which the data bits are tested, must be changed. How would this be done?

Assume that the following priority is to be used: $D_6 > D_3 > D_4$. The simplest program, using rotate instructions, that could test the data bits in this order is listed in Example 2-42.

By examining the last two examples, Examples 2-41 and 2-42, you can see that if the priority of the bits within an eight-bit data word must be changed, the software changes can be awkward and difficult. It is difficult to keep track of the individual bits and the direction in which they must be rotated, so that they are rotated into the carry. A far easier and more memory efficient method of testing individual bits uses ANI instructions (Example 2-43).

In Example 2-43, the three bits that are to be tested are temporarily stored in register B and then copied into register A (moved) for each AND or mask operation.

Example 2-42: The Sequential Testing of Data Bits D_6, D_3, and D_4

```
IN
125      /INPUT THE STATUS WORD.
RLC      /ROTATE D6 INTO THE CARRY.
RLC
JC       /IF D6=1, EXECUTE THE JUMP.
D6IS1
0
RLC      /NOW ROTATE D3 INTO THE CARRY.
RLC
RLC
JC       /IF D3=1, EXECUTE THE JUMP.
D3IS1
0
RRC      /ROTATE D4 INTO THE CARRY.
RRC
JNC      /IF D4=0, EXECUTE THE JUMP.
D4IS0
0
   •
   •
   •
```

Example 2-43: Using ANI Instructions to Test Three Data Bits Within a Word

Program No. 1		Program No. 2	
IN		IN	
125		125	/INPUT THE STATUS.
MOVBA		MOVBA	/SAVE IT IN "B."
ANI		ANI	
004	/TEST D2.	100	/TEST D6.
JNZ	/JUMP IF D2= 1.	JZ	/JUMP IF D6= 0.
D2IS1		D6IS0	
0		0	
MOVAB		MOVAB	
ANI		ANI	
010	/TEST D3.	004	/TEST D2.
JZ	/JUMP IF D3= 0.	JNZ	/JUMP IF D2= 1.
D4IS0		D2IS1	
0		0	
MOVAB		MOVAB	
ANI		ANI	
100	/TEST D6.	010	/TEST D3.
JZ	/JUMP IF D6 =0.	JZ	/JUMP IF D3= 0.
D6IS0		D3IS0	
0		0	
•		•	
•		•	

As you can see, the advantages of using the ANI instructions are numerous. Notice that the program length remains the same even when the order in which the various bits are tested is changed. Also, it is much easier to *see* the order in which the bits are being tested just by looking at the masks (the immediate data bytes) for the ANI instructions.

Loops for Bit Testing (Recursive Bit Testing)

In all of the bit-testing examples, Examples 2-39 through 2-43, a single bit position is only tested once. For example, if bit D_5 is a logic 1, a JNZ instruction might be executed to transfer program execution to another section of the program. If, however, data bit D_5 is a logic 0, some other operation is performed.

Suppose that you wanted the 8080 to wait for a particular bit in a data byte from an input port to be a logic 1 (or logic 0) before the 8080 executes the remainder of the program. How would this program be written?

Example 2-44: Waiting for a Data Bit to be a Logic 0

```
START,  IN      /INPUT THE FLAG WORD FROM INPUT
        125     /PORT 125 (HEX 55).
        ANI     /MASK OUT ALL BUT BIT D3
        010     /WITH 010 (HEX 08).
        JNZ     /IF BIT D3= 1, THE 8080 EXECUTES THE
        START   /JNZ TO "START."
        0
          •     /ONLY WHEN BIT D3 IS A LOGIC 0, WILL THE
          •     /8080 EXECUTE THE INSTRUCTIONS STORED HERE.
```

When the program listed in Example 2-44 is executed, the 8080 microcomputer will remain in the three-instruction *loop* until data bit D_3 of input port 125 (55) goes to a logic 0. When the data bit is a logic 0, the 8080 will no longer execute the JNZ instruction, since the nonzero condition is no longer met. Instead, the 8080 will begin to execute the remainder of the program, starting with the instruction stored after the three-byte jump instruction. If data bit D_3 is a logic 0 before this *loop* is executed, the loop instructions will be executed only once. Will the JNZ instruction be executed? If data bit D_3 is a logic 0 when this section of the program is executed, it will not be executed.

Bit Set/Reset Operations

Just as you can program the 8080 to check individual data bits for a logic 0 or logic 1, you can also program the 8080 to set or clear individual data bits by using AND and OR instructions The AND instructions are generally used to clear individual bits, or groups of bits, to a logic 0. The OR instructions can be used to set individual bits, or groups of bits, to a logic 1. To set data bit D_2 of the A register to a logic 1, you could program the 8080 with the set of instructions in Example 2-45.

Example 2-45: A Bit-Set Operation for Bit D_2

Binary	Octal	Hex	Mnemonic
	Content of the A Register*		
10000010	202	82	MOVAM
			ORI
10000110	206	86	004
10000110	206	86	MOVMA

* After execution of the instruction.

In Example 2-45, only one bit of the data word moved from memory is set to a logic 1. An immediate data byte of 070 (38) could have been used if we wished to set bits D_5, D_4, and D_3 all to logic 1s. We assumed that the data word that was to have a bit set to a logic 1 was already stored in memory. We also assumed that register pair H already contained the proper memory address of the data word.

It would be just as easy to get the data word from an input port, set one or more bits to logic 1, and then latch the new data word out to an output port. Note that the A register must always contain the data word that is to have the bits set.

How can individual data bits, or groups of data bits, be cleared to a logic 0? The ANI instructions can be used. To clear data bits D_5, D_4, and D_2 to a logic 0, the program listed in Example 2-46 could be executed.

Example 2-46: Bit-Clear or Bit-Reset Instructions

Binary	Octal	Hex	Mnemonic
	Content of the A Register*		
10111111	277	BF	MOVAM
			ANI
10001011	213	8B	213
10001011	213	8B	MOVMA

* After execution of the instruction.

In Example 2-46, bits D_5, D_4, and D_2 of the A register are cleared to the logic 0 state. You have already seen this operation in use when we "masked-out" bits in an ASCII character.

CONCLUSION

In conclusion, you have now seen most of the 8080's basic instructions. There are many instructions that we have not yet covered. However, it is our firm belief that you must *know* and be able to *use* these basic instructions before you can proceed with the advanced

8080 instructions. The next chapter will deal with the application of these basic instructions to useful software tasks.

It may come as a surprise to some readers, but even though the 8080 has many more instructions than the ones we have covered, these instructions will constitute between 60% and 80% of most programs. The more advanced and more powerful instructions are the "icing on the cake," and they are used to make the software faster in terms of execution time, smaller in terms of memory usage, or more flexible in terms of adaptability from one project to another.

REFERENCES

1. Rony, P. R., Larsen, D. G., and Titus, J. A. *The 8080A Bugbook®: Microcomputer Interfacing and Programming.* Howard W. Sams & Co., Inc., Indianapolis, IN, 1977.
2. Larsen, D. G., Rony, P. R., and Titus, J. A. *Introductory Experiments in Digital Electronics and 8080A Microcomputer Programming and Interfacing, Book 2.* Howard W. Sams & Co., Inc., Indianapolis, IN, 1977.

3

Subroutines and Use of
the Basic Instructions

So far, you have seen how to combine data movement, logical, mathematical, and jump instructions to create short programs. It soon becomes apparent that programs can be long and tedious to write.

Suppose that you have written a program for a microcomputer-controlled, patient-monitoring system for use in a hospital. In many parts of the program, data relating to the patient will have to be entered into the microcomputer; for example, the patient's name, age, social security account number (SSAN), and address. For this particular program, a teletypewriter or crt could be used for data input. The beginning of the program might perform the tasks shown in Fig. 3-1.

If the terminal (crt) input routine requires 10 to 15 memory locations, you do not want to have to write the same input routine in different sections of the program whenever you need data to be input from the crt. Ideally, you would like to be able to write the routine only once and then use it whenever data has to be entered into the computer by the crt. This idea is shown in Fig. 3-2.

The program could be written so that each time a character is to be input from the crt, the 8080 jumps to the crt routine (on the right side of Fig. 3-2). When this occurs, the input routine software would permit a single character to be input, and then control would be returned to the main program. In Fig. 3-2, data would have to be input from the crt in many different sections of the program. If jump instructions were used to transfer control to the crt input routine, how would control be returned to the main program after a

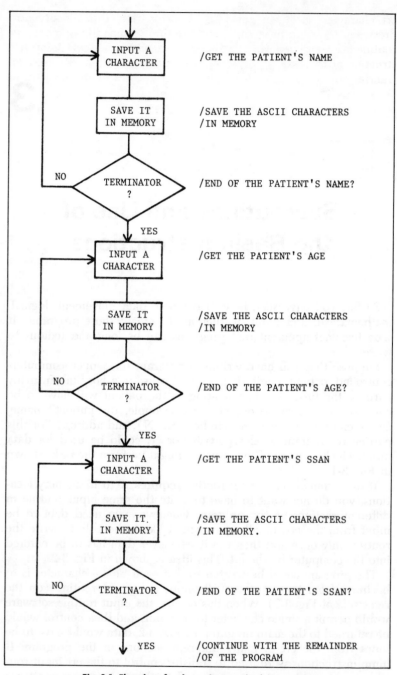

Fig. 3-1. Flowchart for the patient-monitoring program.

crt character has been entered? Unfortunately, the memory addresses in the main program where the three jumps to the crt input routine are contained are all different. Therefore, a single jump instruction at the end of the crt input routine could not be used to transfer control back to three different addresses in the main pro-

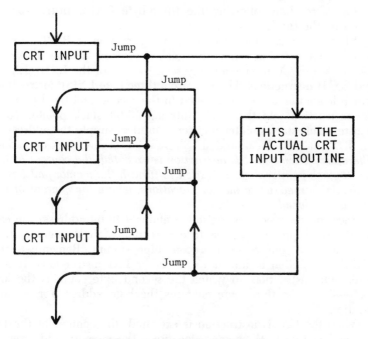

Fig. 3-2. Accessing a single crt input routine.

gram. In fact, it would not be easy for the 8080 to remember or even calculate the proper address for reentry into the main program if you attempt to use the jump instructions. For this reason, a new instruction will be discussed, the CALL instruction, whose op code is 315 (CD).

CALLING SUBROUTINES

The CALL instruction is a three-byte instruction (as were both the conditional and unconditional jump instructions). The second and third bytes of the CALL instruction contain the low and high addresses of the start of the *subroutine* being *called*. When a CALL instruction is executed, program control, or execution, is transferred to the instruction contained in the memory location that is addressed by the low and high address bytes of the CALL instruction. So far, the CALL instruction would appear to perform exactly the same operations as any of the jump instructions.

In Chapter 1, we briefly described an internal 16-bit register called the program counter (PC). This counter contains the 16-bit memory address of the *next* instruction that is to be executed. When a CALL is executed, the 16-bit PC address, which is now pointing to the *instruction* following the three-byte CALL instruction, is saved on the *stack.*

What is a *stack?* The stack is simply a section of R/W memory that you have designated as the stack area. How do you designate the stack area? You have already seen the use of the LXIB, LXID, and LXIH instructions. There is also a three-byte LXISP instruction, which loads the address contained in the second and third bytes of the instruction into the 8080's internal 16-bit stack pointer (SP) register. This stack pointer register is used to supply the address of the R/W memory location that will be used for any stack operation. *Therefore, when a CALL instruction is executed, the content of the 16-bit stack pointer register is used to furnish the memory addresses of available read/write memory locations, where the content of the PC can be saved.*

Since the stack pointer register contains a 16-bit address, you can set the stack pointer address to *any* section of R/W memory that you have in your 8080 microcomputer system. Remember, the LXISP instruction is similar to the other LXI instructions. It is a three-byte instruction, in which the second byte contains the low address and the third byte contains the high address for a stack location.

When the CALL instruction is executed, the content of the PC is saved in two R/W memory locations, the memory addresses of which are supplied by the stack pointer (SP) register. The two-byte address that immediately follows the CALL op code is then placed in the PC, and the 8080 begins execution of the subroutine that starts at that address.

After the 8080 executes the three-byte CALL instruction and all of the instructions in the subroutine that was called, we want the 8080 to continue program execution with the instruction stored in memory immediately *after* the three-byte CALL instruction. In Fig. 3-3, this is the MOVAB instruction at address X+3.

When the CALL in Fig. 3-3 is executed, the *address* of the instruction, MOVAB, is stored on the stack as the *return address* back to the main program. If X is the address of the CALL instruction, the address X+3 is stored "on" the stack. Remember, all addresses used by the 8080 are 16 bits wide, even if you only have one or two thousand words of memory in your 8080 system. How can the 8080 save a 16-bit return address in R/W memory, when memory

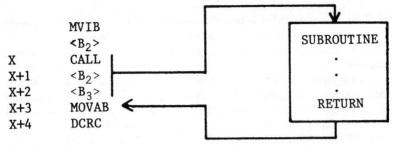

	MVIB	SUBROUTINE
	<B_2>	•
X	CALL	•
X+1	<B_2>	•
X+2	<B_3>	
X+3	MOVAB	RETURN
X+4	DCRC	

Fig. 3-3. The instruction to be executed after a subroutine is finished.

is only eight bits wide? The return address is saved in two consecutive R/W memory locations, as a low and high return address. The 8080 automatically saves this return address on the stack whenever a CALL instruction is executed. This is called *pushing* information onto the stack.

Once the 8080 has executed the instructions in the subroutine, how does it know when to *pop* the return address off of the stack and load it into the PC? For the 8080 to do this, *all subroutines must be ended, in one way or another, with a return instruction.* One of these return instructions is RET, which has an op code of 311 (C9). When the RET instruction is executed at the end of a subroutine, the 8080 automatically pops the return address off of the stack. This 16-bit address is then loaded into the PC, which now points to the instruction immediately following the three-byte CALL instruction. In Fig. 3-3, control would return to the MOVAB instruction.

At this time, you do not have to be concerned with how the return address is actually stored on, or retrieved from, the stack. However, you must make sure that the SP has been loaded with an address for R/W memory before any attempt is made to call a subroutine. As we mentioned, the stack can be located anywhere in R/W memory, and the SP is initialized by executing the three-byte instruction, LXISP. For example, this is done by executing the instructions contained in Example 3-1.

Example 3-1: Loading the Stack Pointer by Means of an LXISP Instruction

Octal	Mnemonic	Hexadecimal
061	LXISP	31
300	<B_2>	C0
003	<B_3>	03

In Example 3-1, the SP within the 8080 is loaded with the address 003 300 (03C0) after the LXISP instruction is executed. For the stack to be useful, this must be an address for R/W memory. As you now know, when a CALL is executed, the return address is pushed onto the stack. When this occurs, is the address contained in the SP incremented or decremented to provide the address of the memory location to be used to store the second byte of the return address?

When information is pushed onto the stack, the stack pointer is decremented, and when information is popped off of the stack, the stack pointer is incremented. If your 8080 system only has 1024 words of R/W memory, it might have addresses of 000 000 through 003 377 (0000 through 03FF). If this is the case, you might set the SP near the top of R/W memory, as was done in Example 3-1, by setting the SP to address 003 300 (03C0). In fact, address 003 300 (03C0) is only a *resting place* for the stack pointer.

If you were to call a subroutine with the SP set to this address, you would find the return address in the memory locations with the addresses of 003 277 and 003 276 (03BF and 03BE). Remember, a 16-bit address is saved on the stack; therefore, two R/W memory locations are required to store the return address. Most 8080 users do not care about the actual order in which the data is stored on the stack. However, for your information, the high address or data byte is always stored on the stack first. Thus, the high-address byte of the return address would be stored in memory location 003 277 (03BF), and the low-address byte of the return address would be stored in memory location 003 276 (03BE). Note that no information is stored in memory location 003 300 (03C0), the address that was used with the LXISP instruction to initialize the SP. From this, you can conclude that *the SP is always decremented to a lower memory address before data or address information is pushed onto the stack. It is incremented to a higher memory address after the data or address information is popped off of the stack.* Note that we said that both data and address information can be saved on the stack, but we have only discussed how address information is stored on the stack when a CALL instruction is executed. We will discuss how data values are stored on the stack in the next chapter.

If you were to examine the stack area in R/W memory after a subroutine had been called, you would still find the return address stored in the R/W memory locations used by the SP. How is this possible? The stack area consists of a section of R/W memory. Therefore, when a return instruction is executed, the contents of the two memory locations pointed to by the SP are read from memory into the PC. Nothing is written into the stack area to clear-out the return address. When a 16-bit value is popped off of the stack, only memory-read operations take place. This is similar to the result obtained when a data movement instruction is executed. If a MOVAB instruction is executed, the content of the B register remains the same because the content of the B register is *duplicated* in the A

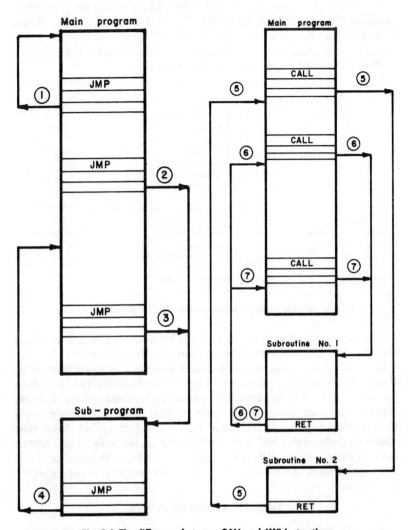

Fig. 3-4. The difference between CALL and JMP instructions.

register. This same duplication process occurs when a return address is popped off of the stack. The content of R/W memory is unaltered when the return address is read from the stack area. However, the next CALL operation will "write over" these two address bytes with the current return address. The stack area is used and reused again and again. You do not need two memory locations on the stack for each CALL or each subroutine.

In Fig. 3-4, there are three call and return loops, labeled 5, 6, and 7. As you can see, each time one of the subroutines is called, it appears as if the subroutine is "inserted" into the main program. When execution of the subroutine is completed, program control is returned to the main program. The order of execution for the software in Fig. 3-4 would appear as it is shown in Fig. 3-5.

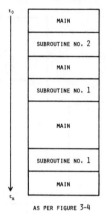

AS PER FIGURE 3-4

Fig. 3-5. Order of program execution when CALL instructions are used.

The first subroutine to be executed is Subroutine No. 2. It is called shortly after the main program is started. After the return instruction at the end of Subroutine No. 2 is executed, a small portion of the main program is executed. A call to Subroutine No. 1 is then executed. After the 8080 finishes executing Subroutine No. 1, it returns to the main program. A major portion of the main program is then executed before Subroutine No. 1 is again called. Note that although Subroutine No. 1 is called twice, it has only been written once in the program. When the 8080 returns from Subroutine No. 1 the second time, the remainder of the main program is executed.

TIME-DELAY SUBROUTINES

We will now describe a typical subroutine that is used to generate a time delay of 0.200 second, or 200 milliseconds, for an 8080 microcomputer operating at 2 MHz (500-ns cycle time). A subroutine such as this can be used when long time delays must be generated under software control. We can take advantage of the fact that every 8080 instruction requires a known time to be executed. The number of *clock cycles* that each 8080 instruction requires is listed in Fig. 3-6.

To determine the time required to execute an instruction, the number of clock cycles required to execute that instruction must be multiplied by the *cycle time* of the microcomputer. Most 8080 microprocessor integrated circuits are driven by a 2-MHz clock, so the cycle time of the 8080 is 500 ns; for a 1-MHz clock, the cycle time is 1000 ns, or 1 μs; and for a 750-kHz clock, the cycle time is 1.33 μs.

Table 3-1 contains the mnemonics for some of the 8080's instructions that have been discussed in this and the previous chapters. It includes the time required to execute each instruction at three different cycle times.

Table 3-1. The Time Required to Execute Some Typical 8080 Instructions

Instruction	Clock Cycles	500 ns	1 μs	1.333 μs
JMP	10	5 μs	10 μs	13.33 μs
OUT	10	5 μs	10 μs	13.33 μs
RAR	4	2 μs	4 μs	5.33 μs
CPI	7	3.5 μs	7 μs	9.33 μs
INRC	5	2.5 μs	5 μs	6.66 μs

The time required to execute a set of the 8080's instructions can be effectively multiplied by causing the microcomputer to loop through the instructions a number of times. Both increment and decrement instructions are particularly useful for this task. In the 200-ms time-delay subroutine (Example 3-2), the content of the E register is decremented until it reaches zero. When this occurs, the content of the D register is decremented. If it is decremented to a nonzero value, the 8080 jumps back to the decrement-register-E loop. Only when both the D and E registers have been decremented to zero will the 8080 return from the subroutine. This is shown in the *flowchart* in Fig. 3-7.

Decisions are made in this program (Fig. 3-7, Example 3-2) based on whether or not the content of a register (D or E) has been decremented to zero. These decision-making steps are represented by the diamonds in the flowchart (Fig. 3-7). What instruction could be used to make the actual decision in the program? The JNZ in-

Example 3-2: A 200-Millisecond Time-Delay Subroutine

```
DELAY1,   MVIE    /LOAD THE E REGISTER WITH 000.
          000     /(OCTAL 000 = HEX 00).
          MVID    /LOAD THE D REGISTER WITH DECIMAL 104.
          150     /(OCTAL 150 = HEX 68).
WAIT,     DCRE    /DECREMENT THE CONTENT OF E.
          JNZ     /IF E IS NONZERO, EXECUTE THE
          WAIT    /JNZ INSTRUCTION TO WAIT.
          0
          DCRD    /NOW E=0, SO DECREMENT THE CONTENT OF D.
          JNZ     /IF D IS NONZERO, EXECUTE THE
          WAIT    /JNZ INSTRUCTION TO WAIT.
          0
          RET     /D=E=0, SO RETURN FROM THE SUBROUTINE.
```

Mnemonic	Description	D_7	D_6	D_5	D_4	D_3	D_2	D_1	D_0	Clock[2] Cycles
MOV r_1, r_2	Move register to register	0	1	D	D	D	S	S	S	5
MOV M, r	Move register to memory	0	1	1	1	0	S	S	S	7
MOV r, M	Move memory to register	0	1	D	D	D	1	1	0	7
HLT	Halt	0	1	1	1	0	1	1	0	7
MVI r	Move immediate register	0	0	D	D	D	1	1	0	7
MVI M	Move immediate memory	0	0	1	1	0	1	1	0	10
INR r	Increment register	0	0	D	D	D	1	0	0	5
DCR r	Decrement register	0	0	D	D	D	1	0	1	5
INR M	Increment memory	0	0	1	1	0	1	0	0	10
DCR M	Decrement memory	0	0	1	1	0	1	0	1	10
ADD r	Add register to A	1	0	0	0	0	S	S	S	4
ADC r	Add register to A with carry	1	0	0	0	1	S	S	S	4
SUB r	Subtract register from A	1	0	0	1	0	S	S	S	4
SBB r	Subtract register from A with borrow	1	0	0	1	1	S	S	S	4
ANA r	And register with A	1	0	1	0	0	S	S	S	4
XRA r	Exclusive Or register with A	1	0	1	0	1	S	S	S	4
ORA r	Or register with A	1	0	1	1	0	S	S	S	4
CMP r	Compare register with A	1	0	1	1	1	S	S	S	4
ADD M	Add memory to A	1	0	0	0	0	1	1	0	7
ADC M	Add memory to A with carry	1	0	0	0	1	1	1	0	7
SUB M	Subtract memory from A	1	0	0	1	0	1	1	0	7
SBB M	Subtract memory from A with borrow	1	0	0	1	1	1	1	0	7
ANA M	And memory with A	1	0	1	0	0	1	1	0	7
XRA M	Exclusive Or memory with A	1	0	1	0	1	1	1	0	7
ORA M	Or memory with A	1	0	1	1	0	1	1	0	7
CMP M	Compare memory with A	1	0	1	1	1	1	1	0	7
ADI	Add immediate to A	1	1	0	0	0	1	1	0	7
ACI	Add immediate to A with carry	1	1	0	0	1	1	1	0	7
SUI	Subtract immediate from A	1	1	0	1	0	1	1	0	7
SBI	Subtract immediate from A with borrow	1	1	0	1	1	1	1	0	7
ANI	And immediate with A	1	1	1	0	0	1	1	0	7
XRI	Exclusive Or immediate with A	1	1	1	0	1	1	1	0	7
ORI	Or immediate with A	1	1	1	1	0	1	1	0	7
CPI	Compare immediate with A	1	1	1	1	1	1	1	0	7
RLC	Rotate A left	0	0	0	0	0	1	1	1	4
RRC	Rotate A right	0	0	0	0	1	1	1	1	4
RAL	Rotate A left through carry	0	0	0	1	0	1	1	1	4
RAR	Rotate A right through carry	0	0	0	1	1	1	1	1	4
JMP	Jump unconditional	1	1	0	0	0	0	1	1	10
JC	Jump on carry	1	1	0	1	1	0	1	0	10
JNC	Jump on no carry	1	1	0	1	0	0	1	0	10
JZ	Jump on zero	1	1	0	0	1	0	1	0	10
JNZ	Jump on no zero	1	1	0	0	0	0	1	0	10
JP	Jump on positive	1	1	1	1	0	0	1	0	10
JM	Jump on minus	1	1	1	1	1	0	1	0	10
JPE	Jump on parity even	1	1	1	0	1	0	1	0	10
JPO	Jump on parity odd	1	1	1	0	0	0	1	0	10
CALL	Call unconditional	1	1	0	0	1	1	0	1	17
CC	Call on carry	1	1	0	1	1	1	0	0	11/17
CNC	Call on no carry	1	1	0	1	0	1	0	0	11/17
CZ	Call on zero	1	1	0	0	1	1	0	0	11/17
CNZ	Call on no zero	1	1	0	0	0	1	0	0	11/17
CP	Call on positive	1	1	1	1	0	1	0	0	11/17
CM	Call on minus	1	1	1	1	1	1	0	0	11/17
CPE	Call on parity even	1	1	1	0	1	1	0	0	11/17
CPO	Call on parity odd	1	1	1	0	0	1	0	0	11/17
RET	Return	1	1	0	0	1	0	0	1	10
RC	Return on carry	1	1	0	1	1	0	0	0	5/11
RNC	Return on no carry	1	1	0	1	0	0	0	0	5/11

NOTES: 1. DDD or SSS – 000 B – 001 C – 010 D – 011 E – 100 H – 101 L – 110 Memory – 111 A.
2. Two possible cycle times, (5/11) indicate instruction cycles dependent on condition flags.

Fig. 3-6. The number of clock cycles

Mnemonic	Description	D7	D6	D5	D4	D3	D2	D1	D0	Clock[2] Cycles
RZ	Return on zero	1	1	0	0	1	0	0	0	5/11
RNZ	Return on no zero	1	1	0	0	0	0	0	0	5/11
RP	Return on positive	1	1	1	1	0	0	0	0	5/11
RM	Return on minus	1	1	1	1	1	0	0	0	5/11
RPE	Return on parity even	1	1	1	0	1	0	0	0	5/11
RPO	Return on parity odd	1	1	1	0	0	0	0	0	5/11
RST	Restart	1	1	A	A	A	1	1	1	11
IN	Input	1	1	0	1	1	0	1	1	10
OUT	Output	1	1	0	1	0	0	1	1	10
LXI B	Load immediate register Pair B & C	0	0	0	0	0	0	0	1	10
LXI D	Load immediate register Pair D & E	0	0	0	1	0	0	0	1	10
LXI H	Load immediate register Pair H & L	0	0	1	0	0	0	0	1	10
LXI SP	Load immediate stack pointer	0	0	1	1	0	0	0	1	10
PUSH B	Push register Pair B & C on stack	1	1	0	0	0	1	0	1	11
PUSH D	Push register Pair D & E on stack	1	1	0	1	0	1	0	1	11
PUSH H	Push register Pair H & L on stack	1	1	1	0	0	1	0	1	11
PUSH PSW	Push A and Flags on stack	1	1	1	1	0	1	0	1	11
POP B	Pop register pair B & C off stack	1	1	0	0	0	0	0	1	10
POP D	Pop register pair D & E off stack	1	1	0	1	0	0	0	1	10
POP H	Pop register pair H & L off stack	1	1	1	0	0	0	0	1	10
POP PSW	Pop A and Flags off stack	1	1	1	1	0	0	0	1	10
STA	Store A direct	0	0	1	1	0	0	1	0	13
LDA	Load A direct	0	0	1	1	1	0	1	0	13
XCHG	Exchange D & E, H & L Registers	1	1	1	0	1	0	1	1	4
XTHL	Exchange top of stack, H & L	1	1	1	0	0	0	1	1	18
SPHL	H & L to stack pointer	1	1	1	1	1	0	0	1	5
PCHL	H & L to program counter	1	1	1	0	1	0	0	1	5
DAD B	Add B & C to H & L	0	0	0	0	1	0	0	1	10
DAD D	Add D & E to H & L	0	0	0	1	1	0	0	1	10
DAD H	Add H & L to H & L	0	0	1	0	1	0	0	1	10
DAD SP	Add stack pointer to H & L	0	0	1	1	1	0	0	1	10
STAX B	Store A indirect	0	0	0	0	0	0	1	0	7
STAX D	Store A indirect	0	0	0	1	0	0	1	0	7
LDAX B	Load A indirect	0	0	0	0	1	0	1	0	7
LDAX D	Load A indirect	0	0	0	1	1	0	1	0	7
INX B	Increment B & C registers	0	0	0	0	0	0	1	1	5
INX D	Increment D & E registers	0	0	0	1	0	0	1	1	5
INX H	Increment H & L registers	0	0	1	0	0	0	1	1	5
INX SP	Increment stack pointer	0	0	1	1	0	0	1	1	5
DCX B	Decrement B & C	0	0	0	0	1	0	1	1	5
DCX D	Decrement D & E	0	0	0	1	1	0	1	1	5
DCX H	Decrement H & L	0	0	1	0	1	0	1	1	5
DCX SP	Decrement stack pointer	0	0	1	1	1	0	1	1	5
CMA	Complement A	0	0	1	0	1	1	1	1	4
STC	Set carry	0	0	1	1	0	1	1	1	4
CMC	Complement carry	0	0	1	1	1	1	1	1	4
DAA	Decimal adjust A	0	0	1	0	0	1	1	1	4
SHLD	Store H & L direct	0	0	1	0	0	0	1	0	16
LHLD	Load H & L direct	0	0	1	0	1	0	1	0	16
EI	Enable Interrupts	1	1	1	1	1	0	1	1	4
DI	Disable interrupt	1	1	1	1	0	0	1	1	4
NOP	No-operation	0	0	0	0	0	0	0	0	4

Courtesy Intel Corp.

required for each 8080 instruction.

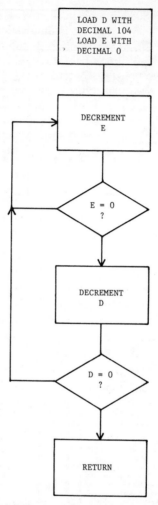

Fig. 3-7. Flowchart for the 200-millisecond time-delay subroutine.

struction could be used. The 8080 will continue to execute the instructions in the 200-millisecond time-delay subroutine until the content of the D and E registers is decremented to zero. Remember, since this is a time-delay *subroutine,* a RET instruction (*RET*urn from the subroutine) must be included at the end of the subroutine.

At the beginning of the DELAY1 subroutine (Example 3-2), the E register is loaded with 000 (00) and the D register is loaded with 150 (68). When the 8080 executes the instruction at WAIT, the content of the E register is decremented by 1. Since E originally contained 000 (00), it is decremented to 377 (FF). Since this is a nonzero result, the 8080 jumps back to the DCRE instruction. When the content of the E register is finally decremented to zero, the 8080 executes the DCRD instruction. If the result of this operation is nonzero, the 8080 jumps back to WAIT, where the DCRE instruction is stored. When the content of the D register is finally decremented to zero, the 8080 returns from the subroutine.

Suppose that you want the 8080 to produce a time delay of 30 seconds. Could the 200-millisecond time-delay subroutine be used to generate this time delay? Yes it could, simply by calling the DELAY1 subroutine 150_{10} times. A subroutine that generates a delay of 30 seconds is listed in Example 3-3.

Example 3-3: A 30-Second Time-Delay Subroutine

HAFMIN,	MVIC	/LOAD C WITH DECIMAL 150.
	226	/(OCTAL 226, HEXADECIMAL 96).
AGN200,	CALL	/CALL THE 200 MILLISECOND
	DELAY1	/DELAY SUBROUTINE.
	0	
	DCRC	/DECREMENT THE CONTENT OF C.
	JNZ	/IF THE CONTENT OF C IS NONZERO,
	AGN200	/THEN CALL THE 200 MILLISECOND
	0	/DELAY SUBROUTINE AGAIN.
	RET	/RETURN AFTER 30 SECONDS.
DELAY1,	MVIE	/LOAD THE E REGISTER WITH 000.
	000	/(OCTAL 000, HEXADECIMAL 00).
	MVID	/LOAD THE D REGISTER WITH DECIMAL 104.
	150	/(OCTAL 150, HEXADECIMAL 68).
WAIT,	DCRE	/DECREMENT THE CONTENT OF E.
	JNZ	/IF E IS NONZERO, EXECUTE THE
	WAIT	/JNZ INSTRUCTION TO WAIT.
	0	
	DCRD	/NOW E IS 000, DECREMENT D.
	JNZ	/IF D IS NONZERO, THEN THE JNZ
	WAIT	/TO WAIT IS EXECUTED.
	0	
	RET	/OTHERWISE, THE 8080 RETURNS IN
		/200 MILLISECONDS.

In Example 3-3, the C register is used to hold a *timing byte*. The timing byte is really a counter for the number of times that the 200-millisecond time-delay subroutine is to be called. Since the C register is loaded with 170 (78), the DELAY1 subroutine is called 150_{10} times. The subroutine listed in Example 3-3 can be simplified, as shown in Example 3-4.

One of the nice features of this delay subroutine is that it can be used to generate a time delay of from 0.200 second to 51.2 seconds. How is this possible? It is possible to generate time delays within this range of values if the C register is first loaded with a timing byte, and then the GENDLY (*GEN*eral-purpose *De*La*Y*) subrou-

tine within HAFMIN is called. If the content of the C register is
001 (01) when GENDLY is called, the subroutine will require 0.200
second to be executed before the 8080 returns to the program that
called GENDLY. If the C register is loaded with 002 (02), the subroutine will require 0.400 second to be executed. Note that the C
register must be loaded with a data value *before* the time-delay subroutine (GENDLY) is called.

Example 3-4: A Simplified 30-Second Time-Delay Subroutine

```
HAFMIN,   MVIC    /LOAD THE C REGISTER WITH DECIMAL 150.
          226     /(OCTAL 226, HEXADECIMAL 96).
GENDLY,   MVID    /LOAD THE D REGISTER WITH DECIMAL 104.
          150     /(OCTAL 150, HEXADECIMAL 68).
          MVIE    /LOAD THE E REGISTER WITH DECIMAL 0.
          000     /(OCTAL 000, HEXADECIMAL 00).
WAIT,     DCRE    /DECREMENT E.
          JNZ     /IF E IS NONZERO, JUMP BACK TO
          WAIT    /THE DCRE INSTRUCTION.
          0
          DCRD    /E IS 0, SO DECREMENT D.
          JNZ     /IF D IS NONZERO, JUMP BACK TO
          WAIT    /THE DCRE INSTRUCTION.
          0
          DCRC    /200 MILLISECONDS HAVE ELAPSED, SO
          JNZ     /DECREMENT C AND JUMP BACK TO THE
          WAIT    /DCRE INSTRUCTION IF C IS NONZERO.
          0
          RET     /THE 8080 HAS NOW DELAYED 30 SECONDS.
```

This gives you a tremendous amount of flexibility in terms of how
the subroutine can be used. You can load a number into the C register before the subroutine is called, and cause a time delay of variable length to occur. What value would have to be loaded into the
C register to produce a time delay of 51.2 seconds? The C register
would have to be loaded with 000 (00) to produce a 51.2-second
time delay. This means that the 0.200-second time-delay section of
the subroutine would be executed 256 times (256 × 0.200 second
= 51.2 seconds).

When a data value is loaded into a register or section of memory
so that a subroutine can access the value, it is called *passing an argument* to the subroutine. This is easily done with the 8080 and is often
done to increase the flexibility of software.

An important point to remember about the time-delay subroutines
listed in Examples 3-2, 3-3, and 3-4 is that the time delay generated
is dependent upon the clock frequency of your 8080 microcomputer.
We obtained a 0.200-second time delay when the DELAY1 subroutine (Example 3-2) was executed on an 8080 microcomputer
that had a 500-ns cycle time. If your microcomputer system has a

faster or slower cycle time, you will have to either increase or decrease the values loaded into registers D and E.

Can you write another 0.200-second time-delay subroutine that performs the same function as Example 3-2, yet uses different instructions? Certainly you could use different INR and DCR instructions, but is there another method? Yes, you could use the register pair increment and decrement instructions (Example 3-5).

Example 3-5: A 0.200-Second Time-Delay Subroutine That Uses a Register Pair Decrement Instruction

```
DELAY1,   LXID    /LOAD REGISTER PAIR D WITH
          032     /16,666 (OCTAL 101 032, HEXADECIMAL
          101     /411A).
DECIT,    DCXD    /DECREMENT REGISTER PAIR D.
          MOVAD   /MOVE THE CONTENT OF D TO A.
          ORAE    /OR IT WITH E.
          JNZ     /IF THE RESUT IS NONZERO, JUMP
          DECIT   /BACK TO THE DCXD INSTRUCTION
          0       /AND DECREMENT IT AGAIN.
          RET     /WHEN REGISTER PAIR D IS DECREMENTED
                  /TO 000 000 (0000), RETURN FROM THE SUBROUTINE.
```

In Example 3-5, register pair D is loaded with the value $16,666_{10}$. We have calculated that this is the number of times that the loop within the subroutine must be executed to produce a delay of 0.200 second.

After loading register pair D with 101 032 (411A), the content of register pair D is decremented by means of the DCXD instruction. The content of the D register is then moved to the A register, where it is ored with the content of the E register. Based on the results of this logical operation, the JNZ to DECIT may or may not be executed. Why were these instructions executed? Remember, the register pair increment and decrement instructions do not affect any of the 8080's flags. Therefore, the MOVAD and ORAE instructions have to be executed to allow the program to determine whether or not the content of register pair D is zero. If the content of register pair D is nonzero, then the result of the ORAE instruction will be a nonzero value in the A register, and the JNZ instruction will be executed.

If desired, a DCRC, a JNZ to DECIT, and a RET instruction could be used to replace the RET instruction at the end of this time-delay subroutine (Example 3-5). This means that the time-delay subroutine must be called with a timing byte in the C register. Only when the content of the C register is decremented to zero will the 8080 return from the subroutine.

How did we determine that $16,666_{10}$ had to be loaded into register pair D to produce a delay of 0.200 second? After the sequence of instructions was written down, the number of cycles required to execute the instructions *within the loop* (*DECIT,* Example 3-5) is determined using Fig. 3-6. The DCXD instruction requires 5 cycles, the MOVAD requires 5 cycles, the ORAE requires 4 cycles, and the JNZ instruction requires 10 cycles. Using a 2-MHz 8080 microcomputer system, 12 μs are required to execute these 24 cycles. By dividing the desired time delay by this time, the number of times that the loop within the subroutine must be executed is determined. Therefore, 200,000 μs divided by 12 μs is 16,666. By executing the DECIT loop within the DELAY1 subroutine (Example 3-5) 16,666 times, a delay of 199.992 ms is really produced. However, we have not taken into account the time required to execute the LXID and RET instructions. These instructions require 20 cycles, or 10 μs. Therefore, the time delay that is really produced by calling this subroutine is 200.002 ms. For most applications, this is more accuracy than is needed.

Using the time-delay subroutine that is listed in Example 3-4, a maximum time delay of only 51.2 seconds is obtainable. However, longer delays may be required. These longer delays may be obtained by calling the HAFMIN or GENDLY subroutines (Example 3-4) a number of times. For instance, to generate a time delay that is one hour long, the 30-second time-delay subroutine (HAFMIN, Example 3-4) could be called 120_{10} times. Example 3-6 shows how this is done.

Example 3-6: A One-Hour Time-Delay Program That Calls the HAFMIN Subroutine

```
START,  LXISP     /SET THE STACK POINTER BECAUSE
        200       /SUBROUTINES WILL BE CALLED.
        000       /(OCTAL 000 200 = HEX 0080).
        MVIB      /SET THE COUNT TO 120 DECIMAL.
        170       /(OCTAL 170 = HEX 78).
AGAIN,  CALL      /CALL THE HALF-MINUTE
        HAFMIN    /DELAY SUBROUTINE.
        0
        DCRB      /DECREMENT THE COUNT.
        JNZ       /IF THE COUNT IS NONZERO, THE
        AGAIN     /JNZ TO "AGAIN" WILL BE EXECUTED
        0         /AND THE HAFMIN SUBROUTINE WILL
        HLT       /BE CALLED AGAIN. HALT WHEN DONE.
```

In Example 3-6, the B register is loaded with 120_{10} (octal 170, hexadecimal 78). This is the number of times that the HAFMIN subroutine is called. In Example 3-6, the timing byte of 120_{10} is loaded into the B register because the HAFMIN subroutine uses the C, D, and E registers. It would have been just as easy to have used the H or L registers rather than the B register.

You have now seen a number of time-delay subroutine examples. You have also seen how the duration of the time delay can be calculated, knowing the cycle time of the 8080 that will execute the program and the number of clock cycles required by each instruction. Knowing this, there is no reason why you could not write a time-delay subroutine that produces a delay of 4.505 ms or a delay of 23 days, 5 hours, 32 minutes, and 19 seconds.

CONDITIONAL CALL AND RETURN INSTRUCTIONS

We have discussed the jump instructions and the CALL and RET instructions. Like the conditional jump instructions, there are also conditional call and return instructions. These instructions are summarized in Table 3-2.

Table 3-2. A Summary of the Jump, Call, and Return Instructions

Condition	Jump			Call			Return		
Unconditional	JMP	303	C3	CALL	315	CD	RET	311	C9
Nonzero	JNZ	302	C2	CNZ	304	C4	RNZ	300	C0
Zero	JZ	312	CA	CZ	314	CC	RZ	310	C8
No Carry	JNC	322	D2	CNC	324	D4	RNC	320	D0
Carry	JC	332	DA	CC	334	DC	RC	330	D8
Odd Parity	JPO	342	E2	CPO	344	E4	RPO	340	E0
Even Parity	JPE	352	EA	CPE	354	EC	RPE	350	E8
Positive Result	JP	362	F2	CP	364	F4	RP	360	F0
Negative Result	JM	372	FA	CM	374	FC	RM	370	F8

Remember that *all* jump and call instructions are three-byte instructions, and that *all* returns are one-byte instructions. Most of the time, you will probably use the conditional jump and the unconditional call and return instructions. However, conditional call and return instructions are very powerful if they are used properly.

Suppose you have messages, as groups of ASCII characters stored in the 8080's memory, and you would like to print them on a teletypewriter or crt. To initially save the ASCII characters in memory, you used a program that let you enter the characters in memory using the teletypewriter or crt keyboard. One special feature of this input program was that whenever a carriage return was typed, both a carriage return and line feed were typed out. This prevented one line from being typed on top of another. However, only the message characters and the carriage-return characters were stored in memory. This allowed you to use one less memory location per line for the storage of the ASCII message, since the line-feed character does not need to be saved.

Now you have to write a program that types out the stored characters. However, every time a carriage return is retrieved from memory and "printed," or output to the printer, a line feed must also be typed out to provide a new line for the remainder of the message. Remember, the line feeds are "understood" and are not stored in memory as ASCII characters. One such program that will generate a line feed after each carriage return is listed in Example 3-7.

Example 3-7: An ASCII Character Print Program Without Line Feeds Stored in Memory

```
START,   LXISP     /SET THE STACK POINTER BECAUSE
         STACK     /SUBROUTINES WILL BE CALLED.
         0         /THIS IS A R/W MEMORY ADDRESS.
         LXIH      /LOAD REGISTER PAIR H WITH THE
         STRING    /MEMORY ADDRESS WHERE THE ASCII
         0         /CHARACTERS ARE STORED IN SEQUENCE.
NXTCHR,  MOVAM     /GET A CHARACTER FROM MEMORY.
         CALL      /PRINT THE CHARACTER ON THE
         TTYOUT    /TELETYPEWRITER OR CRT.
         0
         CPI       /WAS THE CHARACTER PRINTED
         215       /A CARRIAGE RETURN ?
         CZ        /IF YES, THEN CALL THE SUBROUTINE
         LFALSO    /THAT WILL PRINT A LINE FEED.
         0
         INXH      /INCREMENT THE MEMORY ADDRESS IN H&L
         JMP       /AND THEN FETCH ANOTHER CHARACTER
         NXTCHR    /FROM MEMORY AND PRINT IT.
         0

LFALSO,  MVIA      /LOAD THE A REGISTER WITH THE
         212       /ASCII CHARACTER, LINE FEED.
         CALL      /THEN CALL THE TELETYPEWRITER
         TTYOUT    /OR CRT PRINT SUBROUTINE.
         0
         RET

TTYOUT,  MOVBA     /SAVE THE CHARACTER IN B.
TTYO,    IN        /INPUT THE UART'S STATUS WORD.
         001
         ANI       /SAVE ONLY THE TRANSMITTER'S FLAG.
         004       /IF A=004, THE TRANSMITTER (PRINTER) IS READY.
         JZ        /IF A=000, THE TRANSMITTER (PRINTER) IS BUSY.
         TTYO      /SO KEEP WAITING FOR THE TRANSMITTER
         0         /(PRINTER) TO FINISH, BEFORE THE
         MOVAB     /CONTENT OF THE A REGISTER CAN BE PRINTED.
         OUT       /AFTER THE CHARACTER IS MOVED FROM
         000       /B TO A, OUTPUT IT TO THE UART.
         RET       /RETURN WITH THE CHARACTER STILL IN A.
```

The symbolic address, STRING, has been assigned to the memory location that is used to store the first character of the ASCII message which is stored in sequential memory locations. Therefore, the 16-bit address of STRING is stored as the second (STRING) and third (0) bytes of the LXIH instruction. If you were to enter this program into the computer's memory, you would have to determine the proper 16-bit address for the start of the ASCII message, and place this address in the memory locations immediately after the memory location used to store the op code for the LXIH instruction. We have also assigned a symbolic address (STACK) to some R/W memory location. This 16-bit address will be loaded into the SP when the LXISP instruction is executed.

There are four other symbolic addresses that are defined in Example 3-7. These include NXTCHR, LFALSO, TTYOUT, and TTYO. These symbolic addresses are all used as the address bytes in jump and call instructions.

When the program in Example 3-7 is executed, the SP is first loaded with the address for an R/W memory location. The SP is loaded because the program will call subroutines, so return addresses must be saved on the stack. Register pair H is then loaded with the address that points to the first character in the ASCII message stored in memory. At NXTCHR, an ASCII character is moved from memory to the A register, and then the TTYOUT subroutine is called. This subroutine prints the character on the teletypewriter or crt screen. In another section of this chapter, we will discuss I/O device synchronization. For this reason, we will not discuss how the TTYOUT subroutine operates at this time.

The character that is printed is still in the A register when control returns to the main program from the subroutine. Therefore, when the 8080 returns from the subroutine, the content of the A register is compared to the value, 215 (8D), which is the value of the ASCII carriage-return character. If the character that was just printed is a carriage return, as indicated by an equality or "true zero" flag, the LFALSO (Line Feed ALSO) is called by the conditional call instruction, CZ. Only when the ASCII value for a carriage return is read from memory and printed will this subroutine be called. The LFALSO subroutine causes a line feed to be "printed" on the teletypewriter or crt. After the 8080 returns from the LFALSO subroutine, or if the call instruction (CZ) is skipped, the content of register pair H is incremented by 1 (INXH), and then the 8080 jumps back to the instruction associated with the symbolic address, NXTCHR. Therefore, the 8080 transfers program control back to the MOVAM instruction.

How much memory is actually saved by not storing the ASCII line-feed characters in memory? As we mentioned before, if 80 lines of characters are stored in memory, 80 additional memory locations would be required to save the ASCII line-feed characters. However, 80 memory locations are not saved, because a special subroutine (LFALSO) had to be written, and some additional instructions had to be included in the main program (CPI 215 and CZ LFALSO 0). These instructions require 11 memory locations, so if 80 lines of characters are stored in memory, 69 memory locations would be saved. If 11 or fewer lines of ASCII characters were saved in memory, it would be a more efficient use of memory to save the line-feed characters in memory rather than to write a special subroutine, as we did in Example 3-7.

When will the program in Example 3-7 stop printing characters on the teletypewriter? It will never stop, even after the 80 lines of ASCII characters have been printed. This occurs because the 8080 has not been programmed to stop printing after all of the characters in the message have been printed. The "loop" in this program is endless. There is no way for the computer to get out of it or transfer control elsewhere.

To demonstrate the utility of one of the conditional return instructions, a binary-to-ASCII-based, hexadecimal-character-conversion subroutine was written. The subroutine converts the four-bit value contained in the four LSBs (D_3–D_0) in the A register to the appropriate ASCII value for the hexadecimal character. We have assumed that the remaining bits in the A register are zero. Selected ASCII, binary, and hexadecimal equivalents are listed in Table 3-3.

**Table 3-3. The ASCII, Binary, and Hexadecimal
Values for 16 Characters**

ASCII	Binary	Hexadecimal
260	0000	0
261	0001	1
262	0010	2
263	0011	3
264	0100	4
265	0101	5
266	0110	6
267	0111	7
270	1000	8
271	1001	9
301	1010	A
302	1011	B
303	1100	C
304	1101	D
305	1110	E
306	1111	F

The subroutine that was written to convert the binary content of the A register to the corresponding ASCII-based hexadecimal characters is listed in Example 3-8.

Example 3-8: A Binary-to-ASCII-Based, Hexadecimal Conversion Subroutine

```
BINHEX,  ADI    /ADD 260 (HEXADECIMAL B0) TO THE
         260    /CONTENT OF A WHEN THE SUBROUTINE
         CPI    /IS CALLED. THEN COMPARE A TO 272
         272    /(HEXADECIMAL BA). THE 8080 WILL
         RC     /RETURN IF A IS LESS THAN 272 (HEX BA).
         ADI    /IF THE 8080 DOES NOT RETURN, ADD
         007    /007 (HEX 07) TO THE CONTENT OF A
         RET    /AND THEN RETURN WITH ONE OF THE
                /ASCII LETTER CHARACTERS IN A.
```

The subroutine listed in Example 3-8 must be called, with the binary value that is to be converted, in bits D_3–D_0 of the A register. When the 8080 returns from the subroutine, the appropriate ASCII-based hexadecimal character will be contained in the A register.

When the 8080 enters the subroutine, the value 260 (B0) is added (immediately) to the content of the A register. The content of the A register could now be any of the 16 values listed in Table 3-4.

Table 3-4. The Addition of 260 (B0) to the Content of Register A

Content of Register A at Start of Program	Content of Register A After Addition of 260		ASCII Character
Binary	Octal	Hexadecimal	
0000	260	B0	0
0001	261	B1	1
0010	262	B2	2
0011	263	B3	3
0100	264	B4	4
0101	265	B5	5
0110	266	B6	6
0111	267	B7	7
1000	270	B8	8
1001	271	B9	9
1010	272	BA	:
1011	273	BB	;
1100	274	BC	<
1101	275	BD	=
1110	276	BE	>
1111	277	BF	?

By adding 260 (B0) to the content of the A register, the binary values for 0000 through 1001 (0 to 9) are correctly converted to the ASCII characters for these numbers. However, the ASCII characters for the hexadecimal characters A through F (binary 1010 through 1111) are incorrect. Therefore, the CPI 272 instruction determines whether or not the content of the A register is greater than or equal to 272 (BA). The 8080 will return from the subroutine if the carry flag is set to a logic 1, the content of the A register being 260 through 271 (hexadecimal B0 through B9, ASCII 0 through 9). If the content of the A register is 272 or greater, the value 007 (07) is added to the content of the A register. This creates the proper ASCII characters for binary 1010 through 1111. After the 007 (07) is added, the 8080 returns to the main program with the ASCII characters, A through F, in the A register.

There are a number of different methods that can be used to convert from one number system (base) to another. Additional methods will be discussed in the Number Base Conversion chapter. However, you have now seen practical examples that use conditional call and return instructions.

USING THE BASIC INSTRUCTIONS

So far, the following types of instructions have been discussed:

1. The move instructions: register-to-register, memory, and immediate.
2. The increment and decrement instructions: register and memory.
3. The input and output instructions: IN and OUT
4. The simple register pair instructions: LXI, INX, and DCX.
5. The logical and mathematical instructions: ANA, XRA, ORA, CMP, ADD, ADC, SUB, and SBB.
6. The unconditional and conditional jump, call, and return instructions.

I/O DEVICE SYNCHRONIZATION

Only by using all of these instructions can programs be written that perform a task quickly, efficiently, and with a minimum amount of programming effort. However, in order for you to see the microcomputer "do something," there must be I/O devices attached to the microcomputer. These devices could include the microcomputer's front panel, a teletypewriter, crt, floppy disk, paper-tape reader, or paper-tape punch. Many of the program examples in this chapter will use either a teletypewriter or crt as an I/O device because they are very common peripherals. Let us reexamine a very simple teletypewriter output subroutine.

To use the subroutine listed in Example 3-9, we have assumed that the teletypewriter is *interfaced* to the microcomputer; i.e., it is wired to the microcomputer using a Universal Asynchronous Receiver/Transmitter (UART). The data from the microcomputer will be transmitted to the teletypewriter by the UART, and the UART

Example 3-9: A Simple Teletypewriter Output Subroutine

```
TTYOUT,  MOVBA    /SAVE THE CHARACTER IN B.
TTYO,    IN       /INPUT THE UART'S STATUS WORD.
         001
         ANI      /SAVE ONLY THE TRANSMITTER'S FLAG.
         004      /IF A=004, THE TRANSMITTER (PRINTER) IS READY.
         JZ       /IF A=000, THE TRANSMITTER (PRINTER) IS BUSY.
         TTYO     /SO KEEP WAITING FOR THE TRANSMITTER
         0        /(PRINTER) TO FINISH, BEFORE THE
         MOVAB    /CONTENT OF THE A REGISTER CAN BE PRINTED.
         OUT      /AFTER THE CHARACTER IS MOVED FROM
         000      /B TO A, OUTPUT IT TO THE UART.
         RET      /RETURN WITH THE CHARACTER STILL IN A.
```

will receive the transmitted characters from the teletypewriter so that the microcomputer can input the data. It will be assumed that the teletypewriter used in the program examples receives and transmits seven-bit ASCII characters with the parity bit (the MSB) always equal to a logic 1.

The use of UARTs for communications purposes is very common, and a book has been specifically written on the subject.[1] The same hardware functions performed by the UART can also be performed by an assembly language program, often called a *software UART*. A program that performs this function has also been reported.[2]

When the subroutine in Example 3-9 is called, the A register must contain the eight-bit character that is to be transmitted to the teletypewriter. At TTYOUT, the character is saved in the B register. The IN instruction then inputs the *status* of the UART's transmitter section to see if it is busy transmitting a character. If the transmitter is busy, the *transmitter-ready flag bit* of the UART, which is wired to bit D_2 of input port 001 (01), will be a logic 0. When the UART is not transmitting a character, the flag bit will be a logic 1. Other such status bits are input in other bit positions in the *status word.*

After the status word is input, the 8080 performs an ANI instruction with an immediate data byte of 004 (04). This masks-out all the other status bits within the eight-bit word *except* for the transmitter's status bit, D_2. After the ANI instruction is executed, the content of the A register will be 000 (00) if the transmitter is busy, and 004 (04) if the transmitter is not transmitting a character to the teletypewriter. This means that if the UART is presently transmitting a character, the content of the A register will be 000 (00), so the JZ to TTYO is executed.

When the TRANSMITTER-READY flag of the UART finally goes to a logic 1, the content of the A register will be 004 (04) after the ANI instruction is executed. Therefore, the JZ to TTYO is no longer executed. Instead, the next instruction stored in memory after the JZ instruction, is executed. This instruction, MOVAB, duplicates the content of the B register in the A register. An OUT instruction is then executed so that the eight-bit content of the A register is latched, in parallel, by the UART. When a data word is latched (into the UART, the transmission of the character begins automatically. The TRANSMITTER-READY flag is cleared by this operation to signify that the UART is busy transmitting a character. When the eight-bit character has been transmitted to the teletypewriter, the flag is set to the logic 1 condition to indicate the READY condition. After the 8080 executes the OUT instruction, it executes the RET instruction and returns to the program that called the TTYOUT subroutine.

Why are the IN 001, ANI 004, and JZ TTYO instructions executed? This sequence of instructions *synchronizes* the 8080 microcomputer to the teletypewriter. If there was no synchronization, the 8080 could output a new data word every 100 μs to the teletypewriter (by outputting the word to the UART). However, the basic 10-character-per-second teletypewriter requires 100 ms to print one character. This means that the 8080 could output 1000 characters to the slow, mechanical printer before the printer mechanism within the teletypewriter could completely print one character! Because of this difference in speed, the TTYOUT subroutine must be written so that the 8080 waits for the transmitter section of the UART, which is just as slow as the printer, to complete the transmission of the current character before another character is transmitted. As you would expect, the microcomputer spends most of its time waiting for the transmitter (printer) to be ready. This is true of most small microcomputer systems. The microcomputer spends a major portion of its operating time waiting for I/O devices to send or receive data.

In Example 3-9, note that the character that is to be transmitted to the teletypewriter is first saved in the B register. If the character were not saved in the B register, the IN 000 instruction would destroy it, because IN instructions input data words into the A register.

Example 3-10: Printing a B on the Teletypewriter

```
PRINTB,  IN.    /INPUT THE UART'S STATUS BITS.
         001
         ANI    /SAVE ONLY THE TRANSMITTER'S (PRINTER'S)
         001    /STATUS. IF A=000, THE TRANSMITTER IS BUSY.
         JZ     /IF A=004, THE TRANSMITTER IS READY.
         PRINTB
         0
         MVIA   /THE TRANSMITTER IS READY, SO LOAD
         302    /A WITH THE ASCII VALUE FOR A B.
         OUT    /OUTPUT THE EIGHT-BIT CODE TO THE
         000    /TRANSMITTER.
         RET    /AND THEN RETURN FROM THE SUBROUTINE.
```

Suppose you want to print the ASCII character B on the teletypewriter. You could use the subroutine listed in Example 3-10.

In this subroutine (Example 3-10), the 8080 waits for the UART's transmitter (printer) flag to be a logic 1. When it is a logic 1, the A register is loaded with the immediate data byte, 302 (C2), which is the ASCII value for the B character. The content of the A register is then output to the UART for transmission to the teletypewriter or crt. There are a number of different subroutines that can be used to print characters on a teletypewriter or crt. Unfortunately, Example 3-10 is of limited flexibility. You do not want to have to duplicate this subroutine, with its preprogrammed ASCII character, each time a character is to be printed. Instead, you might use the method shown in Example 3-11.

Example 3-11: A Flexible Method of Printing Characters

```
        •
        •
        •
   MVIA    /LOAD THE A REGISTER WITH THE ASCII
   302     /VALUE TO BE TRANSMITTED TO THE PRINTER.
   CALL    /THEN CALL THE TTYOUT SUBROUTINE.
   TTYOUT
   0
        •
        •
        •
```

```
TTYOUT,  MOVBA  /SAVE THE CHARACTER IN B.
TTYO,    IN     /INPUT THE UART'S STATUS WORD.
         001
         ANI    /SAVE ONLY THE TRANSMITTER'S FLAG.
         004    /IF A=004, THE TRANSMITTER (PRINTER) IS READY.
         JZ     /IF A=000, THE TRANSMITTER (PRINTER) IS BUSY.
         TTYO   /SO KEEP WAITING FOR THE TRANSMITTER
         0      /(PRINTER) TO FINISH, BEFORE THE
         MOVAB  /CONTENT OF THE A REGISTER CAN BE PRINTED.
         OUT    /AFTER THE CHARACTER IS MOVED FROM
         000    /B TO A, OUTPUT IT TO THE UART.
         RET    /RETURN WITH THE CHARACTER STILL IN A.
```

If the method shown in Example 3-11 is used, the character to be printed must be loaded into the A register before the TTYOUT subroutine is called. In this example, an MVIA instruction is used to load the ASCII character into the A register. Instructions such as MOVAC and MOVAM could also be used if the ASCII character is already stored in the C register, or the memory location addressed by register pair H.

Few microcomputer users realize that the teletypewriter keyboard *is not* mechanically connected to the printer mechanism, as is the case with an ordinary typewriter. The teletypewriter keyboard and printer are *separate* and *distinct* I/O devices, even though they are housed in the same case. This means that you can write a program that inputs data from the keyboard, and then outputs the same data to the printer. This is called *echoing* a character. A program that performs this function is listed in Example 3-12.

Example 3-12: Echoing a Keyboard Character on the Printer

```
TTYIN,   IN       /INPUT THE UART'S STATUS BITS.
         001
         RAR      /ROTATE THE RECEIVER'S FLAG INTO THE
         JNC      /CARRY. IF THE CARRY IS ZERO, NO KEY
         TTYIN    /IS PRESSED, SO KEEP WAITING.
         0
         IN       /A KEY IS PRESSED, SO INPUT THE
         000      /ASCII CHARACTER INTO THE A REGISTER.
TTYOUT,  MOVBA    /SAVE THE CHARACTER IN B.
TTYO,    IN       /INPUT THE UART'S STATUS WORD.
         001
         ANI      /SAVE ONLY THE TRANSMITTER'S FLAG.
         004      /IF A=004, THE TRANSMITTER (PRINTER) IS READY.
         JZ       /IF A=000, THE TRANSMITTER (PRINTER) IS BUSY.
         TTYO     /SO KEEP WAITING FOR THE TRANSMITTER
         0        /(PRINTER) TO FINISH, BEFORE THE
         MOVAB    /CONTENT OF THE A REGISTER CAN BE PRINTED.
         OUT      /AFTER THE CHARACTER IS MOVED·FROM
         000      /B TO A, OUTPUT IT TO THE UART.
         JMP      /AFTER THE CHARACTER IS OUTPUT, JUMP
         TTYIN    /BACK TO TTYIN SO THAT ANOTHER
         0        /CHARACTER CAN BE INPUT.
```

In Example 3-12, the 8080 waits for the UART to receive a character from the teletypewriter or crt keyboard. When the UART does receive a character, bit D_0, the RECEIVER-FULL flag of input port 001 (01), the status word input port, will go to a logic 1. In the previous examples (Examples 3-9 and 3-10), a different bit in this same input port was used to detect the status of the transmitter (printer). After the status word is input from input port 001 (01), the eight-bit data word is rotated once to the right. This causes the LSB of the A register (the RECEIVER-FULL flag of the UART) to be rotated into the carry. If the carry flag is a logic 0, then no key on the teletypewriter keyboard has been pressed (the receiver is not full). If this is the case, the carry flag will be a logic 0 and the JNC instruction is executed. This will transfer program control back to the IN instruction. The status word input, flag bit testing, and the JNC instructions will continue to be executed until a key on the keyboard is finally pressed.

When a key is pressed and the character has been received by the UART, the RECEIVER-FULL flag (a logic 1) will be rotated into the carry. Now, this true-carry condition means that the JNC instruction will not be executed. Instead, the character received by the UART is inputted into the 8080's A register and then saved in the B register at TTYOUT.

After the ASCII character is input, the program waits for the transmitter section of the UART to be ready (not transmitting a character to the printer of the teletypewriter). It does this by executing the sequence of TRANSMITTER-READY flag-testing instructions that we discussed earlier. When the transmitter section of the UART is ready, the ASCII value for the key that was pressed is moved from the B register into the A register. This ASCII value is then output to the UART, which automatically transmits the character to the teletypewriter printer or to the crt screen.

When the ASCII character is input from the UART, the RECEIVER-FULL flag is reset by the IN command. This is performed by hardware that is external to the microcomputer. This allows the next complete character received by the UART to again set the RECEIVER-FULL flag, indicating that another character has been received by the UART. The UART is a powerful device and there are a number of good references about it.[1, 3, 4]

Why was the data word from the UART's receiver section input into the A register, rather than another of the 8080's general-purpose registers? The reason is that the 8080 can only transfer data between a peripheral device and the A register when the IN and OUT instructions are executed. Therefore, to transmit the ASCII character, it had to be moved from the B register to the A register before it could be output to the UART.

The program used to echo teletypewriter characters (Example 3-12) is a very useful one. It can easily become two subroutines by simply replacing the last instruction (JMP TTYIN) with a return, RET. By calling the subroutine TTYIN. a keyboard character will be input, echoed on the printer, and left in the A and B registers when the 8080 returns from the subroutine. By calling the subroutine TTYOUT, ASCII characters are readily output to the teletypewriter or crt. Remember, though, that if the TTYIN subroutine is called so that a keyboard character can be input, the program will "wait" in the TTYIN loop until a key is pressed. *The microcomputer does nothing else at the time.*

Why was a RAR instruction used to monitor the UART's RECEIVER-FULL flag in the TTYIN section of the subroutine listed in Example 3-12, and an ANI instruction used to monitor the TRANSMITTER-READY flag? If an ANI instruction had been used to monitor the RECEIVER-FULL flag, it would have required two memory locations, one for the ANI instruction and one for the immediate data byte or the mask. The RAR instruction requires only one memory location, so one memory location is saved. However, either the RAR or the ANI instruction could have been used; the result would have been the same.

The same reasoning applies to the choice of an ANI instruction to monitor the TRANSMITTER-READY flag, rather than RAR instructions. The software would have required three RAR instructions to rotate the TRANSMITTER-READY flag into the carry, where it would be sensed for the logic 0 condition with a JNC instruction. By using an ANI instruction, only two memory locations were required, so another memory location was saved.

There is, however, one major fault in using RAR or other rotate instructions for sensing the state of flags. If you want to write the best possible software, why shouldn't you use the rotate instructions in programs that sense the state of flags? The answer has nothing to do with which flags are affected by the RAR instructions versus the ANI instructions. The answer is flexiblility.

Suppose you have written a program that you would like to sell or have other programmers use. Most of the time, other users will not have exactly the same I/O device addresses that you have written into the program. It would be fairly easy for these new users to change the *address bytes* in the I/O instructions to reflect the I/O device addresses that are being used in their systems. However, suppose another user uses bits D_4 and D_5 to sense the status flags of the transmitter and receiver of the UART, while the software you wrote uses bits D_0 and D_2. If you have only used one RAR instruction in the program, the new user will not be able to easily insert a two-byte ANI instruction required to sense either one of the bits, D_4 or D_5, that are input from the UART, in the program. Therefore, you should use ANI instructions in your own I/O routines when you need to test specific flag bits. If this is done, any new user can easily change not only the addresses for the I/O devices, but also the mask byte for the ANI instructions. This is shown in Example 3-13.

Example 3-13: The Flexibility of Using ANI Instructions in I/O Software

IN		IN
001	EASILY CHANGED	360
ANI	TO	ANI
001		040

IN		IN
001	NOT EASILY	360
RAR	CHANGED TO	ANI
		040

TELETYPEWRITER I/O AND CHARACTER MANIPULATIONS

In Example 3-12, an ASCII character can be received from a teletypewriter or crt keyboard, and then echoed on the teletypewriter printer mechanism or the crt screen. A program will now be written that lets you type a message on the teletypewriter keyboard, and which saves the resulting ASCII characters in memory. A program that performs these tasks is listed in Example 3-14.

The program listed in Example 3-14 sets the SP to an R/W memory location because CALL instructions will be executed in the program. Register pair H is then loaded with the R/W memory address of the first 16 sequential locations where the ASCII characters will be stored in memory. In this example, register C will be used as a character counter, and it is initialized with the value 020 (hexadecimal 10, decimal 16). The TTYIN subroutine is then called, so that characters can be input from the teletypewriter keyboard.

The TTYIN causes the 8080 to wait for a key to be pressed, and then inputs the ASCII value for that key into the A register. The

Example 3-14: Input and Save ASCII Characters in Memory

```
INSAV,   LXISP     /SET THE STACK POINTER.
         STACK
         0
         LXIH      /LOAD REGISTER PAIR H WITH AN R/W
         STRING    /MEMORY ADDRESS WHERE THE ASCII
         0         /CHARACTERS CAN BE STORED.
         MVIC      /NUMBER OF CHARACTERS TO INPUT
         020       /AND STORE IS 16 (DECIMAL).
SAVE,    CALL      /GET A TELETYPEWRITER CHARACTER.
         TTYIN
         0
         MOVMA     /SAVE THE CHARACTER IN MEMORY.
         INXH      /INCREMENT THE MEMORY POINTER.
         DCRC      /DECREMENT THE CHARACTER COUNTER.
         JNZ       /16 YET ? NO, GET ANOTHER CHARACTER.
         SAVE
         0
             •
             •
             •

TTYIN,   IN        /INPUT THE UART'S STATUS BITS.
         001
         ANI       /SAVE ONLY THE RECEIVER'S FLAG.
         001       /IF A=001, A KEY IS PRESSED.
         JZ        /IF A=000, NO KEY IS PRESSED.
         TTYIN     /SO KEEP WAITING FOR A KEY
         0         /TO BE PRESSED.
         IN        /A KEY IS PRESSED, SO INPUT THE
         000       /ASCII CHARACTER INTO THE A REGISTER.
         RET       /RETURN WITH THE CHARACTER IN A.
```

8080 then returns from the subroutine. The ASCII character is saved in the memory location addressed by register pair H by the MOVMA instruction. The content of register pair H is then incremented (INXH), and the content of the C register, the character counter, is decremented. How many characters can be entered and saved in memory, using this program? The answer is 16_{10}, because this is the number initially loaded into the C register. The program will continue to save in memory the ASCII characters entered on the keyboard until the content of the C register is decremented to zero. Then, the JNZ instruction that follows the DCRC instruction will no longer be executed, and the 8080 will begin execution of the remainder of the program.

When you type in a 16-character message on the teletypewriter keyboard using this program, will the message also be printed out? The answer is no, because there are no instructions that would cause the ASCII characters to be transmitted to the printer. Therefore, as you entered a message, you would not see it printed on the printer. Of course, the software could be modified so that the message is printed as it is entered. Example 3-15 is the same as Example 3-14, except the TTYIN subroutine now prints the message on the teletypewriter as it is entered. Note the use of ANI instructions rather than RAR instructions

Now that the message is echoed by the software, can you see another limitation of the Input-and-Save program listed in Example 3-15? What happens if you want to enter an ASCII message that is 43 characters long, and the program listed in Example 3-15 is stored in read-only memory (ROM)? There is no way that you can change the character count, which is established by the immediate data byte for the MVIC instruction. Instead of a fixed count, it would be advantageous to have some way of signaling the 8080 that the end of the message had just been typed in. This means that a message that contains 15 or 56 characters could be entered. Can you think of how this could be done? The simplest method is to use one of the keyboard characters as a *software flag*. In Example 3-16, the ASCII value for a question mark (octal 277, hex BF) will be used as the software flag, signaling the 8080 that the end of the message has been entered.

In Example 3-16, after the SP is initialized with an R/W memory address, register pair H is loaded with an R/W memory address where the ASCII characters will be stored. The 8080 then calls the TTYIN subroutine. When a key on the teletypewriter keyboard is pressed, the ASCII value is input from the UART and then output to the transmitter section of the UART. When the 8080 returns from the subroutine, the ASCII value is in the A and B registers. The 8080 then compares the content of the A register (the

Example 3-15: An Input-and-Save Program That Echoes the Message

```
INSAV,   LXISP      /SET THE STACK POINTER.
         STACK
         0
         LXIH       /LOAD REGISTER PAIR H WITH AN R/W
         STRING     /MEMORY ADDRESS WHERE THE ASCII
         0          /CHARACTERS CAN BE STORED.
         MVIC       /NUMBER OF CHARACTERS TO INPUT
         020        /AND STORE IS 16 (DECIMAL).
SAVE,    CALL       /GET A TELETYPEWRITER CHARACTER.
         TTYIN
         0
         MOVMA      /SAVE THE CHARACTER IN MEMORY.
         INXH       /INCREMENT THE MEMORY POINTER.
         DCRC       /DECREMENT THE CHARACTER COUNTER.
         JNZ        /16 YET ? NO, GET ANOTHER CHARACTER.
         SAVE
         0
                •
                •
                •

TTYIN,   IN         /INPUT THE UART'S STATUS BITS.
         001
         ANI        /SAVE ONLY THE RECEIVER'S FLAG.
         001        /IF A=001, A KEY IS PRESSED.
         JZ         /IF A=000, NO KEY IS PRESSED.
         TTYIN      /SO KEEP WAITING FOR A KEY
         0          /TO BE PRESSED.
         IN         /A KEY IS PRESSED, SO INPUT THE
         000        /ASCII CHARACTER INTO THE A REGISTER.
TTYOUT,  MOVBA      /SAVE THE CHARACTER IN B.
TTYO,    IN         /INPUT THE UART'S STATUS WORD.
         001
         ANI        /SAVE ONLY THE TRANSMITTER'S FLAG.
         004        /IF A=004, THE TRANSMITTER (PRINTER) IS READY.
         JZ         /IF A=000, THE TRANSMITTER (PRINTER) IS BUSY.
         TTYO       /SO KEEP WAITING FOR THE TRANSMITTER
         0          /(PRINTER) TO FINISH, BEFORE THE
         MOVAB      /CONTENT OF THE A REGISTER CAN BE PRINTED.
         OUT        /AFTER THE CHARACTER IS MOVED FROM
         000        /B TO A, OUTPUT IT TO THE UART.
         RET        /RETURN WITH THE CHARACTER STILL IN A.
```

received character) and an immediate data byte, 277 (BF). The 277 (BF) is the ASCII value for a question mark. If the character entered is not a question mark, the result of the comparison will be nonzero and the JZ to TERM is not executed. Instead, the ASCII value is stored in the memory location addressed by register pair H (MOVMA), the memory address contained in register pair H is incremented (INXH), and then a JMP instruction is executed (to CHARIN) so that the 8080 can input another character. Note

Example 3-16: Using a Question Mark to Terminate a Message Being Input

```
IANDT,    LXIH      /LOAD REGISTER PAIR H WITH AN R/W
          STRING    /MEMORY ADDRESS WHERE THE ASCII
          0         /CHARACTERS CAN BE STORED.
CHARIN,   CALL      /GET A CHARACTER FROM THE TELE-
          TTYIN     /TYPEWRITER OR CRT AND PRINT IT.
          0
          CPI       /IS THE CHARACTER A QUESTION MARK ?
          277
          JZ
          TERM      /YES, SAVE A TERMINATOR.
          0
          MOVMA     /NO, SAVE THE CHARACTER IN MEMORY.
          INXH      /INCREMENT THE MEMORY POINTER
          JMP       /AND GET ANOTHER CHARACTER FROM THE
          CHARIN    /TELETYPEWRITER OR CRT.
          0
TERM,     MVIM      /NOW SAVE A 000 IN MEMORY AFTER
          000       /THE ASCII CHARACTERS BECAUSE A
            •       /QUESTION MARK WAS TYPED IN.
            •
            •
          ETC


TTYIN,    IN        /INPUT THE UART'S STATUS BITS.
          001
          ANI       /SAVE ONLY THE RECEIVER'S FLAG.
          001       /IF A=001, A KEY IS PRESSED.
          JZ        /IF A=000, NO KEY IS PRESSED.
          TTYIN     /SO KEEP WAITING FOR A KEY
          0         /TO BE PRESSED.
          IN        /A KEY IS PRESSED, SO INPUT THE
          000       /ASCII CHARACTER INTO THE A REGISTER.
TTYOUT,   MOVBA     /SAVE THE CHARACTER IN B.
TTYO,     IN        /INPUT THE UART'S STATUS WORD.
          001
          ANI       /SAVE ONLY THE TRANSMITTER'S FLAG.
          004       /IF A=004, THE TRANSMITTER (PRINTER) IS READY.
          JZ        /IF A=000, THE TRANSMITTER (PRINTER) IS BUSY.
          TTYO      /SO KEEP WAITING FOR THE TRANSMITTER
          0         /(PRINTER) TO FINISH, BEFORE THE
          MOVAB     /CONTENT OF THE A REGISTER CAN BE PRINTED.
          OUT       /AFTER THE CHARACTER IS MOVED FROM
          000       /B TO A, OUTPUT IT TO THE UART.
          RET       /RETURN WITH THE CHARACTER STILL IN A.
```

that a message of any length can now be entered and saved in memory. Only when the question-mark key on the keyboard is pressed, and its ASCII value of 277 (BF) is received by the 8080, will the 8080 execute the JZ to TERM. When the 8080 does jump to TERM, a 000 (00) is saved in memory immediately after the last character saved in memory. The 000 (00) is saved in memory when the MVIM instruction is executed. Will the ASCII value for the question mark be saved in memory too? No, the question-mark code will not be saved in memory; instead a 000 (00) will be saved in memory.

What will happen when a carriage return is typed in? Will both a carriage return and line feed be typed out? No, just a carriage return will be typed out. This means that the second and successive lines will all be typed on top of the first line. To solve this problem, each time a carriage return is entered, both a carriage return and a line feed must be typed out. This is very similar to a problem that we examined in a previous example (Example 3-7). As in this previous example, a conditional call instruction will be used in Example 3-17.

Example 3-17: Printing a Line Feed Upon Entering a Carriage Return

```
IANDT,    LXISP     /LOAD THE SP BECAUSE SUBROUTINES
          STACK     /WILL BE CALLED.
          0
          LXIH      /LOAD REGISTER PAIR H WITH AN R/W
          STRING    /MEMORY ADDRESS WHERE THE ASCII
          0         /CHARACTERS CAN BE STORED.
CHARIN,   CALL      /GET A CHARACTER FROM THE TELE-
          TTYIN     /TYPEWRITER OR CRT AND PRINT IT.
          0
          CPI       /IS THE CHARACTER A QUESTION MARK ?
          277
          JZ
          TERM      /YES, SAVE A TERMINATOR.
          0
          MOVMA     /NO, SAVE THE CHARACTER IN MEMORY.
          INXH      /INCREMENT THE MEMORY POINTER.
          CPI       /WAS A CARRIAGE RETURN TYPED IN ?
          215       /(OCTAL 215 = HEXADECIMAL 8D).
          CZ        /YES, THEN PRINT A LINE FEED SO
          LFALSO    /THAT THE LINES ARE NOT TYPED
          0         /ON TOP OF EACH OTHER
          JMP       /AND GET ANOTHER CHARACTER FROM THE
          CHARIN    /TELETYPEWRITER OR CRT.
          0
TERM,     MVIM      /NOW SAVE A 000 IN MEMORY AFTER
          000       /THE ASCII CHARACTERS BECAUSE A
          •         /QUESTION MARK WAS TYPED IN.
          •
          •
          ETC

LFALSO,   MVIA      /LOAD THE A REGISTER WITH THE
          212       /ASCII CODE FOR A LINE FEED.
          CALL      /THEN CALL THE TELETYPEWRITER
          TTYOUT    /OR CRT PRINT SUBROUTINE.
          0
          RET
```

In Example 3-17, the TTYIN subroutine has not been listed because it is the same TTYIN subroutine that was shown in Example 3-16.

Now that the ASCII characters have been stored in memory, how can the message be typed out on a teletypewriter or crt? In Example 3-14, the C register was loaded with a count. This count determined how many characters could be typed in on the teletypewriter keyboard and saved in the 8080's memory. When the count was zero, no additional characters could be entered. A counter could also be used in a program that prints the characters stored in memory on the teletypewriter or crt (Example 3-18).

Example 3-18: Printing the ASCII Characters Stored in Memory

```
PRINT,  LXISP    /LOAD THE STACK POINTER WITH
        STACK    /AN R/W MEMORY ADDRESS.
        0
        LXIH     /LOAD REGISTER PAIR H WITH THE
        STRING   /MEMORY ADDRESS WHERE THE ASCII
        0        /CHARACTERS ARE STORED.
        MVIC     /LOAD THE C REGISTER WITH THE NUMBER OF
        020      /CHARACTERS TO BE PRINTED (DECIMAL 16).
PRNT1,  MOVAM    /MOVE A CHARACTER FROM MEMORY TO A.
        CALL     /PRINT THE CHARACTER ON THE
        TTYOUT   /TELETYPEWRITER OR CRT.
        0
        INXH     /INCREMENT THE MEMORY ADDRESS IN
        DCRC     /REGISTER PAIR H AND THEN DECREMENT
        JNZ      /THE CHARACTER COUNT IN C.
        PRNT1    /IF THE CONTENT OF C IS NONZERO, THE
        0        /8080 JUMPS BACK TO PRNT1.
          •      /WHEN IT HAS PRINTED ALL THE CHARACTERS,
          •      /THE INSTRUCTIONS STORED HERE ARE EXECUTED.
```

After the SP is loaded with an R/W memory address, and register pair H is loaded with the address where the ASCII characters are stored in memory, the C register is loaded with the number of characters to be printed. At PRNT1, a character is moved from the memory location addressed by register pair H into the A register (MOVAM). The TTYOUT subroutine is then called, so the content of the A register is output to the crt or teletypewriter. When the 8080 returns from the TTYOUT subroutine, the content of register pair H is incremented and the content of the C register is decremented. If the content of the C register is decremented to a nonzero value, the JNZ to PRNT1 is executed. When 16 characters have been printed, the content of the C register is decremented to zero, and the JNZ to PRNT1 is no longer executed. At this point, the 8080 executes the remainder of the program.

This program (Example 3-18) has the same limitations as the input program that used a character counter (Example 3-14). If the ASCII message increases or decreases in length, the count contained in the C register will have to be changed to reflect the length of the new ASCII message. Can a more flexible printer program be written? Yes. Remember that in Examples 3-16 and 3-17, a 000 (00) was saved at the end of the ASCII-based message when the question-mark key was pressed. This can be used to our advantage, as Example 3-19 demonstrates.

Remember, the ASCII line-feed characters are not stored in R/W memory, only the ASCII carriage-return characters. Therefore, the output program in Example 3-19 must generate the ASCII line-feed character after a carriage-return character is output to the teletypewriter or crt. The necessary instructions to do this are shown in this example.

When will the 8080 begin to execute the section of the program starting at the symbolic address END? The 8080 will begin to execute that section when the character, 000 (00), is read from memory prior to the printing process. Remember, the 000 was stored in memory when the question-mark key was pressed. The 000 is a nonprinting character; an ASCII message that is stored in memory can be terminated by just about any nonprinting ASCII character.

What happens if you want to have a question mark in one of your messages? The program listed in Example 3-19 will print a question mark if it was in the ASCII message stored in memory. However, there is no easy way in which the ASCII value for a question mark can be saved in memory. Whenever the question-mark key was pressed (Example 3-16), a 000 (00) was saved in memory, since we selected the question mark as the terminator key for the file input. Instead of using the ASCII question-mark character as the *software flag*, the ASCII value for one of the control characters generated by the teletypewriter could be used. The codes for the control characters are generated by pressing a key on the keyboard while the CTRL key is held down. For example, a CTRL/C is generated by pressing the C key while the CTRL key is held down. Therefore, one of these control codes, rather than the code for a question mark, could be used to terminate the input routine. The only change that would have to be made to Example 3-16 would be to change the immediate data byte of the CPI instruction. This would be changed from a 277 for a question mark, to a 203 for a CTRL/C. With this modification, the input routine would only be terminated when a CTRL/C code is generated. After this modification is made, question marks can be included in any of the ASCII messages, because the 000 terminator is only saved in memory when a CTRL/C is entered.

In summary, the teletypewriter or crt input/output (I/O) subroutines that will be used in the remainder of this book are shown

Example 3-19: Printing an ASCII-Based Message Terminated With 000

```
PRINT,    LXISP      /LOAD THE STACK POINTER WITH AN
          STACK      /R/W MEMORY ADDRESS.
          0
          LXIH       /LOAD REGISTER PAIR H WITH THE
          STRING     /MEMORY ADDRESS WHERE THE ASCII
          0          /CHARACTERS ARE STORED.
PRNT1,    MOVAM      /GET AN ASCII CHARACTER FROM MEMORY.
          CPI        /IS THE CHARACTER THE MESSAGE
          000        /TERMINATOR ?
          JZ         /YES, EXECUTE THE JZ INSTRUCTION.
          END
          0
          CALL       /NO, IT IS NOT A 000, SO PRINT
          TTYOUT     /THE CHARACTER ON THE TELETYPE-
          0          /WRITER OR CRT.
          CPI        /WAS THE CHARACTER THAT WAS PRINTED
          215        /A CARRIAGE RETURN ?
          CZ         /IF IT WAS, THEN PRINT A LINE
          LFALSO     /FEED ALSO.
          0
          INXH       /INCREMENT THE TABLE POINTER
          JMP        /AND THEN GET ANOTHER ASCII CHARACTER.
          PRNT1
          0
END,       •
           •
           •
          ETC


TTYOUT,   MOVBA      /SAVE THE CHARACTER IN B.
TTYO,     IN         /INPUT THE UART'S STATUS WORD.
          001
          ANI        /SAVE ONLY THE TRANSMITTER'S FLAG.
          004        /IF A=004, THE TRANSMITTER (PRINTER) IS READY.
          JZ         /IF A=000, THE TRANSMITTER (PRINTER) IS BUSY.
          TTYO       /SO KEEP WAITING FOR THE TRANSMITTER
          0          /(PRINTER) TO FINISH, BEFORE THE
          MOVAB      /CONTENT OF THE A REGISTER CAN BE PRINTED.
          OUT        /AFTER THE CHARACTER IS MOVED FROM
          000        /B TO A, OUTPUT IT TO THE UART.
          RET        /RETURN WITH THE CHARACTER STILL IN A.


LFALSO,   MVIA       /LOAD THE A REGISTER WITH THE
          212        /ASCII CODE FOR A LINE FEED.
          CALL       /THEN CALL THE TELETYPEWRITER
          TTYOUT     /OR CRT PRINT SUBROUTINE.
          0
          RET
```

in Example 3-20. Although they are slightly different than the subroutines that have been discussed in this chapter, you should not have difficulty in determining exactly how they operate.

Example 3-20: The General-Purpose Teletypewriter I/O Subroutines

TTYIN With Echo and TTYOUT

```
TTYIN,    IN       /INPUT THE UART'S STATUS BITS.
          001
          ANI      /SAVE ONLY THE RECEIVER'S FLAG.
          001      /IF A=001, A KEY IS PRESSED.
          JZ       /IF A=000, NO KEY IS PRESSED.
          TTYIN    /SO KEEP WAITING FOR A KEY
          0        /TO BE PRESSED.
          IN       /A KEY IS PRESSED, SO INPUT THE
          000      /ASCII CHARACTER INTO THE A REGISTER.
          ANI      /REMOVE THE PARITY BIT (D7) FROM
          177      /THE ASCII CHARACTER (OCTAL 177 = HEX 7F).
TTYOUT,   MOVBA    /SAVE THE CHARACTER IN B.
TTYO,     IN       /INPUT THE UART'S STATUS WORD.
          001
          ANI      /SAVE ONLY THE TRANSMITTER'S FLAG.
          004      /IF A=004, THE TRANSMITTER (PRINTER) IS READY.
          JZ       /IF A=000, THE TRANSMITTER (PRINTER) IS BUSY.
          TTYO     /SO KEEP WAITING FOR THE TRANSMITTER
          0        /(PRINTER) TO FINISH, BEFORE THE
          MOVAB    /CONTENT OF THE A REGISTER CAN BE PRINTED.
          OUT      /AFTER THE CHARACTER IS MOVED FROM
          000      /B TO A, OUTPUT IT TO THE UART.
          RET      /RETURN WITH THE CHARACTER STILL IN A.
```

TTYI Without Echo

```
TTYI,     IN       /INPUT THE UART'S STATUS.
          001
          ANI      /SAVE ONLY THE RECEIVER'S STATUS.
          001
          JZ       /IF A=001, A KEY IS PRESSED.
          TTYI     /IF A=000, NQ KEY IS PRESSED.
          0        /IF NO KEY IS PRESSED, KEEP WAITING.
          IN       /A KEY IS PRESSED, SO INPUT THE
          000      /ASCII CHARACTER.
          RET      /AND RETURN WITH IT IN THE A REGISTER.
```

There are now three basic teletypewriter or crt I/O subroutines. The TTYIN subroutine is called when an ASCII character must be received by the 8080 and printed on the printer. Note the ANI instruction that is in the TTYIN subroutine. This instruction eliminates (masks) the parity bit, bit D_7, from the content of the A register after the ASCII character is input from the keyboard device. This means that if the TTYIN subroutine is used to input ASCII characters, it can be used with teletypewriters or crt's that transmit ASCII characters that have odd, even, or no parity. This gives the software tremendous flexibility and adaptability.

The TTYOUT subroutine is called when characters have to be printed on a crt or printed and punched on a teletypewriter. The character to be printed (punched) must be in the A register when this subroutine is called. When the 8080 returns from either the TTYIN or TTYOUT subroutines, the ASCII character will be contained in both the A and B registers.

The TTYI subroutine is called when an ASCII character must be received by the 8080, but the character must not be printed (echoed). The parity bit is not changed by this subroutine, and the character is only contained in the A register when the 8080 returns from the subroutine.

Table 3-5. The ASCII Character Set

Character	Octal	Hex	Character	Octal	Hex
BELL	207	87	?	277	BF
LF	212	8A	@	300	C0
CR	215	8D	A	301	C1
SPACE	240	A0	B	302	C2
!	241	A1	C	303	C3
"	242	A2	D	304	C4
#	243	A3	E	305	C5
$	244	A4	F	306	C6
%	245	A5	G	307	C7
&	246	A6	H	310	C8
'	247	A7	I	311	C9
(	250	A8	J	312	CA
)	251	A9	K	313	CB
*	252	AA	L	314	CC
+	253	AB	M	315	CD
,	254	AC	N	316	CE
−	255	AD	O	317	CF
.	256	AE	P	320	D0
/	257	AF	Q	321	D1
0	260	B0	R	322	D2
1	261	B1	S	323	D3
2	262	B2	T	324	D4
3	263	B3	U	325	D5
4	264	B4	V	326	D6
5	265	B5	W	327	D7
6	266	B6	X	330	D8
7	267	B7	Y	331	D9
8	270	B8	Z	332	DA
9	271	B9	[	333	DB
:	272	BA	\	334	DC
;	273	BB	]	335	DD
<	274	BC	↑	336	DE
=	275	BD	←	337	DF
>	276	BE			

TELETYPEWRITER AND TERMINAL PROGRAMS

Teletypewriter Test Program

One of the simplest and most useful programs that can be written is a teletypewriter and crt test program. In this program, all of the valid printing characters are output to the printer or crt screen. To do this requires some knowledge of the ASCII characters that the teletypewriter or crt can receive, print, or display. The ASCII character set is summarized in Table 3-5. Note that most of the printing characters are within the range of 240 (SPACE) and 337 (←). The only exceptions that we will consider are carriage return (CR, octal 215, hex 8D); line feed (LF, octal 212, hex 8A); and BELL (octal 207, hex 87). Unfortunately, there is no easy method that can be used to print the characters CR, LF, and BELL. Therefore, the program listed in Example 3-21 will be used.

Example 3-21: How to Print a CR, LF, and BELL

```
START,  LXISP    /LOAD THE STACK POINTER WITH AN
        STACK    /ADDRESS FOR R/W MEMORY.
        0
TEST,   MVIA     /LOAD A WITH THE ASCII CHARACTER,
        215      /CARRIAGE RETURN.
        CALL     /THEN PRINT THE CARRIAGE RETURN
        TTYOUT   /ON THE TELETYPEWRITER OR CRT.
        0
        MVIA     /LOAD A WITH THE ASCII CHARACTER,
        212      /LINE FEED.
        CALL     /THEN PRINT THE LINE FEED ON THE
        TTYOUT   /TELETYPEWRITER OR CRT.
        0
        MVIA     /LOAD A WITH THE ASCII CHARACTER,
        207      /BELL.
        CALL     /THEN RING THE BELL IN THE
        TTYOUT   /TELETYPEWRITER OR CRT.
        0
          •
          •
          •
```

This section of the program uses the TTYOUT subroutine that was developed earlier in this chapter. After loading the SP, the character to be printed is moved to the A register, and then the TTYOUT subroutine is called. This must be done three times for the three characters, CR, LF, and BELL.

How does the 8080 cause all of the remaining characters to be printed? Certainly, you do not want to write a program that contains 64 or 67 MVIA instructions all followed by three-byte call instructions that call TTYOUT. Fortunately, all of the ASCII characters with values between 240 (A0) and 337 (DF) are printing

Example 3-22: A Teletypewriter or CRT Test Program

```
START,    LXISP      /LOAD THE STACK POINTER WITH AN
          STACK      /ADDRESS FOR R/W MEMORY.
          0
TEST,     MVIA       /LOAD A WITH THE ASCII CHARACTER,
          215        /CARRIAGE RETURN.
          CALL       /THEN PRINT THE CARRIAGE RETURN
          TYOUT      /ON THE TELETYPEWRITER OR CRT.
          0
          MVIA       /LOAD A WITH THE ASCII CHARACTER,
          212        /LINE FEED.
          CALL       /THEN PRINT THE LINE FEED ON THE
          TTYOUT     /TELETYPEWRITER OR CRT.
          0
          MVIA       /LOAD A WITH THE ASCII CHARACTER,
          207        /BELL.
          CALL       /THEN RING THE BELL IN THE
          TTYOUT     /TELETYPEWRITER OR CRT.
          0
          MVIA       /THE FIRST CHARACTER TO BE PRINTED
          240        /IS A SPACE. (OCTAL 240=HEX A0).
NXTCHR,   CPI
          340        /HAS THE LAST CHARACTER BEEN PRINTED ?
          JZ
          TEST       /YES, START THE PROCESS OVER AGAIN.
          0
          CALL       /NO, PRINT THE CHARACTER.
          TTYOUT
          0
          INRA       /INCREMENT THE VALUE OF THE
          JMP        /CHARACTER TO BE PRINTED
          NXTCHR     /AND THEN PRINT IT.
          0
```

characters. Therefore, the program listed in Example 3-22 can be used to test a teletypewriter or a crt by generating all of the printing characters.

After printing the CR, LF, and BELL characters, the A register is loaded with the value 240 (A0). This is the code for a space. The content of the A register is then compared to the immediate data byte 340 (E0). If the content of the A register is 340 (E0), the 8080 will execute the JZ instruction. This will cause program control to be transferred to the beginning of the program, to TEST. If the content of the A register is not equal to 340 (E0), the content of the A register is printed by means of the call to the TTYOUT subroutine. The content of the A register is then incremented by means of the INRA instruction. The A register initially contained a 240 (A0), so it is first incremented to 241 (A1). When will the content of the A register not be incremented? When the value contained in the A register is 340 (E0). What does the teletypewriter printer output look like? The printout should look like the following:

```
!"#$%&'()*+,−./0123456789:;<=>?@ABCDEFGHIJKLMNOPQRSTUVWXYZ[\]↑ ←
!"#$%&'()*+,−./0123456789:;<=>?@ABCDEFGHIJKLMNOPQRSTUVWXYZ[\]↑ ←
!"#$%&'()*+,−./0123456789:;<=>?@ABCDEFGHIJKLMNOPQRSTUVWXYZ[\]↑ ←
```

One of the nice features of this program is that it can be used to tune-up or adjust the clock that drives the UART interface that is used to communicate between the teletypewriter or the crt and the 8080 microcomputer. You would simply increase or decrease the frequency of the clock to the point at which mistakes begin to appear on the printer. Once the lowest and highest frequencies have been determined, the clock can be adjusted to the center frequency. Although not all 8080 microcomputers use UARTs to communicate with serial devices like a teletypewriter or crt, many microcomputer systems do.

Paper-Tape Reader/Punch Test Programs

How do you know when the paper-tape punch on your teletype-writer is not operating properly? You will probably find out while the microcomputer is punching a 300-foot paper tape. To help you test the paper-tape punch, you could use the program listed in Example 3-23. This program assumes that the paper-tape punch is mechanically linked to the teletypewriter's printer mechanism. In most cases this is true. This means that as far as you are concerned, the printer and paper-tape punch are the *same* device. Therefore, the TTYOUT subroutine can also be used to punch the content of the A register on paper tape. If the punch to be tested is not mechanically linked to the teletypewriter printer, you will have to provide the subroutine that punches the content of the A register on the paper tape. The content of the A register must remain unaltered when the 8080 returns from this subroutine.

When the program in Example 3-23 is started, 100_{10} blank characters (octal 000, hex 00) will be punched on the paper tape first. This occurs because the 8080 calls the BLANK subroutine after loading the SP with an R/W memory address. This subroutine uses the C register as the BLANK character counter, which is initially set to 100_{10} (octal 144, hex 64). The A register is then cleared to 000 (00) and the content of the A register is then punched on paper tape until the content of the C register is decremented to zero. When this occurs, the JNZ to BLANK1 will not be executed, so the 8080 will return control to the main program. Note the use of the XRAA instruction (exclusive-OR the A register with the A register) in this subroutine. This instruction clears the A register to 000 (00).

When control is returned to the main program, the content of the A register is punched on the paper tape when the TTYOUT subroutine is called. The content of the A register is still zero. However, when the 8080 returns from the TTYOUT subroutine, the

Example 3-23: A Paper-Tape-Punch Test Program

```
PTEST,  LXISP    /LOAD THE STACK POINTER WITH AN
        STACK    /ADDRESS FOR R/W MEMORY.
        0
        CALL     /PUNCH 100 BLANK (000) CHARACTERS.
        BLANK
        0
PUNCH,  CALL     /PUNCH THE CONTENT OF THE A REGISTER
        TTYOUT   /(THE PUNCH IS MECHANICALLY LINKED
        0        /TO THE PRINTER UNIT).
        INRA     /INCREMENT THE PUNCH CHARACTER.
        JNZ      /IS IT 000 ? NO, PUNCH ANOTHER CHARACTER.
        PUNCH
        0
        CALL     /YES, IT IS 000, THE NUMBERS 001-377 HAVE
        BLANK    /BEEN PUNCHED, SO PUNCH 100 BLANKS AGAIN.
        0
        HLT      /THEN HALT.

BLANK,  MVIC     /LOAD C WITH DECIMAL 100
        144      /(OCTAL 144 = HEX 64).
        XRAA     /SET A TO ZERO BY EXECUTING THIS INSTRUCTION.
BLANK1, CALL     /PUNCH THE CONTENT OF A ON THE TELE-
        TTYOUT   /TYPEWRITER'S PUNCH.
        0
        DCRC     /DECREMENT THE CHARACTER COUNT
        JNZ      /IF C IS NONZERO, THEN PUNCH
        BLANK1   /ANOTHER BLANK CHARACTER.
        0
        RET      /RETURN WHEN 100 BLANK CHARACTERS
                 /HAVE BEEN PUNCHED ON THE PAPER TAPE.
```

INRA instruction increments the content of the A register by 1, to 001 (01). The zero flag is then tested to see if the content of the A register has been incremented from 377 to 000 (FF to 00). If the content of the A register is nonzero, the JNZ to PUNCH is executed, so that the incremented content of the A register is punched on the paper tape.

When the content of the A register is finally incremented from 377 to 000 (FF to 00), the JNZ to PUNCH will not be executed. Instead, the BLANK subroutine is called again. This will cause an additional 100_{10} blank characters (000 or 00) to be punched on the paper tape. When this task is complete, the 8080 microcomputer will halt.

If the teletypewriter being tested punches 10 characters per inch, a paper tape will be obtained that has 10 inches of blank characters at the beginning, all of the characters from 000 through 377 (00 through FF) punched on 25.6 inches of tape, followed by another 10 inches of blank characters. From this paper tape, it would be very difficult for most programmers to find any but the simplest

Example 3-24: A Paper-Tape-Reader Test Program

```
READER,  LXISP    /LOAD THE STACK POINTER WITH AN
         STACK    /ADDRESS FOR R/W MEMORY.
         0
FRONT,   CALL     /READ A CHARACTER (THE PAPER-TAPE
         TTYI     /READER AND THE KEYBOARD ARE THE SAME
         0        /I-O DEVICE).
         CPI      /WAS A BLANK READ ?
         000
         JZ       /YES, IGNORE ALL BLANKS AT THE BEGINNING
         FRONT    /OF THE PAPER TAPE.
         0
         MVIB     /IT WAS NOT A 000, SET B TO THE FIRST NON-
         001      /ZERO VALUE THAT SHOULD BE READ.
NEXT,    CMPB     /IS THE CHARACTER READ EQUAL TO B ?
         JNZ      /NO, THEN SOMETHING IS WRONG.
         ERROR
         0
         CALL     /GET THE NEXT CHARACTER FROM
         TTYI     /THE PAPER TAPE.
         0
         INRB     /AND INCREMENT THE COMPARISON CHARACTER.
         JNZ      /HAS B BEEN INCREMENTED FROM 377
         NEXT     /TO 000 YET? NO. TEST THE
         0        /NEXT CHARACTER.
         HLT      /YES, WE HAVE TESTED ALL THE NONZERO
                  /CHARACTERS ON THE TAPE, SO HALT.


ERROR,   LXIH     /LOAD REGISTER PAIR H WITH AN AD-
         TEMPO    /DRESS FOR R/W MEMORY SO THAT
         0        /TWO CHARACTERS CAN BE SAVED.
         MOVMB    /SAVE THE COMPARISON CHARACTER.
         INXH     /INCREMENT THE MEMORY ADDRESS.
         MOVMA    /THEN SAVE THE CHARACTER READ.
         MVIA     /NOW PRINT AN * ON THE TELETYPEWRITER
         252      /TO SHOW THAN AN ERROR HAS OCCURRED.
         CALL
         TTYOUT   /YOU SHOULD LOOK AT THE CONTENT OF R/W
         0        /MEMORY TO SEE WHAT ERROR OCCURRED.
         HLT
```

punching errors. To test the paper tape for any missing or incorrect characters, the paper-tape-reader program listed in Example 3-24 could be used. We will assume that the paper-tape reader is operating correctly.

Initially, the SP is loaded with a 16-bit R/W memory address when the LXISP instruction in Example 3-24 is executed. Many teletypewriters function as if the keyboard and paper-tape reader are a single I/O device. That is, when a data word is input from the UART by the microcomputer, it cannot determine whether the data word is from the keyboard or from the paper-tape reader. For this reason, the TTYI subroutine has been used to input one eight-bit character from the paper-tape reader. After reading a character, the 8080 compares it to the immediate data byte, 000 (00). If the data word read from the paper tape is a zero, the zero flag will be true after the CPI instruction is executed. Therefore, the JZ to FRONT is executed. This section of the program has the function of reading and ignoring all of the blank characters at the beginning of the paper tape. When the first nonzero character is read from the paper tape, this section of the program will no longer be executed.

The first nonzero character should be 001 (01). For this reason, the B register is loaded with 001 (01) when the MVIB instruction is executed. The content of the B register is then compared to the content of the A register, which contains the character just read from the paper tape. The first nonzero character read from the paper tape should be 001. If the content of the A and B registers is not equal, the JNZ to ERROR is executed.

At ERROR, register pair H is loaded with a 16-bit address for R/W memory. The content of both the B and A registers is then saved in consecutive memory locations. The A register is then loaded with the ASCII value for an asterisk ($*$), and the character is printed on the teletypewriter by means of the TTYOUT subroutine. This is performed so that you will know that an error has occurred. If an error does occur, you will find the character that the 8080 was expecting from the paper tape stored in the memory location specified in the LXIH instruction, and the character that was actually read from the paper tape stored in the next consecutive memory location at a higher address.

If the first nonzero character is read correctly, the 8080 will read the next paper-tape character, increment the content of the B register, and repeat the comparison process. Only when the content of the B register is incremented from 377 to 000 (FF to 00) will the JNZ to NEXT not be executed. When this occurs, the 8080 will halt. If a correct paper tape was punched by the punch and read correctly by the reader, the 8080 microcomputer will halt after the last nonzero value, 377 (FF), is read from the paper tape. Of course, problems will occur if both the paper-tape reader and punch are not operating properly. One of these devices must be working properly for either or both of these programs to work. More elaborate test programs are possible, but our purpose here has been to introduce you to the basics of teletyptewriter-like I/O.

AN ELECTRONIC LOCK

This program uses a nine-digit number as a key to an electronic lock. Any nine-digit number can be used, but a Social Security Account Number (SSAN) is particularly easy to remember. Just about any method or device can be used to enter the key code numbers into the microcomputer for processing by the lock program. These devices include a 10-key keyboard, thumbwheel switches, a magnetic-badge reader, or a teletypewriter. To keep the program as simple as possible, a teletypewriter will be used to enter the key code numbers.

The numbers for the key will be stored in consecutive memory locations. As the key code is entered on the teletypewriter, the numbers stored in memory will be compared to the numbers entered on the teletypewriter. If the numbers (codes) do not match, an alarm should "sound" because someone is "picking" the lock. If the nine-digit key code is entered correctly, then a door somewhere should open. Two light-emitting diodes (LEDs) will be used to indicate the alarm condition and the open-door condition. The program listed in Example 3-25 performs these tasks.

When the ELOCK program is executed, the stack pointer is first loaded with an address for R/W memory, since the stack will be needed for proper subroutine use. The symbolic address, STACK, has been assigned to this memory location. The B register is then loaded with the digit count, which is the number of digits contained in the key code. In your particular application, this number could be easily increased or decreased, but we have chosen to load the B register with 011 (hex 09, decimal 9). This is the number of digits that are contained in an SSAN. Register pair H is then loaded with the memory address of the location in which the first digit of the key code is stored. This memory location has been assigned the symbolic address, KEY, and the remaining numbers in the key code are stored in consecutive memory locations with higher addresses, starting at KEY. *The key code numbers are stored as their ASCII values.*

By examining these memory locations, can you determine the key code for the lock? These memory locations contain the key code as follows:

$$0,1,2,3,4,5,6,7,8$$

After register pair H is loaded with the address for the first number in the key code, the TTYI subroutine is called. The 8080 will only return from the TTYI subroutine when a key on the teletypewriter keyboard has been pressed. When the 8080 does return, bit D_7 of the ASCII value in the A register is set to zero. This eliminates the parity bit from the ASCII value.

The A register, which now contains the keyboard character, is compared to the content of memory addressed by register pair H. Register pair H addresses the memory location that contains the

Example 3-25: An Electronic Lock Program

```
ELOCK,    LXISP    /SET THE STACK POINTER.
          STACK
          0
          MVIB     /B IS THE DIGIT COUNTER (DECIMAL 9).
          011
          LXIH     /H&L POINT TO THE "KEY"
          KEY      /STORED IN MEMORY.
          0
NEXTIN,   CALL     /GET A CHARACTER FROM THE TELETYPEWRITER.
          TTYI
          0
          ANI      /REMOVE THE PARITY BIT FROM THE
          177      /ASCII CHARACTER.
          CMPM     /COMPARE IT TO THE CONTENT OF MEMORY.
          JNZ      /NOT A MATCH, SOMEONE IS PICKING THE LOCK !
          PICK
          0
          INHX     /THE FIRST DIGIT MATCHED, H&L NOW POINT
          DCRB     /TO THE NEXT DIGIT. DECREMENT THE DIGIT COUNTER.
          JNZ      /ALL NINE DIGITS INPUT YET ?
          NEXTIN   /NO, GET ANOTHER KEY CODE.
          0
OPENIT,   MVIA     /ALL NINE DIGITS WERE INPUT AND THEY
          001      /MATCHED THE KEY CODES STORED
          OUT      /IN MEMORY, SO OPEN THE DOOR.
          156
          HLT

PICK,     MVIA     /SOMEONE IS PICKING THE LOCK, RING THE
          001      /ALARM.
          OUT
          157
          HLT

TTYI,     IN       /INPUT THE UART'S STATUS.
          001
          ANI      /SAVE ONLY THE RECEIVER'S STATUS.
          001
          JZ       /IF A=001, A KEY IS PRESSED.
          TTYI     /IF A=000, NO KEY IS PRESSED.
          0        /IF NO KEY IS PRESSED, KEEP WAITING.
          IN       /A KEY IS PRESSED, SO INPUT THE
          000      /CHARACTER'S ASCII VALUE.
          RET      /AND RETURN WITH IT IN THE A REGISTER.

KEY,      060      /THE NINE-DIGIT KEY IS STORED
          061      /HERE, IN THE PROPER SEQUENCE.
          062
          063
          064
          065
          066
          067
          070
```

first digit of the key code. Therefore, the first key code that is input is compared to the value, 060 (30). If the values are not the same, the JNZ to PICK is executed. At PICK, the LSB of the A register is set to a logic 1, and then output to output port 157 (6F). This logic level could be used to lock a door, turn on an LED, or sound an alarm. The reason that this occurs is because a key was pressed that did not match the sequential key code stored in memory.

If there is a match between the key code in the A register and the content of the corresponding memory location, the JNZ to PICK is not executed. Instead, the memory address contained in register pair H is incremented by 1 (INXH), and the digit count is decremented (DCRB). If the content of B is decremented to a nonzero value, the preceding sequence of instructions is repeated. When the content of B is finally decremented to zero, the JNZ to NEXTIN is not executed. When this occurs, the entire nine-digit key has been entered correctly. Therefore, the LSB of the A register is set to a logic 1, and then output to output port 156 (6E). This logic level could be used to open a door, shut off an alarm system, or light an LED. The microcomputer then comes to a halt.

One of the problems with this program is that there is no way to correct an error, should one occur, when the key code is entered into the microcomputer. Even if you know the proper key code, you might make an error keying it in on the teletypewriter. Therefore, it would be useful if there were an abort key that permitted you to restart the program. At the same time, it would be advantageous for the microcomputer to give you three or four tries at keying in the combination correctly. Even though this increases the possibility of having the lock picked, it is still a very unlikely (1 out of 2.5×10^7) possibility. These two features have been incorporated in the program listed in Example 3-26.

As you can observe, the modifications are very simple. The A key on the teletypewriter keyboard has been assigned to the abort operation by using the number 101 (41) as an immediate data byte for a CPI instruction. This is the value for an ASCII "A." When this program is executed, the SP is loaded with an R/W memory address, and then the count for the number of times that a key code can be entered (four in this example) is loaded into the C register. The PICK section of the program has also been modified, so that the attempt count in the C register must be decremented to zero before the alarm is sounded.

Note that the abort key (A) can be used as often as required. However, the program still only gives you four attempts to enter the key code correctly. When the A key is pressed, the 8080 jumps back to RSTRT, where the digit count is loaded into register B. This means that you can enter another key code on the keyboard.

Example 3-26. An Improved Electronic Lock Program

```
ELOCK,  LXISP    /SET THE STACK POINTER.
        STACK
        0
        MVIC     /NUMBER OF TRIES BEFORE SOUNDING
        004      /THE ALARM.
RSTRT,  MVIB     /B IS THE DIGIT COUNTER (DECIMAL 9).
        011
        LXIH     /H&L POINT TO THE "KEY"
        KEY      /STORED IN MEMORY.
        0
NEXTIN, CALL     /GET A CHARACTER FROM THE
        TTYI     /TELETYPEWRITER.
        0
        ANI      /REMOVE THE PARITY BIT.
        177
        CPI
        101      /IS THE ABORT KEY PRESSED?
        JZ       /YES, RESTART THE PROGRAM.
        RSTRT
        0
        CMPM     /COMPARE IT TO THE CONTENT OF MEMORY.
        JNZ      /NOT A MATCH, SOMEONE MADE AN ERROR
        PICK     /SO SEE HOW MANY ERRORS HAVE BEEN MADE.
        0
        INXH     /THE FIRST DIGIT MATCHED, H&L NOW POINT
        DCRB     /TO THE NEXT DIGIT. DECREMENT THE DIGIT COUNTER.
        JNZ      /ALL NINE DIGITS INPUT YET ?
        NEXTIN   /NO, GET ANOTHER KEY CODE.
        0
OPENIT, MVIA     /ALL NINE DIGITS WERE INPUT AND THEY
        001      /MATCHED THE "KEY" TABLE, OPEN THE DOOR.
        OUT
        156
        HLT

PICK,   DCRC     /FOUR TRIES YET ?
        JNZ      /NO, TRY AGAIN.
        RSTRT
        0
        MVIA     /FOUR TRIES AND STILL WRONG. RING THE
        001      /ALARM.
        OUT
        157
        HLT

TTYI,   IN       /INPUT THE UART'S STATUS.
        001
        ANI      /SAVE ONLY THE RECEIVER'S STATUS.
        001
        JZ       /IF A=001, A KEY IS PRESSED.
        TTYI     /IF A=000, NO KEY IS PRESSED.
        0        /IF NO KEY IS PRESSED, KEEP WAITING.
        IN       /A KEY IS PRESSED, SO INPUT THE
```

```
         000      /CHARACTER'S ASCII CODE.
         RET      /AND RETURN WITH IT IN THE A REGISTER.

KEY,     060
         061      /THIS IS THE NINE-DIGIT KEY,
         062      /STORED IN SEQUENTIAL MEMORY
         063      /LOCATIONS.
         064
         065
         066
         067
         070
```

However, the abort key is only used if you are entering the proper key code, and then forget which numbers you have already entered. If you attempt to enter the code, 123456789, the microcomputer will not be able to match any of these numbers to the first digit of the key code, 0. Therefore, all four "attempts" will be used, even though only a single nine-digit number was entered. This is because the 8080 compares the numbers as they are entered. When the 1 is entered, it is compared to 0, and since they are not equal, the 8080 jumps to the PICK section of the program. At PICK, the attempt counter is decremented. Since C would now contain 003 (03), the 8080 jumps back to RSTRT. At RSTRT, the digit count in B is reinitialized, and then the TTYI subroutine is called a second time. This time, you would incorrectly enter the 2 of the key code, 123456789, which would also be compared to 0, the first number in the key code stored in memory.

The next time through the loop, the 8080 would compare the 3 and 4 entered to the first digit in the key code, 0. Since no matches would occur, the attempt counter would be decremented to zero and the alarm would be sounded.

Do you know why the TTYI subroutine was used to input the ASCII characters from the teletypewriter, rather than the TTYIN subroutine? What are the differences between these two subroutines? The TTYIN subroutine not only lets you enter characters on the teletypewriter keyboard, but the characters are also printed. The TTYI subroutine simply lets you enter the characters on the keyboard. The characters are not printed. Therefore, if someone is looking over your shoulder as you enter the key code, it would be difficult for them to remember it. If the code were printed, it would be far easier for someone else to learn the key code.

SUMMARY

In summary, the following instructions have been discussed in this and the previous chapters:

1. The 63 MOV instructions.
2. The eight MVI instructions.
3. The eight increment (INR) and eight decrement (DCR) instructions.
4. The 64 mathematical and logical instructions: ADD, ADC, SUB, SBB, ANA, XRA, ORA, and CMP.
5. The eight immediate mathematical and logical instructions: ADI, ACI, SUI, SBI, ANI, XRI, ORI, and CPI.
6. The two I/O instructions: IN and OUT.
7. The two instructions: HLT and NOP.
8. The four register-pair load instructions: LXIB, LXID, LXIH, and LXISP.
9. The four register-pair increment (INX) and four decrement (DCX) instructions.
10. The nine jump instructions, one unconditional and eight conditional.
11. The nine call instructions, one unconditional and eight conditional.
12. The nine return instructions, one unconditional and eight conditional.

If you have followed all of the software examples in this book so far, you should be very comfortable with these 202 instructions. Even with these basic instructions, very powerful programs can be written. In the next chapter, we will discuss the more advanced 8080 instructions.

REFERENCES

1. Larsen, D. G., and Rony, P. R. *Interfacing and Scientific Data Communications Experiments.* Howard W. Sams & Co., Inc., Indianapolis, IN, 1978.
2. Field, P. E., Rony, P. R., Larsen, D. G., and Titus, J. A. "Microcomputer Interfacing: A Software UART." *Computer Design,* October 1976, p. 118.
3. Lancaster, D. "Serial Interface." *Byte,* September 1975, p. 23.
4. Titus, J. A. "The UART and How It Works." *Ham Radio,* February 1976, p. 58.

4

The Advanced
8080/8085 Instructions

We have arbitrarily divided the 8080's instruction set into a basic and an advanced section. The Basic Instructions chapter (Chapter 2) covered most of the instructions that the first eight-bit microprocessor, the Intel 8008, could execute, plus some instructions for the 8080 alone. Ths basic instructions are also the ones most frequently used. From 60% to 80% of a program will be composed of these instructions; the rest of the program will contain the instructions described in this chapter.

REGISTER PAIR OPERATIONS

To move data to and from memory locations, register pair H has been used to provide the memory address. You have also seen that, as in register pair H (registers H and L), registers B and C and registers D and E can also be used as register pairs. The instructions that can be used with these register pairs include the INX, DCX, and LXI instructions discussed previously. The 8080 can also use register pairs B and D to address memory, but the data movement instructions that use these register pairs are not as powerful as the data movement instructions associated with register pair H.

Using register pair H, the 8080 can add, subtract, AND, OR, exclusive-OR, or compare the content of a memory location to the content of the A register, as well as increment or decrement the value stored in the memory location. The 8080 can also use the content of register pair H as the address for the source or destination of data in data movement (MOV) instructions. *Using the content of register pairs*

B and D as a memory address, the 8080 can only move data between the A register and a memory location. These data movement instructions are listed in Table 4-1.

Table 4-1. The Data Movement Instructions for Register Pairs B and D

LDAXB	Load the A register with the content of the memory location addressed by register pair B.
LDAXD	Load the A register with the content of the memory location addressed by register pair D.
STAXB	Store the content of the A register in the memory location addressed by register pair B.
STAXD	Store ·the content of the A register in the memory location addressed by register pair D.

Although the instructions LDAXH and STAXH do not exist as such, are there any instructions that perform the same function? Yes, the MOVAM and MOVMA instructions perform the same function. You have now seen the following instructions that use register pairs B and D:

LXIB	LXID
INXB	INXD
DCXB	DCXD
STAXB	STAXD
LDAXB	LDAXD

One application of these instructions is in the movement of a block of data from one area of memory to another. To do this, you must have two addresses, the address for the source of data and the address for the destination of the data. You also must have some way of indicating when all of the data has been moved. This function is performed by a *byte counter*. A program that moves a block of data contained in consecutive memory locations to another section of memory is listed in Example 4-1.

Can you determine where the data is being moved from and to in Example 4-1? The first byte of data is moved from memory location 021 100 (1140) to 021 200 (1180). What will the addresses be for the last data byte that is moved? The last data byte will be moved from memory location 021 022 to 021 222 (1112 to 1192). Could this program be used to move 521 or 623 bytes of data? No, the maximum number of data bytes that this program can move is 256. Why? Because the C register is used to store the byte count. To move 100 or 200 data bytes, the equivalent binary number (01100100 for 100, 11001000 for 200) has to be loaded into the C register. However, to move 256 data bytes, the C register would have to be loaded with 000 (00). When the DCRC instruction is executed after the first byte of data is moved, C will be decremented from 000 (00) to 377 (FF). Since this is a nonzero result, the 8080 will jump back to TRNSFR. The 8080 will then continue to execute the TRNSFR loop until an additional 255 data bytes have been moved. At this point, the C register will be finally decremented to zero.

To remove the limitation of only being able to move 256 data bytes, you can add a few instructions to Example 4-1 and make it more general purpose, as in Example 4-2.

Example 4-1: Moving a Block of Data

```
MOVE,    LXIH    /STARTING ADDRESS FOR THE
         100     /SOURCE OF THE DATA.
         021
         LXID    /STARTING ADDRESS FOR THE
         200     /DESTINATION OF THE DATA.
         021
         MVIC    /NUMBER OF DATA BYTES TO
         023     /BE MOVED.
TRNSFR,  MOVAM   /GET A DATA BYTE USING H&L.
         STAXD   /STORE A DATA BYTE USING D&E.
         INXH    /INCREMENT THE SOURCE ADDRESS.
         INXD    /INCREMENT THE DESTINATION ADDRESS.
         DCRC    /DECREMENT THE BYTE COUNTER.
         JNZ     /MOVED ALL 19 (DECIMAL) DATA BYTES ?
         TRNSFR  /NO, EXECUTE THE JUMP.
         0
           •     /YES, CONTINUE WITH THE PROGRAM.
           •
           •
```

By using register pair B as the byte counter, a maximum of 65,536 data bytes can be moved from one section of memory to another by executing this program (Example 4-2). To move this number of data bytes, register pair B would have to be loaded with 000 000 (0000) so that the first time through the loop, register pair B is decremented from 000 000 to 377 377 (0000 to FFFF). Because register pair B is used as the byte counter, the DCXB instruction is used to decrement the byte count. This instruction does not affect any of the flags, so the MOVAB and ORAC instructions have to be executed to determine when the content of register pair B is 000 000. When register pair B does contain 000 000 (0000), the 8080 will have moved all the required data bytes. In Example 4-2, the number of data bytes is 012 023 (0A13), or decimal 2579. Therefore, only when 2579 data bytes have been moved will the 8080 not execute the TRNSFR loop.

Suppose that you had an *array* of data stored in memory locations 005 000 through 005 200 (0500 through 0580), and you want to move this data to the memory locations 005 100 through 005 300 (0540 through 05C0). Could you use the programs listed in Examples 4-1 or 4-2 to move this array of data? The answer is an emphatic NO! The problem is that you have overlapping data arrays. You want to move the content of 005 000 (0500) to 005 100 (0540), but there is data there that has yet to be moved. In other

Example 4-2: An Improved Data-Block Movement Program

MOVE,	LXIH	/STARTING ADDRESS FOR THE
	100	/SOURCE OF THE DATA.
	021	
	LXID	/STARTING ADDRESS FOR THE
	100	/DESTINATION OF THE DATA.
	051	
	LXIB	/NUMBER OF BYTES TO
	023	/BE TRANSFERRED.
	012	
TRNSFR,	MOVAM	/GET A DATA BYTE USING H&L.
	STAXD	/STORE A DATA BYTE USING D&E
	INXH	/INCREMENT THE SOURCE ADDRESS.
	INXD	/INCREMENT THE DESTINATION ADDRESS.
	DCXB	/DECREMENT THE BYTE COUNTER.
	MOVAB	/IS IT 0 YET ?
	ORAC	
	JNZ	
	TRNSFR	/NO, EXECUTE THE JUMP.
	0	
	•	/YES, CONTINUE WITH THE PROGRAM.
	•	
	•	

words, moving data from 005 000 (0500) to 005 100 (0540) puts the moved data back into the original data array in a memory location the content of which has not yet been moved. You probably would not be able to easily save the value in 005 100 (0540) before writing the moved value into that memory location. This problem is shown in Fig. 4-1.

Can you think of a simple solution to solve this problem? The easiest method of moving the data would be to first move the data from the highest address of the old array (005 200, 0580) to 005 300 (05C0), the highest address in the new array. After this, the 8080 would continue to build the array downward. This avoids writing data from the old array back into the old array. The program listed in Example 4-3 performs this task. The first data byte is moved from 005 200 to 005 300 (0580 to 05C0), and the last data byte is moved from 005 000 to 005 100 (0500 to 0540).

How would you move an array of data values from a higher address to a lower address when the arrays overlap? Suppose that you had an array of data stored in memory from addresses 030 100

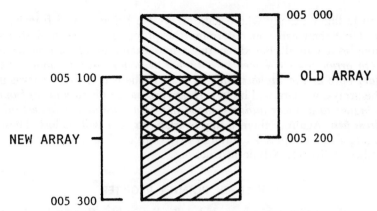

Fig. 4-1. The problem of moving overlapping data arrays.

through 030 250 (1840 through 18A8). If the array had to be moved "down" to addresses 030 000 through 030 150 (1800 through 1868),

Example 4-3: Moving an Overlapping Array From the Top Down

```
MOVE,   LXIH    /STARTING ADDRESS FOR THE
        200     /SOURCE OF THE DATA.
        005
        LXID    /STARTING ADDRESS FOR THE
        300     /DESTINATION OF THE DATA.
        005
        LXIB    /NUMBER OF BYTES TO
        200     /BE TRANSFERRED.
        000
DOWN,   MOVAM   /GET A DATA BYTE FROM THE OLD ARRAY.
        STAXD   /STORE THE DATA BYTE IN THE NEW ARRAY.
        DCXH    /DECREMENT THE SOURCE ADDRESS.
        DCXD    /DECREMENT THE DESTINATION ADDRESS.
        DCXB    /DECREMENT THE BYTE COUNTER.
        MOVAB   /IS IT 0 YET ?
        ORAC
        JNZ
        DOWN    /NO, EXECUTE THE JUMP.
        0
         •      /YES, CONTINUE WITH THE PROGRAM.
         •
         •
```

what would the addresses be for the first and last data bytes that are moved? This is the opposite of the problem that we just had. If the first data byte is moved from address 030 100 to 030 000 (1840 to 1800), none of the data words in the array will be lost. If you move the content of memory location 030 250 to 030 150 (18A8 to 1868), data will be lost since you will be transferring data "back" into the old array. As you can see, it is extremely important for you to know exactly where data arrays are being moved from and to. Only then can you determine the proper sequence of instructions to be used. Based on these two examples, *if you move a data array from a lower to a higher memory address, move the data byte at the highest address first.* If there is overlap between the arrays, no data will be lost. *If you are moving a data array from a higher to a lower address, move the data byte at the lowest address first.* Again, if there is any overlap, no data will be lost. These examples (Examples 4-1 through 4-3) were used to demonstrate the utility of the STAX-type instructions.

THE STACK POINTER REGISTER

Another register that we only briefly discussed is the *stack pointer,* SP. This 16-bit register contains an address that points to a section of R/W memory where return addresses for subroutines are stored. To load the SP with a 16-bit address, the three-byte LXISP instruction (octal 061, hex 31) should be executed. The second and third bytes of this instruction contain the address for an R/W memory location. This instruction is similar in function to the other LXI-type instructions. You can also cause the SP to be incremented or decremented by executing either an INXSP instruction (octal 063, hex 33) or a DCXSP instruction (octal 073, hex 3B). As with the other register pair increment and decrement instructions, no flags are affected when either of these instructions (INXSP and DCXSP) is executed. The SP is a fairly specialized register, as are register pairs B and D. There are no LDAX- or STAX-type instructions associated with the SP. A summary of the register pair instructions that have been discussed so far includes the instructions listed in Table 4-2.

Table 4-2. A Register Pair Instruction Summary

Register Pair Instruction	B	D	H	SP
LXI	YES	YES	YES	YES
INX	YES	YES	YES	YES
DCX	YES	YES	YES	YES
LDAX	YES	YES	YES*	NO
STAX	YES	YES	YES*	NO

* Equivalent instructions exist; LDAXH = MOVAM, STAXH = MOVMA.

With regard to the SP and the SP instructions, we have not been concerned with the method by which return addresses are stored on the stack. We only know that when a call (conditional or unconditional) is executed, a return address is stored in a section of R/W memory that has been allocated by the programmer as the stack area. This area is "allocated" when an LXISP instruction is executed. When a return-type instruction is executed, the return address is popped off of the stack and the 8080 begins to execute the remainder of the program, continuing right after the three-byte CALL instruction.

THE DAD INSTRUCTIONS

The DAD (Double register ADd) instructions cause the content of the specified register pair, B, D, H, or the SP, to be added to the content of register pair H. The result of the *16-bit addition* is automatically stored in register pair H. The op codes for these single-byte instructions are listed in Table 4-3.

Table 4-3. The DAD Instructions

Octal	Mnemonic	Hexadecimal
011	DADB	09
031	DADD	19
051	DADH	29
071	DADSP	39

In the Basic Instructions chapter, the single-precision (eight-bit) add and add-with-carry instructions were discussed. These instructions can be used to (1) add the content of any of the seven general-purpose registers, (2) add the content of memory addressed by register pair H, or (3) add an immediate data byte to the content of the A register. At times, however, you may want to operate on data words larger than eight bits (decimal 0 through 255). Double-precision numbers (16-bit) are often used because they can represent numbers between decimal 0 and 65,535. If you wanted to add two 16-bit numbers, you might use the program listed in Example 4-4.

Example 4-4: Adding Two 16-Bit Numbers

```
ADD16,  MOVAC   /GET ONE OF THE LSBYS.
        ADDL    /ADD THE OTHER LSBY.
        MOVLA   /SAVE THE RESULT'S LSBY IN L.
        MOVAB   /GET ONE OF THE MSBYS.
        ADCH    /ADC THE OTHER MSBY.
        MOVHA   /SAVE THE RESULT'S MSBY IN H.
```

This six-instruction program adds the content of register pair B to the content of register pair H. The 16-bit result is stored in register pair H. Note the use of the ADCH instruction in Example 4-4. This instruction adds the content of the H register, and the carry from the previous addition, to the content of the A register. The result of this addition is left in the A register. Although mathematical programs will be discussed in the next chapter, do you think that this program can be simplified? Yes, it can, by using a single instruction, the DADB instruction.

The DADB instruction, like the other DAD-type instructions, adds the carry generated by the addition of the two LSBYs to the MSBYs when they are added. If a carry is generated by the addition of the two MSBYs, the carry flag will be set to a logic 1. In the Basic Instructions chapter, two types of addition instructions were discussed, ADD and ADC. However, there is only one type of double-precision (16-bit) add instruction and it is the DAD-type instruction. This can be a hindrance if numbers larger than 16 bits have to be added. The reason is that after the first 16-bit addition is performed by a DAD-type instruction, there is no 16-bit add-with-carry instruction. Therefore, additional instructions have to be included in the program to add the carry generated by the first 16-bit addition to the group of 16 bits that are to be added.

The DADH instruction is particularly interesting. Suppose the following 16-bit word is contained in register pair H:

H	L
00000000	00000010

After executing a DADH instruction, what will the content of register pair H be? The content of register H will still be 00000000, but register L will contain 00000100. If another DADH instruction is executed, the content of register H will remain the same, but the content of register L will be 00001000. What has happened? Initially, the content of the L register was 002 (02). After executing the first DADH instruction, the L register contained 004 (04). After the third DADH instruction was executed, the L register contained 010 (08). Based on this information, you should conclude that the content of register pair H is doubled each time a DADH instruction is executed. Remember, when you add a number to itself, you are doubling the size of the number. You can also think of this as multiplication by 2. If register pair H is loaded with 000 001 (0001), what will happen to the content of register pair H when a number of DADH instructions are executed? Consider the results shown in Table 4-4.

Based on the results shown in Table 4-4, you can consider the DADH instruction not only as a doubling instruction, but also as a logical shift-left operation in which the MSB is lost or moved into the carry. It is not a rotate operation since data are not rotated back into the LSB of the 16-bit word. What will the content of

H	L
00000000	00000001
00000000	00000010
00000000	00000100
00000000	00001000
00000000	00010000
00000000	00100000
00000000	01000000
00000000	10000000
00000001	00000000
00000010	00000000
00000100	00000000
00001000	00000000

register pair H be after executing the program listed in Example 4-5? The loop in Example 4-5 is executed a total of 20_{10} times. After the 15th execution of the DADH instruction, the content of register pair H will be as follows:

H	L
10000000	00000000

The next time the DADH instruction is executed, both registers H and L will contain 000 (00). However, the carry will be a logic 1. Both registers will contain 000 (00) for the remainder of the program. Remember, there is an eight-bit carry from the L register into the H register.

Example 4-5: Executing 20 DADH Instructions

```
BY2,      LXIH      /LOAD REGISTER PAIR H WITH 000 001
          001       /(OCTAL 000 001 = HEX 0001 =
          000       /BINARY 00000000 00000001).
          MVIB      /LOAD B WITH THE COUNT, DECIMAL 20
          024       /(OCTAL 024 = HEX 14).
DOUBLE,   DADH      /ADD H&L TO H&L, SAVE THE RESULT IN H&L.
          DCRB      /DECREMENT THE COUNTER.
          JNZ       /IF B IS NONZERO, EXECUTE THE
          DOUBLE    /JNZ INSTRUCTION TO DOUBLE.
          0
          HLT       /WHEN B=000, THE 8080 EXECUTES THIS HALT.
```

The contents of the carry and registers H and L for the remainder of the loop are shown in Table 4-5.

The DADSP instruction is an interesting instruction because it gives you the ability to determine the address currently contained in the stack pointer register (SP). In most programs, this is not important because nothing unusual is being done with the stack.

Table 4-5. The Contents of the Carry and Registers
H and L for the Remainder of the Loop

Carry	H	L
0	00001000	00000000
0	00010000	00000000
0	00100000	00000000
0	01000000	00000000
0	10000000	00000000
1	00000000	00000000
0	00000000	00000000
0	00000000	00000000
0	00000000	00000000
0	00000000	00000000

However, debug, system monitor, and operating system programs often inform the user of the location to which the SP currently points, whether it has overrun a program or data storage area, or whether it has exceeded a certain size. To determine the current content of the SP, you could program the 8080 with the program listed in Example 4-6.

Example 4-6: Determining the Address Contained in the Stack Pointer Register (SP)

```
LXIH    /LOAD REGISTER PAIR H WITH OCTAL
000     /000 000 (HEX 0000).
000
DADSP   /ADD THE SP TO REGISTER PAIR H
  •     /AND SAVE THE RESULT IN REGISTER PAIR H.
  •
  •
```

After the sequence of instructions in Example 4-6 is executed, the content of register pair H will be the address that is currently contained in the SP. The content of the SP will not be altered by this instruction sequence. Like many of the other 8080 instructions, the content of a register is *unaltered* after an instruction has been executed that uses it as a source register. After the instructions in Example 4-6 are executed, the stack can still be used. However, the content of register H will be the current SP address. What will be the content of register pair H when the sequence of instructions listed in Example 4-7 is executed?

The content of register pair H will be 002 303 (02C3) after the instructions are executed. The SP is initially set to 002 300 (02C0). After the three INXSP instructions are executed, the address in the SP is 002 303 (02C3). The DCXSP instruction causes the content of the SP to be decremented by 1 to 002 302 (02C2). Register pair H is then loaded with 000 001 (0001), and the SP is then added

Example 4-7: Incrementing and Decrementing the SP

```
LXISP    /LOAD THE STACK POINTER REGISTER.
300
002
INXSP    /INCREMENT THE STACK POINTER.
INXSP    /INCREMENT THE STACK POINTER.
INXSP    /INCREMENT THE STACK POINTER.
DCXSP    /DECREMENT THE STACK POINTER.
LXIH     /LOAD L WITH 001, H WITH 000.
001
000
DADSP    /ADD THE SP TO REGISTER PAIR H
  •      /AND SAVE THE RESULT IN REGISTER PAIR H.
  •
  •
```

to the content of register pair H by means of the DADSP instruction. Therefore, 002 302 + 000 001 results in 002 303 (02C2 + 0001 = 02C3) being stored in register pair H.

THE DIRECT LOAD AND STORE INSTRUCTIONS

In a previous example, you saw that the content of the SP could be added to the content of register pair H. However, suppose that you already have a 16-bit number stored in register pair H. Can the SP address still be determined by executing the following instruction sequence?

```
LXIH     /LOAD REGISTER PAIR H WITH OCTAL
000      /000 000 (HEX 0000).
000
DADSP    /ADD THE SP TO REGISTER PAIR H
  •      /AND SAVE THE RESULT IN REGISTER PAIR H.
  •
  •
```

Yes it can, if the content of register pair H is saved prior to executing these instructions. You could save the content of register pair H in another register pair, but quite often another register pair is not available. Before adding the SP to register pair H, you could save the content of register pair H in R/W memory. How could you do this? Consider the instructions in Example 4-8.

Where in memory will the content of register pair H be saved? The content of the L register will be saved in memory location 060 015 (300D), and the content of the H register will be saved in memory location 060 016 (300E). Of course, this method has the disadvantage that it requires the use of register pair D to ultimately save register pair H in R/W memory. Even if you use STAX-type instructions, you would still have to use register pair B or D to hold the address 060 015 (300D) for the L register, and 060 016 (300E)

Example 4-8: Saving the Content of Register Pair H in R/W Memory

```
MOVEL   /SAVE THE LOW ADDRESS IN E.
MOVDH   /SAVE THE HIGH ADDRESS IN D.
LXIH    /LOAD REGISTER PAIR H WITH THE ADDRESS
015     /060 015 (HEX 300D).
060
MOVME   /SAVE THE LOW ADDRESS IN 060 015
INXH    /(HEX 300D). THEN INCREMENT THE ADDRESS.
MOVMD   /SAVE THE HIGH ADDRESS IN 060 016 (HEX 300E).
LXIH    /NOW LOAD REGISTER PAIR H WITH 000 000
000     /(HEX 0000).
000
DADSP   /ADD THE SP TO REGISTER PAIR H AND
  •     /SAVE THE RESULT IN REGISTER PAIR H.
  •
  •
```

for the H register. To solve this problem of saving the content of register pair H in memory, the SHLD instruction can be used.

The SHLD (Store *H* and *L* *D*irect) instruction is a three-byte instruction in which the second and third bytes contain a 16-bit memory address. This instruction enables us to save the content of register pair H in R/W memory without using the content of another register pair as an address. The use of the SHLD instruction in a program would appear as shown in Example 4-9.

Example 4-9: Using the SHLD Instruction

```
SHLD    /SAVE THE CONTENT OF REGISTER PAIR H
015     /IN THE R/W MEMORY LOCATIONS SPECIFIED
060     /BY THE SECOND AND THIRD BYTES.
```

Since a single eight-bit memory location has been specified in Example 4-9, how can the 8080 save the content of both the H and L registers? The content of the L register will be saved in memory location 060 015 (300D), and the content of the H register will be saved in the next consecutive memory location at a higher address, 060 016 (300E).

Should the address used in the SHLD instruction be for R/W or read-only memory? Most, if not all, of the time, the address used in the SHLD instruction should be for R/W memory. However, there will be some examples in which the address is not that of R/W memory, as in the use of an SHLD instruction to communicate with a memory-mapped I/O device. It is important to note that two consecutive memory locations are required to save the content of register pair H in R/W memory. Therefore, when a program is written using the SHLD instruction, two memory locations must be reserved for the storage of both registers.

The problem of saving register pair H and then adding the SP to register pair H is now greatly simplified (Example 4-10).

Example 4-10: Using the SHLD Instruction Before Executing a DADSP Instruction

```
SHLD    /SAVE THE LOW ADDRESS IN 060 015 (HEX 300D).
015     /AND SAVE THE HIGH ADDRESS IN 060 016 (HEX 300E).
060
LXIH    /LOAD REGISTER PAIR H WITH OCTAL 000 000
000     /(HEX 0000).
000
DADSP   /ADD THE SP TO REGISTER PAIR H AND
  •     /SAVE THE RESULT IN REGISTER PAIR H.
  •
  •
```

Note that no additional registers were used when saving register pair H in R/W memory.

Another instruction that is similar to the SHLD instruction is the LHLD (*Load H and L Direct*) instruction. This three-byte instruction loads register pair H with the content of two consecutive memory locations. The address of the first memory location is specified in the second and third bytes of the instruction. As in the SHLD instruction, the address specified is really the address of the memory location that will be used as the source of the data with which to load the L register. The address specified, plus one, will be used as the address of the memory location used to load the H register. To load register pair H with the content of two consecutive memory locations, the LHLD instruction can be executed (Example 4-11).

Example 4-11: Loading Register Pair H With an LHLD Instruction

```
LHLD    /LOAD REGISTER L WITH THE CONTENT OF
020     /MEMORY LOCATION 024 020 (HEX 1410)
024     /AND LOAD H WITH THE CONTENT OF MEMORY
  •     /LOCATION 024 021 (HEX 1411).
  •
  •
```

After executing this instruction, what will be contained in register pair H? The L register will be loaded with the content of memory location 024 020 (1410), and the H register will be loaded with the content of memory location 024 021 (1411). What will be the content of register pair H after the sequence of instructions in Example 4-12 is executed?

In Example 4-12, register pair H is loaded with the content of memory locations 060 015 and 060 016 (300D and 300E). Register pair H is then loaded with the 16-bit immediate data byte, 000 000 (0000), when the LXIH instruction is executed. The content of the

Example 4-12: Testing Your Knowledge of the LHLD Instruction

```
LHLD    /LOAD REGISTER PAIR H WITH THE CONTENT OF
015     /MEMORY LOCATIONS 060 015 AND 060 016,
060     /(HEX 300D AND 300E).
LXIH    /LOAD REGISTER PAIR H WITH THE OCTAL
000     /VALUES 000 000 (HEX 0000).
000
DADSP   /ADD THE SP TO REGISTER PAIR H AND
  •     /SAVE THE RESULT IN REGISTER PAIR H.
  •
  •
```

SP is then added to register pair H. As you might guess, there was no reason to use the LHLD instruction in Example 4-12. A final example for saving and restoring register pair H, while still being able to determine the content of the SP, is listed in Example 4-13.

Example 4-13: Determining the SP Address Without Disturbing Register Pair H

```
SHLD    /SAVE REGISTER PAIR H IN MEMORY LOCATIONS
020     /024 020 (L) AND 024 021 (H)
024     /(HEX 1412 AND 1413).
LXIH    /LOAD REGISTER PAIR H WITH 000 000
000     /(HEX 0000).
000
DADSP   /ADD THE STACK POINTER TO H&L.
SHLD    /SAVE THE LOW BYTE OF THE
022     /SP IN 024 022 AND THE HIGH BYTE
024     /OF THE SP IN 024 023 (HEX 1412 & 1413).
LHLD    /GET THE PREVIOUS H&L BACK AGAIN FROM
020     /MEMORY LOCATIONS 024 020 AND 024 021
024     /(HEX 1410 AND 1411).
  •     /CONTINUE WITH THE REMAINDER OF
  •     /THE PROGRAM.
  •
```

After executing this portion of the program (Example 4-13), register pair H will appear to be unaltered. The current content of the SP will be stored in R/W memory locations 024 022 and 024 023 (1412 and 1413). In this example, memory locations 024 020 and 024 021 (1410 and 1411) were used as temporary storage locations for register pair H. After this program is executed, these two memory locations will still contain the content of register pair H when the SHLD instruction was executed. Note that the addresses specified in the two SHLD instructions differ by two.

There are no equivalents of the SHLD and LHLD instructions for register pairs B and D. However, you will soon be given some easy methods that can be used to save these register pairs in R/W memory.

There are two instructions that are similar to SHLD and LHLD. These are the instructions STA (STore A direct) and LDA (LoaD A direct). Both of these instructions are three-byte instructions in which the second and third bytes contain a 16-bit memory address.

The LDA instruction is used to load the A register with the content of the memory location specified by the second and third bytes of the instruction. In previous software examples, register pair B, D, or H had to be loaded with a memory address so that an LDAXB, LDAXD, or MOVAM could be executed to load the A register with an eight-bit data word. However, the LDA instruction specifies the memory location in its second and third bytes, so a register pair does not have to be used to address memory.

The STA instruction is used to store the content of the A register in the memory location specified by the second and third bytes of the instruction. This means that a register pair does not have to be used to address memory so that an STAXB, STAXD, or MOVMA instruction can be executed. Examples 4-14 and 4-15 contain some examples of how the STA and LDA instructions can be used.

Example 4-14: The Use of the LDA Instruction

LDA	LDA
132	COUNT
001	0

Example 4-15: The Use of the STA Instruction

STA	STA
307	CHAR
034	0

In Example 4-14, the A register is loaded with the content of the memory location addressed by the second and third bytes of the instruction, memory location 001 132 (015A). The content of this memory location will remain unaltered when the LDA instruction is executed. A symbolic address can also be used as the second and third bytes of the LDA instruction, as Example 4-14 demonstrates. For this particular LDA instruction, the A register is loaded with the content of the memory location assigned the symbolic address, COUNT.

In Example 4-15, the content of the A register is stored in memory location 034 307 (1CC7), and the memory location assigned the symbolic address, CHAR. The A register remains unaltered when an STA instruction is executed. There are no single-register instructions equivalent to either the STA or LDA instructions for the other 8080 general-purpose registers.

Suppose you need to determine whether or not a particular memory location contains the data word 215 (8D). How would you do this? You should now be able to think of many different methods to perform this task, including some of the examples in Example 4-16.

Example 4-16: Determining Whether or Not a Memory Location Contains 215 (8D)

LXIH	LXIH	LDA
123	123	123
062	062	062
MOVAM	MVIA	CPI
CPI	215	215
215	CMPM	

In the first two methods (Example 4-16), register pair H and the A register are used to determine whether the content of the memory location addressed by register pair H contains 215 (8D). You might have to save the content of register pair H before the LXIH instruction is executed. To do this, an SHLD and an LHLD instruction could be used. However, this means that these two methods would require two additional instructions that require a total of six memory locations for storage. The last method, which uses an LDA instruction, is not only shorter, but it uses only the A register rather than both register A and register pair H.

USING THE STACK FOR THE STORAGE OF DATA, ADDRESSES, AND STATUS INFORMATION

In all of the previous examples, the stack has been used to store return addresses when subroutines are called. When the call instruction is executed, the return address, in the form of two eight-bit values, is automatically pushed onto the stack. When a return instruction is executed, the last two eight-bit values are automatically popped off of the stack and loaded into the program counter (PC).

Suppose you have data values in registers B, C, D, E, H, and L. If you call a subroutine and eventually return to the main program, will the same data values still be contained in these registers? There is no way to be sure of this. You would have to examine the subroutine on an instruction-by-instruction basis, noting which registers were used, to determine whether or not the content of any of the registers had changed. If you had called the one-hour-delay subroutine (Example 3-6) in Chapter 3, the data values in registers B, C, D, and E would have been altered because the time-delay subroutine uses these registers for its own purposes.

Can you overcome this serious limitation? You could store the content of all the registers in a section of R/W memory before the subroutine is called. After the 8080 returns from the subroutine, the data would then have to be retrieved from R/W memory. The software required for this operation is cumbersome, and it requires the use of two of the 8080's general-purpose registers to address R/W memory locations where the data values are to be stored.

One of the nice features of the 8080 is that you can utilize the stack to temporarily store the content of the general-purpose registers, even while a subroutine is being executed. You can actually store all of the registers (A through E, H, and L) and the five 8080 flags on the stack anytime you need to. Though the content of individual registers cannot be pushed onto or popped off of the stack, the content of the register pairs can be saved on the stack. The op codes for the push and pop instructions for register pairs B, D, H, and the *processor status word (PSW)* are listed in Table 4-6.

When the 8080 executes either a PUSHPSW or a POPPSW instruction, a total of 16 bits of information [the A register and the flag word containing the five flags (carry, zero, sign, parity, and auxiliary carry) and three *dummy* bits] is pushed onto or popped off of the stack. *Therefore, all transfers to and from the stack are as two eight-bit bytes (16 bits).* You should recall that this is also the case for the call- and return-type instructions; all addresses are stored and retrieved to and from the stack as two eight-bit bytes.

Table 4-6. A Summary of the Register Pair Stack Instructions

Octal	Mnemonic	Hexadecimal
305	PUSHB	C5
325	PUSHD	D5
345	PUSHH	E5
365	PUSHPSW	F5
301	POPB	C1
321	POPD	D1
341	POPH	E1
361	POPPSW	F1

All PUSH and POP instructions are single-byte instructions.

The effect that these instructions have on the content of the memory locations addressed by the stack pointer, M(SP), the stack pointer plus one, M(SP+1), the stack pointer minus one, M(SP−1), and the stack pointer minus two, M(SP−2) is shown in Fig. 4-2.

To *effectively* use these instructions, you have to be sure that the data is pushed onto the stack and popped off of the stack in *reverse* order. This is because the stack is a last-on, first-off stack. This is easily seen in Example 4-17.

The push and pop order in Example 4-17 is correct; the order in which the registers are popped off of the stack is the reverse of the

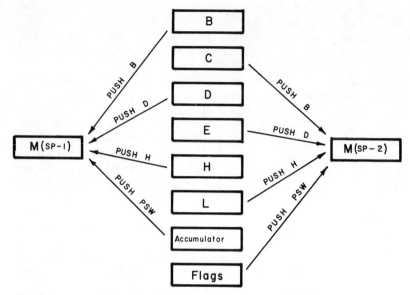

(A) After any one of these instructions has been executed, the stack pointer address has been decremented by two.

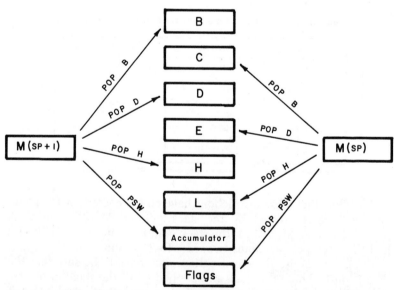

(B) After any one of these instructions has been executed, the stack pointer address has been incremented by two.

Fig. 4-2. Diagrams illustrating the PUSH and POP operations, each of which involves a register pair and two memory locations.

Example 4-17: The Proper Use of the Stack to Save the Content of the Registers

```
PUSHH       /SAVE H&L ON THE STACK.
PUSHPSW     /SAVE A AND THE FLAGS ON THE STACK.
PUSHB       /SAVE B&C ON THE STACK.
CALL
COUNT       /CALL THE SUBROUTINE CALLED "COUNT."
0
POPB        /POP B&C OFF OF THE STACK.
POPPSW      /POP A AND THE FLAGS OFF OF THE STACK.
POPH        /POP H&L OFF OF THE STACK.
```

order in which they were pushed onto the stack. For instance, register pair H was the first pushed on and the last popped off. In Example 4-17, the subroutine COUNT did not affect the content of register pair D, so there was no need to save register pair D on the stack. If you could examine the actual content of the stack when the call to COUNT is executed, you would see the results as shown in Table 4-7. We will assume that the stack pointer is set to 024 100 (1440) with an LXISP instruction prior to the execution of this program (Example 4-17).

Table 4-7. The Content of the Stack After a PUSHH, PUSHPSW, PUSHB, and a CALL Instruction Have Been Executed

Octal Stack Address		Hexadecimal Stack Address	
Initial SP—024 100		1440	
024 077	Register H	143F	} PUSHH
024 076	Register L	143E	
024 075	Register A	143D	} PUSHPSW
024 074	The Flag Word	143C	
024 073	Register B	143B	} PUSHB
024 072	Register C	143A	
024 071	HI Return Address	1439	} CALL
Current SP—024 070	LO Return Address	1438	

Note that since the return address is the last entry on the stack, it must be the first off of the stack. Why was a return address stored on the stack? It was stored there because a CALL instruction was executed by the 8080. When the return instruction at the end of the subroutine is executed, the return address will be popped off of the stack and loaded into the PC. This will be the address of the next instruction that is to be executed. After the return address is popped off of the stack, the SP will point to memory location 024 072 (143A). The next instruction executed after the 8080 returns from the COUNT subroutine is POPB, so the values for the B and C registers are popped off of the stack into registers B and C (register pair B). The SP now points to memory location 024 074 (143C). After the PSW (the A register and the flag word) is popped off of the stack, the SP will point to 024 076 (143E). When the POPH instruction is finally executed, the SP will point to 024 100 (1440). As long as the push and pop instructions are used properly and executed in the proper order, no problems should occur during the use of the stack for storage operations.

Suppose the program in Example 4-18 is executed. What would the content of the registers be after the last instruction, POPB, has been executed? This program may appear to be very complex, but it is relatively simple. Before calling the subroutine, GUESS, register pairs B, D, and H are loaded with data values. These values are then pushed onto the stack. In the GUESS subroutine, the 8080 executes some increment and decrement instructions that alter the content of registers B, C, D, H, and L. However, since the content of register pairs D, H, and B is popped off of the stack when the 8080 returns to the main program, it really does not matter how the content of the registers is altered by the subroutine. All that needs to be done is to determine the order in which the register pairs are pushed and popped.

Register pair D was the last register pair pushed onto the stack, and the first register pair popped off of the stack. Therefore, it will contain the value, 020 020 (1010), when the POPD instruction is executed. After register pair D is popped off of the stack, register pair H is popped off of the stack. Register pair H was also the second to the last register pair pushed onto the stack. Because of this, register pair H will contain 123 001 (5301) when the POPH instruction is executed. Register pair B was the first register pair to be pushed onto the stack, and the last register pair to be popped off of the stack, so it will contain 002 100 (0240).

In general, the push and pop instructions may be thought of as data movement instructions. Like the move instructions, the content of the register pairs is *duplicated* in a section of R/W memory (the stack area) whenever a push instruction is executed. Therefore, when a PUSHB instruction is executed, register pair B contains the same data values after the instruction is executed that it contained before the instruction was executed. Likewise, when data values are popped off of the stack and back into register pairs, the R/W memory that is used by the stack still contains the data values written into memory when the push instruction was executed.

You have now seen that the push and pop instructions allow you a great deal of flexibility in writing programs. Data values can be temporarily saved on the stack before a subroutine is called, and then retrieved from the stack when program control is returned to the main program from the subroutine. Of course, these instructions

Example 4-18: Pushing and Popping Data Values On and Off the Stack

```
LXISP    /LOAD THE STACK POINTER BECAUSE PUSH
STACK    /AND POP INSTRUCTIONS WILL BE EXECUTED.
0
LXIH     /LOAD REGISTER PAIR H. L IS LOADED
001      /WITH 001, H WITH 123
123      /(HEX 5301).
LXIB     /LOAD REGISTER PAIR B, C IS LOADED
100      /WITH 100, B WITH 002
002      /(HEX 0240).
LXID     /LOAD REGISTER PAIR D. BOTH THE E
020      /AND D REGISTERS ARE LOADED WITH 020
020      /(HEX 1010).
PUSHB    /SAVE B&C ON THE STACK.
PUSHH    /SAVE H&L ON THE STACK.
PUSHD    /SAVE D&E ON THE STACK.
CALL     /CALL THE SUBROUTINE WITH THE
GUESS    /SYMBOLIC ADDRESS OF "GUESS."
0
POPD     /POP D&E OFF OF THE STACK.
POPH     /POP H&L OFF OF THE STACK.
POPB     /POP B&C OFF OF THE STACK.
   •
   •
   •

GUESS,   INXH     /INCREMENT REGISTER PAIR H.
         DCXB     /DECREMENT REGISTER PAIR B.
         INRD     /INCREMENT THE CONTENT OF D.
         JNZ      /HAS D BEEN DECREMENTED TO 000 ?
         GUESS    /NO, EXECUTE THE LOOP AGAIN.
         0
         RET      /YES, RETURN TO THE MAIN PROGRAM.
```

can be used in any section of a program. They do not have to be executed just before and just after a call instruction. This brings up an interesting point. Would the push and pop instructions be executed before and after the call instruction, or would they actually be executed at the beginning and end of the subroutine? These differences are shown in Example 4-19.

Placing the push and pop instructions in one place, in the subroutine, is far better than having to repeat such instructions before and after every call to the subroutine. Remember, this is the reason why the subroutine was originally written; to eliminate the duplication of a particular sequence of instructions. With the push and pop instructions located within the subroutine, the subroutine causes the content of register pairs B and H to be saved on the stack as soon as the subroutine is executed. Just before the return instruction is executed, register pairs B and H are popped off of the stack. No matter when the stack is used, you will still have to

Example 4-19: When to Push and Pop

	Program No. 1				Program No. 2	
	•				•	
	•				•	
	PUSHH	/SAVE H&L.			•	
	PUSHB	/SAVE B&C.			CALL	
	CALL	/EXECUTE THE			TEST	
	TEST	/SUBROUTINE.			0	
	0				•	
	POPB	/RETRIEVE B&C.			•	
	POPH	/RETRIEVE H&L.			•	
	•				•	
	•				•	

TEST,	MVIB			TEST,	PUSHH	/SAVE H&L.
	123				PUSHB	/SAVE B&C.
	LXIH				MVIB	
	134				123	
	036				LXIH	
COUNT,	MVIM				134	
	000				036	
	INXH			COUNT,	MVIM	
	DCRB				000	
	JNZ				INXH	
	COUNT				DCRB	
	0				JNZ	
	RET				COUNT	
					0	
					POPB	/RETRIEVE B&C.
					POPH	/RETRIEVE H&L.
					RET	

ensure that there is enough room on the stack for all of these data words. You do this at the time that the stack pointer is initialized by means of an LXISP instruction. Since the stack pointer is decremented when values are pushed onto the stack, the stack will normally start at or near the R/W memory location with the highest available address with "open" memory "below" it.

You also know that *all* subroutines must contain (1) the same number of push and pop instructions, and (2) a conditional or unconditional return instruction. If these conditions are not met, the stack may run away; that is, it may grow very large very quickly. If this occurs, a program and/or data stored in R/W memory will be destroyed. A runaway stack is almost always fatal. Unfortunately, it is very easy to make the stack run away. A typical example is listed in Example 4-20.

Example 4-20: How Not to Call a Subroutine

```
TEST,  CALL  /CALL THE "TEST" SUBROUTINE.
       TEST
       0
       INRA  /INCREMENT A WHEN THE 8080 RETURNS.
```

Although most programmers would not make this particular error, it is very easy to make this type of error when you have subroutines nested 15 levels deep, or when you have a program that is one- or two-thousand instructions long. What will R/W memory contain if the stack does run away? Generally, R/W memory will be filled with identical 16-bit values, the *return address* for the call instruction, or the register pair data stored by the "push" for which there is no equivalent, corresponding "pop." In Example 4-20, memory would be filled with the 16-bit memory address of the location in which the INRA instruction is stored.

THE RESTART INSTRUCTIONS—ONE-BYTE CALL INSTRUCTIONS

How can you cause the 8080 to execute a subroutine? The 8080 has to execute a call instruction in your program. The call instruction is a three-byte instruction, and it differs from a jump instruction in that a return address is stored on the stack when the call instruction is executed. There are also single-byte instructions, called *restart* instructions, which perform the same function as the call instruction, except that the subroutines that are called by them must reside in memory starting at specific addresses. There are eight restart instructions, which are summarized in Table 4-8.

Table 4-8. A Summary of the Restart Instructions

| Instruction | Op Code | | Memory Address Called | |
	Octal	Hex	Octal	Hex
RST0	307	C7	000 000	0000 *
RST1	317	CF	000 010	0008
RST2	327	D7	000 020	0010
RST3	337	DF	000 030	0018
RST4	347	E7	000 040	0020
RST5	357	EF	000 050	0028
RST6	367	F7	000 060	0030
RST7	377	FF	000 070	0038

* Identical to hardwired RESET.

When one of the restart instructions is executed, the 8080 branches to the specific memory location listed in Table 4-8. At the same time, a return address is saved on the stack. This is the same sequence of events that occurs when a call instruction is executed. However, with a single-byte instruction, how can a 16-bit address be specified? It *cannot*. The address that the 8080 branches to when any of these restart instructions is executed is fixed and you cannot change it. No matter which restart instruction is executed, the high portion of the memory address that the 8080 branches to is always 000 (00). The low address varies, depending on which restart instruction is executed. Also note that if the octal numbering system is used, it is very easy to remember the low addresses that the restart instructions branch to (RST0, low=000; RST1, low=010; RST2, low=020; RST3, low=030; etc.). *Even though the restart instructions are single-byte call instructions, a return address is saved on the stack when one of these instructions is executed.* A simple example that uses a restart instruction is listed in Example 4-21.

Example 4-21: Using a Restart Instruction to Call a Subroutine

```
          •
          •
          MVIA      /LOAD THE A REGISTER WITH 001.
          001
          RST7      /EXECUTE A RESTART 7 INSTRUCTION.
          OUT       /OUTPUT THE CONTENT OF THE A
          123       /REGISTER TO OUTPUT PORT 123.
          •
          •

          *000 070
SETUP,    LXID      /LOAD REGISTER PAIR D.
          001       /LOAD E WITH 001, D WITH 000.
          000
          MVIH      /LOAD H WITH 030.
          030
          RET       /RETURN TO THE MAIN PROGRAM.
```

This is the first example that you have seen that uses an asterisk. The asterisk is used to define a starting address for a program, a subroutine, or an array of data. When the source program is assembled by an *assembler program,* the asterisk causes the assembler to begin typing out new addresses during the assembled listing of the program. All this means is that the subroutine, SETUP (Example 4-21), is stored in memory starting at address 000 070 (0038).

Although this program does not perform a particularly useful function, it does demonstrate the use of a restart instruction (RST7) to call a subroutine. When this program is executed, the RST7 instruction will cause a return address, which is the memory address of the location in which the OUT instruction is stored, to be pushed onto the stack. The 8080 will then branch to memory address 000 070 (0038) and execute the subroutine. Of course, there must be a subroutine at the address that is called by the restart instruction. When the return instruction at the end of the subroutine is executed, the return address is popped off of the stack and used as the address for the next instruction to be executed. In conclusion, you have seen how a single-byte restart instruction can perform the same function as a three-byte call instruction. In fact, the program in Example 4-21 could have been written with a call instruction (Example 4-22).

Example 4-22: Using a Call Instruction Rather Than a Restart Instruction

```
       •
       •
     MVIA
     001      /LOAD THE A REGISTER WITH 001.
     CALL     /CALL THE SETUP SUBROUTINE.
     SETUP
     0
     OUT      /OUTPUT THE CONTENT OF THE A REGISTER
     123      /TO OUTPUT PORT 123.
       •
       •

           *000 070
SETUP,     LXID     /LOAD REGISTER PAIR D.
           001      /LOAD E WITH 001 (HEX 01).
           000      /LOAD D WITH 000 (HEX 00).
           MVIH     /LOAD H WITH 030 (HEX 18).
           030
           RET      /RETURN TO THE MAIN PROGRAM.
```

One of the disadvantages of using a three-byte call instruction is the fact that two memory locations are required to store the address bytes of the subroutine in the instruction. The amount of memory saved by using restart instructions, rather than call instructions, may or may not be important to you. It would seem that one limitation in using the restart instructions is that the subroutine that is called must be eight or fewer memory locations long. This is because there are only eight memory locations between the addresses to which the restart instructions branch. Is this really true? No, it is not. Even though there are only eight memory locations between the restart instruction's branch addresses, you could use the technique shown in Example 4-23 when you wish to call subroutines that are longer than eight memory locations, using restart instructions for the call function.

If restart instructions are used in a program rather than call instructions, two memory locations in a program can be saved. This is not a very great savings, unless you can use restart instructions in many places throughout the program. How many memory locations can be saved if restart instructions are used 50 times? One hundred memory locations would be saved. This is very important if you have to "squeeze" a 1056-byte program into a 1024-byte read-only memory (ROM). One of the problems associated with the use of restart instructions is the fact that I/O devices, interfaced to the 8080 by means of an interrupt, may also use restart instructions. This means that restart instructions cannot be used "casually." This problem will be discussed in the chapter on interrupts.

Example 4-23: Using Restart Instructions With Long Subroutines

```
          *001 000
START,    MVIA
          001          /LOAD THE A REGISTER WITH 001.
          RST7         /EXECUTE THE RESTART 7 INSTRUCTION.
          OUT          /OUTPUT THE CONTENT OF THE A REGISTER
          123          /TO OUTPUT PORT 123.
            •
            •

          *000 070
SETUP,    LXIB         /LOAD REGISTER C WITH 001, B WITH 000.
          001
          000
          JMP          /LINK TO THE REMAINDER OF
          MORE         /SUBROUTINE AT SYMBOLIC
          0            /ADDRESS "MORE."

          *001 200
MORE,     MVIH         /LOAD THE H REGISTER WITH 030.
          030
          MVID         /LOAD THE D REGISTER WITH 023.
          023
DECIT,    DCRD         /DECREMENT THE D REGISTER.
          JNZ          /IS THE D REGISTER 000 ?
          DECIT        /NO, JNZ TO DECIT.
          0
          RET          /D=000, RETURN.
```

WORKING WITH REGISTER PAIR H

It has already been shown that the 8080 can move data to and from memory when an address is contained in register pairs B, D, or H. Instructions have also been discussed that cause the content of register pair H to be moved to and from memory. These are the SHLD and LHLD instructions. There are four additional instructions that use registers H and L as a register pair.

Register Pair Exchange Operations

The first to be discussed will be the XCHG instruction, which has an op code of 353 (EB). This instruction causes *the contents of register pair D and register pair H to be exchanged.* After this instruction is executed, the content of the E register will be in the L register, L in E, D in H, and H in D. Note that this instruction swaps, or exchanges, the 16-bit contents of these two register pairs. What will be contained in register pairs D and H when the program in Example 4-24 is executed?

After the XCHG instruction is executed, register H will contain 002 (02), L will contain 001 (01), register D will contain 004 (04), and the E register will contain 003 (03). Of course, if this is the

Example 4-24: Using the XCHG Instruction

```
SWAP,   LXID    /LOAD REGISTER PAIR D.
        001     /LOAD E WITH 001 (HEX 01).
        002     /LOAD D WITH 002 (HEX 02).
        LXIH    /LOAD REGISTER PAIR H.
        003     /LOAD L WITH 003 (HEX 03).
        004     /LOAD H WITH 004 (HEX 04).
        XCHG    /EXCHANGE THE CONTENTS OF D&E WITH H&L.
          •
          •
```

desired end result, the program listed in Example 4-25 could have just as easily been executed.

Example 4-25: Using LXI Instructions Rather Than an XCHG Instruction

```
EQUIV,  LXID
        003
        004
        LXIH
        001
        002
```

Can you think of two other ways in which the contents of register pairs H and D can be exchanged? If not, see Example 4-26.

Example 4-26: Equivalent Instructions for the XCHG Instruction

```
                        MOVAH
                PUSHD   MOVHD
                PUSHH   MOVDA
   XCHG   =     POPD  = MOVAL
                POPH    MOVLE
                        MOVEA
```

You have already seen how to move the content of register pair H to and from memory by means of the SHLD and LHLD instructions. Suppose that you need to save the content of register pair D in memory. How would you do this? The instructions listed in Example 4-27 could be used. This program saves the content of register pair H on the stack, and then loads register pair H with the R/W memory address that is assigned to the symbolic address, STORE. The content of the E register is then saved in the R/W memory locations addressed by register pair H. The memory address is then incremented (INXH), and the content of the D register is then saved in memory. The original content of register pair H is then popped off of the stack, and the 8080 continues executing the remainder of the program.

By using the XCHG instruction, a much simpler program can be written (Example 4-28).

Example 4-27: Saving Register Pair D in R/W Memory

.
.

```
PUSHH    /SAVE REGISTER PAIR H ON THE STACK.
LXIH     /LOAD REGISTER PAIR H WITH THE ADDRESS
STORE    /ASSIGNED TO THE SYMBOLIC ADDRESS
0        /OF "STORE."
MOVME    /SAVE THE CONTENT OF REGISTER E IN MEMORY.
INXH     /INCREMENT THE MEMORY ADDRESS IN REGISTER PAIR H.
MOVMD    /SAVE THE CONTENT OF REGISTER D IN MEMORY.
POPH     /POP REGISTER PAIR H OFF OF THE STACK.
```

.
.

Example 4-28: An Improved Method of Saving Register Pair D in R/W Memory

.
.

```
XCHG     /EXCHANGE REGISTER PAIRS D AND H.
SHLD     /SAVE THE CONTENT OF REGISTER PAIR H
STORE    /IN TWO CONSECUTIVE MEMORY LOCATIONS, STARTING
0        /AT THE SYMBOLIC ADDRESS OF "STORE."
XCHG     /EXCHANGE REGISTER PAIRS D AND H TO THEIR
.        /ORIGINAL VALUES.
```

.

The instructions listed in Example 4-28 initially exchange the content of register pair D with the content of register pair H. The data values that are to be saved in R/W memory are now in register pair H. The content of register pair H is then saved in R/W memory when the SHLD instruction is executed. The content of the L register is saved in the memory location with the symbolic address, STORE, and the content of the H register is saved at memory address STORE+1. After the data values are saved in memory, the contents of register pairs D and H are again exchanged. The contents of register pairs D and H are now the same as before this sequence of instructions was executed.

Example 4-29: Using an LHLD Instruction to Load Register Pair D With the Content of Memory

.
.

```
XCHG     /EXCHANGE REGISTER PAIRS D AND H.
LHLD     /LOAD REGISTER PAIR H WITH THE
STORE    /CONTENT OF "STORE."
0
XCHG     /EXCHANGE REGISTER PAIRS D AND H AGAIN.
```

.
.

A similar sequence of instructions can also be used to load register pair D with the content of two consecutive memory locations (Examples 4-29 and 4-30). As you will see, by using an XCHG instruction, three memory locations are saved, the program is easier to understand, and it will take less time to be executed.

Example 4-30: Using Move Instructions to Load Register Pair D With the Content of Memory

```
    •
    •
PUSHH     /SAVE REGISTER PAIR H ON THE STACK.
LXIH      /LOAD REGISTER PAIR H WITH THE
STORE     /MEMORY ADDRESS OF "STORE."
0
MOVEM     /LOAD THE E REGISTER WITH MEMORY.
INXH      /INCREMENT THE MEMORY ADDRESS.
MOVDM     /LOAD THE D REGISTER WITH MEMORY.
POPH      /POP REGISTER PAIR H OFF OF THE STACK.
    •
    •
```

You have now been given some efficient methods of saving the contents of register pairs D and H in R/W memory, including those listed in Example 4-31.

Example 4-31: Saving Register Pairs D and H in Memory

To Save Register Pair H	To Save Register Pair D
SHLD	XCHG
TEMPO	SHLD
0	TEMPO
	0
	XCHG

However, how can the content of register pair B be saved in memory? Remember that there is no exchange instruction for register pairs B and H. The program listed in Example 4-32 could be used to save the content of register pair B in memory.

Example 4-32: Saving Register Pair B in Memory

```
    •
    •
PUSHH     /SAVE REGISTER PAIR H ON THE STACK.
PUSHB     /SAVE REGISTER PAIR B ON THE STACK.
POPH      /POP REGISTER PAIR B INTO REGISTER PAIR H.
SHLD      /SAVE THE CONTENT OF REGISTER PAIR
TEMPO     /H (B) IN R-W MEMORY.
0
POPH      /RESTORE THE CONTENT OF REGISTER PAIR H.
    •
    •
```

In Example 4-32, register pair H is pushed onto the stack. Register pair B is then pushed onto and then popped off of the stack *into register pair H*. This acts as a register-pair-to-register-pair data movement step. The content of register pair H (the value initially stored in register pair B) is then stored in R/W memory when the SHLD instruction is executed. At this point, the original content of register pair H is still on the stack, and the 16-bit value that was initially in register pair B is now in register pair H. By simply popping the content of register pair H off of the stack and into register pair H again, the 8080 can continue on with the remainder of the program, and the contents of these two register pairs appear to be undisturbed. Note that a complete exchange between register pairs B and H has not taken place.

Example 4-33: Exchanging Register Pair B With Either Register Pair D or H

To Exchange Register Pairs B and D	To Exchange Register Pairs B and H
PUSHB	PUSHB
PUSHD	PUSHH
POPB	POPB
POPD	POPH
or	or
PUSHD	PUSHH
PUSHB	PUSHB
POPD	POPH
POPB	POPB

If you really need to exchange the content of register pair B with either register pair D or register pair H, it is very easy to do so. The PSW register pair could also be exchanged if you needed this operation.

An Improved Array Movement Program

At the beginning of this chapter, programs were used to move blocks (arrays) of data from one section of memory to another. One of the programs used is listed in Example 4-34.

Suppose you need to make the program listed in Example 4-34 (1) as general purpose as possible, and (2) put the program in ROM and still be able to change the initial address, final address, and byte count. This means that the addresses, 021 100 and 051 100 (1140 and 2940), or the byte count, (012 023, 0A13), might not always be the proper address or count values to use. What you want to do is store the initial address, final address, and byte count somewhere in R/W memory and then have the block movement program access these values. The program listed in Example 4-35 performs this task.

The first instruction in Example 4-35 loads register pair H with the contents of two consecutive memory locations, starting at the symbolic address, BC. This 16-bit value is then pushed onto the stack and then popped off of the stack into register pair B. Register pair B has now been loaded with the byte count (BC). Register pair H is then loaded with the contents of the two consecutive memory locations, starting at the symbolic address, FA. This is the final

Example 4-34: A Data-Block Movement Program

```
MOVE,     LXIH      /STARTING ADDRESS FOR THE
          100       /SOURCE OF THE DATA.
          021
          LXID      /STARTING ADDRESS FOR THE
          100       /DESTINATION OF THE DATA.
          051
          LXIB      /NUMBER OF BYTES TO
          023       /BE TRANSFERRED.
          012
TRNSFR,   MOVAM     /GET A DATA BYTE USING H&L.
          STAXD     /STORE A DATA BYTE USING D&E.
          INXH      /INCREMENT THE SOURCE ADDRESS.
          INXD      /INCREMENT THE DESTINATION ADDRESS.
          DCXB      /DECREMENT THE BYTE COUNTER.
          MOVAB     /IS IT 0 YET ?
          ORAC
          JNZ
          TRNSFR    /NO, EXECUTE THE JUMP.
          0
            •       /YES, CONTINUE WITH THE PROGRAM.
            •
            •
```

address that the data is to be moved to. The contents of register pairs D and H are then exchanged, so that the final address (FA) is now in register pair D. Register pair H is then loaded with the initial address (IA) of the array of data to be moved. Register pairs B, D, and H have now been loaded with the byte count, final address, and initial address. The movement of the block of data is then performed when the 8080 executes the TRNSFR loop.

Loading the Program Counter

Another instruction that uses register pair H is the PCHL instruction, which has an octal op code of 351 (E9). This instruction is a single-byte jump instruction. However, any 16-bit address can be specified! How can this be done with a single-byte instruction? This is accomplished by loading the 16-bit content of register pair H into the program counter (PC), the only operation performed by the PCHL instruction.

Example 4-35: Using LHLD Instructions to Access the Addresses and Count

```
MOVE,    LHLD    /LOAD REGISTER PAIR H WITH THE CONTENT
         BC      /OF MEMORY ASSIGNED THE SYMBOLIC ADDRESS "BC."
         0
         PUSHH   /PUSH THE VALUE ON THE STACK
         POPB    /AND THEN POP IT OFF INTO B&C.
         LHLD    /NOW LOAD H&L WITH THE FINAL ADDRESS
         FA      /SAVED IN MEMORY AT THE SYMBOLIC ADDRESS
         0       /"FA."
         XCHG    /EXCHANGE D&E WITH H&L. THE FINAL ADDRESS IS IN D&E.
         LHLD    /LOAD H&L WITH THE INITIAL ADDRESS.
         IA
         0
TRNSFR,  MOVAM   /GET A DATA BYTE USING H&L.
         STAXD   /STORE A DATA BYTE USING D&E.
         INXH    /INCREMENT THE SOURCE ADDRESS.
         INXD    /INCREMENT THE DESTINATION ADDRESS.
         DCXB    /DECREMENT THE BYTE COUNTER.
         MOVAB   /IS IT 0 YET ?
         ORAC
         JNZ
         TRNSFR  /NO, EXECUTE THE JUMP.
         0
             •   /YES, CONTINUE WITH THE PROGRAM.
             •
             •


BC,      023     /THIS IS THE BYTE COUNT.
         012
FA,      100     /THIS IS THE FINAL ADDRESS.
         040
IA,      100     /THIS IS THE INITIAL ADDRESS.
         021
```

Since the PC points to where the next instruction to be executed is stored in memory, the PCHL instruction performs the same function as the unconditional jump, JMP.

You can think of the PCHL instruction as: load the *PC* with the contents of registers *H* and *L*. There are few, if any, simple program examples that really demonstrate the power of this instruction. However, the program listed in Example 4-36 should give you an idea of how the PCHL instruction can be used.

Example 4-36: Using the PCHL Instruction

```
                    LXIH
                    345
                    005
                    PCHL
```

If this sequence of instructions (Example 4-36) is executed, at what address is the instruction op code stored that is to be executed after the PCHL instruction is executed? The instruction op code must be stored in 005 345 (05E5), the address loaded into register pair H by the LXIH instruction.

Stack Exchange Operations

The XTHL instruction, which has an op code of 343 (E3), is also a very sophisticated instruction. It exchanges the content of register pair H with the last two bytes stored on the stack (the content of a register pair or a 16-bit return address).

If you need to determine, or examine, the last two eight-bit bytes that are stored on the stack, a POPB, POPD, or POPH instruction could be executed. However, the use of one of these instructions would mean that we must have a "free" register pair into which we can pop the values of interest. You cannot make a register pair available by executing a push instruction, since the next pop instruction would just reload this "saved" data back into a register pair. Also, if a pop instruction is executed, the content of the SP will be incremented by two. Since the XTHL instruction exchanges the *content* of register pair H with the last two bytes stored on the stack, without affecting the stack pointer's address, the data values can be restored to their original "position" simply by executing another XTHL instruction.

Suppose you wrote a program so that a subroutine could determine the address of the instruction op code to which control would be returned after the completion of the subroutine. The XTHL instruction could be used for this purpose. This permits a program to determine the point from which the subroutine was called.

In Example 4-37, each time the 8080 enters the TEST subroutine, the return address on the stack and the content of register pair H are exchanged. In this example, what would the content of register pair H be after each XTHL instruction in the TEST subroutine is executed? Observe that the TEST subroutine is called from three different points in the program. The content of register pair H would be 001 203, 001 207, and 001 213 (0183, 0187, and 018B) after each call, respectively. After the 8080 has performed the first XTHL instruction, the return address contained in register pair H could be altered or simply examined before the address was put back on the stack by the second XTHL, at the end of the subroutine, when it is executed. If the address in register pair H is altered, the second XTHL instruction will place a *modified* address back on the stack.

Loading the Stack Pointer From Register Pair H

The LXISP instruction can be used to load the stack pointer. However, if this instruction is used in a program that is stored in ROM, the two address bytes of the LXISP instruction *cannot* be

Example 4-37: Using the XTHL Instruction

```
         *001 200
START,   CALL        /CALL THE TEST SUBROUTINE.
         TEST
         0
         INRA        /INCREMENT THE CONTENT OF THE A REGISTER.
         CALL        /CALL THE TEST SUBROUTINE.
         TEST
         0
         INRB        /INCREMENT THE CONTENT OF THE B REGISTER.
         CALL        /CALL THE TEST SUBROUTINE.
         TEST
         0
         HLT         /HALT.

TEST,    XTHL        /EXCHANGE H&L AND THE LAST TWO ENTRIES ON THE STACK.
          •
          •
          •
         XTHL        /EXCHANGE H&L AND THE LAST TWO ENTRIES ON THE STACK.
         RET         /RETURN TO THE MAIN PROGRAM.
```

changed. You have already seen examples using the LXISP instruction; the SPHL instruction performs a similar function. The SPHL instruction, which has an op code of 371 (F9), is also very similar to the PCHL instruction that was just discussed. You can think of the SPHL instruction as: load the *SP* with the contents of registers *H* and *L*.

With this instruction, you can load any 16-bit value into register pair H and then execute an SPHL instruction to load these values into the SP. Of course, the value will remain in register pair H after the SPHL instruction is executed. The sequence of instructions listed in Example 4-38 will load the SP by means of an SPHL instruction.

Example 4-38: Using the SPHL Instruction

Program No. 1	Program No. 2
LXISP	LXIH
300	300
012	012
	SPHL

By using the SPHL instruction, the stack pointer can be easily loaded with different 16-bit values to suit particular applications, even if the program containing the SPHL instruction is in ROM. Can you write a program that will load the SP with a 16-bit address that is stored in two consecutive memory locations?

By using this program (Example 4-39), you would store the desired SP address in two memory locations; specifically, 020 234 and 020 235 (109C and 109D). The low SP address would be contained

Example 4-39: Changing the SP for a Program in ROM

```
SETSP,  LHLD  /LOAD REGISTER PAIR H WITH THE CONTENT OF
        234   /020 234 AND 020 235 (HEX 109C
        020   /AND 109D).
        SPHL  /NOW LOAD THE SP WITH THE CONTENT
              /OF REGISTER PAIR H.
```

in memory location 020 234 (109C), and the high SP address would be contained in memory location 020 235 (109D).

You have now seen a number of new 8080 instructions that use registers H and L as a register pair. These new instructions are summarized in Table 4-9.

Table 4-9. A Summary of the Register Pair H Instructions

LXIH	XTHL
$<B_2>$	XCHG
$<B_3>$	
	LHLD
INXH	$<B_2>$
DCXH	$<B_3>$
	SHLD
DADSP	$<B_2>$
DADH	$<B_3>$
DADD	PCHL
DADB	SPHL

ADDITIONAL A REGISTER (ACCUMULATOR) INSTRUCTIONS

There are two additional single-byte instructions that operate on the content of the A register, and two single-byte instructions that operate on the carry, that will be discussed in this chapter. One of the instructions that operates on the content of the A register is CMA, or CoMplement the content of the A register, which has an op code of 057 (2F). When this instruction is executed, it causes the content of the A register to be complemented, or inverted, on a bit-by-bit basis. What will the content of the A register be after the two instructions in Example 4-40 are executed?

To determine what the content of the A register is after the CMA instruction is executed, the content of the A register can be thought of as an eight-bit binary word. Therefore, 127 (57) is equivalent to binary 01010111. When the CMA instruction is executed, the content of the A register is complemented to 10101000 (octal 250, hex A8). A more complex program that uses the CMA instruction is listed in Example 4-41.

Example 4-40: A Simple CMA Example

•
•

```
MVIA    /LOAD THE A REGISTER WITH 127
127     /(OCTAL 127 = HEX 57).
CMA     /COMPLEMENT THE CONTENT OF A.
```
•
•

Example 4-41: Another Program That Uses the CMA Instruction

```
USECMA,  LXIB    /LOAD REGISTER PAIR B WITH THE
         000     /VALUE 012 000 (HEX 0A00).
         012
         DCRB    /DECREMENT THE CONTENT OF THE B REGISTER.
         MOVAB   /MOVE THE CONTENT OF B TO A.
         CMA     /COMPLEMENT THE CONTENT OF THE A REGISTER.
```
•
•

In this second example that uses the CMA instruction, the B register is loaded with the value, 012 (0A), when the LXIB instruction is executed. The content of the B register is then decremented by 1 to 011 (09) when the DCRB instruction is executed. After the complementing operation, the A register contains 366 (F6). This result is shown in binary as follows:

$$00001001 \text{ complemented to } 11110110$$

The complemented result is the *1s complement* of the content of the A register. It is called the 1s complement because 1s are complemented to 0s, and 0s are complemented to 1s. Quite often, the *2s complement* of a binary number is required for mathematical operations. The 2s complement of a number is that number which, when added to the original number, produces a result of zero. For instance, the 2s complement of the binary number 00000011 is 11111101. The 2s complement is actually 1 more than the 1s complement, or the 1s complement plus 1. For example,

$$
\begin{array}{r}
00000011 \text{ binary 3} \\
+\ 11111101 \text{ 2s complement of binary 3} \\
\hline
1 \quad 00000000 \text{ the result is zero}
\end{array}
$$

The 8080's CMA instruction produces the 1s complement of the number contained in the A register. Can you write a program that produces the 2s complement of the number contained in the A register? The program is very simple (Example 4-42).

If you could examine the content of the A register as these instructions are executed, you would see,

A Register	After Execution of Instruction
XXXXXXXX	•
XXXXXXXX	•
XXXXXXXX	MVIA
00000011	003
11111100	CMA
11111101	INRA
11111101	•
11111101	•

Example 4-42: Generating the 2s Complement of a Number

```
       •
       •
MVIA   /LOAD THE A REGISTER WITH
003    /OCTAL 003 (HEX 03).
CMA    /COMPLEMENT THE CONTENT OF A.
INRA   /INCREMENT THE CONTENT OF A.
       •
       •
```

There is another instruction that operates on the content of the A register, and it is the DAA instruction. However, this instruction will not be discussed until the next chapter.

THE CARRY INSTRUCTIONS

The two instructions that are associated with the carry are the set-the-carry and complement-the-carry instructions. The set-the-carry instruction sets the carry to a logic 1 when it is executed. If the carry is a logic 0 before the instruction is executed, it will be a logic 1 after the instruction is executed. If the carry is already a logic 1, then the set-the-carry instruction will have no effect on the state of the carry.

The complement-the-carry instruction complements the state of the carry. If the carry is a logic 1, then it is complemented to the logic 0 state by the complement-the-carry instruction. If the carry is a logic 0, then it will be complemented to the logic 1 state.

The STC instruction (Set-The-Carry) has an op code of 067 (37). The CMC instruction (CoMplement-the-Carry) has an op code of 077 (3F). Both of these instructions are single-byte instructions and they both affect the state of the carry flag.

The program listed in Example 4-43 has a subroutine that uses the STC instruction to notify the main program that an error has occurred.

In this example, the TEST subroutine moves the content of memory addressed by register pair H to the A register. The content of A is then compared to the immediate data byte, 233 (9B). If the value read from memory is equal to 233 (9B), the 8080 returns from

Example 4-43: Using the STC Instruction to Flag an Error Condition

```
        •
        •
CALL     /CALL THE TEST SUBROUTINE.
TEST
0
CC       /IF THE CARRY FLAG IS A LOGIC ONE,
ERROR    /CALL THE ERROR SUBROUTINE.
0        /OTHERWISE, THIS INSTRUCTION IS SKIPPED.
        •
        •
```

```
TEST,  MOVAM   /GET THE CONTENT OF MEMORY INTO REGISTER A.
       CPI     /COMPARE IT TO THE IMMEDIATE DATA BYTE
       233     /233 (HEX 9B).
       RZ      /IF THE CONTENT OF A IS 233 (HEX 9B), RETURN.
       STC     /IF A IS NOT 233 (9B), SET THE CARRY TO A ONE.
       RET     /NOW RETURN TO THE MAIN PROGRAM.
```

the subroutine. The carry is a logic 0 as a result of the comparison.

If the value read from memory is not 233 (9B), the 8080 sets the carry to a logic 1 and then returns from the subroutine. When the 8080 returns from the subroutine, the state of the carry flag is tested. If the carry flag is a logic 1, which indicates that an error condition exists, the ERROR subroutine is called. Otherwise, the conditional call instruction (CC) is skipped and the 8080 executes the instruction stored in memory after the three-byte CC instruction.

We will consider both the STC and CMC instructions to be logical instructions. Therefore, the state of the carry flag reflects the results of these instructions when they are executed.

The single-byte instruction, CMC, can be used by mathematical programs. Suppose that you need to ensure that the carry is a logic 0 before a certain section of a program is executed. Since the 8080 has no clear-carry instruction, can you write a program to do this?

Example 4-44: Clearing the Carry

```
        •
        •
STC
CMC
        •
        •
```

This simple program sets the carry to a logic 1 regardless of its current state, and then complements it to a logic 0. Rather than use this sequence of instructions, you can clear the carry and also clear the A register to all 0s by executing a single, single-byte instruction. What is this instruction? If the 8080 executes the instruction, XRAA (exclusive-or the A register with the A register), both the A register and the carry will be cleared to the logic 0 state. A subtract A from A (SUBA) instruction also has the same effect.

FINAL THOUGHTS

In many of the subroutines listed in this book, we have not included push instructions at the beginning of the subroutine, and pop instructions at the end of the subroutine. This would make many of the subroutine listings longer, and you would learn little if we had done this. Of course, if you want to use the subroutines in this book in your own programs, you may want to add push and pop instructions to the subroutines. However, some of the subroutines use conditional return instructions. Extreme care must be exercised when push and pop instructions are added to this type of subroutine. In fact, if push and pop instructions are added, the conditional return instructions are often changed to other instructions that perform the same task. For instance,

```
                                    TESTA,   PUSHD
                                             PUSHH
                                             INRA
                                             JNZ
                                             ANOTO
    TESTA,  INRA                              0
            RZ                                POPH
            INXB       Changed to:           POPD
            RET                               RET
                                    ANOTO,   INXB
                                             POPH
                                             POPD
                                             RET
```

As you see, adding push and pop instructions can increase the complexity of a simple subroutine. Of course, in this particular example, there was no real reason why register pairs D and H had to be saved on the stack.

We have now discussed 244 of the 8080's instructions. The remainder of this book will concern the application of these instructions to software problems.

5

Mathematical Routines

Quite often, data values from an experiment or a peripheral device have to be converted from one unit of measurement to another unit of measurement. This means that a pressure expressed in pounds per square inch (psi) might have to be converted to torr, or a torque in foot-pounds might have to be converted to newton-meters. To accomplish this conversion task, mathematical routines can be used. As you have already seen, the 8080 usually operates on eight-bit data words. However, you have also seen that the 8080 can execute some instructions that operate on 16 bits of data. These include the LXIH, DCXB, INXD, and DADH instructions.

The first mathematical routines and subroutines that will be discussed operate on fixed-point numbers. This means that the decimal point is in a fixed location, regardless of the size of the numbers being operated upon. There are no exponents associated with fixed-point numbers. Later in this chapter, floating-point numbers, which do have an exponent, will be briefly discussed.

INTEGER ADDITION

The simplest addition that the 8080 can perform is the addition of two eight-bit numbers. The source of one of the eight-bit numbers must be the A register. The source of the other number that is added may be (1) the content of any of the general-purpose registers (A through E, H, and L), (2) the content of memory addressed by register pair H, or (3) an immediate data byte. Two examples in Chapter 2 (Examples 2-13 and 2-15) showed how eight-bit numbers can be added together. There was also an example (2-17) where the 16-bit content of register pair B was added to the content of register pair D using ADD- and ADC-type instructions. In Chapter 4, the DAD-type instructions were discussed. These instructions can be used to add the content of any register pair to the content of register pair H. Example 4-5 showed a 16-bit addition, a *double-precision* addition where the content of register pair H was added to itself a number of times. The 8080 can also add 24-bit, 32-bit, or larger numbers. Programs that operate on numbers larger than eight bits are often called *multiprecision* or *multibyte* programs.

Suppose that two four-byte (32-bit) numbers have to be added together. The 8080 does not have enough registers to hold this much information (eight bytes). How could the 8080 be used to add these two numbers? One of the four-byte numbers could be stored in memory, and the other number could be stored in registers B, C, D, and E. Register pair H could then be used to address the memory locations where one of the numbers is stored. The subroutine listed in Example 5-1 adds the content of four sequential memory locations, starting at the symbolic address, DATA, to the content of registers E, D, C, and B in sequence. Before this subroutine is called, these registers have to be loaded with one of the 32-bit numbers (eight bits each) that is to be added, and the four sequential memory locations would have to be loaded with the other 32-bit number. When the 8080 returns from this subroutine, the result of the addition will be stored in registers B, C, D, and E.

Where is the MSBY and LSBY of the result stored? The MSBY will be stored in the B register and the LSBY will be stored in the E register when the 8080 returns from the subroutine.

Note the fact that the 8080 will only return from this subroutine, after the MOVBA instruction is executed, if the carry is a logic 0. If the carry is a logic 1, the 8080 will not execute the RNC instruction. Instead, it will begin to execute the instructions starting at ERROR. Why is this included in the subroutine? Suppose the number 000 000 000 001 (00000001) is added to 377 377 377 377 (FFFF-FFFF). What will the result of this addition be? The carry will be a logic 1 and the content of the B, C, D, and E registers will be 000 (00). Of course, the result of this addition is not 000 000 000 000 (00000000). Therefore, instructions must be included in the subroutine that save the *final carry* or notify the microcomputer operator that the result of the addition is larger than the storage space allocated for the storage of the result. In this example, four registers (32 bits) were allocated for the storage of the result, but the result is really 33 bits long (including the carry).

Unfortunately, this subroutine (Example 5-1) is very inflexible. To add two three-byte numbers, the MSBYs in both 32-bit numbers would have to be set to 000 (00). If two five-byte numbers need to be added, an entirely new subroutine would have to be written. In

Example 5-1: A 32-Bit Addition Subroutine

/THIS SUBROUTINE ADDS THE CONTENT OF FOUR CONSEC-
/UTIVE MEMORY LOCATIONS TO THE CONTENT OF REGISTERS
/B, C, D, AND E. REGISTER E CONTAINS THE LEAST
/SIGNIFICANT BYTE, AS DOES THE MEMORY LOCATION
/WITH THE LOWEST MEMORY ADDRESS.

```
ADDIT,   LXIH      /SET H&L TO POINT TO THE
         DATA      /FOUR DATA WORDS STORED
         0         /IN MEMORY.
         MOVAM     /GET THE FIRST WORD
         ADDE      /AND ADD E TO IT.
         MOVEA     /THEN SAVE THE RESULT IN E.
         INXH      /INCREMENT H&L TO THE NEXT WORD.
         MOVAM     /GET THE SECOND WORD.
         ADCD      /ADD D AND THE CARRY TO IT.
         MOVDA     /AND SAVE THE RESULT IN D.
         INXH      /INCREMENT H&L TO THE THIRD WORD.
         MOVAM     /MOVE THE THIRD WORD TO A.
         ADCC      /ADD C AND THE CARRY TO IT.
         MOVCA     /SAVE THE RESULT IN C.
         INXH      /INCREMENT H&L TO THE LAST WORD.
         MOVAM     /MOVE THE LAST WORD TO A.
         ADCB      /ADD B AND THE CARRY TO IT.
         MOVBA     /SAVE THE MOST SIGNIFICANT BYTE
         RNC       /OF THE RESULT IN B. RETURN IF
ERROR,   •         /THE CARRY IS ZERO. IF THE CARRY
         •         /IS A ONE, THE RESULT OF THE
         •         /ADDITION IS GREATER THAN 32 BITS
         •         /(4 BYTES). SO PERFORM SOME "ERROR
         RET       /INSTRUCTIONS" AND THEN RETURN.

DATA,    207       /THE FOUR DATA BYTES ARE
         051       /STORED IN MEMORY HERE.
         372
         165
```

Example 5-1, one ADD- and three ADC-type instructions were required to add four-byte numbers. To add five-byte numbers, would
an additional ADD- or ADC-type instruction be required? An additional ADC-type instruction would be required. The best solution
to this problem would be to write a general-purpose subroutine,
where large or small numbers can be added together as the situation
requires.

It was demonstrated in the 0.200-second time-delay subroutine
(Example 3-4) that arguments (the number of times that the 0.200-
second loop is executed) can be passed to the subroutine. This same
technique can be used to "tell" a multiprecision addition subroutine
how many eight-bit bytes are in each number that is to be added.
Since the number of data bytes will be variable, it would be ad-

vantageous to add together two numbers as they reside in sequential memory locations, since under some circumstances, there might not be enough general-purpose registers to store all of the bytes in one of the numbers. Therefore, some method will have to be developed to access two different areas of memory at the same time, since each number that is to be added will be stored in a different section of memory. Has there already been an example in which two different sections of memory were accessed simultaneously? Yes, when data values were moved from one section of memory to another using STAXD and LDAXD instructions (Example 4-1). A diagram of the movement of data during the addition of multiprecision numbers would appear as shown in Fig. 5-1.

The program will have to obtain a data value from one section of memory, add the content of another memory location to the value, and then store the result back in memory. The result is stored in place of one of the numbers that was just added. A subroutine that can add these variable-length numbers is shown in Example 5-2.

In this subroutine, register pair H is used to address the memory region where one of the numbers is stored, and register pair D is used to address the memory region where the other number is

Example 5-2: A Multiprecision Addition Subroutine

```
/THIS SUBROUTINE MUST BE ENTERED WITH THE FOLLOWING
/CONDITIONS. REGISTER PAIR H POINTS TO THE LEAST
/SIGNIFICANT BYTE OF ONE WORD AND REGISTER PAIR
/D POINTS TO THE LEAST SIGNIFICANT BYTE OF THE
/OTHER WORD. BOTH WORDS ARE STORED WTH THE LEAST
/SIGNIFICANT BYTE IN THE LOWEST MEMORY LOCATION.
/THE CONTENT OF THE C REGISTER EQUALS THE NUMBER
/OF BYTES TO BE ADDED (1–256 DECIMAL).


START,    LDAXD    /GET THE FIRST BYTE USING D&E AS A POINTER.
          ADDM     /ADD THE CONTENT OF MEMORY ADDRESSED
STRT1,    MOVMA    /BY H&L AND THEN STORE IT BACK IN MEMORY.
          INXH     /INCREMENT THE POINTERS TO THE NEXT
          INXD     /SIGNIFICANT BYTE OF THE NUMBERS.
          DCRC     /DECREMENT THE BYTE COUNTER.
          JZ       /DONE ALL THE BYTES YET? YES, THEN
          CHKCRY   /CHECK THE CARRY FOR AN "OVERFLOW"
          0        /ERROR.
AGAIN,    LDAXD    /OTHERWISE, GET THE NEXT BYTE USING D&E.
          ADCM     /ADD-WITH-CARRY THE CONTENT OF MEMORY.
          JMP      /THEN SAVE THE RESULT, INCREMENT THE
          STRT1    /MEMORY ADDRESSES, AND DECREMENT THE
          0        /BYTE COUNTER.
CHKCRY,   RNC      /IF THE CARRY IS A LOGIC ZERO, THEN
          •        /RETURN. OTHERWISE, SIGNAL THE MAIN
          •        /PROGRAM THAT THE RESULT IS LARGER
          •        /THAN THE ALLOCATED STORAGE SPACE.
          RET      /THEN RETURN FROM THE SUBROUTINE.
```

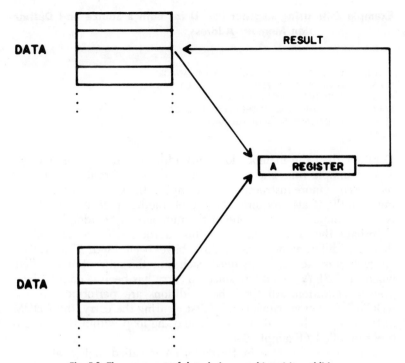

DATA

RESULT

A REGISTER

DATA

Fig. 5-1. The movement of data during a multiprecision addition.

stored. The result of the addition is stored in the memory locations addressed by register pair H. Note that an ADD-type instruction still has to be used at the beginning of the subroutine to perform the addition of the LSBYs, because the carry must not be involved in this first addition. Remember, when register pair D is used to address memory locations for data transfer instructions, the data source (destination) must be the A register. Thus, one eight-bit byte must be moved to register A from the location addressed by register pair D before the mathematical operation can be performed. The content of the memory location addressed by register pair H is then added to the content of the A register with the ADDM or ADCM instruction. The result of the addition is then stored in the memory location addressed by register pair H. Because the memory location addressed by register pair H is both the source and destination for data, the number previously stored in these memory locations is replaced with a byte of the result from the addition. The addition could have been performed in a slightly different manner and the same result obtained.

If the instructions in Example 5-3 were used, the result would have been stored in the memory locations addressed by register pair

Example 5-3: Using Register Pair D for Both a Source and Destination Memory Address

```
    •
    •
MOVBM   /LOAD B WITH THE CONTENT OF MEMORY.
LDAXD   /LOAD A WITH MEMORY ADDRESSED BY D&E.
ADDB    /ADD THE CONTENT OF B TO A.
STAXD   /SAVE THE SUM IN THE MEMORY LOCATION
    •   /ADDRESSED BY REGISTER PAIR D.
    •
```

D rather than the memory locations addressed by register pair H, as in Example 5-2. The disadvantage of this subroutine is that it requires one more instruction to accomplish the same task and, more importantly, it also requires the use of another register, the B register, to temporarily store one of the numbers to be added.

Perhaps the only limitation of this subroutine (Example 5-2) is that two different add instructions have been used. The ADDM instruction is executed only once, each time the subroutine is called, when the LSBYs are added, since no carry has been generated by a previous addition. All the other additions are performed by the ADCM instruction. However, by first clearing the carry, the ADCM instruction can be used exclusively and the loop within the subroutine simplified (Example 5-4).

When the subroutine in Example 5-4 is called, a logical exclusive-OR between the A register and itself is performed. This causes

Example 5-4: Elimination of the ADDM Instruction From the Subroutine (Example 5-2)

```
/ENTER THIS SUBROUTINE WITH THE FOLLOWING CONDITIONS.
/H&L POINT TO THE LSBY OF ONE NUMBER. D&E POINT TO
/THE LSBY OF THE OTHER NUMBER. BOTH NUMBERS ARE
/STORED WITH THE LSBYS IN THE LOWEST MEMORY LO-
/CATIONS. C = NUMBER OF BYTES TO ADD (1–256).

START,   XRAA    /CLEAR A AND THE CARRY TO ZERO.
STRT1,   LDAXD   /GET A BYTE FROM MEMORY ADDRESSED BY D&E.
         ADCM    /ADD THE CONTENT OF MEMORY ADDRESSED
         MOVMA   /BY H&L, THEN STORE THE RESULT BACK IN
         INXH    /MEMORY. INCREMENT BOTH DATA BUFFER
         INXD    /POINTERS.
         DCRC    /DECREMENT THE BYTE COUNTER.
         JNZ     /ADDED ALL THE BYTES? NO, THEN
         STRT1   /ADD THE CONTENT OF THE NEXT TWO
         0       /MEMORY LOCATIONS.
CHKCRY,  RNC     /IF THE CARRY IS A LOGIC ZERO,
         •       /RETURN. OTHERWISE SIGNAL THE MAIN
         •       /PROGRAM THAT THE RESULT IS LARGER
         •       /THAN THE ALLOCATED STORAGE SPACE.
         RET     /THEN RETURN FROM THE SUBROUTINE.
```

the A register to be cleared to zero and, more importantly, it also causes the carry to be cleared to a logic 0. Therefore, by including the XRAA instruction in the subroutine, the ADCM is the only addition instruction required.

When this subroutine is first called, the XRAA instruction causes the carry to be cleared so that the ADCM instruction adds a carry of zero to the sum of the two LSBYs. Of course, the second time through the loop, the carry (logic 1 or logic 0) is added to the result, since the 8080 now jumps to STRT1, rather than to START, where the carry would be cleared. The largest number that can be added by calling this subroutine is 256 bytes long. Why does the subroutine limit the numbers to this length? This is because only one eight-bit register, the C register, is used as the byte counter. However, this subroutine can still accommodate even the largest numbers (2^{2048}, or numbers that are 2048 bits long; $2^{333} > 1 \times 10^{100}$).

What must the content of the C register be, when the START subroutine in Example 5-4 is called, for a 256-byte number to be added? The C register must contain 000 (00). After the LSBYs of the numbers are added and stored in memory, the content of the C register is decremented from 000 (00) to 377 (FF). Since this is a nonzero result, the loop in the START subroutine is executed an additional 255 times. This means that the instructions within the loop are executed 256 times.

Note that when the content of the C register is decremented to zero, the instructions at the end of the subroutine test the carry for a logic-1 condition. If the carry is a logic 0, the 8080 simply returns from the subroutine. If the carry is a logic 1, additional instructions must be executed to either save the final carry or notify the microcomputer operator that the result stored in memory is not the proper result.

The only deficiency of Example 5-4 is that the result is stored in the same memory locations that are used to store one of the numbers being added. It would be advantageous to store the result in a third area of memory so that an addend is not "lost." Therefore, register pairs B, D, and H will all be used to hold memory addresses. These addresses will be the two addresses of the memory locations where the numbers to be added are stored, and the address of the memory locations where the result will be stored. Even so, a byte counter is still needed—the C register in Example 5-4. The only register not being used to hold an address is the A register. However, it cannot be used to hold the byte count because it is used to add the two numbers together. How can this improved subroutine be written?

When the subroutine in Example 5-5 is called, not only must three addresses have been loaded into register pairs B, D, and H, but a byte count must have also been loaded into the A register. When the

8080 begins executing the subroutine, the A register and the flags are immediately pushed onto the stack (PUSHPSW). After the PUSHPSW instruction is executed, the A register and carry are cleared. The content of memory addressed by register pair D is then moved to the A register, the content of memory addressed by register pair H is then added to the content of the A register, and the result is stored in the memory location addressed by register pair B. All three memory addresses are then incremented by 1. The XTHL instruction then causes the content of register pair H to be exchanged with the last two bytes on the stack. What are the last two bytes on the stack?

Example 5-5: A Multiprecision Addition Subroutine With Three Memory Addresses

```
/ENTER THIS SUBROUTINE WITH THE FOLLOWING CONDITIONS.
/H&L POINT TO THE LSBY OF THE FIRST NUMBER. D&E
/POINT TO THE LSBY OF THE SECOND NUMBER. BOTH NUM-
/BERS ARE STORED WITH THE LSBYS IN THE LOWEST MEMORY
/LOCATIONS. B&C POINT TO WHERE THE RESULT WILL BE
/STORED. ENTER WITH REGISTER A CONTAINING THE
/NUMBER OF EIGHT-BIT BYTES TO BE ADDED.

                        /FIRST SAVE THE BYTE COUNT IN A
START,      PUSHPSW     /AND THE FLAGS ON THE STACK.
            XRAA        /CLEAR A AND THE CARRY TO ZERO.
AGAIN,      LDAXD       /GET ONE OF THE BYTES TO BE ADDED.
            ADCM        /ADD THE OTHER BYTE AND THE CARRY TO IT.
            STAXB       /THEN SAVE THE RESULT IN MEMORY.
            INXH        /INCREMENT ALL THREE MEMORY ADDRESSES.
            INXD
            INXB
            XTHL        /EXCHANGE H&L AND THE TOP OF THE STACK.
            DCRH        /(H=A=BYTE COUNT). DECREMENT THE COUNT.
            XTHL        /RESTORE H&L AND A AND THE FLAGS.
            JNZ         /DID WE DECREMENT H (REALLY A)
            AGAIN       /TO 000? IF NOT, ADD ANOTHER
            0           /TWO BYTES.
            JC          /WHEN ALL THE BYTES HAVE BEEN ADDED,
            CHKCRY      /CHECK THE CARRY FOR AN "OVERFLOW"
            0           /FROM THE LAST ADDITION.
            POPPSW      /THE CARRY IS A 0, POP THE PSW OFF
            RET         /OF THE STACK AND THEN RETURN.
CHKCRY,     •           /THE CARRY IS A LOGIC ONE,
            •           /SO NOTIFY THE MAIN
            •           /PROGRAM THAT THE RESULT IS LARGER
            •           /THAN THE ALLOCATED STORAGE SPACE.
            POPPSW      /THEN POP THE PSW OFF OF THE STACK
            RET         /AND RETURN FROM THE SUBROUTINE.
```

When the subroutine is called, a return address is pushed onto the stack. The first instruction in the subroutine is a PUSHPSW, so the last two bytes on the stack are the A register and the flags. When the XTHL instruction is executed, the content of register pair H is put on the stack, the previous content of the A register is loaded into the H register, and the flags are loaded into the L register *from the stack*. The content of the H register, now the byte count, is then decremented by 1 when the DCRH instruction is executed. After decrementing the content of the H register, the content of register pair H and the last two bytes on the stack are again exchanged. At this point, it would appear as if nothing had taken place between the stack and register pair H, the two XTHL instructions having no *net* effect. However, the *result* of the DCRH instruction (decrement the byte count) is indicated by the state of the zero flag, which is then tested by a JNZ instruction. If the content of the byte count is nonzero, the JNZ to AGAIN is executed.

When the byte count is finally decremented to zero, the JNZ to AGAIN is no longer executed. This means that all of the bytes in the multiprecision number have been added, so the 8080 needs to return from the subroutine. However, before it does return from the subroutine, the state of the carry must be tested to see if there was a final carry from the addition of the two MSBYs. If there is no final carry, the JC to CHKCRY is not executed. Instead, the A register and the flags are popped off of the stack (POPPSW), and the return (RET) instruction is executed. Why was the POPPSW instruction executed? We really don't care about the values popped off of the stack into the A register and the flags, but if the POPPSW instruction was not executed, these last two bytes on the stack would have been used by the RET instruction as a return address. This would cause the program to continue at some unknown address, the real return address being left on the stack. Therefore, it is extremely important to have as many pop instructions as there are push instructions and *vice versa*. *Stack operations are not trivial!*

If the carry was a logic 1 after the addition of the two MSBYs was performed, the JC to CHKCRY would have been executed. At CHKCRY additional instructions would be required to save the final carry or indicate to the microcomputer operator that the carry is in a logic-1 state, and that the result stored in memory is not the correct result.

Why is it that the byte count, which was temporarily contained in the H register, can be decremented without affecting the carry flag, which reflects the result of the last addition performed, and which must be preserved for the next ADCM instruction? The only reason that the carry flag is not affected by the DCRH instruction is that the decrement instructions affect all of the flags *except* the carry flag. The only way that you would know this is by looking up the characteristics of the DCR-type instructions in one of the 8080 manufacturers' catalogs. This brings up an important point. When you are using a new instruction, look up the instruction in the 8080 specifications and find out exactly what the instruction does and what flags are, or are not, affected by the instruction when it is executed.

You have now seen a number of multiprecision addition subroutines that you can use to solve your own software problems. In the next section of this chapter, we will apply what we have learned from the addition subroutines to multiprecision subtraction subroutines.

INTEGER SUBTRACTION

A number of subtraction examples were listed in Chapter 2 (Examples 2-19, 2-21, 2-23, and 2-25). These examples showed how single- and double-precision numbers can be subtracted from one another. However, as larger and larger numbers are subtracted from one another, the 8080's general-purpose registers will not be able to store the numbers being subtracted. Instead, the general-purpose registers will be used to store the memory addresses where the two numbers that are to be subtracted are stored.

In Example 5-2, an ADDM and an ADCM instruction had to be executed so that the carry was not added to the sum of the LSBYs. The subroutine listed in Example 5-4 contained fewer instructions because the carry was cleared to a logic 0 by an XRAA instruction. An XRAA instruction can also be executed to clear the carry in a multiprecision subtraction subroutine (Example 5-6).

Example 5-6: A Multiprecision Subtraction Subroutine

```
/ENTER THIS SUBROUTINE WITH THE FOLLOWING CONDITIONS.
/H&L POINT TO THE LSBY OF ONE NUMBER. D&E POINT TO
/THE LSBY OF THE OTHER NUMBER. BOTH NUMBERS ARE
/STORED WITH THE LSBYS IN THE LOWEST MEMORY LO-
/CATIONS. C = NUMBER OF BYTES TO SUBTRACT (1–256).

MSUB,     XRAA      /CLEAR A AND THE CARRY TO 0.
MSUB1,    LDAXD     /GET A BYTE FROM MEMORY ADDRESSED BY D&E.
          SBBM      /SUBTRACT THE CONTENT OF MEMORY ADDRESSED
          MOVMA     /BY H&L, THEN STORE THE RESULT BACK IN
          INXH      /MEMORY. INCREMENT BOTH DATA BUFFER
          INXD      /POINTERS.
          DCRC      /DECREMENT THE BYTE COUNTER.
          JNZ       /SUBTRACTED ALL THE BYTES? NO,
          MSUB1     /SO SUBTRACT THE CONTENT OF THE
          0         /NEXT TWO MEMORY LOCATIONS.
CHKCRY,   RNC       /IF THE CARRY IS A LOGIC ZERO, RETURN.
          •         /OTHERWISE, SIGNAL THE MAIN
          •         /PROGRAM THAT A FINAL
          •         /BORROW HAS OCCURRED.
          RET       /THEN RETURN FROM THE SUBROUTINE.
```

When the MSUB subroutine is called, the A register and the carry are cleared when the XRAA instruction is executed. The A register is then loaded with the content of memory addressed by register pair D. The content of memory addressed by register pair H is then subtracted from the content of the A register. The first time that the SBBM instruction is executed, the carry is a logic 0, so the state of the carry will not affect the result of subtracting the two LSBYs. If the MSUB1 loop is executed any additional times, the carry will be subtracted from the content of the A register and, in addition, the carry will reflect whether or not a *borrow* has occurred. After the subtraction is performed, the result is stored in the memory location addressed by register pair H. This result byte writes over the number that was just subtracted from the content of the A register. After saving the subtraction result in memory, the memory addresses in register pairs D and H are incremented, and the byte count is decremented. At this point, a decision is made indicating whether or not the MSUB1 loop will be executed again. If the byte count is nonzero after the DCRC instruction is executed, the 8080 executes a JNZ to MSUB1. If the byte count is decremented to zero, the 8080 will return from the subroutine if the subtraction of the two MSBYs did not produce a borrow. If the carry is a logic 1, the RNC instruction will not be executed when the C register is decremented to zero. Instead, the instructions starting at ERROR will be executed. If a borrow does occur, a larger number has been subtracted from a smaller number. Therefore, the instructions at ERROR can be used to pass an argument back to the main program, or indicate to the microcomputer operator that a borrow has occurred.

The same techniques used in the multiprecision addition subroutine (Example 5-5) can also be used in a multiprecision subtraction subroutine. In this way, the result of the subtraction is saved in a third section of memory, so that both the minuend and subtrahend are preserved. To do this, register pair D contains the memory address that points to the minuend stored in memory, register pair H points to the subtrahend, and register pair B points to the result. The A register is used again as the byte counter, and this register contains the number of bytes in the two numbers that are to be subtracted. The subroutine listed in Example 5-7 has these features incorporated in it. This multiprecision subtraction subroutine is the same as the multiprecision addition subroutine (Example 5-5) except that an SBBM instruction has been used instead of an ADCM instruction.

When the subroutine is called, the A register must contain the number of bytes in the numbers being subtracted, and register pairs B, D, and H must contain memory addresses for the result, minuend, and subtrahend. The first instruction in the subroutine (PUSHPSW) saves the byte count, contained in the A register, on the stack. The A register and the carry are then cleared to zero by the XRAA instruction. The content of the memory location addressed by register pair D is then moved to the A register, and the content of memory addressed by register pair H is subtracted from the content of A. The result of the subtraction is saved in the memory location addressed by register pair B. The three memory addresses are then incremented.

By executing the XTHL instruction, the last two bytes on the stack, the A register and flags, are exchanged with the content of register pair H. Therefore, after the XTHL instruction is executed, the address from register pair H is on the stack, and the values present in register A and the flags are found in register pair H. In this way, we have been able to use stack locations in place of registers. The byte count, now in register H, is decremented by 1 when the DCRH instruction is executed, and it is put back on the stack, along with the flag byte, when the second XTHL instruction is executed. At the same time, the address that was originally stored in register pair H is retrieved by the XTHL instruction. The zero flag (set or cleared by the DCRH instruction) is then tested by the JNZ to AGAIN instruction.

If the byte count has been decremented to a nonzero value, the 8080 jumps back to AGAIN. This permits two additional bytes to be subtracted. If the byte count is decremented to zero, the carry flag is tested by software instructions. If the carry is zero, indicating that a borrow did not occur when the two MSBYs were subtracted, the A register and the flags are popped off of the stack, and then the 8080 returns to the main program. If the carry is a logic 1, which means that a borrow did occur when the two MSBYs were subtracted, the JC to CHKCRY is executed. These instructions can be used to indicate to the main program that a larger number has been subtracted from a smaller number.

Do you know why the subroutine could not be ended with the following sequence of instructions?

```
        •
        •
      XTHL
      DCRH
      XTHL
      RZ
      JMP
      AGAIN
      0
```

You should realize that this sequence of instructions does not check for a borrow after the two MSBYs are subtracted, and these

Example 5-7: A Multiprecision Subtraction Subroutine That Accesses Three Different Sections of Memory

```
/ENTER THIS SUBROUTINE WITH THE FOLLOWING CONDITIONS.
/H&L POINT TO THE LSBY OF THE SUBTRAHEND. D&E
/POINT TO THE LSBY OF THE MINUEND. BOTH NUM-
/BERS ARE STORED WITH THE LSBYS IN THE LOWEST MEMORY
/LOCATIONS. B&C POINT TO WHERE THE RESULT WILL BE
/STORED. ENTER WITH REGISTER A CONTAINING THE
/NUMBER OF EIGHT-BIT BYTES TO BE SUBTRACTED.
```

```
                      /FIRST SAVE THE BYTE COUNT IN A
START,    PUSHPSW     /AND THE FLAGS ON THE STACK.
          XRAA        /CLEAR A AND THE CARRY TO ZERO.
AGAIN,    LDAXD       /GET ONE OF THE MINUEND BYTES.
          SBBM        /SUBTRACT ONE OF THE SUBTRAHEND BYTES.
          STAXB       /THEN SAVE THE RESULT IN MEMORY.
          INXH        /INCREMENT ALL THREE MEMORY ADDRESSES.
          INXD
          INXB
          XTHL        /EXCHANGE H&L AND THE TOP OF THE STACK.
          DCRH        /(H=A=BYTE COUNT). DECREMENT THE COUNT.
          XTHL        /RESTORE H&L AND A AND THE FLAGS.
          JNZ         /DID WE DECREMENT H (REALLY A)
          AGAIN       /TO 000? IF NOT, SUBTRACT ANOTHER
          0           /TWO BYTES.
          JC          /IF THE CARRY IS A 1, THEN A LARGER
          CHKCRY      /NUMBER HAS BEEN SUBTRACTED FROM A
          0           /SMALLER NUMBER, SO TELL THE MAIN PROGRAM
          POPPSW      /THE CARRY IS A 0, POP THE PSW OFF
          RET         /OF THE STACK AND THEN RETURN.
CHKCRY,   •           /THE CARRY IS A LOGIC ONE, SO PRINT
          •           /AN ERROR MESSAGE OR PERFORM SOME
          •           /OTHER ACTION.
          POPPSW      /THEN GET THE PSW OFF OF THE STACK
          RET         /AND RETURN FROM THE SUBROUTINE.
```

instructions also do not "clean up" the stack before the return instruction is executed. When the subroutine is called, the A register and the flags are pushed onto the stack. Therefore, before *any* return instruction is executed, these values must be popped off of the stack. If they are not, these values will be used as the 16-bit return address when the RZ instruction is executed. This will cause the program to return to an unknown point in the program.

All of the multiprecision addition and subtraction programs and subroutines have obeyed a simple rule that was used in the Basic Instructions chapter: *when multibyte numbers are being added or subtracted, the least-significant byte (LSBY) of the number must be added or subtracted first.* When this is done, the carry can be added to or subtracted from the more significant bytes of the number.

In the next section of this chapter, single and multiprecision multiplication subroutines will be discussed. These subroutines are far more complex than the addition and subtraction programs and subroutines that have been discussed in this and previous chapters. However, the methods used to perform multiplication are very similar to the methods you already know.

INTEGER MULTIPLICATION

Most programmers realize that numbers can be multiplied by performing successive additions, and that numbers can be divided by performing successive subtractions. A simple multiplication subroutine that multiplies a 16-bit number by another 16-bit number to produce a 16-bit result is listed in Example 5-8. This subroutine performs the multiplication of the two numbers by performing successive additions.

Ordinarily, multiplication subroutines like this are not used because of the long program execution times that they may require. Suppose the numbers 2046 and 3 were to be multiplied. If the multiplication of these numbers is performed by the successive addition subroutine, one of these numbers would have to act as a counter to keep track of the number of successive additions. For instance, the number 2046 might be added to itself thrice:

$$(2046 + 2046 + 2046) = 2046 \times 3$$

This means that the addition loop within the subroutine would have to be executed only three times. However, this requires the binary equivalent for 3 to be loaded into register pair D, and the binary equivalent for 2046 to be loaded into register pair H. What will happen if the value 2046 is loaded into register pair D, and the value 3 is loaded into register pair H? Since register pair D contains the count, the loop within the subroutine would be executed 2046 times, so that 3 is added to itself 2045 times! Just by switching the register pairs in which these numbers are stored, the loop will be executed either three or 2046 times. This is unsatisfactory because of the long time delays that this can cause. Therefore, more sophisticated multiplication subroutines are commonly used.

Examine the following multiplication of 203 by 114. This multiplication may be thought of as $(4 \times 203) + (10 \times 203) + (100 \times 203)$. Notice that when 203 is multiplied by the tens or hundreds digit, both 1s in this example, the result of their multiplication is shifted to the left to increase the significance of the result. This is done because the numbers in the multiplier increase by powers of ten as the numbers are read from right to left. Therefore, the result of the multiplication must also increase by powers of ten.

Example 5-8: Multiplication by Successive Addition

/THIS IS AN UNSIGNED INTEGER MULTIPLY SUB-
/ROUTINE THAT "USES" SUCCESSIVE ADDITIONS.
/ENTER THIS SUBROUTINE WITH H&L CONTAINING ONE OF
/THE 16-BIT NUMBERS TO BE MULTIPLIED AND D&E CON-
/TAINING THE OTHER 16-BIT NUMBER. RETURN FROM THE
/SUBROUTINE WITH THE 16-BIT RESULT IN B&C. L, E,
/AND C ARE THE LSBYS AND H, D, AND B ARE THE MSBYS.

MULTP,	LXIB	/SET THE REGISTER PAIR THAT WILL
	000	/CONTAIN THE RESULT TO 000 000.
	000	
MULA,	MOVAE	/D&E ARE USED AS THE WORD COUNT-
	ORAD	/ER. IS THE COUNT = 000 000 ?
	RZ	/YES, RETURN WITH THE RESULT IN B&C.
	XRAA	/NO, CLEAR A AND THE CARRY TO 0.
	MOVAL	/GET THE LSBY OF THE NUMBER TO ADD.
	ADDC	/ADD THE LSBY OF THE PARTIAL RESULT
	MOVCA	/AND SAVE THE RESULT IN C.
	MOVAH	/THEN GET THE MSBY OF THE NUMBER TO ADD.
	ADCB	/ADD B AND THE CARRY TO IT.
	MOVBA	/SAVE THE MSBY OF THE RESULT IN B.
	DCXD	/DECREMENT THE MULTIPLIER IN D&E.
	JMP	/THEN SEE IF THE MULTIPLICAND
	MULA	/HAS BEEN ADDED TO ITSELF THE
	0	/REQUIRED NUMBER OF TIMES.

$$
\begin{array}{r}
203 \\
\times\ 114 \\
\hline
812 \\
203 \\
+\ 203 \\
\hline
23142
\end{array}
$$

While our shorthand notation of the preceding multiplication does not show them, there are understood to be 0s in the results of the multiplication. This clearly shows "power-of-ten" multiplication:

$$
\begin{array}{r}
203 \\
\times\ 114 \\
\hline
812 \\
2030 \\
+\ 20300 \\
\hline
23142
\end{array}
$$

This same idea is applied to binary multiplication:

$$
\begin{array}{r}
0110 \\
\times\ 0011 \\
\hline
0110 \\
0110 \\
0000 \\
+\ 0000 \\
\hline
0010010 = 18_{10}
\end{array}
\qquad
\begin{array}{r}
6_{10} \\
\times\ 3_{10} \\
\hline
18_{10}
\end{array}
$$

As you can see, the results of the multiplication are the same, whether the multiplication is performed in the decimal or in the binary numbering system because the result, 0010010, equals $(1 \times 16) + (1 \times 2)$, or 18. This is the first example of binary multiplication. Since binary digits may be either 1 or 0, the multiplier must be examined on a bit-by-bit basis for a 1 or a 0. Starting from right to left, the multiplier is examined, one bit at a time, for a 1. If a 1 is found, the multiplicand is added to the accumulating result in the proper position. Remember that there is really no "multiplication" as such, as in the decimal multiplication example. A 1 simply indicates that the multiplicand must be added to the accumulating result. Why? Remember, the multiplication of any number by 1 is the same as using the number alone; i.e., $1 \times X = X$.

If required, the multiplier can also be examined from left to right, rather than from right to left. This means that the MSB of the multiplier is examined first. As bits to the right of the MSB are examined, the multiplicand would also have to be shifted to the right. This is shown in Example 5-9.

Example 5-9: A Decimal and Binary Multiplication, Where the MSB of the Multiplier is Examined First

$$
\begin{array}{r}
43_{10} \\
\times\ 53_{10} \\
\hline
215 \\
+\ 129 \\
\hline
2279_{10}
\end{array}
\qquad
\begin{array}{r}
00101011 \\
\times\ 00110101 \\
\hline
00000000 \\
00000000 \\
00101011 \\
00101011 \\
00000000 \\
00101011 \\
00000000 \\
+\qquad 00101011 \\
\hline
000100011100111 = 2279_{10}
\end{array}
$$

To check the result of the binary multiplication, $(1 \times 2048) + (1 \times 128) + (1 \times 64) + (1 \times 32) + (1 \times 4) + (1 \times 2) + (1 \times 1) = 2279_{10}$.

Which method is better, shifting the numbers to the left or to the right? It really does not matter whether the multiplier is shifted to the left or to the right as long as the *partial result* or *accumulated result*, or *the number that the multiplicand is added to*, is shifted in the same direction.

In the Basic Instructions chapter, methods were discussed that could be used to detect whether or not a bit was a logic 1. Rotate instructions that can be used to perform the shifting operation were also discussed, and the changes in the contents of the A register as the rotate instructions were executed were also shown. Therefore, the development of a subroutine that performs a multiplication using the test-and-shift method is relatively simple.

Example 5-10: An Eight-Bit by Eight-Bit Multiplication Subroutine

```
/THE CONTENT OF REGISTER D IS THE MULTIPLIER AND REG-
/ISTER E CONTAINS THE MULTIPLICAND. THE 16-BIT  RESULT
/WILL BE STORED IN REGISTER PAIR B (B=MSBY,  C=LSBY).
/THE NUMBERS TO BE MULTIPLIED MUST BE IN REGISTERS
/D AND E BEFORE THE SUBROUTINE IS CALLED.

MP88,    LXIB     /SET THE REGISTER PAIR THAT WILL BE
         000      /USED TO STORE THE RESULT OF THE
         000      /MULIPLICATION TO 000 000 (0000).
         MVIL     /LOAD THE L REGISTER WITH THE
         010      /NUMBER OF BITS IN THE MULTIPLIER.
NXTBIT,  MOVAD    /MOVE THE MULTIPLIER INTO A.
         RAR      /ROTATE ONE BIT OF IT INTO THE CARRY.
         MOVDA    /SAVE THE MULTIPLIER BACK IN D.
         JNC      /IF THE CARRY IS A LOGIC 0, JUST
         NOADD    /ROTATE THE PARTIAL RESULT. IF IT IS
         0        /1, ADD THE MULTIPLICAND TO THE RESULT.
         MOVAB    /GET THE MSBY OF THE PARTIAL RESULT.
         ADDE     /ADD THE MULTIPLICAND.
         MOVBA    /SAVE THE RESULT BACK IN B.
NOADD,   MOVAB    /NOW ROTATE THE 16-BIT RESULT
         RAR      /ONCE TO THE RIGHT.
         MOVBA
         MOVAC    /NOW ROTATE ANY CARRY FROM THE MSBY
         RAR      /INTO THE MSB OF THE LSBY.
         MOVCA    /SAVE THE LSBY BACK IN C.
         DCRL     /HAVE ALL 8 BITS OF THE MULTIPLIER
         JNZ      /BEEN TESTED YET? IF NOT, JUMP
         NXTBIT   /BACK AND TEST ANOTHER ONE.
         0
         RET      /YES, ALL THE BITS HAVE BEEN TESTED.
                  /RETURN WITH THE RESULT IN B&C.
```

The first instruction in this subroutine (Example 5-10) clears register pair B, the register pair that will be used to store the 16-bit result of the multiplication. The L register is then loaded with 010 (08), the number of times that the multiplication loop within the subroutine is to be executed. This is also the number of bits within the multiplier that must be tested for a logic 1 or a logic 0. After these registers are initialized, the content of the D register, which is the multiplier, is moved to the A register, rotated to the right once, and the result is stored back in the D register. As a result of the RAR operation, the LSB of the A register (the multiplier) is rotated into the carry. If a logic 1 is rotated into the carry, the multiplicand must be added to the partial result. Therefore, the JNC to NOADD is not executed. If a logic 0 is rotated into the carry, the JNC to NOADD is executed, and no addition takes place.

If a 1 is rotated into the carry, the multiplicand is added to the partial result that is stored in register pair B. The content of the B register, where the MSBY of the result will be stored, is moved to the A register where the content of the E register, the multiplicand, is added to it by an ADDE instruction. After the addition of the multiplicand to the MSBY of the partial result, the entire 16-bit partial result stored in register pair B is rotated one bit to the right. The bit count contained in register L is then decremented, and if the result of this operation is nonzero, there are additional bits within the multiplier that must be tested.

If a logic 0 from the multiplier is rotated into the carry, the multiplicand must not be added to the partial result in register pair B. Therefore, the JNC to NOADD is executed, where the content of register pair B is rotated to the right, one bit position, even though the multiplicand was not added to the B register. The bit count contained in the L register is then decremented, and if the result is nonzero, another bit within the multiplier must be tested.

When the content of the L register is finally decremented to zero, all of the bits within the multiplier have been tested, and the 8080 can return from the subroutine with the 16-bit result of the multiplication contained in register pair B. The MSBY of the result is in the B register and the LSBY of the result is in the C register. Just to make certain that these 8080 operations are understood, let us examine the content of the registers as the subroutine is executed. The multiplication of 32_{10} by 5_{10} will be performed. Initially, B = 00000000, C = 00000000, L = 010, D = 00000101, and E = 00100000.

1. Get and rotate the multiplier, 00000101 (00000101 is rotated to 00000010; the carry is a 1).
2. Since the carry is a 1, add the multiplicand to the partial result and save the partial result in register pair B.

$$
\begin{array}{ll}
00000000 & \text{register B (partial result)} \\
+\,00100000 & \text{register D (multiplicand)} \\
\hline
00100000 &
\end{array}
$$

3. Now rotate the partial result that is stored in register pair B (00100000 00000000 rotates to 00010000 00000000).
4. Decrement the bit count; L now contains 007 (07), which is nonzero.
5. Get and rotate the multiplier, 00000010 (00000010 is rotated to 00000001; the carry is a 0).
6. Since the carry is a 0, just rotate the partial result; no addition is performed (00010000 00000000 rotates to 00001000 00000000).
7. Decrement the bit count; L now contains 006 (06), which is nonzero.
8. Get and rotate the multiplier, 00000001 (00000001 is rotated to 00000000; the carry is a 1).
9. Since the carry is a 1, add the multiplicand to the partial result and save the partial result in register pair B.

$$
\begin{array}{ll}
00001000 & \text{register B (partial result)} \\
\underline{+\,00100000} & \text{register D (multiplicand)} \\
00101000 &
\end{array}
$$

10. Now rotate the partial result that is stored in register pair B (00101000 00000000 rotates to 00010100 00000000).
11. Decrement the bit count; L now contains 005 (05), which is nonzero.

Since there are no more 1s in the multiplier, the only action that is performed by the 8080 for the remainder of the subroutine is the rotation of the partial result contained in register pair B. The effect of the rotate instructions on the content of register pair B, and the content of the L register, the bit count, are as follows:

Register Pair B	The L Register
00010100 00000000 rotates to 00001010 00000000;	L = 004 (04)
00001010 00000000 rotates to 00000101 00000000;	L = 003 (03)
00000101 00000000 rotates to 00000010 10000000;	L = 002 (02)
00000010 10000000 rotates to 00000001 01000000;	L = 001 (01)
00000001 01000000 rotates to 00000000 10100000;	L = 000 (00)

Now that the content of the L register has been decremented to zero, the 8080 returns from the MP88 subroutine (Example 5-10). The MSBY of the result is stored in the B register, and the LSBY of the result is stored in the C register. As you would expect, $5_{10} \times 32_{10} = 160_{10}$, or $5_8 \times 40_8 = 240_8$, and $240_8 = 160_{10} = 10100000_2$. Therefore, the result obtained from the multiplication is correct. You should now realize why the multiplicand was added to the MSBY of the partial list. It is eventually rotated to the right into the LSBY.

It has already been shown that the DADH instruction rotates the content of register pair H one bit to the left. Therefore, this instruction can be used in an eight-bit by eight-bit multiplication subroutine, as shown in Example 5-11.

Example 5-11: Using DADH Instructions in an Eight-Bit by Eight-Bit Multiplication Subroutine

```
/THE CONTENT OF THE C REGISTER IS THE MULTIPLICAND AND
/THE CONTENT OF THE D REGISTER IS THE MULTIPLIER. THE
/16-BIT RESULT WILL BE STORED IN REGISTER PAIR H (H=MSBY,
/L=LSBY). THE C AND D REGISTERS MUST BE LOADED
/BEFORE THE SUBROUTINE IS CALLED.

MP88A,    MVIA    /LOAD THE A REGISTER WITH THE NUMBER
          010     /OF BITS IN THE MULTIPLIER.
          MVIB    /SET THE MSBY OF REGISTER PAIR B
          000     /TO 000 (00).
          LXIH    /LOAD REGISTER PAIR H, WHICH WILL BE
          000     /USED TO STORE THE RESULT, TO 000
          000     /000 (0000).
NXTBIT,   XCHG    /MOVE THE MULTIPLIER IN D TO H.
          DADH    /ROTATE REGISTER PAIR H LEFT ONE BIT.
          XCHG    /GET THE MULTIPLIER BACK INTO D.
          JNC     /IF A ZERO IS ROTATED INTO THE CARRY,
          NOADD   /JUST ROTATE THE RESULT, OTHERWISE,
          0
          DADB    /ADD THE MULTIPLICAND TO THE RESULT.
NOADD,    DCRA    /HAVE ALL 8 BITS BEEN TESTED YET?
          RZ      /YES, THEN RETURN FROM THE SUBROUTINE.
          DADH    /NO, ROTATE THE RESULT IN H&L BY 1 BIT.
          JMP     /THEN TEST THE NEXT BIT IN THE MULTIPLIER.
          NXTBIT
          0
```

In Example 5-11, the multiplier is contained in the D register, the multiplicand is contained in the C register, and when the multiplication is complete, the result is stored in register pair H. When the subroutine is called, the A register is loaded with the bit count, 010 (08). The B register, the MSBY of register pair B, is loaded with 000. The C register, the LSBY of register pair B, already contains the multiplicand. This means that a DADB instruction can be executed to add the multiplicand to the partial result in register pair H. The LXIH instruction clears register pair H because this is the register pair that will be used to hold the partial and the final result.

At NXTBIT, the contents of register pairs D and H are exchanged. The multiplier that was in the D register is now in the H register. It does not matter what is moved from the E register to the L register. The partial result, in register pair H, is now in register pair D. By using a DADH instruction, the multiplier is "shifted" one bit position to the left by adding register pair H to itself. The shifted multiplier bits are put back into register pair D when the second XCHG instruction is executed. After the shift operation is performed by the addition operation (DADH), the carry is either a 1 or a 0, reflecting the state of the MSB in register pair D prior to the XCHG, DADH, and XCHG program sequence. This type of shift is shown in Example 5-12.

Example 5-12: Shifting the Content of Register Pair D With XCHG and DADH Instructions

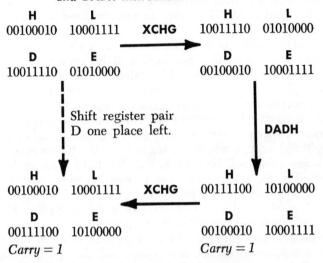

If the MSB of register pair D is a 0, the carry contains a 0 after the DADH instruction is executed. In this case, the multiplicand must not be added to the partial result contained in register pair H. Therefore, the JNC to NOADD is executed, and the bit count, which is contained in the A register, is decremented. If the count is decremented to zero, the 8080 returns from the subroutine with the result of the multiplication in register pair H. If the bit count is nonzero, the 8080 shifts the content of register pair H, the partial result, one bit position to the left by executing a DADH instruction. The next bit of the multiplier is then tested. Only when all eight bits of the multiplier have been tested will the subroutine be completed.

If, however, the carry is a logic 1 as a result of shifting a logic 1 from the MSB of register pair D into the carry, as explained previously, the content of register pair B, the multiplicand, is added to the content of register pair H, the partial result. After the addition, the 8080 continues executing the subroutine as described previously. Based on this description, you should now understand why the content of the B register must initially be set to 000 (00) when the C register contains the multiplicand. When the content of register pair B is added to the content of register pair H, the MSBY of register pair B must be zero.

As we mentioned previously, it does not matter whether the multiplier is shifted to the left or to the right. However, the partial sum must also be shifted in the same direction. In Example 5-10, both the multiplier and the partial sum were shifted to the right. In Example 5-11, a DADH instruction was used to shift the multiplier to the left, and a DADH instruction was also used to shift the partial result to the left.

As the last integer multiplication example, a 16-bit by 16-bit multiplication subroutine that produces a 32-bit result will be examined. In all of the previous multiplication examples, the multiplier, the multiplicand, and the result have been contained in the 8080's general-purpose registers. This is not possible in this new multiplication subroutine, because four registers would be needed to store the result, as well as two registers each for the multiplier and the multiplicand, and an additional register for the bit counter. Therefore, a few tricks will be used so that the R/W memory locations addressed by the stack pointer can be used for temporary storage.

At the beginning of the subroutine (Example 5-13), the A register is loaded with the number of bits in the multiplier, 16 (decimal), the number of times that the loop within the subroutine must be executed. Since register pair H is used to store 16 bits of the result, it is loaded with 000 000 (0000) and then pushed onto the stack. There are now four eight-bit storage locations that have been initialized to zero. Of course, as a result of the XCHG, DADH, and XCHG instruction sequence, the content of register pair D has been shifted one bit position to the left, and the carry now contains the value of the MSB contained in register pair D prior to the shift.

At this point in the program, a decision is made based on the state of the carry. If the carry is a 1, the multiplicand must be added to the 32-bit partial result, so the multiplicand contained in register pair B is added to the content of register pair H. If a carry occurs as a result of this 16-bit addition, a 1 must be added to the most-significant 16 bits of the result, currently on the stack. This is why, after loading register pair H with 000 000 (0000), the content of register pair H was pushed on the stack. If a carry does occur due to this addition, register pair H and the last two bytes on the stack are exchanged when the XTHL instruction is executed. The most-significant 16 bits of the result are then incremented by the INXH instruction, and then put back on the stack by the second XTHL instruction. Note that the addition of 1 to a number is the same as incrementing the number by 1. Also observe that at this

Example 5-13: A 16-Bit by 16-Bit Multiplication Subroutine (32-Bit Result)

```
/THIS SUBROUTINE MULTIPLIES THE CONTENT OF REGISTER
/PAIR D BY THE CONTENT OF REGISTER PAIR B. THE 32-
/BIT RESULT WILL BE CONTAINED IN REGISTER PAIR
/H (THE TWO LEAST SIGNIFICANT BYTES) AND REGISTER
/PAIR D (THE TWO MOST SIGNIFICANT BYTES).

MP1616,  MVIA      /LOAD THE A REGISTER WITH THE NUMBER
         020       /OF BITS IN THE MULTIPLIER.
         LXIH      /SET REGISTER PAIR H AND THE LAST
         000       /ENTRY ON THE STACK
         000       /TO 000 000 (0000).
         PUSHH
NXTBIT,  XCHG      /GET THE MULTIPLIER INTO H&L.
         DADH      /ROTATE THE MSB INTO THE CARRY.
         XCHG      /PUT THE MULTIPLIER BACK INTO D&E.
         JNC       /IF THE CARRY IS ZERO, DON'T ADD
         NOADD     /THE MULTIPLICAND TO THE PARTIAL
         0         /RESULT IN H&L AND THE STACK.
         DADB      /IF 1, ADD B&C TO H&L, RESULT IN H&L.
         JNC       /SHOULD A 1 BE ADDED TO THE TWO
         NOADD     /MOST SIGNIFICANT BYTES OF THE
         0         /RESULT STORED ON THE STACK?
         XTHL      /YES, EXCHANGE H&L AND THE STACK ENTRY.
         INXH      /INCREMENT THE 16-BIT MSBY BY ONE.
         XTHL      /THEN SAVE IT BACK ON THE STACK.
NOADD,   DCRA      /DECREMENT THE BIT COUNT.
         JNZ       /THE COUNT IS NONZERO, SO
         NOTEND    /TEST ANOTHER BIT OF THE MUL-
         0         /TIPLIER.
         POPD      /POP THE 16-BIT RESULT MSBY OFF THE STACK.
         RET       /THEN RETURN WITH THE RESULT IN D&E AND H&L.
NOTEND,  DADH      /ROTATE THE LSBY OF THE RESULT LEFT.
         XTHL      /GET THE MSBY INTO H&L.
         PUSHPSW   /SAVE THE COUNT AND CARRY ON THE STACK.
         DADH      /ROTATE THE MSBY ONCE TO THE LEFT.
         POPPSW    /POP THE COUNT AND CARRY OFF OF THE STACK.
         JNC       /WAS THERE A CARRY FROM THE LSBY?
         NOCMSB    /NO, THEN DO NOT ADD ONE TO THE MSBY.
         0
         INXH      /INCREMENT THE MSBY BY ONE.
NOCMSB,  XTHL      /PUT THE MSBY BACK ON THE STACK
         JMP       /AND TEST ANOTHER BIT IN THE MULTIPLIER.
         NXTBIT
         0
```

point in the program, push and pop instructions cannot be used to move the most-significant 16 bits of the result off of the stack and into a register pair simply because there is no register pair available to hold the 16-bit number. Therefore, the XTHL instruction is used. Remember, all stack transfers involve 16-bit values.

If the carry is a logic 0 as a result of rotating the multiplier contained in register pair D, the multiplicand is not added to the partial result. No matter what the state of the carry is, or whether or not the multiplicand is added to the partial result, the program always reaches the bit count decrement instruction (DCRA) at NOADD, where the count is operated upon. If the bit count is zero, the most-significant 16 bits are popped off of the stack and into register pair D, and the return instruction (RET) is executed. When this occurs, the most-significant 16 bits of the result are in register pair D, and the least-significant 16 bits of the result are in register pair H.

If the bit count is nonzero, the 32-bit partial result has to be shifted to the left by one bit position. This 32-bit shift is performed at NOTEND. The least-significant 16 bits of the result are in register pair H, and the most-significant 16 bits of the result are on the stack. Since the partial result has to be shifted to the left, the least-significant 16 bits must be shifted first. In this way, any carry from the LSBs may be shifted into the MSBs when they are shifted. The DADH instruction at NOTEND shifts the least-significant 16 bits to the left by one bit position. At this point in the program, the carry is either a logic 1 or a logic 0 as a result of the DADH instruction. After the DADH instruction is executed, the least-significant and most-significant 16 bits of the result are exchanged by the XTHL instruction. Now the problem is to shift the carry into the MSBs of the partial result. How is this done?

It is difficult, because the DAD-type instructions do not add the previous carry to the numbers currently being added. However, the DAD-type instructions do affect the carry, so that the carry produced by the first DADH instruction can be saved on the stack prior to executing a DADH instruction that shifts the 16 MSBs. For this reason, the PUSHPSW instruction is executed to save the carry on the stack. The 16 MSBs are then shifted to the left one bit position when the DADH instruction is executed. The carry from the previous DADH instruction must now be added to the 16 MSBs. The A register and the flags are popped off of the stack, and the 8080 makes a decision based on the state of the carry. If the carry is zero, no carry is added to the MSBs. If the carry is a 1, the most-significant 16 bits in register pair H must be incremented by 1. At NOCMSB (*NO* *C*arry into the *MSBs*), the 16 LSB are put back on the stack, and register pair H contains the 16 LSBs of the shifted partial result when the XTHL instruction is executed. After this XTHL instruction is executed, the 8080 jumps to NXTBIT, where the next bit in the multiplier is tested.

Although all the multiplication subroutines vary in size and complexity, they are all very similar in operation. Only Example 5-8 used successive additions, all the other multiplication subroutines used the test-and-shift method. More properly, this is called an *add-and-shift algorithm*. One point you should remember when working with multiplication programs is that the maximum number of bits in the result is equal to the number of bits in the multiplier plus the number of bits in the multiplicand. This means that if two 16-bit numbers are multiplied, a 32-bit result can be obtained. If a 16-bit and an eight-bit number are multiplied, the result can be up to 24 bits long. This is important to remember, so that enough storage space is allocated for the storage of the result. *This means that if Example 5-8 is used to multiply two 16-bit numbers, the 8080 will return from the subroutine with only the 16 LSBs of the result in register pair B. The 16 MSBs will be lost.*

INTEGER DIVISION

In the multiplication section of this chapter, Example 5-8 performed the multiplication operation by adding the multiplicand to itself the number of times specified by the multiplier. For instance,

$$15 = 5 \times 3 = 5 + 5 + 5 = 3 + 3 + 3 + 3 + 3$$

In division, the *divisor* can be *subtracted* from the *dividend a number of times*. Each time the subtraction is performed without producing a borrow, a count can be incremented by 1. This resulting count is the *integer quotient* of the division. When completed, any number less than the divisor, but greater than zero, is the *remainder* of the division. Therefore, in the division of 15 by 3,

$$15 - 3 = 12; \qquad \text{count} = 1$$
$$12 - 3 = 9; \qquad \text{count} = 2$$
$$9 - 3 = 6; \qquad \text{count} = 3$$
$$6 - 3 = 3; \qquad \text{count} = 4$$
$$3 - 3 = 0; \qquad \text{count} = 5$$

In this example, the quotient of the division is 5 and the remainder is 0. In the division of 7 by 4,

$$7 - 4 = 3 \qquad \text{count} = 1$$
$$3 - 4 = -1 \qquad \text{a borrow is generated}$$
$$4 + (-1) = 3 \qquad \text{remainder}$$

The quotient of this division is 1 and the remainder is 3. Of course, this procedure is very cumbersome for large numbers, so division is often performed by a shorthand method.

It does not matter whether the division is performed using decimal or binary numbers, the result of the division is the same because

Example 5-14: Decimal and Binary Division

```
        00101010                    042
101 ⌐ 11010010            5 ⌐ 210
      − 0                       − 0
      ────                      ────
       11                        21
      − 00                      − 20
      ────                      ────
       110                       10
      − 101                     − 10
      ─────                     ────
        11                        0
      − 00
      ────
       110
      − 101
      ─────
        10
       − 00
       ────
        101
       − 101
       ─────
         00
        − 00
        ────
          0
```

$00101010 = (1 \times 32) + (1 \times 8) + (1 \times 2) = 42_{10}$. Unfortunately, most division problems are not this simple. In the following division problem:

$$2151 \; \rceil \; 12{,}835$$

a quotient of either 5 or 6 might be tried first,

$$5 \times 2151 = 10{,}755$$
$$6 \times 2151 = 12{,}906$$

Only by multiplying the quotients and the divisor, and subtracting the result from the dividend, can the proper quotient be determined.

```
   12,835            12,835
 − 10,755          − 12,906
 ────────          ────────
    2,080             − 71
```

From this example, it is easy to see that the first part of the quotient must be 5.

In the binary division example in Example 5-14, the divisor was subtracted from the first bit of the dividend. If a borrow occurred as a result of the subtraction, which it did, a 0 is entered in the quotient, and the divisor is added to the result of the subtraction so that the original value of the dividend is restored. If no borrow occurs during the subtraction, a 1 is entered into the quotient, and the result of the subtraction is used for the next subtract-and-test process. This process is shown in Example 5-15.

Example 5-15: Using the Subtract-and-Test Method to Divide 1101-0010 by 101

$$101 \sqrt{ 11010010}$$

0011010010	Dividend.
− 1010000000	Divisor.
1001010010	Borrow occurs, quotient bit = 0,
+ 1010000000	so add divisor to result.
0011010010	
− 101000000	Shift divisor, try again.
1110010010	Borrow occurs, quotient bit = 0,
+ 101000000	so add divisor to result.
0011010010	
− 10100000	Shift divisor, try again.
0000110010	No borrow, quotient bit = 1.
− 1010000	No addition, shift divisor, try again.
1111100010	Borrow occurs, quotient bit = 0,
+ 1010000	so add divisor to result.
0000110010	
− 101000	Shift divisor, try again.
0000001010	No borrow, quotient bit = 1.
− 10100	No addition, shift divisor, try again.
1111110110	Borrow occurs, quotient bit = 0,
+ 10100	so add divisor to result.
0000001010	
− 1010	Shift divisor, try again.
0000000000	No borrow, quotient bit = 1.
− 101	No addition, shift divisor, try again.
1111111011	Borrow occurs, quotient bit = 0,
+ 101	so add divisor to result.
0000000000	

Eight shifts and subtractions have been performed, so the dividend has been divided by the quotient. The result is 00101010_2, the same as before.

One of the simplest integer division subroutines that can be written divides an eight-bit number by another eight-bit number. The result and remainder of this division are also eight bits. In Example 5-16, the dividend contained in the E register is divided by the divisor contained in the D register. The 8080 returns from the subroutine with the quotient in the H register and the remainder in the C register.

Example 5-16: An Eight-Bit by Eight-Bit Division Subroutine

```
/THIS IS A DIVISION SUBROUTINE THAT DIVIDES AN
/EIGHT-BIT NUMBER BY ANOTHER EIGHT-BIT NUMBER.
/THIS SUBROUTINE MUST BE CALLED WITH THE DIVISOR
/IN THE D REGISTER AND THE DIVIDEND IN THE E REGISTER.
/THE RESULT WILL BE CONTAINED IN THE H REGISTER
/WHEN THE 8080 RETURNS FROM THE SUBROUTINE.

DIV88,   LXIH     /LOAD THE L REGISTER WITH 010
         010      /(DECIMAL 8) AND LOAD THE H REGISTER
         000      /WITH 000 (THE RESULT WILL BE IN H).
         MVIC     /LOAD THE C REGISTER WITH 000, BECAUSE
         000      /PART OF THE DIVIDEND WILL BE STORED IN C.
NXTBIT,  MOVAE    /MOVE THE DIVIDEND TO THE A REGISTER.
         RAL      /ROTATE THE MSB OF A INTO THE CARRY.
         MOVEA    /SAVE THE DIVIDEND BACK IN E.
         MOVAC    /GET THE PARTIAL DIVIDEND STORED IN C.
         RAL      /ROTATE THE CARRY INTO THE LSB OF A.
         SUBD     /SUBTRACT THE DIVISOR FROM THIS NUMBER.
         JNC      /IF THE CARRY=0, NO BORROW WAS PRO-
         NOADD    /DUCED. THEREFORE, ROTATE THE QUOTIENT.
         0        /OTHERWISE, ADD THE DIVISOR TO THE
         ADDD     /RESULT OF THE SUBTRACTION.
NOADD,   MOVCA    /SAVE THE PARTIAL DIVIDEND BACK IN C.
         CMC      /COMPLEMENT THE CARRY
         MOVAH    /AND THEN ROTATE THE CARRY INTO
         RAL      /THE LSB OF THE H REGISTER.
         MOVHA
         DCRL     /HAVE ALL 8 BITS BEEN TESTED?
         JNZ      /NO, ROTATE ANOTHER BIT OF THE
         NXTBIT   /DIVIDEND AND TRY SUBTRACTING
         0        /AGAIN.
         RET      /RETURN WITH THE ANSWER IN H.
```

This subroutine performs the same operations that were performed in Example 5-15. The first instruction of the subroutine (LXIH) loads register pair H with 000 010 (0008). In effect, this loads the L register with the bit count, the number of bits in the dividend. At the same time, the H register is cleared, since it will be used to store the quotient, or the result of the division. The C register is also used as a temporary storage register, so it is also cleared.

In Example 5-15, the first subtraction actually subtracted the divisor from the *first bit* of the dividend. The other LSBs are not affected since zero is subtracted from them, yielding no net effect. Thus, we could have ignored all but the subtraction of the divisor from the MSB of the dividend:

$$\begin{array}{r} 00000001 \\ -\ 00000101 \\ \hline 11111100 \end{array}$$
content of register A; partial dividend
content of register D; divisor
a borrow is generated

In the program, this is exactly what is done. The content of the C register (used for temporary storage) is placed in the A register, and the MSB of the dividend, which was previously rotated into the carry, is rotated into the LSB of the A register. This is the "partial" dividend. Now, the divisor in the D register is subtracted from the partial dividend. If a borrow is generated by this subtraction, the carry will be a logic 1.

If there is no borrow (carry = 0), the divisor was smaller than the partial dividend, thus the quotient must have a 1 placed in the proper bit position to show this. This is done by saving the result of the subtraction in the C register (the new partial dividend), and then by rotating a logic 1 into the partial result, stored in the H register.

If a borrow did occur, the divisor was greater than the partial dividend. In this case, the divisor is added to the result of the subtraction. After this is done, the next LSB of the dividend is rotated into the partial dividend, and the process is repeated seven more times, because there are eight bits in the dividend.

Is there any reason why the H register must be cleared? Remember, the H register is used to save the quotient of the division. Unlike the multiplication subroutines, where a partial sum had to be stored in a register or registers, the divide subroutine uses rotate instructions to rotate the quotient from the carry, a bit at a time, into the H register. To do this, the content of the H register is moved to the A register, the carry is rotated into the A register, and the result is saved back in the H register (MOVAH, RAL, MOVHA). Since this sequence of instructions is performed eight times, it does not matter what is contained in the H register when the subroutine is called, because whatever is in the H register at the start of the program is rotated out by the time the 8080 returns from the subroutine.

One of our objectives, which has been mentioned throughout this book, is to use as few memory locations, instructions, or registers as possible. In the next division subroutine, an improved version of Example 5-16, the A, B, and C registers are used, but register pair

H is not used. Instead, the quotient of the division is returned in the E register.

The improved version of the subroutine (Example 5-17) is four memory locations shorter and uses one less register. One of the first changes that should be noted is that the bit count, which is contained in the B register, is decimal 9 rather than decimal 8. You should also observe that the bit count is decremented in the middle of the subroutine rather than at the end of the subroutine. At the end of the subroutine, the carry is simply complemented, and then the 8080 jumps back to NXTBIT, which is near the beginning of the subroutine.

Example 5-17: An Improved Eight-Bit by Eight-Bit Division Subroutine

```
/THIS SUBROUTINE MUST BE CALLED WITH THE DIVISOR IN
/THE D REGISTER AND THE DIVIDEND IN THE E REGISTER.
/THE RESULT WILL BE CONTAINED IN THE REGISTER
/WHEN THE 8080 RETURNS FROM THE SUBROUTINE.

DIV88A,   LXIB    /LOAD THE C REGISTER WITH 000 (USED
          000     /TO STORE PART OF THE DIVIDEND) AND
          011     /LOAD B WITH DECIMAL 9.
NXTBIT,   MOVAE   /MOVE THE DIVIDEND TO THE A REGISTER.
          RAL     /ROTATE THE MSB OF A INTO THE CARRY.
          MOVEA   /SAVE THE DIVIDEND BACK IN E.
          DCRB    /HAVE ALL 8 BITS BEEN TESTED YET?
          RZ      /YES, THE RESULT IS IN E.
          MOVAC   /NO, GET THE PARTIAL DIVIDEND INTO A.
          RAL     /ROTATE THE PARTIAL DIVIDEND LEFT.
          SUBD    /SUBTRACT THE DIVISOR FROM IT.
          JNC     /IF NO "BORROW" DO NOT ADD THE DIVISOR
          NOADD   /TO THE RESULT OF THE SUBTRACTION.
          0
          ADDD    /ADD THE DIVISOR TO THE RESULT.
NOADD,    MOVCA   /SAVE THE PARTIAL DIVIDEND IN C.
          CMC     /COMPLEMENT THE CARRY.
          JMP     /THEN JUMP BACK AND ROTATE THE CARRY
          NXTBIT  /INTO THE LSB OF E AND THE MSB
          0       /OF E INTO THE CARRY AND TEST ANOTHER BIT.
```

By eliminating the instructions MOVAH, RAL, and MOVHA the carry is still set or cleared to the proper state by the CMC instruction. The JMP to NXTBIT is then executed. At NXTBIT, the content of the E register is moved to the A register, where it is rotated one bit to the right. The new content of the A register is then saved in the E register. How is the quotient saved in the E register? When the E register is moved to the A register and rotated, the MSB of A is rotated into the carry. At the same time, the carry, which really represents one bit of the quotient, is rotated into the LSB of the A register. Therefore, after eight rotate instructions are executed, the quotient will be contained in the E register. If this is true, why was the bit count set to decimal 9? Let us assume that the DCR-type instruction for the bit count is still at the end of the subroutine *and* that the bit count is initially set to decimal 8. We still want the quotient to be rotated into the E register. These instructions are listed in Example 5-18.

Example 5-18: An Improper Method of Ending the DIV88A Subroutine (Example 5-17)

```
        •
        •
        MOVCA   /SAVE THE PARTIAL DIVIDEND IN C.
NOADD,  CMC     /COMPLEMENT THE CARRY.
        DCRB    /TESTED ALL 8 BITS OF THE DIVIDEND?
        JNZ     /NO, THEN TEST ANOTHER ONE.
        NXTBIT
        0
        RET     /YES, THE COUNT IS ZERO, THE ANSWER IS IN E.
```

It would appear that this sequence of instructions would work properly, since the DCRB instruction does not affect the carry. However, when the loop is executed for the last time, the carry is complemented to reflect the last and least-significant bit of the quotient. However, the content of the B register will be decremented from 001 to 000 (01 to 00), and this last bit of the quotient will not be rotated into the quotient. Since the beginning of the subroutine rotates a single bit of the dividend into the carry, and a single bit of the quotient out of the carry and into the quotient, the DCRB instruction had to be moved *and* the bit count had to be increased from decimal 8 to 9. This means that the rotate section of the subroutine (the instructions before the RZ instruction) is executed nine times, and the subtraction section of the subroutine is only executed eight times. Is the remainder of the division saved in a register? Yes, it is saved in the C register.

By using the same type of instructions, a subroutine that divides a 16-bit number by another 16-bit number is easy to write. For this subroutine, the following numbers must be stored simultaneously:

> 16-bit divisor,
> 16-bit dividend,
> 16-bit partial dividend,
> 16-bit quotient,
> 16-bit remainder,
> 8-bit bit count.

Because of these storage requirements, R/W memory will be used to store some of these numbers.

Example 5-19: A 16-Bit by 16-Bit Division Subroutine

/THIS SUBROUTINE DIVIDES THE 16-BIT QUANTITY IN REGISTER
/PAIR D BY THE 16-BIT QUANTITY IN REGISTER PAIR B.
/THE RESULT WILL BE STORED IN REGISTER PAIR D AND
/THE REMAINDER IN REGISTER PAIR B, WHEN THE 8080
/RETURNS FROM THE SUBROUTINE.

```
DV1616,  LXIH    /LOAD REGISTER PAIR H WITH THE MEMORY
         TEMP    /ADDRESS FOR THE SYMBOLIC ADDRESS
         0       /TEMP. THIS IS AN R/W MEMORY ADDRESS.
         MOVMC   /SAVE THE LSBY OF THE DIVISOR IN MEMORY.
         INXH    /INCREMENT THE MEMORY ADDRESS.
         MOVMB   /SAVE THE MSBY OF THE DIVISOR IN MEMORY.
         INXH    /INCREMENT THE MEMORY ADDRESS.
         MVIM    /THEN SAVE THE DIVISOR'S BIT COUNT
         021     /IN MEMORY (DECIMAL 17).
         LXIB    /LOAD REGISTER PAIR B WITH 000 000
         000     /(0000). IT WILL BE USED TO STORE
         000     /THE PARTIAL DIVIDEND.
NXTBIT,  LXIH    /LOAD REGISTER PAIR H WITH THE MEM-
         COUNT   /ORY ADDRESS WHERE THE BIT COUNT
         0       /(021 INITIALLY) IS STORED.
         MOVAE   /GET THE LSBY OF THE DIVISOR INTO A.
         RAL     /ROTATE THE MSB INTO THE CARRY.
         MOVEA   /SAVE THE LSBY OF THE DIVIDEND BACK IN E.
         MOVAD   /THEN GET THE MSBY OF THE DIVIDEND.
         RAL     /ROTATE THE MSB INTO THE CARRY.
         MOVDA   /SAVE THE DIVIDEND'S MSBY IN D.
         DCRM    /DECREMENT THE BIT COUNT IN MEMORY.
         RZ      /RETURN IF THE COUNT IS 0.
         MOVAC   /OTHERWISE, ROTATE THE MSB OF THE
         RAL     /DIVIDEND INTO THE PARTIAL DIVIDEND
         MOVCA   /STORED IN REGISTERS B AND C.
         MOVAB
         RAL
         MOVBA
         DCXH    /DECREMENT THE MEMORY ADDRESS SO THAT
         DCXH    /H&L POINT TO THE DIVISOR IN MEMORY.
         MOVAC   /GET THE LSBY OF THE PARTIAL DIVIDEND.
         SUBM    /SUBTRACT THE LSBY OF THE DIVISOR.
         MOVCA   /SAVE THE RESULT BACK IN C.
         INXH    /INCREMENT THE ADDRESS.
         MOVAB   /GET THE MSBY OF THE PARTIAL DIVIDEND.
         SBBM    /SUBTRACT-WITH-BORROW THE DIVISOR IN MEMORY.
         MOVBA   /SAVE THE RESULT BACK IN B.
         JNC     /IF THE CARRY IS 0, DO NOT ADD
         NOADD   /THE DIVISOR TO THE RESULT OF THE
         0       /PREVIOUS SUBTRACTION.
         DCXH    /THE DIVISOR IS LARGER THAN THE
         MOVAC   /PARTIAL DIVIDEND, SO THE DIVISOR
         ADDM    /MUST BE ADDED TO THE RESULT OF
         MOVCA   /THE SUBTRACTION SO THAT THE PRE-
         INXH    /VIOUS VALUE OF THE PARTIAL DIVIDEND
         MOVAB   /IS RE-ESTABLISHED.
         ADCM
```

```
        MOVBA
NOADD,  CMC      /COMPLEMENT THE CARRY.
        JMP      /THEN TEST ANOTHER BIT IN THE
        NXTBIT   /DIVISOR.
        0

TEMP,   0        /THESE MEMORY LOCATIONS ARE USED TO
        0        /STORE THE DIVISOR AND THE BIT
COUNT,  0        /COUNT.
```

As you can see, this subroutine is fairly long. It could be made shorter by using some of the 8080's more powerful instructions, but it has purposely been kept simple so that it is as easy as possible to understand. When this subroutine is called, the dividend must be contained in register pair D and the divisor must be in register pair B.

Because some numbers must be stored in R/W memory, the program loads register pair H with an address for an R/W memory location. The contents of registers C, B, and the bit count are then saved in R/W memory. The bit count is 021 (decimal 17) because there are 16 bits in the dividend, and the rotate loop within the subroutine must be executed an additional time so that the last bit of the quotient is saved in the appropriate register pair. Register pair B is then cleared because this is the register pair that is used to hold the partial dividend. At NXTBIT, register pair H is loaded with the R/W memory address where the bit count is stored (assigned the symbolic address, COUNT). The 16-bit dividend contained in register pair D is then rotated once to the left. The carry is either a logic 1 or a logic 0 as a result of this rotation. As was noted in the previous example, this sequence of six instructions not only rotates the MSB of the dividend into the carry, but it also causes the carry to be rotated into the LSB of register pair D. This technique is used to rotate the quotient, bit-by-bit, into register pair D.

After the dividend has been rotated, the bit count stored in R/W memory is decremented. When the count reaches zero, the subroutine is completed. If the count is nonzero after the DCRM instruction is executed, the RZ instruction is not executed. The MSB of the dividend, which is now in the carry, is rotated into the LSB of the partial dividend that is stored in register pair B. Note that the DCRM instruction does not affect the content of the carry.

As was the case in the previous subroutine, once the partial dividend is formed, the divisor has to be subtracted from it. The divisor is contained in R/W memory, so the memory address contained in register pair H must be decremented twice so that it points to the LSBY of the divisor. The address is decremented by the two DCXH instructions. The LSBY of the partial dividend (the content of the C register) is moved to the A register, and the content of memory addressed by register pair H is subtracted from the content of the A register (SUBM). The result of the subtraction is saved in the C register. The memory address contained in register pair H is then incremented by 1 so that the address points to the memory location containing the MSBY of the divisor.

The MSBY of the partial dividend, stored in the B register, is moved to the A register, and the content of memory addressed by register pair H is subtracted-with-borrow from A (SBBM). Why is the instruction SBBM rather than SUBM used? The SBBM instruction is used because there may have been a borrow generated when the LSBY of the divisor was subtracted from the LSBY of the partial dividend. The SBBM instruction not only subtracts the content of memory from the A register, but it also subtracts the content of the carry from the A register. Of course, the carry contains any borrow. If no borrow occurs from this *entire* 16-bit subtraction, then the partial dividend is equal to or larger than the divisor. If there is a borrow as a result of the 16-bit subtraction, then the partial dividend is smaller than the divisor, and the divisor must be added to the result of the 16-bit subtraction to restore the partial dividend to its original value. To do this, both ADDM and ADCM instructions are executed. If there is no borrow as a result of the 16-bit subtraction, the 8080 jumps to NOADD.

At NOADD, the carry is complemented to reflect whether or not a borrow occurred as a result of the 16-bit subtraction. This carry bit is then rotated into the LSB of register pair D at the time that the next MSB of the dividend contained in register pair D is rotated left into the carry.

Where is the quotient or the result of the division stored? The quotient is stored in register pair D. In many cases, the dividend is not a multiple of the divisor. Therefore, there may be a remainder after all 16 bits of the dividend have been tested. Is this remainder saved? Yes, the 16-bit remainder is saved in register pair B.

Do you think that the 16-bit by 16-bit division subroutine (Example 5-19) can be used to divide a 16-bit number by an eight-bit number? Yes it can, but you would have to ensure that the B register, the MSBY of the divisor, contains 000 (00) before the subroutine is called. The subroutine can also be used to perform an eight-bit by eight-bit division if you set both registers B and D, the MSBYs of the divisor and dividend, respectively, to 000 (00).

This subroutine (Example 5-19) can also be used to divide fractional quantities! This is done by assuming that a 16-bit number represents either an eight-bit number with an eight-bit fraction, or a 16-bit fraction alone. In other words, you assume that there is a decimal point (an implied decimal point) between the two eight-bit numbers or in front of the 16-bit number. Actually, it is called a *binary point* because we are working with binary numbers and binary fractions. For instance,

Previous	Present
XXXXXXXX YYYYYYYY	XXXXXXXX . YYYYYYYY
Represents numbers between 0 and 65,535	Represent numbers between 0 and 255.996
	. XXXXXXXX YYYYYYYY
	Represents numbers between 0 and 0.9998

For integer numbers, the farther to the left that a bit is from the binary point, the larger is the number. Therefore, binary 1000 is larger than binary 0110. For fractional numbers, the farther to the right that a bit is from the binary point, the smaller is the number. This means that binary .0001 is smaller than binary .1010. For an eight-bit fractional number, the significance of the individual bits is as follows:

0.5	0.25	0.125	0.0625	0.03125	0.015625	0.0078125	0.00390625
. X	X	X	X	X	X	X	X

To divide a 16-bit number (eight-bit integer and eight-bit fraction) by an eight-bit integer, the eight-bit divisor would be loaded into the C register, and the B register would be loaded with the MSBY of the divisor, 000 (00). The 16-bit dividend would be loaded into register pair D, with the integer portion of the dividend in register D, and the fractional portion of the dividend in register E. The integer and fractional quotient would be returned in register pair B (integer in the B register; fraction in the C register). The following two examples demonstrate these ideas.

To divide 20.5 by 4, register pairs B and D would be loaded with the following binary numbers:

B	C	D	E
00000000	00000100	0001010	. 1

The result of this division is 5.125; this result is returned in register pair D:

D	E
00000101 .	00100000

This result is $5 + 1/8$, or 5.125. The number 20.5 can also be divided by 5:

$$\begin{array}{cc|cc}
\textbf{B} & \textbf{C} & \textbf{D} & \textbf{E} \\
00000000 & 00000101 & 00010100 \,.\, & 10000000
\end{array}$$

The result that we obtain is 00000100 . 00011001. Is this correct? Yes, because the decimal equivalent for this result is $4 + 0.0625 + 0.03125 + 0.00390625$, which is 4.09765. Unlike integer numbers, binary fractional numbers can only *approximate* a true decimal fraction. With an eight-bit fractional number, the result can be no more accurate than $1/256$, or 0.00390625. Therefore, 4.09765 is as close as the microcomputer can come to the correct result when using an eight-bit fraction. If a 16-bit fraction is used, the microcomputer can come within $1/65,535$, or 1.526×10^{-5} of the correct result. Of course, there are many situations where the microcomputer will determine the exact fractional result, such as the division of 5 by 10, or the division of 9 by 36.

BCD MATHEMATICS

For many individuals, the programs used to convert ASCII characters to binary numbers, to mathematically process the binary numbers, and then to convert the binary numbers back to ASCII characters for output to a teletypewriter or crt can be very difficult and time consuming to write. An easier method of manipulating data would be to convert the ASCII characters to BCD (*B*inary-*C*oded *D*ecimal), process the numbers using BCD mathematical routines, and then convert the BCD results back to ASCII characters. The ASCII characters could then be printed on a teletypewriter. Table 5-1 contains BCD numbers and their binary equivalents.

**Table 5-1. The Binary Equivalents
of the BCD Numbers**

BCD	Binary
0	0000
1	0001
2	0010
3	0011
4	0100
5	0101
6	0110
7	0111
8	1000
9	1001

There are no BCD numbers with the binary values of 1010 through 1111. These would be the octal numbers 12 through 17 or the hexadecimal characters A through F. Since the numbers that the 8080 usually operates on are eight bits long, two four-bit BCD numbers are often *packed* into one eight-bit word.

You have already seen that the 8080 has instructions that can be used for addition and subtraction, and through the proper use of these instructions, the 8080 can multiply and divide numbers as well. However, all of these instructions, programs, and subroutines have operated upon binary numbers. How can the 8080 add and subtract BCD numbers? Surprisingly enough, the same addition and subtraction instructions that have already been discussed can be used.

To add the BCD numbers 32 and 47, some very simple instructions can be executed. These instructions are listed in Example 5-20.

Example 5-20: Adding Two Packed BCD Numbers

```
    •
    •
MVIA   /LOAD THE A REGISTER WITH THE
062    /PACKED BCD DATA BYTE, 32.
ADI    /ADD THE PACKED BCD IMMEDIATE
107    /DATA BYTE, 47.
    •  /THE RESULT IS LEFT IN THE
    •  /A REGISTER.
```

In the A register, these two packed BCD numbers would be added as follows:

$$
\begin{array}{rr}
0011\ 0010 & 32 \\
+\ 0100\ 0111 & +\ 47 \\
\hline
0111\ 1001 & 79
\end{array}
$$

Of course, 79 is the correct answer. However, suppose you need to add two numbers such as 59 and 2:

$$
\begin{array}{rr}
0101\ 1001 & 59 \\
+\ 0000\ 0010 & +\ 02 \\
\hline
0101\ 1011 & ?
\end{array}
$$

The result is *not the 61 that we would expect*. Instead, the tens digit of the BCD number is still 5, but the units digit is an illegal BCD number for which there is no decimal equivalent. To solve this problem, the 8080 instruction DAA, or *Decimal Adjust the Accumulator*, will be discussed. The DAA instruction has an op code of 047 (27). This instruction *adjusts* the content of the A register so that a valid BCD number is left in the A register after it is executed. *The 8080 must be programmed so that this instruction is executed after all addition instructions that operate on BCD numbers.* This means that to add 59 and 2, the program listed in Example 5-21 should be used.

The proper answer, 61 decimal, obtained by executing this sequence of instructions, is saved in the B register as a two-digit, packed BCD number. As was shown previously, the 8080 obtains a result of 0101 1011 after the ADI instruction is executed. However, the DAA instruction adjusts this result of 0110 001. How does the 8080 do this?

Example 5-21: A Proper BCD Addition Routine

```
    •
    •
MVIA    /LOAD THE A REGISTER WITH THE
131     /PACKED BCD DATA BYTE, 59.
ADI     /ADD TO IT THE PACKED BCD
002     /VALUE 02.
DAA     /DECIMAL ADJUST THE CONTENT OF A.
MOVBA   /SAVE THE BCD RESULT IN
    •   /THE B REGISTER.
    •
```

If the least-significant BCD digit (the four LSBs in the A register) is greater than BCD 9, or if the *auxiliary carry (AC)* is a logic 1, BCD 6 is added to the content of the A register. If the most-significant BCD digit (the four MSBs of the A register) is greater than 9, or the carry is a logic 1, a BCD 60 is added to the content of the A register. This last addition is equivalent to adding 6 to the most-significant BCD digit. Therefore, in the addition of BCD 59 to BCD 2, a result of 0101 1011 is obtained. Since the least-significant digit is greater than BCD 9 (1001), BCD 6 is added to the content of the A register when the DAA instruction is executed.

$$\begin{array}{r} 0101\ 1011 \\ +\ 0000\ 0110 \\ \hline 0110\ 0001 \end{array}$$

Carry = 0
Auxiliary Carry = 1

Note that the auxiliary carry is now set to a logic 1, but the eight-bit carry is set to a logic 0. *The DAA instruction is the only instruction that can test the state of the auxiliary carry.* Since the most-significant packed BCD digit contained in the A register is less than 1010, a BCD 60 is not added to the content of the A register.

Suppose that BCD 99 is added to BCD 3:

$$\begin{array}{r} 1001\ 1001 \\ +\ 0000\ 0011 \\ \hline 1001\ 1100 \end{array}$$

A result of 1001 1100 is obtained. Since 1100 is greater than 1001 (BCD 9), the DAA instruction adds BCD 6 to the content of the A register. However, as a result of this addition,

$$\begin{array}{l} 1001\ 1100 \text{ result} \\ +\ 0000\ 0110 \text{ "added" by the DAA operation} \\ \hline 1010\ 0010 \text{ result of DAA} \end{array}$$

$Carry = 1$
$Auxiliary\ Carry = 1$

the most-significant digit of the packed BCD number is greater than BCD 9 (1001). Therefore, BCD 60 must be added to the content of the A register.

$$\begin{array}{l} 0101\ 0010 \text{ result of the first DAA operation} \\ +\ 0110\ 0000 \text{ "added" by the second DAA operation} \\ \hline 0000\ 0010 \text{ final result of DAA} \end{array}$$

$Carry = 1$
$Auxiliary\ Carry = 0$

The result in the A register is now BCD 02, and the carry is a logic 1. The result of the addition, $99 + 3 = 102$, is three BCD digits; the two BCD digits contained in the A register represent the two least-significant digits of the result. The carry bit, which is a logic 1, indicates that if there is a hundreds BCD digit stored somewhere, it should be increased by 1, or perhaps the carry should be saved.

The 8080 can also subtract BCD numbers, but it is very clumsy in this respect. Instead of subtracting two two-digit BCD numbers and then adjusting the result with the DAA instruction, the minuend must be added to the 10s complement of the subtrahend. This is the same as saying $23 - 13 = 23 + (-13)$. This means that to subtract BCD 26 from BCD 54, the 10s complement of BCD 26 must first be determined. This is obtained by subtracting 26 from 100 ($100 - 26 = 74$). This 10s complement of 26 can now be added to 54 and the result adjusted with the DAA instruction.

$$54 - 26 = 54 + (100 - 26)$$

$$\begin{array}{ll} 0101\ 0100 & 54 \\ +\ 0111\ 0100 & (100 - 26) = 74 \\ \hline 1100\ 1000 & \text{result} \end{array}$$

$$Carry = 0$$
$$Auxiliary\ Carry = 0$$

The result of this addition still has to be adjusted with the DAA instruction. As you can see, this adjustment only requires that BCD 60 be added to the content of the A register.

$$
\begin{array}{ll}
1100\ 1000 & \text{result} \\
+\ 0110\ 0000 & \text{BCD 60 (due to DAA)} \\
\hline
0010\ 1000 &
\end{array}
$$

$$Carry = 1$$
$$Auxiliary\ Carry = 0$$

The final result of this addition of the 10s complement of 26 to 54 is 28, which is the result that is obtained from $54 - 26$.

If this seems like a difficult method to use for "subtracting" BCD numbers, your impression is correct. Now the only remaining problem left to be solved is how to obtain the 10s complement using software instructions. Note that a BCD 100 requires a three-digit BCD number for storage. As you know, the 8080 can only hold a single two-digit BCD number in either a register or memory location. Therefore, the subtrahend is subtracted from 99, a two-digit BCD number, and the result of this subtraction is incremented by 1 to form the 10s complement. Therefore, the subtraction of 26 from 54 can be summarized as follows:

$$54 - 26 = 54 + [(99 - 26) + 1]$$

To add the BCD content of the B register to the BCD content of the C register, the program listed in Example 5-22 could be executed.

Example 5-22: Adding the BCD Content of Register C to Register B

```
        •
        •
MOVAB   /MOVE THE CONTENT OF B TO A.
ADDC    /ADD THE CONTENT OF C TO A.
DAA     /DECIMAL ADJUST THE RESULT.
        •
        •
```

To subtract the BCD content of the C register from the BCD content of the B register, a more complex sequence of instructions is required (Example 5-23).

As you can see in Example 5-23, the 9s complement is formed by loading the A register with the immediate data byte, 99 (BCD). The content of the C register is then subtracted from the content of the A register. This 9s complement is then incremented to form

Example 5-23: Subtracting the BCD Content of Register C From Register B

- •
- •

```
MVIA    /LOAD THE A REGISTER WITH THE
231     /PACKED BCD VALUE 99.
SUBC    /SUBTRACT C TO FORM THE 9'S COMPLEMENT.
INRA    /INCREMENT A TO FORM THE 10'S COMPLEMENT.
ADDB    /ADD THE MINUEND TO A.
DAA     /DECIMAL ADJUST THE CONTENT OF A.
  •     /THE RESULT OF THE BCD "SUBTRACTION"
  •     /IS NOW IN THE A REGISTER.
```

the 10s complement. The content of the B register is then added to the content of the A register. The content of the A register is then adjusted with the DAA instruction, and the result of the "subtraction" is left in the A register.

FOUR-DIGIT BCD OPERATIONS

To add the BCD content of register pair B to the BCD content of register pair D requires a slightly more complex program (Example 5-24).

Example 5-24: Adding the BCD Content of Register Pair B to Register Pair D

- •
- •

```
BPLUSD,  MOVAE   /MOVE THE BCD LSBY OF ONE NUMBER TO A.
         ADDC    /ADD THE BCD LSBY OF THE OTHER NUMBER.
         DAA     /DECIMAL ADJUST THE RESULT.
         MOVLA   /SAVE THE BCD LSBY OF THE RESULT IN L.
         MOVAD   /LOAD A WITH THE BCD MSBY OF ONE NUMBER.
         ADCB    /ADD THE BCD MSBY OF THE OTHER NUMBER.
         DAA     /DECIMAL ADJUST THE RESULT.
         MOVHA   /SAVE THE BCD MSBY OF THE RESULT IN H.
```

- •
- •

Where is the result of the four-digit BCD addition stored? The LSBY of the BCD result is stored in the L register and the MSBY of the BCD result is stored in the H register. Remember, the carry may also contain a logic 1, depending on the size of the BCD numbers that are added. This carry may have to be saved.

Suppose that you need to subtract multiprecision BCD numbers, such as 522 − 146. How would this be done? First, the 9s complement of 146 would have to be determined. Then 1 would have to be added to this value so that the 10s complement of the number is obtained. After this, the minuend and the 10s complement of the subtrahend could be added and adjusted. These operations are summarized as follows:

$$
\begin{array}{r}
99\ 99 \\
-\ 01\ 46 \\
\hline
98\ 53
\end{array}
\quad \text{subtrahend} \\
\quad \text{9s complement}
$$

A 1 would have to be added to this result to form the 10s complement.

$$
\begin{array}{r}
98\ 53 \\
+\ 00\ 01 \\
\hline
98\ 54
\end{array}
$$

The 10s complement of 146 (98 54) can now be added to 522.

$$
\begin{array}{r}
05\ 52 \\
+\ 98\ 54 \\
\hline
03\ 76
\end{array}
$$

Carry = 1
Auxiliary Carry = 0

After *both* of these two-digit BCD numbers are added together, a DAA instruction has to be executed. When performing this type of subtraction, the program listed in Example 5-25 can be used to generate the 10s complement of the BCD content of register pair B.

After these instructions are executed, the BCD content of register pair B could be added to the BCD content of register pair D. Since these addition instructions were listed in Example 5-24, the addition instructions could be executed right after the 10s complement of the BCD content of register pair B is determined. In fact, these instructions could be stored in memory, as listed in Example 5-26.

Both of these subroutines, COMPB (*COMP*lement register pair *B*) and BPLUSD (register pair *B PLUS* register pair *D*), can now be called at any time. The COMPB subroutine will first determine the 10s complement for the BCD content of register pair B. The addition of the BCD content of register pair B to register pair D will then be performed at BPLUSD. This has the *net effect* of subtracting the BCD content of register pair B from the BCD content of register pair D. However, the BPLUSD subroutine can also be called on its own, causing the BCD content of register pair B to be added to the BCD content of register pair D.

Both of these subroutines would be far more general-purpose in nature if the BCD numbers were contained in memory. In this manner, long or short BCD numbers could be added or subtracted. To generate the 10s complement of a BCD number contained in memory, the subroutine listed in Example 5-27 could be executed.

Example 5-25: Determining the 10s Complement of the BCD Content of Register Pair B

```
/THIS SECTION OF THE PROGRAM CALCULATES THE 10'S
/COMPLEMENT OF THE CONTENT OF REGISTER PAIR B.
/FIRST THE 9'S COMPLEMENT IS DETERMINED AND THEN
/THE RESULT IS INCREMENTED, BY ADDING ONE, TO
/FORM THE 10'S COMPLEMENT.

COMPB,  MVIA     /LOAD THE A REGISTER WITH BCD 99.
        231      /(OCTAL 231 = HEX 99).
        SUBC     /SUBTRACT THE LSBY OF THE SUBTRA-
        MOVCA    /HEND AND SAVE THE RESULT IN C.
        MVIA     /LOAD THE A REGISTER WITH BCD 99
        231      /AGAIN. (OCTAL 231 = HEX 99)
        SBBB     /SUBTRACT-WITH-BORROW, THE MSBY
        MOVBA    /AND SAVE THE RESULT IN B.
        MOVAC    /NOW INCREMENT THE NUMBER BY ONE.
        ADI
        001
        DAA      /DECIMAL ADJUST THE RESULT.
        MOVCA
        MOVAB    /GET THE MSBY OF THE NUMBER.
        ACI      /ADD IN ANY CARRY FROM THE LSBY.
        000
        DAA      /THEN ADJUST THE RESULT.
        MOVBA    /THE 10'S COMPLEMENT OF REGISTER
          •      /PAIR B IS NOW STORED IN REGISTER
          •      /PAIR B.
```

Example 5-26: Complementing the BCD Content of Register Pair B and Then Adding the Result to the BCD Content of Register Pair D

```
COMPB,  MVIA     /LOAD THE A REGISTER WITH BCD 99.
        231      /(OCTAL 231 = HEX 99).
        SUBC     /SUBTRACT THE LSBY OF THE SUBTRAHEND.
          •
          •
          •
        DAA      /DECIMAL ADJUST THE CONTENT OF A.
        MOVBA    /THE 10'S COMPLEMENT IS IN B&C.
BPLUSD, MOVAE    /MOVE THE BCD LSBY OF ONE NUMBER TO A.
        ADDC     /ADD THE LSBY OF THE OTHER NUMBER.
        DAA      /DECIMAL ADJUST THE RESULT.
          •
          •
          •
        DAA      /DECIMAL ADJUST THE MSBY.
        MOVHA    /SAVE THE BCD MSBY IN H.
        RET      /RETURN WITH THE BCD RESULT IN
                 /REGISTER PAIR H.
```

This subroutine requires that register pair H points to the memory location containing the two least-significant digits of the BCD number that is to be complemented. Also, the more-significant words of the number must be stored at sequentially higher memory addresses, and the C register must be loaded with the number of memory locations that have been used to store the BCD number. This is one-half the number of BCD digits, two per location.

Basically, there are two sections to the subroutine. The first section determines the 9s complement, and the second section adds 1 to the 9s complement to produce the 10s complement.

Example 5-27: A 10s Complement Subroutine That Complements a BCD Number Stored in Memory

```
/THIS SUBROUTINE DETERMINES THE 10'S COMPLEMENT
/OF A BCD NUMBER STORED IN R/W MEMORY.
/ENTER THE SUBROUTINE WITH REGISTER PAIR H LOADED WITH
/THE R/W MEMORY ADDRESS FOR THE LSBY OF THE NUMBER.
/THE LSBY IS STORED AT THE LOWEST MEMORY ADDRESS.
/ENTER WITH C EQUAL TO THE NUMBER OF PACKED BCD WORDS
/(HALF THE NUMBER OF BCD DIGITS).


COMP1,    PUSHH     /SAVE THE MEMORY ADDRESS ON THE STACK.
          PUSHB     /SAVE THE WORD COUNT ON THE STACK.
          XRAA      /SET THE A REGISTER AND THE CARRY TO 0.
CMPNXT,   MVIA      /LOAD THE A REGISTER WITH BCD 99.
          231       /(OCTAL 231 = HEX 99).
          SBBM      /SUBTRACT THE CONTENT OF MEMORY FROM IT.
          MOVMA     /SAVE THE 9'S COMPLEMENT IN MEMORY.
          INXH      /INCREMENT THE MEMORY ADDRESS.
          DCRC      /DECREMENT THE WORD COUNT.
          JNZ       /IF THE COUNT IS NONZERO, THE
          CMPNXT    /JUMP IS EXECUTED SO THAT THE 9'S
          0         /COMPLEMENT OF ANOTHER WORD IS FOUND.
          POPB      /DONE ALL THE WORDS, POP THE COUNT
          POPH      /AND THE MEMORY ADDRESS OFF OF THE STACK.
          STC       /SET THE CARRY TO A LOGIC ONE.
ADD1,     MOVAM     /GET ONE OF THE 9'S COMPLEMENT VALUES.
          ACI       /ADD THE CARRY AND 000 TO IT.
          000
          DAA       /DECIMAL ADJUST THE RESULT.
          MOVMA     /SAVE THE 10'S COMPLEMENT IN MEMORY.
          INXH      /INCREMENT THE MEMORY ADDRESS.
          DCRC      /DECREMENT THE WORD COUNT.
          JNZ       /IF THE COUNT IS NONZERO, THE CARRY
          ADD1      /MUST BE ADDED TO ANOTHER PACKED
          0         /BCD WORD.
          RET       /FOUND THE 10'S COMPLEMENT, RETURN.
```

At COMP1, the memory address contained in register pair H and the memory location count contained in the C register, are saved on the stack. The carry and the A register are then cleared by the

XRAA instruction. The A register is then loaded with BCD 99 (octal 231, hex 99), and the BCD content of memory is subtracted from the BCD content of the A register by the SBBM instruction. Since the XRAA instruction was executed before this first pass through the subroutine, the SBBM instruction produces the same result as an SUBM instruction does because the carry is zero. However, when the loop is executed successive times, the SBBM instruction carries the borrow into the more-significant BCD words. After the subtraction has taken place, the 9s complement of the number is saved in the same memory location where the number was originally stored. The memory address is then incremented and the word count is decremented. Only when the content of the C register is decremented to zero is the JNZ to CMPNXT not executed. This means that the entire BCD number, no matter how large, has been complemented to the 9s complement.

The second section of the program, starting just before the symbolic address ADD1, determines the 10s complement of the BCD number stored in memory. First, the memory address counter is popped off of the stack and into register C. The address of the first memory location used to store the BCD number is also popped off the stack. The carry is then set to a logic 1 (STC), and the first BCD number is moved from memory to the A register. An ACI 000 instruction is then executed. Doesn't a 1 have to be added to the 9s complement to form the 10s complement? It does, and this subroutine does it by setting the carry to a logic 1, and using an ACI instruction to add the logic 1 into the BCD number. The first time through the loop, the carry is added to the content of the A register. Since the carry is initialized to the logic 1 state, a 1 is added to the content of the A register. After the content of the A register is decimal adjusted, the 10s complement of the number is stored back in memory. The memory address is incremented and the memory location counter is decremented. If this count is nonzero, which means that there are more BCD digits to be incremented, the JNZ to ADD1 is executed. When the content of the C register is finally decremented to zero, the 8080 returns from the subroutine. The 10s complement of the number is now stored in R/W memory, where the original number was stored.

Once the 10s complement of the subtrahend has been formed, the addition of the two BCD numbers is straightforward (Example 5-28). This subroutine should look very familiar. It is one of the integer addition subroutines that was written in the integer addition section of this chapter (Example 5-4). The only difference is that a DAA instruction has been added, and the final carry is no longer checked. Because you have already seen this subroutine in essentially the same form, we will not explain how it functions.

Example 5-28: Adding Two BCD Numbers That Are Stored in Memory

```
/ENTER THIS SUBROUTINE WITH REGISTER PAIR H POINTING TO
/ONE OF THE BCD NUMBERS TO BE ADDED AND REGISTER PAIR
/D POINTING TO THE OTHER NUMBER. THE RESULT WILL BE
/STORED IN MEMORY USING REGISTER PAIR H AS THE ADDRESS.
/REGISTER C MUST CONTAIN THE NUMBER OF WORDS TO
/BE ADDED (2 BCD DIGITS PER WORD).
```

```
BCDADD,   XRAA    /CLEAR THE A REGISTER AND THE CARRY.
ADD1,     LDAXD   /GET ONE OF THE PACKED BCD WORDS.
          ADCM    /ADD THE CARRY AND THE OTHER WORD.
          DAA     /DECIMAL ADJUST THE RESULT.
          MOVMA   /SAVE THE BCD RESULT IN MEMORY.
          INXH    /INCREMENT THE MEMORY ADDRESSES
          INXD    /CONTAINED IN REGISTER PAIRS D AND H.
          DCRC    /DECREMENT THE WORD COUNT IN C.
          JNZ     /IF THE COUNT IS NONZERO, ANOTHER
          ADD1    /TWO WORDS MUST BE ADDED.
          0
          RET     /RETURN WITH THE BCD ANSWER IN MEMORY.
```

For the sake of brevity, we will not include any BCD multiplication or division subroutines in this book. Looking back at the BCD examples that we have seen so far, it is easy to see why. Is there any overwhelming reason why BCD mathematical operations should be used? Probably not. Although the use of BCD numbers does mean that ASCII-to-binary and binary-to-ASCII subroutines do not have to be written, the actual BCD mathematical subroutines can be much longer and more complex than the equivalent binary subroutines. Besides, a four-word (32-bit) binary number can represent numbers between 0 and 4,294,967,295. The same 32-bit word can only represent the BCD numbers between 0 and 99,999,999. The storage capacity for 8-, 16-, and 24-bit words is shown in Table 5-2.

Table 5-2. The Storage Capacity of Binary and BCD Words

Word Length	Binary	BCD
8 bits	0–255	0–99
16 bits	0–65,535	0–9999
24 bits	0–16,777,215	0–999,999

A few last comments about the DAA instruction are in order. First, to use the DAA instruction, the mathematical *addition* operations must take place in the A register. You *cannot* load register pairs D and H with BCD numbers, add them with a DADD instruction, and then adjust the result of the addition by moving the L or

H register to the A register and executing a DAA instruction. Also, to increment a BCD number by 1, use an ADI 001 or ACI 001 instruction and then adjust the result with a DAA instruction. The content of the A register cannot be incremented by 1 (INRA), and the result adjusted with the DAA instruction. If a BCD number must be decremented by 1, simply add a BCD 99 to it and adjust the result. Finally, *the DAA instruction does not perform a binary-to-BCD number-base conversion.* You cannot add two *binary* numbers and convert the result to BCD simply by executing a DAA instruction. *If you use the DAA instruction, the implication is that BCD numbers are being added, or their 10s complement are being "subtracted."*

FLOATING-POINT MATHEMATICAL OPERATIONS

One of the limitations of the fixed-point mathematical routines and subroutines that have been discussed in this chapter is that it would be almost impossible to represent numbers such as 6.02×10^{23} or 8.76×10^{-14}. These numbers are either too large or too small to be easily represented in a three- or four-word binary number. For this reason, floating-point numbers and floating-point mathematical programs are used. Floating-point numbers have both a *fraction* and an *exponent*. In the two preceding numbers, the fractions are 6.02 and 8.76, and the exponents for these numbers are 23 and -14. In floating-point format, there is not only a sign for the exponent, but there is also a sign for the fraction. When integer mathematical routines were discussed, it was assumed that all of the numbers were positive.

Are the following numbers equal in sign and magnitude?

$$6.02 \times 10^{23} \qquad .602 \times 10^{24} \qquad 60.2 \times 10^{22}$$

Yes, they are equal even though the exponents and fractions are different. When floating-point mathematical software is actually used, these same numbers might be printed out by the microcomputer as,

$$6.02E + 23 \qquad .602E + 24 \qquad 60.2E + 22$$

In this instance, the E indicates that the following digits express a signed decimal exponent. To represent any of these numbers in floating-point format, three or four eight-bit memory locations or registers can be used. Two formats that are used to represent floating-point numbers are:

$$S_x XXXXXXX \qquad S_f.FFFFFFF \qquad FFFFFFFF$$
$$S_x S_f XXXXXX \qquad .FFFFFFFF \qquad FFFFFFFF$$

In the upper example, there is an eight-bit word, S_xXXXXXXX. This represents the sign (S_x) of the exponent, and the seven-bit exponent (XXXXXXX) of the floating-point number. In general, if the sign bit is a logic 1, the sign is negative; if it is a logic 0, the sign is positive. This applies to the sign of both the fraction and the exponent. The sign bit for the fraction is in the word, S_f.FFFFFFF. In this particular floating-point number, there is a seven-bit binary exponent and a 15-bit binary fraction. In the second example, the sign bits for both the exponent and fraction are contained in the same eight-bit word. Therefore, the exponent is only a six-bit binary word and the fraction is a 16-bit binary word.

In the middle word, or byte, of these floating-point numbers, there is a *binary point*, which is present in all floating-point numbers. In the preceding examples, the binary point is to the left of the MSB of the fraction. This means that all floating-point numbers that use this format will be represented as *fractional numbers*. The binary point in these numbers is what the decimal point is to decimal numbers. To meet this requirement of the floating-point number format, the numbers 6.02×10^{23} and 8.76×10^{-14} would have to be represented as $.602 \times 10^{24}$ and $.876 \times 10^{-13}$. If the binary or decimal point is moved to the left, the exponent of the corresponding binary or decimal number must be incremented by 1. If the binary or decimal point is moved to the right, the exponent of the corresponding binary or decimal number must be decremented by 1.

As you may recall from the discussion of fractional numbers in the integer division section of the chapter, if the bit closest to the binary point is a logic 1, the number is 0.5 or greater. The values that can be assigned to the other bit positions decrease by a factor of 0.5 the farther away from the binary point the numbers are. Can you determine the proper eight-bit integer and eight-bit fractional value for the number 24.133? Using the first floating-point format, the answer is,

00000101   0.1100000

This number is really $(0.5 + 0.25) \times 2^5$, or $.75 \times 32$, or 24, which is as close to the value 24.133 as is possible with an eight-bit fractional quantity. What are the values for the following fractions?

0.1000000

0.1001000

The value for the first fraction is 0.5, and the value for the second fraction is .5625. If a number had to be multiplied by 56.25, what would be the equivalent two-word floating-point number? For a two-word floating-point number, the format can be assumed to be

$S_xXXXXXXX$ $S_fFFFFFFF$. For the number 56.25, the floating-point equivalent would be,

$$56.25 = 5.625 \times 10^1 = .5625 \times 10^2$$

$$00000110 \qquad 0.1110000$$

The binary number is $(0.5 + 0.25 + 0.125) \times 2^6$, or 0.875×64, or 56. Since the signs of both the exponent and fraction are positive, there must be zeros in bit D_7 of both the fraction and exponent. What are the decimal equivalents for the following numbers, assuming the same two-word floating-point format ($S_xXXXXXXX$ $S_f.FFFFFFF$)?

$$10000010 \qquad 0.101000$$
$$10000010 \qquad 1.101000$$
$$00000010 \qquad 1.101000$$

The numbers are $.625 \times 2^{-2}$, or 0.15625; -0.625×2^{-2}, or -0.15625; and -0.625×2^2, or -2.5.

One of the problems with the use of floating-point numbers is the fact that people still think in decimal, while the microcomputer thinks in binary (no matter whether floating-point or integer). For this reason, floating-point conversion programs often have conversion subroutines so that decimal numbers may be entered and converted to the required floating-point format. Within this conversion subroutine, another subroutine is probably called that *floats* the binary equivalent of the decimal number to the proper floating-point format. Quite often, these subroutines can be called separately, so that the decimal input subroutine does not have to be executed just to float a binary number. The binary number that is floated may be left in the *floating-point accumulator* (*FPA*). The FPA is *not* another accumulator within the 8080 integrated circuit. Instead, it is simply a few consecutive R/W memory locations where the subroutines within the floating-point software can fetch and store one of the numbers that is to be mathematically operated upon. The result of one of the floating-point operations (addition, subtraction, multiplication, or division) is generally left in the FPA.

Usually, there is another subroutine within the floating-point program that converts the floating-point number to a fixed-point binary number. This is called the *fix* subroutine, because it fixes the binary point of the number. In general, positive or negative integer values can be produced by this subroutine. The binary number that results from the fix operation may be left in the FPA or in another section of R/W memory.

There is also a *normalization* subroutine within most floating-point software. This subroutine performs the following type of conversion:

Exponent	Fraction		Exponent	Fraction
00001011	0.0011011	converted to	00001001	0.1101100

In floating-point operations, the number operated upon must be within the range of $0.5 \leq X < 1$. This means that the number in the preceding example must be rotated to the left, two bit positions so that the first bit that is a logic 1 is rotated into bit D_6. Why isn't the first bit that is a logic 1 rotated into bit D_7? Remember, the first bit of the fraction is often the sign bit; therefore, the first logic 1 bit of the fraction must not be rotated into the sign bit. Of course, during this rotation, the sign bit must not change. By rotating the first bit that is a logic 1 into bit D_6, the number has to be 0.5 or greater, but it is impossible for it to be equal to 1 because the value of 1 can only be approached by binary fractional values, no matter how many bits of significance they have. Each time the fraction is rotated once to the left, the exponent must be decremented by 1.

The most common *floating-point package* (a *package* is just a collection of useful floating-point routines and subroutines) can perform the four basic mathematical operations: addition, subtraction, multiplication, and division. In other sections of this chapter, multiprecision addition and subtraction subroutines were used as examples. Routines and subroutines that are very similar to such routines could be used as a starting point for writing a floating-point addition or subtraction subroutine.

In floating-point addition, the following two numbers can be added directly:

$$5.02 \times 10^{13}$$
$$+ \, 4.17 \times 10^{13}$$
$$\overline{9.19 \times 10^{13}}$$

The only reason that these two numbers can be added is because they are equal to each other in terms of magnitude. The numbers,

$$5.02 \times 10^{13}$$
$$+ \, 2.43 \times 10^{12}$$
$$\overline{5.263 \times 10^{13}}$$

can also be added. However, if you were to perform this addition with pencil and paper, you would probably first change the number 2.43×10^{12}, to $.243 \times 10^{13}$. In a similar manner, how would the numbers 5.02×10^{13} and 3.79×10^3 be added? The chances are that you would not even bother to add these numbers, since 3.79×10^3 is equal to $.000000000379 \times 10^{13}$, which is not within the significance of the number 5.02×10^{13}. The result of the addition would be $5.02 \, 10^{13}$. Probably the smallest number that could be added to 5.02×10^{13} would be 1×10^{11}, or possibly 5×10^{10}. Any number smaller than this would not change the result of the addition. No matter what size the exponents are in the two numbers being added, if they are not equal, one of the exponents must be *aligned* with the other exponent. For the number 3.79×10^3, the exponent would have to be aligned (increased) until it was 13. As you have already seen, to increase the value of the exponent, the fraction must be rotated to the right. To perform this alignment, the smaller of the two numbers must be found. Once this is done, the exponent of the smaller number would be increased, and the fraction rotated to the right. However, as a result of the alignment, the number 3.79×10^3 would be insignificant when compared to the number 5.02×10^{13}. This means that the numbers cannot be aligned; that is, one of the numbers is much smaller than the other number. If numbers cannot be aligned, then no addition takes place. Instead, the larger of the two numbers is found and placed in the FPA. For a mathematical operation to be performed, one of the numbers must be in the FPA. Therefore, if the numbers cannot be aligned, the larger of the two numbers may already be in the FPA, so no additional operations would take place in the floating-point addition subroutine.

If the numbers can be aligned, then the addition will take place. However, before the addition is performed, the fractions of both numbers must be rotated to the right by one bit position. This prevents any carry from the addition of the seven-bit MSBYs of the fractions from entering into bit D_7 of the MSBY of the fraction. Remember, bit D_7 of the MSBY of the fraction contains the sign of the fraction. Suppose that the following two numbers, both in floating-point format, are to be added:

Exponent	Fraction
00000010	0.1011100
00000010	+ 0.1001000
00000010	1.0100100

This result is incorrect because the sign of the result is now negative despite the fact that two positive numbers were added. To add these numbers properly, they first have to be rotated to the right, and the exponents increased by 1.

Exponent	Fraction
00000011	0.0101110
00000011	+ 0.0100100
00000011	0.1010010

What is the result of this addition? The result is $(0.5 + 0.125 + 0.015625) \times 2^3$, or 0.640625×8, or 5.125. Before the numbers were rotated, they had values of 0.71875×2^2, or 2.875, and 0.5625×2^2, or 2.25.

When addition is performed, the sign of the result is also the sign of the number with the largest absolute value. For instance, $5 + (-3) = 2$. The largest number is 5, so the sign stays positive. With $3 + (-7)$, the 7 is the largest number, so the sign of the result is the same as the sign of the 7, which is negative. Of course, there is the special case of $3 + (-3)$, where the sign of the result is positive. In some floating-point packages, the result of this addition would be negative; that is, there is both a positive and negative zero!

Now that the concepts of floating-point addition have been discussed, it is easy to understand the floating-point subtraction process. To subtract two floating-point numbers, the 2s complement of the subtrahend is obtained. The floating-point addition subroutine is then called. The addition is performed, and the result of the "subtraction," which may or may not be left in the FPA, will remain. This can be done because,

$$25 - 13 = 25 + (-13)$$

In reality, floating-point multiplication and floating-point division are easier than floating-point addition. This statement is true because the fractions of the multiplier and multiplicand do not have to be aligned, and the numbers do not have to be rotated once to the right before the multiplication can be performed. In multiplication, the exponents of the two numbers are simply added, and the fractions are multiplied as per integer multiplication. In floating-point division, the exponents are subtracted and the fractions are divided. You have already seen integer multiplication and division subroutines. These subroutines could be used to operate on the fraction portion of the floating-point numbers that are being multiplied or divided. The only hard work associated with either of these two operations is keeping track of the sign of the fraction of the result.

When multiplication is performed, the sign combinations of the fraction can be as follows:

Multiplier	Multiplicand	Result
+	+	+
+	−	−
−	+	−
−	−	+

Since a minus sign is a logic 1 in the floating-point format that has been discussed, we obtain the following truth table:

Multiplier	Multiplicand	Result
0	0	0
0	1	1
1	0	1
1	1	0

From this truth table, you should see that the sign of the result can be determined by exclusive-ORing the sign of the multiplier with the sign of the multiplicand. As you will remember, when two 16-bit numbers are multiplied, a 32-bit result can be obtained. Therefore, in floating-point multiplication, some additional memory locations have to be reserved for the FPA, which will be twice as large after a multiplication is performed. For a three-word fraction, six consecutive memory locations would have to be reserved for the fraction of the FPA.

Floating-point division is only slightly more complex. The division of the fraction could be performed by one of the integer division subroutines that were discussed in a previous section of this chapter. The exponent of the result would simply be the result of subtracting the exponent of the divisor from the exponent of the dividend. Like multiplication, if the signs of the divisor and dividend are the same, the result of the division will be positive. If the signs are different, the sign of the result of the division will be negative.

We have not discussed many of the finer points that are required to make a general-purpose floating-point package; e.g., the possible error conditions that can result and how to prevent them. Suppose the result of a multiplication or addition is larger than the FPA can hold, or division by zero is attempted? To learn about these and other interesting features of floating-point packages, we recommend the references at the end of this chapter.

SPECIAL FUNCTIONS

Some floating-point packages not only perform the four basic functions, they can also be used to determine logarithms, or the sine and cosine of an angle. The remainder of this chapter will summarize the formulas used to calculate values for these functions.

Sine

For all real values of X (in radians), a series can be used to determine the sin (X),

$$\sin X = X - \frac{X^3}{3!} + \frac{X^5}{5!} - \frac{X^7}{7!} + \frac{X^9}{9!} \cdots$$

Written in another way,

$$\sin X = X - 0.166666(X^3) + 0.008333(X^5) - 0.000198(X^7) + 0.0000028(X^9)$$

Cosine

For all real values of X, the cosine of an angle in radians can also be calculated using a series,

$$\cos X = 1 - \frac{X^2}{2!} + \frac{X^4}{4!} - \frac{X^6}{6!} + \frac{X^8}{8!} \cdots$$

This equation can also be simplified,

$$\cos X = 1 - 0.50000(X^2) + 0.041667(X^4) - 0.001389(X^6) + 0.000025(X^8)$$

Tangent

The tangent of an angle, expressed in radians, can be calculated using the equations used to calculate the sine and cosine of an angle, using the identity,

$$\tan X = \frac{\sin X}{\cos X}$$

Logarithm

Exponential logarithms can also be calculated with a series expansion,

$$\log_e (1+X) = X - \frac{X^2}{2} + \frac{X^3}{3} - \frac{X^4}{4}$$

This equation can only be used for the values, $-1 < X \leq 1$. To calculate a base-10 logarithm, the preceding formula can be used, and the result multiplied by 2.30258,

$$\log_e X = \frac{\log_{10} X}{\log_{10} e} = (\log_e 10)\,(\log_{10} X) = 2.30258 \log_{10} X$$

You have now seen a number of mathematical programs and subroutines that can be used to manipulate mathematical quantities. These programs and subroutines can be used in accounting, surveying, scientific problem solving, navigation, and business applications. Depending on the application, you may have to use integer or floating-point mathematical programs.

REFERENCES

1. Wadsworth, N. *Machine Language Programming for the 8008 and Similar Microcomputers*. Scelbi Computer Consulting, Inc., Milford, CT, 1975.
2. *PDP-8 Floating Point System Programmer's Reference Manual*, No. DEC-08-YQYB-D. Digital Equipment Corporation, Maynard, MA, 1969.
3. Rony, P. R., Titus, J. A., Titus, C. A., and Larsen, D. G. "Microcomputer Interfacing: Integer Addition and Subtraction." *American Laboratory*, Vol. 10, No. 2, 1978, p. 153.

6

Number-Base Conversion

All computers have to have a method of entering digital information. This information may be data or instructions from memory, from a teletypewriter, from a card reader, from a digital cassette, or from a floppy disk. This information may be ASCII, EBCDIC, (Extended-Binary-Coded-Decimal-Interchange-Code), binary or Gray code. For the 8080 to operate on this information, it must consist of a string of logic 1s and 0s. However, it is very difficult for programmers to remember strings of logic 1s and 0s when the instructions or data values are being entered into a microcomputer. For this reason, the octal and hexadecimal numbering systems are used to represent such strings.

THREE-DIGIT, ASCII-BASED, OCTAL-TO-BINARY

The first number-base-conversion problem that we will address is that of converting three-digit octal numbers to eight-bit binary numbers. The octal digits will be represented by three ASCII characters (ASCII-based). An operator will press the keys numbered 0 through 7 on a teletypewriter or crt. The ASCII characters thus generated will be received by the microcomputer and will then be packed into an eight-bit word through the use of a computer program. This binary information is then saved in a register or memory location. For instance, when the keys 3, 2, and 3 are pressed in sequence, a binary 11010011 must be saved in memory, since $323_8 =$ 11010011_2. If the keys 0 through 7 are pressed, the teletypewriter will produce the codes listed in Table 6-1.

It is fortunate that the least-significant digit of the code, in either octal or hexadecimal, is identical to the number of the key that is

Table 6-1. Octal, Hexadecimal, and Binary Values for the ASCII Characters 0 Through 7

Key	Character Values		
	Octal	Hex	Binary
0	260	B0	10110000
1	261	B1	10110001
2	262	B2	10110010
3	263	B3	10110011
4	264	B4	10110100
5	265	B5	10110101
6	266	B6	10110110
7	267	B7	10110111

pressed. Note that when any one of these keys is pressed, the tele-typewriter will transmit the corresponding binary codes listed in Table 6-1. If the keys 1, 2, and 5 are pressed in sequence, the codes 261 (B1), 262 (B2), and 265 (B5) will be transmitted. The computer program will have to mask-out the five MSBs that are transmitted, and then pack the remaining bits of information into the most-significant two bits, the middle three bits, and the least-significant three bits, respectively. This eight-bit byte is then placed in a register or a memory location.

If the 1, 2, and 5 keys are pressed in sequence, binary 01010101 will have to be saved. The first character that will be received by the 8080 will be an ASCII "1." The six MSBs will have to be masked-out, and the remaining two bits will then have to be rotated into the MSBs of the A register, as shown in Example 6-1.

Example 6-1: A Routine That Inputs and Saves a Value in the Two MSBs of the A Register

```
CALL    /GET A TELETYPEWRITER CHARACTER.
TTYIN
0
ANI     /REMOVE THE 6 MSB'S
003     /SAVING THE 2 LSB'S.
RRC     /ROTATE THE VALUE RIGHT INTO THE
RRC     /MOST SIGNIFICANT BITS OF THE WORD.
  •
  •
  •
```

The CALL instruction calls the TTYIN subroutine, which inputs a single character from the teletypewriter or crt. The ANI 003 instruction then sets the six MSBs of the A register to zero. The contents of the A register are then rotated to the right twice. This causes bit D_0 to be rotated into bit D_6, and bit D_1 to be rotated into bit D_7. Of course, these bits could have also been rotated into bits D_6 and

D_7 by executing six RLC instructions. However, this would mean that the program would be four instructions longer. Now that the ASCII character "1" has been received and processed, the ASCII character "2" will be received next, so the 01000000 contained in the A register will have to be saved before the next ASCII character can be input into the 8080. To receive and process the entire three-digit octal value, the program listed in Example 6-2 can be used. This program expects that three ASCII values from keyboard keys 0 through 7 will be input. It cannot detect nonvalid keys such as "A," "?," or "9."

Instead of using the instruction ANI 003, what other two-byte instruction could be used? The two-byte instruction SUI 060 could be used.

Example 6-2: An ASCII-Based, Octal-to-Binary Conversion Subroutine

```
OCTIN,  CALL    /GET THE MOST SIGNIFICANT DIGIT
        TTYIN   /FROM THE TELETYPEWRITER.
        0
        ANI     /REMOVE THE 6 MSB'S FROM
        003     /THE ASCII VALUE (10110XXX).
        RRC     /ROTATE THE VALUE RIGHT INTO THE
        RRC     /MOST SIGNIFICANT BITS OF THE WORD.
        MOVCA   /SAVE THE VALUE IN C.
        CALL    /GET THE NEXT CHARACTER FROM THE
        TTYIN   /TELETYPEWRITER.
        0
        ANI     /REMOVE THE 5 MSB'S FROM THE
        007     /ASCII VALUE ALSO (10110XXX).
        RLC     /ROTATE THE VALUE LEFT INTO THE
        RLC     /MIDDLE THREE BITS OF THE A REGISTER.
        RLC
        ADDC    /ADD THE FIRST DIGIT TO IT.
        MOVCA   /SAVE THE COMBINED WORD IN C.
        CALL    /NOW GET THE LEAST SIGNIFICANT DIGIT
        TTYIN   /OF THE WORD.
        0
        ANI     /REMOVE THE 5 MSB'S FROM THE
        007     /ASCII VALUE (10110XXX).
        ADDC    /COMBINE THE WORDS. THE BINARY
        RET     /VALUE IS NOW IN THE A REGISTER.
```

Remember, the TTYIN subroutine masks-out the parity bit (bit D_7) from all of the teletypewriter characters that are received (Chapter 3). Therefore, if a 260 (B0) is received and processed by the TTYIN subroutine, the value 060 (30) is present in the A register when control is returned to the calling program. If the subroutine listed in Example 6-2 is used, what would the content of the A register be when the 8080 returns from the subroutine if the 1, 9, and 2 keys on the teletypewriter were pressed in the order given?

The content of the A register would be 112 (4A). Why? Remember that when a number is entered, it is ANDed with an immediate data byte of 003 (03) or 007 (07). Since the 9 key was the second key pressed, it is ANDed with 007 (07). Since the ASCII value for 9 is 271,

$$\begin{array}{ll} 00111001 & \text{Content of A} \\ \underline{00000111} & \text{ANI data byte} \\ 00000001 & \text{Content of A after ANI} \end{array}$$

the content of the A register will be 001 (01). Therefore, instead of having a binary 9 (1001) in the middle three bits, there is a 001. Of course, if the ASCII-based, octal-to-binary conversion subroutine has been properly written, the 8080 should not process the ASCII characters 8 and 9 because they are not valid octal numbers. In fact, the 8080 should ignore all the ASCII characters other than 0 through 7. Therefore, an improved version of the ASCII-based, octal-to-binary conversion subroutine is listed in Example 6-3.

Example 6-3: An Improved ASCII-Based, Octal-to-Binary Conversion Subroutine

```
OCTIN,    LXID     /LOAD REGISTER PAIR D WITH 000 003
          003      /(0003). E WILL CONTAIN 003 (03)
          000      /AND D WILL CONTAIN 000 (00).
OCTIN1,   CALL     /GET A TELETYPEWRITER OR CRT CHARACTER
          TTYIN    /(IT WILL BE PRINTED ON THE TELETYPE-
          0        /WRITER OR CRT) AND RETURN WITH IT IN A.
          CPI      /THE PARITY BIT (D7) = 0
          060      /IS THE VALUE LESS THAN AN ASCII 0 ?
          JC       /YES, THEN IGNORE THE CHARACTER.
          OCTIN1
          0
          CPI      /IS IT EQUAL TO OR GREATER THAN
          070      /THE VALUE FOR AN ASCII 8 ?
          JNC      /YES, THEN THE CARRY IS CLEARED, SO
          OCTIN1   /JUMP IF IT IS EQUAL TO OR GREATER
          0        /THAN THE CODE FOR ASCII 8.
          ANI      /OK, IT'S ASCII 0 THROUGH 7, SET ALL
          007      /THE BITS EXCEPT D2, D1, AND D0 TO ZERO.
          MOVBA    /SAVE THE NUMBER TEMPORARILY IN B.
          MOVAD    /GET THE PREVIOUS DIGITS AND ROTATE
          RLC      /THEM TO THE LEFT THREE TIMES. THIS
          RLC      /WILL INCREASE THEIR SIGNIFICANCE AND
          RLC      /MAKE ROOM FOR THE NUMBER JUST ENTERED.
          ADDB     /ADD THE NUMBER JUST ENTERED.
          MOVDA    /SAVE THE NEW BINARY NUMBER IN D.
          DCRE     /DECREMENT THE DIGIT COUNTER.
          JNZ      /IF THE COUNT IS NOT ZERO,
          OCTIN1   /GET ANOTHER CHARACTER.
          0
          RET      /RETURN WITH THE BINARY VALUE IN D.
```

The first instruction of this subroutine initializes register pair D with 000 003 (0003). The 003 (03) is loaded into the E register. This will be used as a digit counter; that is, the number of ASCII-based octal digits that can be packed into an eight-bit word. The D register is loaded with 000 (00) because it will be used for temporary storage. Starting at OCTIN1, the 8080 calls the TTYIN subroutine so that a character may be received by the microcomputer from the teletypewriter. When the 8080 returns from the subroutine, the content of the A register, which is the ASCII character, is immediately compared to the value 060 (30). This is the seven-bit ASCII value for the 0 key. If the character received by the 8080 is less than the value for an ASCII 0, the JC to OCTIN1 is executed. This section of the subroutine causes the 8080 to ignore all ASCII characters that have values less than 060.

The second CPI instruction compares the content of the A register to 070 (38). This instruction determines whether or not the content of the A register is 067 (2F) or less. Since the values for the ASCII characters 0 through 7 are between 060 and 067 (30 and 37), the carry flag will be true after the second comparison if a 0 through 7 is received. If the 8 key on the keyboard is pressed, or any other key that produces a key code greater than 067 is pressed, the JNC instruction will be executed, and the 8080 will again call the TTYIN subroutine. This group of four instructions causes the 8080 to ignore all values that do not represent the characters 0 through 7. This is a good illustration of the use of successive comparisons to filter out a set of values rather than one value alone.

Only if one of the keys, 0 through 7, is pressed will the 8080 execute the ANI instruction. The ANI 007 instruction causes only data bits D_0, D_1, and D_2 to be saved in the A register. This binary value is then saved in the B register. The previous one- or two-digit packed value is then moved from register D, the temporary storage register, to the A register. Three RLC instructions are then executed, so that "room" is created in bit positions D_0, D_1, and D_2 of the A register for the binary code of the ASCII-based octal digit that was just entered. After the RLC instructions are executed, the content of the B register is added to the A register. Since only bits D_0, D_1, and D_2 of the A register can be nonzero, due to the use of the ANI instruction, the ADDB instruction combines the previous binary value with the binary value for the key that was just pressed. An ORAB instruction could have also been used. After the ADDB instruction is executed, the new eight-bit word is saved in the D register, and the digit count in the E register is decremented by 1. If the content of the E register is nonzero after the DCRE instruction is executed, the 8080 executes the JNZ to OCTIN1, where the microcomputer waits for another teletypewriter character to be entered. Only when three valid keys (0 through 7) on the teletypewriter keyboard have been pressed, which means that the content of the E register has been decremented to zero, will the 8080 execute the RET instruction. When it does, the binary equivalent of the three octal digits that were entered is in the D register.

What would the content of the D register be if a 477 is entered on the teletypewriter keyboard? Because the D register is only eight bits long, the content of the D register would be 077. This is shown in the following:

477   **077**
100 111 111 to 00 111 111

Therefore, if a 777 is entered, the D register will contain 11111111_2, or 377.

EIGHT-BIT, BINARY-TO-ASCII-BASED OCTAL

Unlike the ASCII-based, octal-to-binary conversion subroutine, where a general-purpose mask (ANI 007) and three rotate instructions (RLC) could be used, the same techniques cannot be used in the binary-to-ASCII-based octal conversion subroutine. To see why, examine octal 156,

01 101 110

To convert a binary word to the appropriate ASCII-based octal digits, the ASCII characters 0 through 7 (260 through 267) will have to be printed on the teletypewriter or crt. To do this, the value to be printed, 000_2 through 111_2, has to be moved to the least-significant bits of the A register. A 260 would then have to be added to the content of the A register, and the resulting ASCII numeric character printed. To position the bits for the number 01101110, the 01 in the two MSBs would have to be rotated to the right six times or to the left twice. The 101 in the middle three bits would have to be rotated to the right three times, and the 110 would not have to be rotated at all. A subroutine that converts the binary content of the memory location addressed by register pair H to the three appropriate ASCII characters and prints them on a teletypewriter or crt is listed in Example 6-4.

The first instruction in this example loads the content of the memory location addressed by register pair H into the A register of the 8080. The ANI instruction masks-out all but bits D_6 and D_7 of the A register. These two bits are rotated to the left twice; this rotates them into bit positions D_0 and D_1 of the A register. The BCDOUT subroutine, which adds 260 to the content of the A register, is then called and prints the character on the teletypewriter.

Example 6-4: A Binary-to-ASCII-Based, Octal Conversion Subroutine

```
/THIS SUBROUTINE CONVERTS THE BINARY VALUE STORED IN
/THE MEMORY LOCATION ADDRESSED BY REGISTER PAIR H
/INTO A THREE-DIGIT, ASCII-BASED, OCTAL NUMBER.

BINOCT,   MOVAM    /GET A BINARY VALUE FROM MEMORY.
          ANI      /THE MOST SIGNIFICANT DIGIT
          300      /MUST BE PRINTED FIRST.
          RLC      /ROTATE THE TWO MSB'S INTO THE LSB'S.
          RLC
          CALL     /NOW CALL THE BCDOUT SUBROUTINE, WHICH
          BCDOUT   /WILL ADD 260 TO THE CONTENT
          0        /OF THE A REGISTER AND PRINT IT.
          MOVAM    /NOW THE MIDDLE DIGIT MUST BE PRINTED.
          ANI      /MASK OUT ALL BUT THE MIDDLE 3 BITS.
          070
          RRC      /THEN ROTATE THEM INTO THE
          RRC      /3 LSB'S.
          RRC
          CALL     /ADD 260 TO THE CONTENT OF
          BCDOUT   /THE A REGISTER AND PRINT THE RESULT.
          0
          MOVAM    /NOW PRINT THE RIGHT HAND DIGIT.
          ANI      /MASK OUT ALL BUT THE 3 LSB'S.
          007
          CALL     /THEN ADD 260 TO THE NUMBER AND PRINT
          BCDOUT   /THE CHARACTER.
          0
          RET      /RETURN FROM THE SUBROUTINE.

BCDOUT,   ADI      /ADD 260 TO THE CONTENT OF THE A REGISTER.
          260      /(THIS IS B0 IN HEXADECIMAL).
          CALL     /PRINT THE ASCII CHARACTER
          TTYOUT   /ON THE TELETYPEWRITER OR CRT.
          0
          RET      /THEN RETURN FROM "BCDOUT."

TTYOUT,   MOVBA    /SAVE THE CHARACTER IN B.
TTYO,     IN       /INPUT THE UART'S STATUS WORD.
          001
          ANI      /SAVE ONLY THE TRANSMITTER'S FLAG.
          004      /IF A=004, THE TRANSMITTER (PRINTER) IS READY.
          JZ       /IF A=000, THE TRANSMITTER (PRINTER) IS BUSY.
          TTYO     /SO KEEP WAITING FOR THE TRANSMITTER
          0        /(PRINTER) TO FINISH, BEFORE THE
          MOVAB    /CONTENT OF THE A REGISTER CAN BE PRINTED.
          OUT      /AFTER THE CHARACTER IS MOVED FROM
          000      /B TO A, OUTPUT IT TO THE UART.
          RET      /RETURN WITH THE CHARACTER STILL IN A.
```

Before the 260 is added to the content of the A register, the A register can only contain an octal 000, 001, 002, or 003, because only two bits were left in the A register by the ANI 300 instruction. After adding 260 to the content of A, the result could be 260, 261, 262, or 263.

After the addition, the 8080 calls the TTYOUT subroutine, which prints the ASCII character contained in the A register on the teletypewriter or crt. After the 8080 prints the character using the TTYOUT subroutine, control returns to the RET instruction in the BCDOUT subroutine. This RET instruction then returns control to the second MOVAM instruction in the BINOCT subroutine. This program can be simplified by changing the CALL to TTYOUT in the BCDOUT subroutine to a JMP to TTYOUT. The RET instruction at the end of the BCDOUT subroutine can then be eliminated (Example 6-5).

When the program listed in Example 6-4 is executed, a return address is saved on the stack when the BCDOUT subroutine is called. A second return address is then saved on the stack when the TTYOUT subroutine is called. The RET instruction at the end of the TTYOUT subroutine then causes the 8080 to return to the BCDOUT subroutine, and the RET instruction at the end of this subroutine causes the 8080 to return to the BINOCT subroutine. By changing the CALL to TTYOUT to a JMP to TTYOUT, a return address is saved on the stack when the BCDOUT subroutine is called. The JMP to TTYOUT then causes the content of the A register to be printed on the teletypewriter. The RET instruction at the end of TTYOUT then causes the 8080 to return to BINOCT rather than BCDOUT. Note that BCDOUT and TTYOUT are still general-purpose subroutines, and they can be called by any other program or subroutine, not just BINOCT. By jumping to TTYOUT rather than calling it, one memory location is saved by not having a RET instruction at the end of BCDOUT, and two R/W memory locations used by the stack are also saved. Only one return address is saved on the stack rather than two.

Example 6-5: A Modified and Simpler BCDOUT Subroutine

```
BCDOUT,  ADI      /ADD 260 (B0) TO THE CONTENT OF A TO
         260      /CREATE AN ASCII CHARACTER.
         JMP      /THEN JUMP TO THE TELETYPEWRITER OR CRT
         TTYOUT   /PRINTER SUBROUTINE SO THAT THE CHAR-
         0        /ACTER IN THE A REGISTER IS PRINTED.
```

If you ever have a subroutine that ends in the following manner:

```
                    CALL
                    XXX
                    YYY
                    RET
```

it can be simplified by writing,

```
JMP
XXX
YYY
```

After the 8080 prints the first character on the teletypewriter, control returns to the BINOCT subroutine. The content of the same memory location addressed by register pair H is loaded into the A register. However, the content of the A register is ANDed with 070 this time. This means that the A register will only have nonzero data in the middle three bits, D_5, D_4, and D_3. These three bits are then rotated three times to the right into bit positions D_2, D_1, and D_0. The BCDOUT subroutine is then called, and the ASCII equivalent for the middle three bits (D_5, D_4, and D_3) of the content of memory is then printed. It is easy to see how the remaining three bits of the eight-bit word are treated. This subroutine might be called the "brute-force" method, because it does not contain any convenient loops that can be used to make the program more compact.

The program listed in Example 6-6 does use a loop to perform the binary-to-ASCII-based octal conversion. This subroutine is not only longer, but it is also more complex than the subroutine listed in Example 6-4. For this reason, a detailed description will not be given.

Example 6-6: A Binary-to-ASCII-Based, Octal Conversion Subroutine That Uses a Loop

```
/THIS SUBROUTINE USES A LOOP TO CONVERT THE BINARY
/VALUE STORED IN THE MEMORY LOCATION ADDRESSED BY
/REGISTER PAIR H TO A THREE-DIGIT, ASCII-BASED,
/OCTAL NUMBER.

BINOCT,  MOVAM   /GET A BINARY CHARACTER FROM MEMORY.
         ANI     /MASK OUT ALL BUT THE MSB'S.
         300
         MVIC    /LOAD THE ROTATE COUNTER WITH 002
         002     /(THREE ROTATES FOR EACH COUNT).
         CALL    /THIS WILL CAUSE THE CONTENT OF THE
         BNOCT   /A REGISTER TO BE ROTATED RIGHT 6 TIMES.
         0       /THEN ADD 260 (B0) AND PRINT THE RESULT.
         MOVAM   /GET THE BINARY WORD AGAIN.
         ANI     /MASK OUT ALL BUT THE 3 MIDDLE BITS.
         070
         MVIC    /SET THE ROTATE COUNTER TO 1
         001     /SO ONLY 3 ROTATES WILL BE EXECUTED.
         CALL    /AFTER THE ROTATE INSTRUCTIONS ARE
         BNOCT   /EXECUTED, 260 WILL BE ADDED AND THE
         0       /RESULT PRINTED.
         MOVAM   /GET THE BINARY VALUE AGAIN.
         ANI     /NO ROTATES ARE NEEDED, GO DIRECTLY
         007     /TO THE ADDITION INSTRUCTION (ADI).
```

```
                JMP
                BNOCT1
                0
BNOCT,          RRC        /ROTATE THE CONTENT OF THE A
                RRC        /REGISTER TO THE RIGHT THREE TIMES.
                RRC
                DCRC       /DECREMENT THE COUNT.
                JNZ        /NOT 0, ROTATE IT THREE MORE TIMES.
                BNOCT
                0
BNOCT1,         ADI        /NOW ADD 260 (B0) TO THE A REGISTER.
                260
                JMP        /THEN JUMP TO THE TELETYPEWRITER
                TTYOUT     /SUBROUTINE THAT HAS BEEN USED IN
                0          /THE PREVIOUS EXAMPLES.
```

**Example 6-7: A Comparison of the "Brute-Force" and Loop Methods
for Converting a Binary Word to ASCII-Based Octal
Characters**

OLD—WITHOUT LOOP

NEW—WITH LOOP

```
BINOCT,    MOVAM                    BINOCT,    MOVAM
           ANI                                 ANI
           300                                 300
           RLC                                 MVIC
           RLC                                 002
           CALL                                CALL
           BCDOUT                              BNOCT
           0                                   0
           MOVAM                               MOVAM
           ANI                                 ANI
           070                                 070
           RRC                                 MVIC
           RRC                                 001
           RRC                                 CALL
           CALL                                BNOCT
           BCDOUT                              0
           0                                   MOVAM
           MOVAM                               ANI
           ANI                                 007
           007                                 JMP
BCDOUT,    ADI                                 BNOCT1
           260                                 0
           JMP
           TTYOUT                   BNOCT,     RRC
           0                                   RRC
                                               RRC
                                               DCRC
                                               JNZ
                                               BNOCT
                                               0
                                    BNOCT1,    ADI
                                               260
                                               JMP
                                               TTYOUT
                                               0
```

A side-by-side comparison of the two subroutines is made in Example 6-7. As you can see, the "brute-force," or *pipeline*, method requires nine fewer memory locations and one fewer register. Clearly, the use of a loop in a program may not always be the best way to write a program or subroutine. One of the shortest binary-to-ASCII-based octal conversion subroutines is listed in Example 6-8.

Example 6-8: A Short Binary-to-ASCII-Based, Octal Conversion Subroutine

```
/THIS SUBROUTINE CONVERTS THE BINARY VALUE STORED IN
/THE MEMORY LOCATION ADDRESSED BY REGISTER PAIR H
/INTO A THREE-DIGIT, ASCII-BASED, OCTAL NUMBER.


BINOCT,   MOVAM    /GET A BINARY VALUE FROM MEMORY.
          ANI      /THE MOST SIGNIFICANT DIGIT
          300      /MUST BE PRINTED FIRST.
          RLC      /ROTATE THE TWO MSB'S INTO THE LSB'S.
          RLC
          CALL     /NOW CALL THE BCDOUT SUBROUTINE, WHICH
          BCDOUT   /WILL ADD 260 TO THE CONTENT
          0        /OF THE A REGISTER AND PRINT IT.
          MOVAM    /NOW THE MIDDLE DIGIT MUST BE PRINTED.
          ANI      /MASK OUT ALL BUT THE MIDDLE 3 BITS.
          070
          RRC      /THEN ROTATE THEM INTO THE
          RRC      /3 LSB'S.
          RRC
          CALL     /ADD 260 TO THE CONTENT OF
          BCDOUT   /THE A REGISTER AND PRINT THE RESULT.
          0
          MOVAM    /NOW PRINT THE RIGHT HAND DIGIT.
          ANI      /MASK OUT ALL BUT THE 3 LSB'S.
          007
BCDOUT,   ADI      /ADD 260 TO THE A REGISTER
          260      /(THIS IS B0 IN HEXADECIMAL).
          JMP      /PRINT THE ASCII CHARACTER
          TTYOUT   /ON THE TELETYPEWRITER OR CRT.
          0
```

TWO-DIGIT, ASCII-BASED, HEXADECIMAL-TO-BINARY

Some programmers prefer to use the hexadecimal numbering system rather than the octal numbering system when programming the 8080. For this reason, ASCII-based hexadecimal-to-binary and binary-to-ASCII-based hexadecimal conversion subroutines are needed. For those readers not familiar with the hexadecimal numbering system, Table 6-2 is presented.

After the number 9, the letter A is used to represent 1010 rather than the number 10. Notice the discontinuity between the ASCII

Table 6-2. The Hexadecimal Numbering System

Hexadecimal Character	Binary Value	ASCII Value	
0	0000	260	B0
1	0001	261	B1
2	0010	262	B2
3	0011	263	B3
4	0100	264	B4
5	0101	265	B5
6	0110	266	B6
7	0111	267	B7
8	1000	270	B8
9	1001	271	B9
A	1010	301	C1
B	1011	302	C2
C	1100	303	C3
D	1101	304	C4
E	1110	305	C5
F	1111	306	C6

values for the characters 9 (271, B9) and A (301, C1). For the ASCII values that are given in Table 6-2, it has been assumed that the MSB of the eight-bit value is always a logic 1. This is the parity bit of the ASCII value. Depending on the teletypewriter or crt used, this bit may be either a logic 1 or 0. Our examples have assumed a logic 1.

In a previous example, it was very easy to convert the ASCII characters 0 through 7 to binary values. In fact, the subroutine only required the use of an AND mask and some rotate instructions. A more complex conversion subroutine is required to convert ASCII-based hexadecimal characters to binary because the four LSBs of the ASCII value for the letter keys do not correspond to the required binary numbers. For example, ASCII A (11000001) must be converted to 00001010. One of the nice features of using hexadecimal numbers is that only two hexadecimal digits are required per eight-bit binary number. As you know, three octal digits are required per eight-bit binary number. Quite often, this is the strongest argument given for using hexadecimal rather than octal numbers when programming the 8080. Some typical examples of binary, octal, and hexadecimal numbers are shown in Table 6-3.

Table 6-3. Some Binary, Octal, and Hexadecimal Numbers

Binary	Octal	Hexadecimal
00000000	000	00
01000000	100	40
10000000	200	80
11001010	312	CA
11111111	377	FF

A subroutine that converts two hexadecimal numbers, obtained from a teletyptwriter or crt ASCII keyboard, to an eight-bit binary number, is listed in Example 6-9. The HEXBIN subroutine can be called at any time. When the subroutine is called, two hexadecimal numbers can be entered on the teletypewriter or crt keyboard. The

Example 6-9: An ASCII-Based, Hexadecimal-to-Binary Conversion Subroutine

```
/THIS SUBROUTINE CONVERTS TWO ASCII-BASED HEX-
/ADECIMAL CHARACTERS INTO AN EIGHT-BIT BINARY WORD.


HEXBIN,  CALL     /GET A HEXADECIMAL CHARACTER (ASCII)
         HEXIN    /FROM THE TELETYPEWRITER'S KEYBOARD.
         0
         RLC      /ROTATE THE BINARY EQUIVALENT INTO
         RLC      /THE 4 MSB'S.
         RLC
         RLC
         MOVCA    /SAVE THE VALUE IN C TEMPORARILY.
         CALL     /GET THE SECOND AND LAST HEXADECIMAL
         HEXIN    /CHARACTER FROM THE KEYBOARD.
         0
         ADDC     /ADD THE TWO DIGITS TOGETHER
         RET      /AND RETURN WITH THE VALUE IN A.
HEXIN,   CALL     /GET A CHARACTER FROM THE KEYBOARD.
         TTYIN
         0
         CPI      /IS THE CODE LESS THAN 060 (0) ?
         060
         JC       /YES, THEN IGNORE IT.
         HEXIN
         0
         CPI      /IS IT LESS THAN : (0-9) ?
         072
         JC       /YES, THEN A NUMBER (0-9) WAS
         NOLET    /ENTERED, SO JUMP TO NOLET.
         0
         CPI      /NOT 0-9, IS IT A-F ?
         101      /IS IT LESS THAN ASCII A ?
         JC       /YES, THEN IGNORE IT.
         HEXIN
         0
         CPI      /IS IT LESS THAN ASCII G ?
         107
         JNC      /NO, THEN IGNORE IT.
         HEXIN
         0
         ADI      /ADD 011 (09) TO A THROUGH F TO
         011      /CONVERT THEM TO EQUIVALENT BINARY NUMBERS.
NOLET,   ANI      /NOW SAVE ONLY THE FOUR LSB'S.
         017
         RET
```

equivalent binary number will be in the A register when the 8080 returns from the subroutine.

When the HEXBIN subroutine is entered, the HEXIN subroutine is immediately called. At the beginning of HEXIN, the 8080 calls the TTYIN subroutine, so the 8080 waits for a crt or teletypewriter key to be pressed. As shown previously, the TTYIN subroutine inputs the ASCII character and masks-out the parity bit (D_7) by executing an ANI 177 instruction. When control returns to the HEXIN subroutine, the A register may contain any one of the 16 values listed in Table 6-4, if a valid hexadecimal number key is pressed.

After returning from TTYIN, the CPI 060 instruction checks for all characters that have ASCII values less than and not equal to 060 (30), which is the ASCII value for 0. No hexadecimal numbers have values less than this. If a key is pressed that produces a value less than 060 (30), the 8080 executes the JC to HEXIN. In this manner, the 8080 ignores nonvalid hexadecimal numbers with ASCII values less than 060 (30). By executing the CPI 072, the 8080 checks to see if the ASCII value for the keys 0 through 9 is in the A register. If the content of the A register is less than 072, the carry flag is set to a logic 1 by the CPI 072 instruction. Therefore, the 8080 does a JC to NOLET (*NO*t a *LET*ter) if one of the numeric keys 0 through 9 is pressed. At NOLET, the 8080 executes an ANI instruction that further masks the ASCII value contained in the A register. The result is that bits D_7 through D_4 are set to

Table 6-4. The Content of the A Register After Receiving an ASCII Character

Key	Content of A
0	00110000
1	00110001
2	00110010
3	00110011
4	00110100
5	00110101
6	00110110
7	00110111
8	00111000
9	00111001
A	01000001
B	01000010
C	01000011
D	01000100
E	01000101
F	01000110
The parity bit has been set to zero by TTYIN.	

zero, so that the ASCII values for the numbers 0 through 9 (260 through 271, B0 through B9) are converted to 0000 through 1001. These are the appropriate binary values for the numbers in the hexadecimal numbering system. After the ANI instruction at NOLET is executed, the 8080 returns to HEXBIN.

Suppose that instead of one of the numbers, 0 through 9, being entered, one of the letter keys is pressed. If this occurs, the 8080 does not perform the JC to NOLET because all of the ASCII values for the letters are greater than 072. Instead, the 8080 executes the CPI 101 instruction. Since the smallest value for an ASCII letter is 101 (41), the ASCII value for the letter A, the 8080 must check to see if any key that produces a value greater than 071 but less than 101 is pressed. If one of these keys is pressed, the 8080 will ignore it by jumping on a true carry (JC) to HEXIN. If the ASCII value is 101 or greater, the 8080 executes the CPI 107 instruction. If one of the letter keys, A through F, is pressed, the carry is cleared as a result of this instruction. If any key is pressed that produces an ASCII value greater than 106, the 8080 executes the JNC to HEXIN, which causes the value to be ignored. The purpose of the four CPI instructions is to "bracket" the valid ASCII hexadecimal key values. That is, only if one of the number keys, 0 through 9, or one of the letter keys, A through F, is pressed, will be 8080 execute the instructions at the end of the HEXIN subroutine. However, notice that 011 (09) is added to the ASCII values for the letter keys, A through F, before the four MSBs are set to zero at NOLET. If a number key is pressed, the 8080 simply masks-out the four MSBs. Why is 011 (09) added to the ASCII values for the valid ASCII-based hexadecimal letters? The four LSBs of the ASCII value for A are 0001. However, a hexadecimal A has to be converted to binary 1010. Therefore, 1001 must be added to the ASCII values for the hexadecimal letters to convert them to the proper binary value.

Table 6-5. The Conversion of ASCII-Based
Hexadecimal Letters to Binary Numbers

Letter	ASCII Value	After ADI 011	After ANI 017
A	01000001	01001010	00001010
B	01000010	01001011	00001011
C	01000011	01001100	00001100
D	01000100	01001101	00001101
E	01000101	01001110	00001110
F	01000110	01001111	00001111

When the 8080 returns from HEXIN to HEXBIN, register A contains the four-bit binary value for the ASCII-based hexadecimal character that was typed in. If any invalid hexadecimal characters are entered, the 8080 will remain in the HEXIN subroutine until a 0 through 9 or an A through F is entered. Because two hexadecimal characters comprise a single eight-bit number, the first four binary bits of information must be rotated four bit positions to the left. Remember, the first character entered represents the most-significant character of the two-character hexadecimal number. After rotating the first binary value four bit positions to the left, the value is saved in the C register. At this point, the 8080 calls the HEXIN subroutine a second time so that the second and least-significant character can be entered. When the 8080 returns from HEXIN the second time, the A register contains the proper binary value for the second hexadecimal character. The two values, one contained in the C register and one contained in the A register, are then combined when the ADDC instruction is executed. The 8080 then returns from the HEXBIN subroutine with the binary value for the two ASCII-based hexadecimal characters in the A register.

EIGHT-BIT, BINARY-TO-ASCII-BASED HEXADECIMAL

Now that hexadecimal characters from a teletypewriter or crt can be converted to the proper eight-bit binary number, a binary-to-ASCII-based hexadecimal conversion subroutine will be written. Before the subroutine in Example 6-10 is called, the binary value that is to be converted into two ASCII-based hexadecimal characters must be contained in the A register. As the conversion process takes place, the ASCII-based hexadecimal characters will be printed on the teletypewriter or crt.

When the BINHEX subroutine is called, the content of the A register, the binary number that is to be converted to ASCII-based hexadecimal, is saved in the C register. The four LSBs are then masked-out when the ANI 360 instruction is executed. If the A register contains

$$1111\ 1110$$

before the ANI instruction is executed, it will contain

$$1111\ 0000$$

afterward. The four MSBs are rotated into the four LSBs of A. The content of the A register could be between 0000 0000 and 0000 1111 now (00 through 0F). At this point in the subroutine, the content of A has to be printed on the teletypewriter or crt. Therefore, the PHEX (Print a HEXadecimal character) subroutine is called. At PHEX, the content of the A register is compared to 012 (0A). If the content of the A register is 0000 0000 through 0000 1001 (00 through 09), the carry flag is set by this comparison, indicating

Example 6-10: A Binary-to-ASCII-Based, Hexadecimal Conversion Subroutine

```
/THIS SUBROUTINE CONVERTS THE CONTENT OF THE A
/REGISTER TO TWO ASCII-BASED HEXADECIMAL CHARACTERS
/THAT ARE PRINTED ON A TELETYPEWRITER OR CRT.

BINHEX,   MOVAC    /SAVE THE BINARY NUMBER IN C.
          ANI      /SAVE THE FOUR MSB'S IN THE A REGISTER
          360      /BY ANDING IT WITH 360 (F0).
          RRC      /NOW ROTATE THE FOUR MSB'S INTO THE
          RRC      /FOUR LSB'S.
          RRC
          RRC
          CALL     /THEN PRINT THE HEXADECIMAL CHARACTER
          PHEX     /EQUIVALENT OF THE CONTENT OF
          0        /THE A REGISTER.
          MOVAC    /GET THE ORIGINAL BINARY NUMBER INTO A.
          ANI      /NOW JUST SAVE THE FOUR LSB'S.
          017
PHEX,     CPI      /SHOULD A NUMBER OR LETTER BE PRINTED ?
          012      /A 0000 - 1001 (0-9) ?
          JC       /YES, IT SHOULD BE A NUMBER.
          NMBOK
          0
          ADI      /NO, IT'S A LETTER, SO ADD 007 (07).
          007
NMBOK,    ADI      /NOW ADD 260 TO CONVERT IT TO
          260      /AN ASCII CHARACTER.
          JMP      /THEN JUMP TO THE PRINTER SUBROUTINE.
          TTYOUT
          0
```

that the content of A is equal to binary 0 through 9, thus ASCII 0 through 9 must be printed. As a result of this comparison, the JC to NMBOK is executed if the content of A is less than 0000 1010.

At NMBOK, 260 (B0) is added to the content of register A to convert the binary content of register A to a numeric ASCII character. This character is then printed when the 8080 jumps to the TTYOUT subroutine.

If the content of the A register is 0000 1010 through 0000 1111, the carry is cleared by the CPI 012 (0A) instruction. Therefore, the JC to NMBOK is not executed. Instead, 007 (07) is added to the content of A, after which 260 (B0) is added. The ASCII character is then printed when the 8080 jumps to the TTYOUT subroutine. For the numbers 1010 through 1111, a total of 267 (B7) has to be added to the content of the A register. If A contained 0000 1010, then

$$
\begin{array}{r}
0000\ 1010 \\
+\ 1011\ 0111 \\
\hline
1100\ 0001
\end{array}
$$

This means that 0000 1010 is converted to 1100 0001, the ASCII value for the letter A. These two consecutive add instructions, which add a total of 267 (B7) to the content of A, convert the binary numbers 1010 through 1111 to the proper ASCII-based hexadecimal characters A through F, which have values of 301 through 306 (C1 through C6).

After the character is printed by the TTYOUT subroutine, the RET instruction at the end of the TTYOUT subroutine is executed. This causes the 8080 to return to the BINHEX subroutine. The MOVAC instruction moves the eight-bit content of register C to register A. The four MSBs are then masked-out, or set to zero, by the instruction ANI 017. The next instruction that is executed is CPI 012. This is the first instruction in the PHEX subroutine, although this time the PHEX subroutine is executed even though it was not called. The 8080 was programmed so that the BINHEX subroutine "runs into" the PHEX subroutine. Some programmers might consider this a trick to save memory; others may feel that this is the only way that the subroutine should have been written in the first place. This is similar to the TTYIN subroutine (Example 3-20) which can be used for input and output (echo) or output alone (TTYOUT). As you can observe, the BINHEX subroutine might have been written as in Example 6-11.

As you can see, there are a number of CALL instructions that are immediately followed by RET instructions. By eliminating these situations, a more condensed version of the subroutine is produced. The only problem with the more condensed version of the subroutine is that it may be more difficult to understand when examined for the first time.

The BINHEX can be condensed even further by eliminating an ANI instruction (Example 6-12).

Now that the conversions between the binary, octal and hexadecimal numbering systems have been discussed, conversion subroutines for decimal and binary will be discussed.

THREE-DIGIT, ASCII-BASED, DECIMAL-TO-BINARY

If mathematical operations are to be performed, many decimal numbers may have to be loaded into the 8080 microcomputer. As you have already seen, most of the 8080's mathematical operations are performed on binary numbers. Therefore, there has to be some method of converting decimal numbers to binary and, after the microcomputer calculates a result, converting the binary result to decimal notation. Once the result is in decimal, it can be printed on a teletypewriter or crt. As you already know, decimal numbers can be expressed as integers multiplied by powers of 10. For example,

$$237 = (2 \times 10^2) + (3 \times 10^1) + (7 \times 10^0)$$

or

$$237 = (2 \times 100) + (3 \times 10) + (7 \times 1)$$

Since only one digit of a number can be entered into the 8080 microcomputer at a time, there will have to be a multiply-by-10 routine or subroutine in a general-purpose, ASCII-based, decimal-to-binary conversion subroutine. In this type of multiplication routine, when a 93 is entered, the 9 must be multiplied by 10 before

Example 6-11: A Longer Binary-to-ASCII-Based, Hexadecimal Conversion Subroutine

/THIS SUBROUTINE CONVERTS THE CONTENT OF THE A
/REGISTER TO TWO ASCII-BASED HEXADECIMAL CHARACTERS
/THAT ARE PRINTED ON A TELETYPEWRITER OR CRT.

```
BINHEX, MOVCA   /SAVE THE BINARY NUMBER IN C.
        ANI     /SAVE THE FOUR MSB'S IN THE A REGISTER
        360     /BY ANDING IT WITH 360 (F0).
        RRC     /NOW ROTATE THE FOUR MSB'S INTO THE
        RRC     /FOUR LSB'S.
        RRC
        RRC
        CALL    /THEN PRINT THE HEXADECIMAL CHARACTER
        PHEX    /EQUIVALENT OF THE CONTENT OF
        0       /THE A REGISTER.
        MOVAC   /GET THE ORIGINAL BINARY NUMBER INTO A.
        ANI     /NOW JUST SAVE THE FOUR LSB'S.
        017
        CALL
        PHEX    /NOW PRINT THE LEAST SIGNIFICANT DIGIT
        0       /OF THE HEXADECIMAL WORD.
        RET     /THEN RETURN TO THE CALLING PROGRAM.
PHEX,   CPI     /SHOULD A NUMBER OR LETTER BE PRINTED ?
        012     /A 0000 - 1001 (0-9) ?
        JC      /YES, IT SHOULD BE A NUMBER.
        NMBOK
        0
        ADI     /NO, IT'S A LETTER, SO ADD 007 (07).
        007
NMBOK,  ADI     /NOW ADD 260 TO CONVERT IT TO
        260     /AN ASCII CHARACTER.
        CALL    /THEN CALL THE TTYOUT SUBROUTINE
        TTYOUT  /WHICH WILL PRINT THE CONTENT OF A ON
        0       /A TELETYPEWRITER OR CRT.
        RET     /THEN RETURN TO THE BINHEX SUBROUTINE.
```

Example 6-12: A Very Short Binary-to-ASCII-Based, Hexadecimal Conversion Subroutine

```
/THIS SUBROUTINE CONVERTS THE CONTENT OF THE A
/REGISTER TO TWO ASCII-BASED HEXADECIMAL CHARACTERS
/THAT ARE PRINTED ON A TELETYPEWRITER OR CRT.

BINHEX,   MOVCA   /SAVE THE BINARY NUMBER IN C.
          RRC     /NOW ROTATE THE FOUR MSB'S INTO THE
          RRC     /FOUR LSB'S.
          RRC
          RRC
          CALL    /THEN PRINT THE HEXADECIMAL CHARACTER
          PHEX    /EQUIVALENT OF THE CONTENT OF
          0       /THE A REGISTER.
          MOVAC   /GET THE ORIGINAL BINARY NUMBER INTO A.
PHEX,     ANI     /NOW JUST SAVE THE FOUR LSB'S.
          017
          CPI     /SHOULD A NUMBER OR LETTER BE PRINTED ?
          012     /A 0000 - 1001 (0-9) ?
          JC      /YES, IT SHOULD BE A NUMBER.
          NMBOK
          0
          ADI     /NO, IT'S A LETTER, SO ADD 007 (07).
          007
NMBOK,    ADI     /NOW ADD 260 TO CONVERT IT TO
          260     /AN ASCII CHARACTER.
          JMP     /THEN JUMP TO THE PRINTER SUBROUTINE.
          TTYOUT
          0
```

being added to the 3. A general-purpose, ASCII-based, decimal-to-binary conversion subroutine is listed in Example 6-13. This subroutine has the same problem as the three-digit, ASCII-based, octal-to-binary conversion subroutine. That is, numbers can be entered that are not "properly" converted. In Example 6-3, the number 777 can be entered, but it will be converted to 1111111. In Example 6-13, only the numbers between 0 and 255 can be entered and converted properly. If numbers between 256 and 999 are entered, they will not be converted to the proper binary number.

At the start of the DECBIN subroutine, two of the 8080's registers are initialized. The D register is loaded with 003 (03), which is the number of ASCII-based decimal digits that can be input by the subroutine. The C register is used for temporary storage, so it is initialized to 000 (00). One memory location could be saved by using one of the register pairs rather than registers C and D. At DECIT, the TTYIN subroutine is called. The instructions from DECIT down to the ANI instruction cause the 8080 to input only valid decimal ASCII characters, 0 through 9. This bracketing function is also in many of our previous software examples in this chapter. The ANI instruction "filters" out only the BCD code for

Example 6-13: An ASCII-Based, Decimal-to-Binary Conversion Subroutine

```
/THIS SUBROUTINE CONVERTS A THREE-DIGIT, ASCII-BASED
/DECIMAL NUMBER INTO A BINARY EQUIVALENT.


DECBIN,   MVID      /THIS IS THE NUMBER OF DECIMAL DIGITS
          003       /THAT MAY BE ENTERED (000 TO 255).
          MVIC      /CLEAR C BECAUSE IT WILL BE USED
          000       /AS A TEMPORARY STORAGE REGISTER.
DECIT,    CALL      /GET A KEYBOARD CHARACTER.
          TTYIN
          0
          CPI       /IS THE KEY CODE LESS THAN ASCII 0 ?
          060
          JC        /YES. IGNORE THE CODE AND WAIT
          DECIT     /FOR ANOTHER KEY TO BE PRESSED.
          0
          CPI       /IS IT LESS THAN : (0-9) ?
          072
          JNC       /NO. IGNORE IT AND WAIT FOR
          DECIT     /ANOTHER KEY TO BE PRESSED.
          0
          ANI       /NOW MASK OUT THE FOUR MSB'S, LEAVING
          017       /THE FOUR LSB'S.
          MOVBA     /SAVE THE DECIMAL DIGIT IN B.
          MOVAC     /GET THE TEMPORARY NUMBER IN C.
          RLC       /MULTIPLY THE NUMBER BY TWO.
          RLC       /MULTIPLY BY TWO AGAIN (TOTAL = X4).
          ADDC      /ADD THE ORIGINAL NUMBER (TOTAL = X5).
          RLC       /MULTIPLY BY TWO (TOTAL = X10).
          ADDB      /ADD THE PREVIOUS CHARACTER CODE.
          MOVCA     /SAVE THE NEW BINARY NUMBER IN C.
          DCRD      /DECREMENT THE DIGIT COUNTER.
          JNZ       /THREE DIGITS YET ?
          DECIT
          0
          RET       /THREE DIGITS WHERE ENTERED, RETURN WITH
                    /THE BINARY NUMBER IN C.
```

Table 6-6. The ASCII-Based Decimal Characters

Character	Binary Equivalent
ASCII 1	00000001
ASCII 2	00000010
ASCII 3	00000011
ASCII 4	00000100
ASCII 5	00000101
ASCII 6	00000110
ASCII 7	00000111
ASCII 8	00001000
ASCII 9	00001001

each valid digit. Any one of the following numbers could now be in the A register, depending on the key pressed (Table 6-6).

No matter what the content of register A is, it is saved in the B register after the ANI instruction is executed. The content of the C register is then moved to the A register, and a number of rotate and addition instructions are then executed. What do these instructions do?

Suppose the number 93 must be entered into a particular 8080 program. If the 9 is entered, you would expect it to be stored in a register in the following format,

$$00001001$$

However, when the 3 is entered, the 9 has to be multiplied by 10, the result being 90, or the equivalent binary number,

$$01011010$$

After the multiplication by 10 is performed, the binary value for 3 can be added to the binary value for 90, to form the desired result, 93 (01011101_2). How does the multiplication by 10 take place? From our discussion of multiplication, you should remember that multiplication by 2 is the same as rotating the number to the left once. To divide a number by 2, the number simply has to be rotated to the right once.

If A contains 00000001, the rotation of A to the left three times would be the same as multiplication by 2^3, or 8. If the content of register A was rotated to the left five times, the content of register A would be multiplied by 2^5, or 32. Fortunately, the content of register A can easily be multiplied by 9, 31, or even 62 by using rotate and other simple instructions.

In the DECBIN subroutine, a number has to be multiplied by 10. You already know

$$A \times 10 = (A \times 5) \times 2$$

Therefore, to multiply the content of the C register by 10, the instructions listed in Example 6-14 can be executed.

Example 6-14: Multiplying the Content of Register C by 10

```
    •
    •
MOVAC   /MOVE THE NUMBER FROM C TO A.
RLC     /MULTIPLY THE NUMBER BY TWO.
RLC     /MULTIPLY IT BY TWO AGAIN (TOTAL = X4).
ADDC    /ADD THE ORIGINAL NUMBER (TOTAL = X5).
RLC     /MULTIPLY THE RESULT BY TWO (TOTAL = X10).
    •
    •
```

This is the same sequence of instructions used in the DECBIN subroutine (Example 6-13). After the content of register C has been multiplied by 10 (the previous values entered), the content of the B register (the latest value entered) is added to it. The result of this addition is saved back in register C, and the digit count in register D is decremented. The D register was initially loaded with 003 because three decimal digits are to be entered and converted into one eight-bit binary number. If the result of the DCRD is non-zero, the 8080 does a JNZ to DECIT. This means that three ASCII-based decimal digits have not been entered yet, and the computer waits for another valid ASCII character. If three valid ASCII-based decimal keys have been pressed, the binary equivalent of the decimal number entered on the teletypewriter or crt keyboard is in the C register when the 8080 returns from the subroutine.

To enter the number 93, what keys would have to be pressed? Since the 8080 executes the loop within the DECBIN subroutine three times, the 0, 9, and 3 keys would have to be pressed to enter the number 93. If just the 9 and 3 keys were pressed, the 8080 would never return from the DECBIN subroutine. It would still be waiting for the third key to be pressed.

One of the difficulties with the three-digit, ASCII-based, octal-to-binary conversion subroutine in Example 6-3 is the fact that numbers larger than 377 cannot be entered and converted properly. The same problem exists for the DECBIN subroutine (Example 6-13). What will the content of the C register be after the number 256 is entered? The content of the C register will be 000 (00). Remember, an *eight-bit binary number* can only represent the decimal numbers 0 through 255. Therefore, 256 would be too large to be contained in the C register alone.

There are many, many cases in which we often need to work with numbers larger than decimal 255. This means that an ASCII-based, double- or triple-precision, decimal-to-binary conversion subroutine that will provide 16- or 24-bit results (0–65,535 or 0–1.67 $\times 10^7$) is very desirable. As you may recall, the multiplication-by-10 section of Example 6-13 appeared as follows:

```
MOVBA   /SAVE THE DECIMAL DIGIT IN B.
MOVAC   /GET THE TEMPORARY NUMBER IN C.
RLC     /MULTIPLY THE NUMBER BY TWO.
RLC     /MULTIPLY BY TWO AGAIN (TOTAL = X4).
ADDC    /ADD THE ORIGINAL NUMBER (TOTAL = X5).
RLC     /MULTIPLY BY TWO (TOTAL = X10).
ADDB    /ADD THE PREVIOUS CHARACTER CODE.
MOVCA   /SAVE THE NEW BINARY NUMBER IN C.
```

However, double-precision "rotates" similar to those used in the multiply and divide subroutines would have to be used to convert a decimal number into a 16-bit binary number. The instructions listed in Example 6-15 are just the instructions required to perform a double-precision multiply-by-10. Based on this section of the conversion subroutine, can you determine where the binary result of the conversion is stored? The MSBY of the result will be stored in register D and the LSBY of the result will be stored in register E.

Instead of using instructions such as those shown in Example 6-15, the same task of converting an ASCII-based decimal number to a 16-bit binary number can be accomplished by using some of the 8080's instructions that operate on 16-bit data values (Example 6-16).

Example 6-15: A Portion of a Double-Precision, ASCII-Based, Decimal-to-Binary Conversion Subroutine

```
/THIS IS A PORTION OF THE DOUBLE-PRECISION
/DECIMAL-TO-BINARY CONVERSION SUBROUTINE.
/IT CAN BE USED TO CONVERT THE NUMBERS BETWEEN
/0 AND 65,535 TO BINARY EQUIVALENTS.
/ONLY THE DOUBLE-PRECISION ROTATE SECTION OF THE
/SUBROUTINE IS SHOWN BELOW.

          •
          •
        MOVBD   /SAVE THE MSBY IN B TEMPORARILY.
        MOVCE   /SAVE THE LSBY IN C TEMPORARILY.
        CALL    /MULTIPLY THE NUMBER CONTAINED IN
        ROT1    /REGISTER PAIR D BY TWO.
        0
        CALL    /NOW MULTIPLY THE CONTENT OF REG-
        ROT1    /ISTER PAIR D BY TWO AGAIN (TOTAL = ×4).
        0
        MOVAC   /NOW A DOUBLE-PRECISION ADDITION IS
        ADDE    /PERFORMED AFTER WHICH THE NUMBER
        MOVEA   /APPEARS TO BE MULTIPLIED BY 5.
        MOVAB   /GET THE MSBY OF THE TEMPORARY VALUE.
        ADCD    /ADD THE MSBY OF THE TIMES FOUR NUMBER.
        MOVDA   /SAVE THE MSBY.
        CALL    /MULTIPLY THE RESULT BY TWO AGAIN.
        ROT1    /NOW THE RESULT IS 10 TIMES LARGER.
        0
          •
          •
ROT1,   MOVAE   /GET THE LSBY OF THE TEMPORARY VALUE.
        RLC     /ROTATE IT TO THE LEFT.
        MOVEA   /THEN SAVE THE LSBY BACK IN E.
        MOVAD   /THEN GET THE MSBY OF THE TEMPORARY VALUE.
        RLC     /ROTATE THE CARRY FLAG INTO IT.
        MOVDA   /THEN SAVE THE MSBY BACK IN D
        RET     /AND RETURN.
```

A flowchart for the double-precision conversion subroutine is shown in Fig. 6-1.

As you can see in Example 6-16, the use of 16-bit data manipulation instructions makes the subroutine much simpler. A section of this subroutine is based on the fact that multiplication by two is the same as adding the number to itself:

$$2 \times 5 = 5 + 5 = 10$$

$$2 \times 13 = 13 + 13 = 26$$

In Example 6-16, register pair H is loaded with 000 000 (0000). This register pair is used to store a temporary result as well as the final result of the conversion. Register C is used as a digit counter. Since a 16-bit binary number can represent 65,535, a five-digit ASCII-based decimal number can be entered and converted, as long as the number is not larger than 65,535. Thus, 05207 would be a valid entry; 99956 would not.

After initializing register pair H and register C, the usual call and compare instructions are executed to ensure that only decimal numbers are processed by the subroutine. After a character is received, an immediate data byte of 060 is subtracted from the content of register A. This performs the same function as the ANI 017 instructions in the previous examples. Since the TTYIN subroutine removes the parity bit from the ASCII values, the SUI 060 instruction can be used with any teletypewriter or crt regardless of the device's parity. After the subtraction, the content of register pair H is pushed on the stack and then popped off of the stack into register pair D. Register pair D and H now contain the *same* 16-bit value. An XCHG instruction cannot be used here to replace these two instructions. By executing the DADH instruction, the content of register pair H is multiplied by two. Execution of the same instruction a second time results in the content of register pair H being multiplied by four. A DADD instruction adds the original content of register pair H (now in register pair D) to the content of register pair H so that the content of register pair H now appears to be multiplied by five. The reason that the PUSHH, POPD instruction sequence was executed was to preserve the original number for the multiplication by five. The third DADH instruction completes the multiplication of the original 16-bit number by 10.

The character that is input into the A register from the teletypewriter or crt is then stored in the E register, and the D register is set to 000. By setting D to 000, a new decimal number can be easily added to the times-10 product of the previous digits simply by executing a DADD instruction. The result of the multiplication-by-10 and the addition is now stored in register pair H. The digit count contained in the C register is then decremented. If the content of the C register is decremented to a nonzero result, the JNZ to DECIN1 is executed to permit another decimal character to be

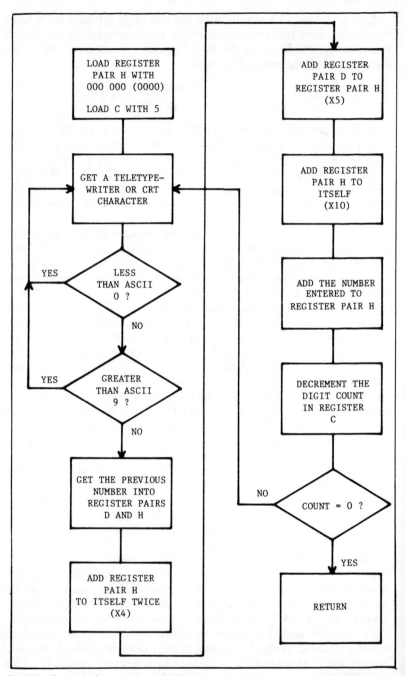

Fig. 6-1. Flowchart for a 16-bit, ASCII-based, decimal-to-binary conversion subroutine.

Example 6-16: A 16-Bit, ASCII-Based, Decimal-to-Binary Conversion Subroutine

```
/THIS ASCII-BASED DECIMAL-TO-BINARY CONVERSION
/SUBROUTINE PRODUCES A DOUBLE-PRECISION
/(16-BIT) RESULT. THE SUBROUTINE USES SOME OF
/THE 8080'S MORE SOPHISTICATED INSTRUCTIONS, MAKING
/THE SOFTWARE FASTER AND SHORTER IN LENGTH.


DECBIN,   LXIH      /SET REGISTER PAIR H TO 000 000 (0000).
          000       /REGISTER PAIR H WILL BE USED TO STORE
          000       /THE BINARY EQUIVALENT OF THE DECIMAL NUMBER.
          MVIC      /C WILL BE USED AS THE DIGIT COUNTER.
          005
DECIN1,   CALL      /GET A TELETYPEWRITER OR CRT CHARACTER.
          TTYIN     /PRINT IT AND RETURN WITH IT
          0         /IN THE A REGISTER (D7 ALREADY = 0).
          CPI       /IS IT LESS THAN AN ASCII 0 ?
          060
          JC        /YES. THEN IGNORE THE CHARACTER
          DECIN1    /AND GET ANOTHER ONE.
          0
          CPI       /IT WAS EQUAL TO OR GREATER THAN 060.
          072       /IS IT LESS THAN AND NOT EQUAL TO 072 ?
          JNC       /NO. IT IS EQUAL TO OR GREATER THAN
          DECIN1    /072 (BA), SO IGNORE IT ALSO.
          0
          SUI       /IT WAS A VALID ASCII NUMBER, STRIP OFF
          060       /BITS D7, D6, D5 AND D4.
          PUSHH     /SAVE THE NUMBER IN H&L ON THE STACK.
          POPD      /POP THE NUMBER OFF THE STACK INTO D&E.
          DADH      /ADD H&L TO H&L; RESULT IN H&L (×2).
          DADH      /ADD H&L TO H&L; RESULT IN H&L (×4).
          DADD      /ADD D&E TO H&L; RESULT IN H&L (×5).
          DADH      /ADD H&L TO H&L; RESULT IN H&L (×10).
          MOVEA
          MVID
          000
          DADD      /ADD THE ENTRY TO THE SUM.
          DCRC      /DECREMENT THE DIGIT COUNTER.
          JNZ
          DECIN1    /NOT 5 DIGITS YET, SO GET ANOTHER.
          0
          RET       /ALL 5 ENTERED, EXIT WITH THE
                    /BINARY EQUIVALENT IN REGISTER PAIR H.
```

entered. If the content of the C register is decremented to zero, the 8080 returns from the subroutine with the 16-bit binary number that is equivalent to the decimal number that was entered in register pair H. Note that this subroutine still does not permit the numbers 76128 or 68921 to be entered. They are simply too large to be represented by a 16-bit binary number. In this subroutine, too, five key actuations must occur, so 57 must be entered as 00057.

EIGHT-BIT, BINARY-TO-ASCII-BASED DECIMAL

Once the decimal numbers have been converted to binary and appropriate mathematical operations performed, it would be desirable to print the result in ASCII-based decimal numbers. If the result is printed in binary, octal, or hexadecimal, it would be difficult to relate the answer to the decimal numbers that were previously entered. Therefore, a subroutine that converts binary numbers to decimal will be discussed.

If you think of decimal numbers as integers times a power of 10, it will greatly simplify the process of converting binary numbers to decimal numbers. To convert an eight-bit binary number to a decimal number, successive subtractions are performed. For example, to determine the number of 100s in the decimal number 237, 100 is subtracted from 237 until the result of the subtraction is negative. Each time 100 is subtracted from the number being converted, and the result is still not negative, a *100s count* is incremented by 1:

$$
\begin{array}{r}
237 \\
-\ 100 \\
\hline
137 \quad \text{100s count} = 1 \\
-\ 100 \\
\hline
37 \quad \text{100s count} = 2 \\
-\ 100 \\
\hline
-\ 63 \\
+\ 100 \\
\hline
37
\end{array}
$$

To determine the number of 10s in the number, 10 is subtracted from the remainder of the last 100s subtraction. Like the 100s subtraction, each time 10 is subtracted from the remainder and the result is not negative, the *10s count* is incremented by 1:

$$
\begin{array}{r}
37 \\
-\ 10 \\
\hline
27 \quad \text{10s count} = 1 \\
-\ 10 \\
\hline
17 \quad \text{10s count} = 2 \\
-\ 10 \\
\hline
7 \quad \text{10s count} = 3 \\
-\ 10 \\
\hline
-\ 3 \\
+\ 10 \\
\hline
7
\end{array}
$$

To determine the number of units, 1 could be subtracted from the remainder of the 10s subtraction. However, the remainder already represents the number of units in the number being converted. To perform these successive subtractions on a binary number, the binary equivalent of 100 (octal 144, hex 64), and 10 (octal 012, hex 0A) must be used. These numbers are used in the eight-bit, binary-to-decimal conversion subroutine listed in Example 6-17.

Example 6-17: An Eight-Bit, Binary-to-Decimal Conversion Subroutine

```
/THIS SUBROUTINE PERFORMS A BINARY-TO-DECIMAL
/CONVERSION. THE SUBROUTINE MUST BE CALLED
/WITH THE BINARY NUMBER TO BE CONVERTED, IN THE
/A REGISTER. THE 8080 RETURNS FROM THE SUB-
/ROUTINE WITH THE DECIMAL EQUIVALENTS IN REGISTERS
/E (HUNDREDS), D (TENS), AND C (UNITS).

BINDEC,    LXID      /SET D=E=000 (00).
           000
           000
           MVIC      /SET C=000 (00).
           000
SUB100,    SUI       /SUBTRACT DECIMAL 100 FROM A.
           144       /(144 OCTAL=100 DECIMAL)
           JC        /A BORROW OCCURRED, ADD
           ADD100    /100 TO THE CONTENT OF A.
           0
           INRE      /INCREMENT THE HUNDREDS COUNTER BY 1.
           JMP       /TRY THE SUBTRACTION AGAIN.
           SUB100
           0
ADD100,    ADI       /TOO LARGE A SUBTRACTION WAS ATTEMPTED
           144       /SO ADD 100 (DECIMAL) TO A.
SUB10,     SUI       /NOW SUBTRACT 10 (DECIMAL) FROM A.
           012
           JC        /BORROW OCCURRED, BETTER ADD 10
           UNITS     /(DECIMAL) TO THE CONTENT OF A.
           0
           INRD      /INCREMENT THE TENS COUNTER BY 1.
           JMP       /TRY THE SUBTRACTION AGAIN.
           SUB10
           0
UNITS,     ADI       /ADD DECIMAL 10 TO THE CONTENT OF A.
           012
           MOVCA     /SAVE THE NUMBER OF UNITS IN C.
           RET       /RETURN WITH THE ANSWER IN E, D, AND C.
```

When the conversion process is complete, the number of 100s is contained in the E register, the number of 10s in the D register, and the number of units in the C register. As you may have observed, this subroutine must be called with the binary number to be converted contained in the A register.

This subroutine (Example 6-17) is relatively straightforward. At the beginning of the subroutine, registers C, D, and E are set to 000 because they will be used to store the results of the conversion. An immediate data byte of 100_{10} is then subtracted from the content of register A. If the A register contained 237_{10}, it now contains 137_{10}. No borrow occurs, so the 8080 does not execute the JC to ADD100. Instead, the content of the E register is incremented by 1, so it now contains 001. The 8080 then jumps back to SUB100. Decimal 100 is again subtracted from the content of register A, so register A now contains 37_{10}. No borrow occurs, so the content of the E register is incremented to 002, and the 8080 again jumps back to SUB100. When 100_{10} is subtracted from 37_{10} a borrow does occur because a larger number was subtracted from a smaller number. Therefore, the 8080 does a JC to ADD100 at which point 100_{10} is added back to the content of the A register. The content of the A register is now 37_{10}. Note that the largest number that can be contained in the E register when the 8080 returns from the subroutine is 002, since the largest number that can be contained in an eight-bit register is 255_{10}.

When a borrow finally occurs, the JC to ADD100 is executed, and 100_{10} (octal 144, hex 64) is added to the content of the A register to yield the remainder from the last "valid" subtraction. The SUB10 loop is then executed to subtract 10_{10} from the content of register A. Each time 10_{10} can be subtracted from A without producing a borrow condition, the D register is incremented. When a borrow finally occurs, the 8080 does a JC to UNITS, at which 10_{10} is added to the content of register A. Since this addition has the effect of preserving the remainder from the last valid subtraction of 10_{10}, the result represents the number of units. The number of units is then stored in the C register.

Now that the eight-bit, binary-to-decimal conversion has taken place, where are the results of the conversion stored? The number of 100s in the binary number is stored in the E register, the number of 10s is stored in the D register, and the number of units is stored in the C register. With these numbers stored in these registers, the next problem is to write a subroutine that will print the decimal equivalent for the binary number on a teletypewriter or crt. The subroutine listed in Example 6-18 can be used for this purpose.

Which character is printed first, the 100s or the units digit? The 100s digit is printed first, because the printer prints from left to right. Since only ASCII characters can be printed on the teletypewriter or crt, the BCDOUT subroutine is used to create and print the appropriate numeric ASCII characters.

There is one simplification to the BINDEC subroutine that has to do with the initialization of registers C, D, and E. These registers

Example 6-18: A Subroutine That Prints the Decimal Result of the Eight-Bit, Binary-to-Decimal Conversion

```
/THIS SUBROUTINE PRINTS THE ASCII CHARACTERS CONTAINED
/IN THE E, D AND C REGISTERS ON THE TELETYPEWRITER.
/THE RET INSTRUCTION AT THE END OF THE TTYOUT SUB-
/ROUTINE CAUSES CONTROL TO RETURN TO THE PROGRAM
/THAT CALLED DECPNT.

DECPNT,   MOVAE    /GET THE NUMBER OF HUNDREDS, CONVERT
          CALL     /IT TO ASCII,  THEN PRINT THE ASCII
          BCDOUT   /CHARACTER.
          0
          MOVAD    /NOW GET THE NUMBER OF TENS, CONVERT
          CALL     /IT TO ASCII, THEN PRINT THE ASCII
          BCDOUT   /CHARACTER TO THE RIGHT OF THE
          0        /HUNDREDS CHARACTER.
          MOVAC    /THEN GET THE NUMBER OF UNITS,
BCDOUT,   ADI      /ADD 260 (B0) TO THE CONTENT OF A TO
          260      /CONVERT THE NUMBER TO AN ASCII NUMBER,
          JMP      /THEN PRINT THE CONTENT OF THE A
          TTYOUT   /REGISTER ON THE TELETYPEWRITER.
          0
```

are initially loaded with 000 and then incremented, depending on the results of the subtractions performed in the BINDEC subroutine. When the entire eight-bit binary number is converted, the DECPNT subroutine could be called to print the result on the teletypewriter or crt. In DECPNT, the BCDOUT subroutine is called. This subroutine adds 260 (B0) to the content of register A before the ASCII number is printed. It would be easier if the C, D, and E registers were initialized with 260 (B0). This would mean that the DECPNT subroutine could call or jump directly to the TTYOUT subroutine, and the BCDOUT subroutine could be eliminated. These changes are listed in Example 6-19.

By initially loading the C, D, and E registers with 260 (B0) there is no need to call or jump to BCDOUT. Instead, the TTYOUT subroutine can be called or jumped to, because the content of the C, D, and E registers is already in the form of numeric ASCII characters. Of course, if some other routine or subroutine needs to use the BCDOUT subroutine, there is no advantage to initializing the three registers with 260 (B0).

SIXTEEN-BIT, BINARY-TO-ASCII-BASED DECIMAL

One of the limitations of the BINDEC subroutine (Example 6-17) is that it can only convert an eight-bit binary number to decimal digits. Therefore, a 16-bit, binary-to-ASCII-based decimal conversion subroutine will be written. The largest number that can be con-

Example 6-19: Simplifying the BINDEC and DECPNT Subroutines

```
/THIS IS A SIMPLER BINARY-TO-ASCII-BASED DECIMAL
/CONVERSION SUBROUTINE. THE SUBROUTINE MUST BE
/CALLED WITH THE BINARY NUMBER TO BE CONVERTED
/IN THE A REGISTER. THE ASCII-BASED DECIMAL
/EQUIVALENT WILL BE PRINTED ON THE TELETYPE-
/WRITER OR CRT IN THE FORM OF A THREE-DIGIT NUMBER.
BINDEC,  LXID     /SET D=E=260 (ASCII 0).
         260
         260
         MVIC     /ALSO SET C=260 (ASCII 0).
         260
           •
           •
           •
         ADI      /ADD DECIMAL 10 TO THE CONTENT OF A.
         012
         ADDC     /ADD 260 TO THE RESULT.
         MOVCA    /SAVE THE RESULT IN REGISTER C.
DECPNT,  MOVAE    /GET THE MOST SIGNIFICANT DIGIT
         CALL     /THEN PRINT IT (IT IS ALREADY
         TTYOUT   /A VALID ASCII CHARACTER).
         0
         MOVAD    /GET THE TENS DIGIT
         CALL     /AND PRINT IT.
         TTYOUT
         0
         MOVAC    /FINALLY, GET THE NUMBER OF UNITS
         JMP      /AND PRINT IT. THE RET INSTRUCTION AT
         TTYOUT   /THE END OF "TTYOUT" WILL CAUSE THE 8080
         0        /TO RETURN TO THE MAIN PROGRAM THAT
                  /CALLED THIS SUBROUTINE.
```

verted using this program is 65,535, which means that the result of the conversion will be up to five digits long. This means that five memory locations will be used to store the five-digit result.

To make the subroutine as short and as simple as possible, some of the 8080's 16-bit data manipulation instructions will be used, specifically the DAD-type instructions. In the previous BINDEC subroutine, the decimal numbers 100 and 10 had to be *subtracted* from the binary number that was being converted. How can the DAD-type instructions be used to perform this subtraction? You may remember that subtraction is the same as *adding a negative number* to the minuend:

$$
\begin{array}{r} 32 \\ + \; (-28) \\ \hline 5 \end{array}
\qquad\qquad
\begin{array}{r} 127 \\ + \; (-31) \\ \hline 96 \end{array}
$$

Therefore, in the conversion of a 16-bit binary number to ASCII-based decimal, instead of subtracting 10,000 from the 16-bit binary number, a −10,000 will be added to the binary number by executing a DAD-type instruction. The negative equivalent of 10,000 is its 2s complement. The five-digit result is stored in memory when the conversion is complete, and the 16-bit number that is to be converted must be in register pair D when the subroutine is called.

When the 8080 enters the DPBDEC subroutine (Example 6-20), register pair H is loaded with the address for the R/W memory location assigned the symbolic address, UNIT. The C register is then loaded with the digit count, which is five. Starting with the instructions at SETTO0, the data byte 260 (B0) is moved to five consecutive R/W memory locations, UNIT, TEN, HUN, THOU, and TTHOU, the memory locations that will be used to accumulate the number of units, 10s, 100s, 1000s, and 10,000s that the binary number can be converted to.

Example 6-20: A 16-Bit, Binary-to-ASCII-Based, Decimal Conversion Subroutine

```
/THIS IS A DOUBLE-PRECISION, BINARY-TO-ASCII-BASED
/DECIMAL CONVERSION SUBROUTINE. THE NUMBER TO BE
/CONVERTED MUST BE CONTAINED IN REGISTER PAIR D WHEN
/THIS SUBROUTINE IS CALLED. THE FIVE-DIGIT DECIMAL
/EQUIVALENT WILL BE PRINTED ON THE TELETYPEWRITER
/OR CRT.

DPBDEC,   LXIH      /LOAD REGISTER PAIR H WITH THE ADDRESS
          UNIT      /WHERE THE FIVE-DIGIT DECIMAL
          0         /RESULT WILL BE STORED IN R/W MEMORY.
          MVIC      /REGISTER C IS USED AS A DIGIT COUNTER
          005       /AND THERE ARE FIVE DIGITS.
SETTO0,   MVIM      /NOW ZERO THE FIVE MEMORY LOCATIONS
          260       /BY STORING ASCII ZEROS IN THE STORAGE
          INXH      /LOCATIONS. INCREMENT THE ADDRESS.
          DCRC      /DECREMENT THE DIGIT COUNTER.
          JNZ       /IS THE COUNT 0? NO, SAVE ANOTHER 260 (B0).
          SETTO0
          0
          DCXH      /DECREMENT THE MEMORY ADDRESS.
          LXIB      /NOW LOAD REGISTER PAIR B WITH
          360       /A  −10,000 (2'S COMPLEMENT).
          330
          CALL      /NOW ADD THE −10,000 TO THE CONTENT
          DIGIT     /OF REGISTER PAIR D, UNTIL A
          0         /BORROW OCCURS.
          LXIB      /NOW LOAD REGISTER PAIR B WITH
          030       /A  −1000 (2'S COMPLEMENT)
          374
          CALL      /AND THEN ADD THE −1000 TO THE
          DIGIT     /CONTENT OF REGISTER PAIR D UNTIL
          0         /A BORROW OCCURS.
          LXIB      /NOW REGISTER PAIR B IS LOADED WITH
          234       /A  −100 (2'S COMPLEMENT)
          377
          CALL      /AND THE ADDITION PROCESS IS REPEATED.
          DIGIT
          0
```

```
            LXIB      /FINALLY, THE 8080
            366       /ADDS −10 (2'S COMPLEMENT) TO
            377       /THE CONTENT OF REGISTER
            CALL      /PAIR D.
            DIGIT
            0
            MOVAE     /GET THE NUMBER OF UNITS.
            ADI       /ADD 260 (ASCII) 0 TO IT.
            012
            MOVMA     /SAVE THE RESULT IN MEMORY.
            LXIH      /AFTER THE CONVERSION, THE NUMBER IS PRINTED.
            TTHOU     /REGISTER PAIR H IS LOADED WITH THE
            0         /ADDRESS WHERE THE MSBY IS STORED.
            MVIC      /THERE WILL BE FIVE DIGITS PRINTED.
            005
PRINT,      MOVAM     /GET THE ASCII CHARACTER.
            CALL      /PRINT IT ON THE CRT OR TTY.
            TTYOUT
            0
            DCXH      /DECREMENT THE MEMORY ADDRESS POINTER.
            DCRC      /DECREMENT THE DIGIT COUNT.
            JNZ       /THE COUNT IS NONZERO, SO
            PRINT     /PRINT ANOTHER DIGIT.
            0
            RET       /WHEN THE COUNT =0, RETURN.
DIGIT,      PUSHH     /SAVE THE MEMORY POINTER ON THE STACK.
            XCHG      /GET THE NUMBER BEING CONVERTED INTO H&L.
            DADB      /ADD THE 2'S COMPLEMENT TEST NUMBER.
            JNC       /IF A BORROW, THE CARRY IS TRUE.
            ADDIT
            0
            XCHG      /NO BORROW, GET H&L AND D&E BACK PROPERLY.
            POPH      /POP THE MEMORY ADDRESS OFF THE STACK.
            INRM      /INCREMENT THE MEMORY COUNT BY 1
            JMP       /AND TRY THE SUBTRACTION AGAIN.
            DIGIT     /ONLY WHEN THE CARRY IS TRUE, WILL THE
            0         /8080 GET OUT OF THIS LOOP.
ADDIT,      MOVAC     /NOW FORM THE 2'S COMPLEMENT OF THE
            CMA       /2'S COMPLEMENT.
            MOVEA
            MOVAB
            CMA
            MOVDA
            INXD      /D&E NOW CONTAIN THE POSITIVE NUMBER.
            DADD      /ADD IT TO THE TEST NUMBER.
            XCHG
            POPH      /POP THE MEMORY POINTER OFF OF THE STACK.
            DCXH      /NOW DECREMENT THE MEMORY POINTER.
            RET       /RETURN TO THE MAIN PROGRAM.

UNIT,       0         /THESE FIVE CONSECUTIVE R/W MEMORY LO-
TEN,        0         /CATIONS, STARTING FROM A LOWER ADDRESS
HUN,        0         /AND GOING TO A HIGHER ADDRESS,
THOU,       0         /ARE USED TO STORE THE ASCII-BASED DECIMAL
TTHOU,      0         /EQUIVALENTS FOR THE BINARY NUMBER IN
                      /REGISTER PAIR D.
```

With the binary number that is to be converted in register pair D, register pair B is loaded with the value that is to be subtracted. To facilitate the 16-bit subtraction, the 2s complement of the value will be used in a double-precision addition using DAD-type instructions. The DIGIT subroutine saves the address of the memory location used to accumulate the digit total. This "frees" register pair H so that DAD-type instructions can be used. The following steps "subtract" the test value from the 16-bit binary number through the use of a DADB instruction, the test value being in register pair B and the binary value that is being converted in register pair H. The addition of the 2s complement value to the binary number continues until a carry occurs. This indicates that the binary value was smaller than the test value. For each successful noncarry-generating addition, the accumulating result in memory is incremented by 1. The next example shows this in operation:

$$\text{Value to be converted} = 37521$$
$$\text{1st test value} = 10,000$$
$$\text{Initial value of TTHOU} = 260$$

37521		TTHOU = 260
− 10000		
27521	no carry	TTHOU = 261
− 10000		
17521	no carry	TTHOU = 262
− 10000		
7521	no carry	TTHOU = 263
− 10000		
− 2479	carry	TTHOU = 263 (no increment)

In the last subtraction, a carry occurs, so the 2s complement for 10,000 must not be added to the number being converted. The TTHOU memory location contains the correct ASCII value for the character "3." The next step is the subtraction of 1000, but first the remainder must be restored from −2479 to 7521. This is accomplished by adding 10,000 back to the remainder, −2479. This is all done in the DIGIT subroutine.

After the 8080 adds 10,000 to the remainder, the memory address in register pair H is decremented so that it points to THOU. The 8080 then returns to the calling program. The remainder of the DPBDEC subroutine then goes on to test the binary number for 1000s, 100s, and 10s, by loading the 2s complement of each number in register pair B, and then calling the DIGIT subroutine. The result of each "test" properly increments the content of the corresponding memory location, THOU, HUN, and TEN, respectively. There is no need to test for the UNITS; they are the final remainder.

After the DIGIT subroutine is called for the last time, the number of units is left in the E register. Decimal 10 is added to this, and the result is saved in UNITS. After completing the conversion, the five ASCII-based decimal characters are printed on a teletypewriter or crt. The section of the DPBDEC subroutine that prints the result is listed in Example 6-21 for your convenience.

Example 6-21: The Printer Instructions in the DPBDEC Subroutine (Example 6-20)

```
        MOVME   /THE NUMBER IN MEMORY.
        LXIH    /AFTER THE CONVERSION, THE NUMBER IS PRINTED.
        TTHOU   /REGISTER PAIR H IS LOADED WITH THE
        0       /ADDRESS WHERE THE MSBY IS STORED.
        MVIC    /THERE WILL BE FIVE DIGITS PRINTED.
        005
PRINT,  MOVAM   /GET THE ASCII CHARACTER.
        CALL    /PRINT IT ON THE CRT OR TTY.
        TTYOUT
        0
        DCXH    /DECREMENT THE MEMORY ADDRESS POINTER.
        DCRC    /DECREMENT THE DIGIT COUNT.
        JNZ     /THE COUNT IS NOW NONZERO, SO
        PRINT   /PRINT ANOTHER DIGIT.
        0
        RET     /WHEN THE COUNT =0, RETURN.
```

Since the most-significant digit must be printed first (the printer moves from left to right), register pair H is loaded with the address for the symbolic address, TTHOU. The C register is then loaded with the number of digits that are to be printed (005). The most-significant digit is loaded into register A, and the TTYOUT subroutine is called. After the character is printed, the memory address is decremented so that it points to the next digit of lesser significance. The digit counter is also decremented, and if it is decremented to a nonzero number, the print loop is executed again. When the content of register C is finally decremented to zero, the 8080 returns from the DPBDEC subroutine to the calling program. The content of register pair D will have been converted to ASCII-based decimal digits, each of which is stored in R/W memory. The result of the conversion will also have been printed on a teletypewriter or crt.

TO CONVERT OR NOT, THAT IS THE QUESTION

At some time, you may want the 8080 to count events. These events could be external; i.e., I/O related, such as the number of people through a turnstile or the number of cars through an intersection. The events could be internal, such as the number of times the number 215 (8D) or 302 (C2) occurs in a 4K block of memory. The count might even be the number of times an interrupt occurs within a 24-hour period. Once these events are counted, you will probably want them to be printed out on some type of output device.

A simple INR- or INX-type instruction could be used to count these events, and the number could be printed using one of the binary-to-ASCII-based, decimal conversion subroutines that we have just finished discussing. However, the size, complexity, and inflexibility of these subroutines can place severe restraints on their use. For instance, what happens if a triple-precision (three-byte) binary number must be converted to ASCII-based decimal? This would require a long subroutine, particularly if Example 6-20 was expanded to handle 24-bit data words.

To solve this problem, a flexible, easy-to-use counter program will be written. One of the requirements for this program is that the accumulated numbers be easily converted to ASCII values for output to a teletypewriter or crt. As an example, let us develop a microcomputer-controlled car counter. This counter can be set up at any intersection, and it will count the number of cars that pass through the intersection. At the end of one week, the computer will print the number of cars that have been counted. If this number were printed in binary, octal, or hexadecimal, it would be difficult for anyone using the system to quickly interpret the results of the car count. Therefore, a decimal number must be printed. The first question to ask is, "How many cars can be expected to pass through the intersection in one week?" We will assume that the number is not larger than 65,535. If the software is written properly, it should be *easy* to reprogram the 8080 microcomputer so that a larger number of cars can be counted.

The car-counter problem can be subdivided into two parts. The first part is the software that actually performs the count; the second part prints the result. In one of these parts, some type of number-base conversion may be necessary. Since the number of cars cannot exceed 65,535, it would be easy to write a program that uses a register pair as a counter. This is shown in Example 6-22.

At the beginning of the week, the program in Example 6-22 is started. Register pair H is loaded with the number 000 000 (0000), and then the CAR subroutine is called. *Only when a car passes over the sensor, buried in the pavement, does the 8080 return from the CAR subroutine.* At this time, it is not important to know how this is done in software. However, when the 8080 does return from the CAR subroutine, the content of register pair H is incremented by 1 (INXH), and the 8080 then does a JMP to NXTCAR, where the

Example 6-22: A Program That Uses Register Pair H for the Car Count

```
              •
              •
          LXIH     /LOAD REGISTER PAIR H WITH 000 000
          000      /(0000) BECAUSE IT WILL BE USED
          000      /TO CONTAIN THE CAR COUNT.
NXTCAR,   CALL     /WAIT FOR A CAR TO RUN OVER THE
          CAR      /SENSOR IN THE STREET.
          0
          INXH     /A CAR IS OVER THE SENSOR, INCREMENT
          JMP      /THE COUNT AND THEN JUMP AND WAIT
          NXTCAR   /FOR ANOTHER CAR.
          0
              •
              •
```

8080 waits for another car to pass over the sensor. At the end of a week, register pair H contains the binary count of the number of cars that passed over the sensor. This count must then be converted to ASCII-based decimal, and the characters printed. The double-precision (16-bit) DPBDEC subroutine (Example 6-20) could be used to perform this conversion. The content of register pair H would simply have to be moved to register pair D before the DPBDEC subroutine is called. However, as you have seen, this subroutine requires 79 memory locations, plus the five R/W memory locations used to store the ASCII equivalents of the decimal numbers. What will happen if, as is possible, the number of cars going through the intersection exceeds 65,535? A larger number would be difficult to work with because a triple-precision conversion subroutine would be needed. To solve this problem, a more flexible program can be used, as seen in Example 6-23.

Without a doubt, this program is more complex than the initial counter program (Example 6-22). However, the count that this program produces does not have to be converted from binary to ASCII-based decimal before it can be printed. Note that to keep Examples 6-22 and 6-23 as simple as possible, there are no instructions that cause the count to be printed at the end of the week. The counter and conversion/printer programs are separate and distinct.

How does this car-counter program work? The first six instructions load four consecutive R/W memory locations with the value 260 (B0), starting at the symbolic address UNIT. Since the numbers produced by this counter program are to be printed on a teletypewriter or crt, the contents of these consecutive R/W memory locations are initialized with the ASCII value for the character, 0. The number of memory locations initialized with 260 (B0) is determined by the value of the immediate data byte for the MVIC in-

Example 6-23: A Car-Counting Program

```
/THIS PROGRAM USES SIMILAR CONCEPTS THAT WERE
/EMPLOYED IN PREVIOUS SUBROUTINES.

INIT,     LXIH      /LOAD REGISTER PAIR H WITH THE ADDRESS
          UNIT      /OF THE MEMORY LOCATION ASSIGNED THE
          0         /SYMBOLIC ADDRESS "UNIT."
          MVIC      /THERE ARE FOUR DIGITS IN THE NUMBER.
          004       /MAXIMUM COUNT = 9999.
NXT0,     MVIM      /SAVE A 260 IN THE MEMORY LOCATION
          260       /ADDRESSED BY REGISTER PAIR H.
          INXH      /INCREMENT THE MEMORY ADDRESS.
          DCRC      /DECREMENT THE DIGIT COUNT.
          JNZ       /IS THE COUNT 0? NO, DO ANOTHER.
          NXT0      /THESE INSTRUCTIONS INITIALIZE FOUR
          0         /MEMORY LOCATIONS WITH ASCII 0.
COUNT,    LXIH      /LOAD REGISTER PAIR H WITH THE ADDRESS
          UNIT      /ASSIGNED TO THE SYMBOLIC ADDRESS "UNIT."
          0
NXTCAR,   CALL      /WAIT FOR A CAR TO PASS OVER
          CAR       /THE SENSOR IN THE STREET.
          0
CNTUP,    INRM      /INCREMENT THE CONTENT OF MEMORY.
          MOVAM     /HAS IT BEEN INCREMENTED PAST ASCII 9?
          CPI
          272       /ASCII 9 = 271.
          JC        /NO, THEN JUMP TO COUNT AND WAIT
          COUNT     /FOR ANOTHER CAR TO PASS OVER THE
          0         /SENSOR IN THE STREET.
          MVIM      /YES, THEN REINITIALIZE THIS MEMORY
          260       /LOCATION.
          INXH      /INCREMENT THE MEMORY ADDRESS.
          JMP
          CNTUP     /AND INCREMENT THE NEXT MEMORY LOCATION.
          0

UNIT,     0         /THESE ARE FOUR R/W MEMORY LOCATIONS THAT
TEN,      0         /ARE USED TO STORE THE CAR COUNT, AS
HUN,      0         /ASCII NUMERIC CHARACTERS.
THOU,     0
```

struction, between the symbolic address INIT and NXT0. After these four memory locations have been initialized, the 8080 begins to execute the instructions starting at COUNT. At COUNT, register pair H is loaded with the address for UNIT. The CAR subroutine is then called. The 8080 does not return from the CAR subroutine until a car has passed over the sensor in the street. This is the same situation as in the previous counter program (Example 6-22). However, when the 8080 returns from the CAR subroutine now, a completely different set of instructions is executed.

At CNTUP, the content of the memory location addressed by register pair H is incremented by 1. Register pair H currently points to UNIT. After the content of memory is incremented, it is moved to the A register and compared to the immediate data byte 272 (BA). If the content of memory is less than 272 (BA), the JC to COUNT is executed. The first time through the loop, the content of memory is incremented from 260 (B0) to 261 (B1); therefore, the JC to COUNT is executed. Note that 272 (BA) is one more than the value of an ASCII 9. Therefore, only when the content of the UNIT memory location is incremented past the ASCII value for 9 (271, B9) to 272 (BA), will the JC to COUNT not be executed. When this occurs, the MVIM 260 instruction is executed. This loads memory location UNIT with the ASCII value for 0.

The memory address contained in register pair H is then incremented by 1, so that it now addresses the memory location assigned the symbolic address TEN. The JMP to CNTUP is then executed and causes the content of the TENs memory location to be incremented by 1. It is then checked to see if it is less than 272 (BA). The 8080 continues to execute the CNTUP loop until the incremented content of one of the memory locations is less than 272 (BA). The 8080 then does a JC to COUNT, where the memory address in register pair H is reinitialized to point the UNITs memory location.

What would the content of memory be after 394 cars had passed through the intersection?

Memory Location	Octal Content	Hex Content	ASCII Equivalent
UNIT	264	B4	4
TEN	271	B9	9
HUN	263	B3	3
THOU	260	B0	0

What would be contained in these same four R/W memory locations if 2153 cars have passed over the sensor in the street?

Memory Location	Octal Content	Hex Content	ASCII Equivalent
UNIT	263	B3	3
TEN	265	B5	5
HUN	261	B1	1
THOU	262	B2	2

As you can see, the four R/W memory locations from UNIT to THOU are used as a cascaded counter, where each memory location is used to store a count of between 0 and 9 (as the equivalent ASCII values). By using these four memory locations, the 8080 can count between 0000 and 9999. You should have a full understanding of how this subroutine operates. There should be no doubt as to why the four memory locations were initialized with 260 (B0) rather than 000 (00).

Now that the car count is stored in memory as ASCII numeric characters (0 through 9), the subroutine required to print the count is very simple, as shown in Example 6-24. The first instruction of the NMBOUT subroutine loads register pair H with the address assigned to the symbolic address THOU. The C register is then loaded with the digit count, which is four, because a four-digit ASCII-based decimal number is to be printed. The content of the memory location addressed by register pair H is then loaded into register A, and the TTYOUT subroutine is called. Since the values are stored in R/W memory as ASCII characters, a binary-to-ASCII-based, decimal conversion subroutine does not have to be called. After the ASCII character is printed on the teletypewriter, the 8080 returns to the DCXH instruction in NMBOUT. This instruction decrements the address contained in register pair H so that it now points to HUN. The digit count in register C is also decremented; if it is nonzero, the JNZ to NXTOUT is executed. This causes the next ASCII character to be printed. This subroutine continues to be executed until all four ASCII characters have been printed. When all the characters have been printed, the 8080 returns to the section of the program that called the NMBOUT subroutine.

Why was the ASCII number contained in the memory location THOU printed first? This digit was printed first because it was as-

Example 6-24: Printing the ASCII-Based Car Count Stored in R/W Memory

```
/THIS SUBROUTINE PRINTS THE CONTENT OF MEMORY LOCATIONS
/THOU, HUN, TEN AND UNIT ON A CRT OR TELETYPEWRITER.
/SINCE THE CONTENT OF MEMORY IS ALREADY ASCII, THIS
/SUBROUTINE IS VERY SIMPLE. OBSERVE THAT THE CONTENT
/OF THOU IS PRINTED FIRST.

NMBOUT,  LXIH     /LOAD REGISTER PAIR H WITH THE ADDRESS
         THOU     /WHERE THE THOUSAND'S DIGIT
         0        /IS STORED.
         MVIC     /SET THE DIGIT COUNT TO 4.
         004
NXTOUT,  MOVAM    /GET AN ASCII CHARACTER FROM MEMORY.
         CALL     /PRINT IT ON THE CRT OR TTY.
         TTYOUT
         0
         DCXH     /DECREMENT THE MEMORY ADDRESS.
         DCRC     /DECREMENT THE DIGIT COUNTER.
         JNZ      /IS THE COUNT 0? NO, PRINT ANOTHER.
         NXTOUT
         0
         RET      /ALL THE CHARACTERS WERE PRINTED, SO RETURN.
```

sumed that the printer moved from left to right. Therefore, the most-significant digit of the result must be printed first.

What changes would have to be made to software Examples 6-23 and 6-24 if the microcomputer were moved to an intersection where up to 99,999 cars per week could pass over the sensor? Would the software be easy to change? Yes, it would be extremely easy to change the software. Only the digit counters in the software would have to be changed, and there are only two instructions that would have to be changed. The immediate data byte for the MVIC instruction in the INIT section of Example 6-23, which initializes four R/W memory locations to 260 (B0), would have to be changed from four to five, to accommodate the numbers 0 through 99,999. The data byte for the MVIC instruction in the NMBOUT subroutine (Example 6-24) would also have to be changed from four to five. Also, the address bytes of the LXIH instruction in NMBOUT (Example 6-24) would have to be increased by one so that the 10,000s digit is printed. The advantage of using this ASCII-based decimal counter is the fact that it is very easy to change the program so that larger and smaller counts can be accommodated. Only three changes are required, and they are very simple to make.

USING THE DAA INSTRUCTION IN COUNTER PROGRAMS AND SUBROUTINES

The counter program that was just developed (Example 6-23) might be called an ASCII/BCD counter. You have already seen two different types of counters, a binary counter and the ASCII/BCD counter. Is there another type of counter that should be easy to implement on the 8080? Yes, a BCD counter that uses the DAA instruction. In Example 6-25, the DAA instruction is used in a program that can count from 0 to 9999.

Since the DAA instruction operates on packed BCD words (that is, there are two BCD digits per eight-bit word), only two R/W memory locations have to be initialized. These two memory locations can hold a count between 0 and 9999. Since the DAA instruction is being used, these memory locations must be initialized to 000 rather than the ASCII value for 0. This initialization is performed by the INIT section of Example 6-25.

At COUNT, the actual process of counting the cars begins. Reg-signed the symbolic address UNITEN. This memory location is signed the symbolic address, UNITEN. This memory location is used to store the units count (bits D_3–D_0) and the 10s count (bits D_7–D_4) for the number of cars. The CAR subroutine is then called, and when a car passes over the sensor, the 8080 returns to the MOVAM instruction. The content of the UNITEN memory loca-

Example 6-25: A BCD Counter That Uses the DAA Instruction (0–9999)

```
INIT,    LXIH      /INITIALIZE TWO MEMORY LOCATIONS
         UNITEN    /BECAUSE EACH MEMORY LOCATION
         0         /CAN HOLD TWO BCD DIGITS.
         MVIC      /C IS THE MEMORY LOCATION COUNTER
         002       /AND THERE ARE 2 MEMORY LOCATIONS IN USE.
         XRAA      /SET A TO 000 (00).
NXT0,    MOVMA     /SAVE THE CONTENT OF A IN MEMORY.
         INXH      /INCREMENT THE MEMORY ADDRESS.
         DCRC      /DECREMENT THE MEMORY LOCATION COUNTER.
         JNZ
         NXT0      /THERE IS STILL ANOTHER ONE TO
         0         /INITIALIZE.
COUNT,   LXIH      /REGISTER PAIR H POINTS TO UNITEN.
         UNITEN
         0
NXTCAR,  CALL      /WAIT FOR A CAR TO PASS OVER THE
         CAR       /SENSOR THAT IS IN THE STREET.
         0
         MOVAM     /A CAR PASSED OVER THE SENSOR.
         ADI       /SO INCREMENT THE CAR COUNT.
         001       /ADDING ONE IS THE SAME AS INCREMENTING.
CNTUP,   DAA       /DECIMAL ADJUST THE BCD RESULT.
         MOVMA     /SAVE THE ADJUSTED RESULT IN MEMORY.
         JNC       /THERE WAS NO CARRY, SO GO WAIT
         COUNT     /FOR ANOTHER CAR.
         0
         INXH      /INCREMENT THE MEMORY ADDRESS.
         MOVAM     /GET THE NEXT TWO MSBY'S.
         ACI       /ADD THE CARRY INTO THE 2 MSBY'S.
         000
         JMP       /THEN DECIMAL ADJUST THE RESULT BY
         CNTUP     /JUMPING TO CNTUP AND CHECKING THIS
         0         /RESULT FOR AN ADDITIONAL CARRY.
```

tion is then moved to the A register, and 001 is added to it. The result of this addition is decimally adjusted when the DAA instruction is executed, and the adjusted result is stored back in the same memory location. If there is no carry as a result of the DAA instruction (that is, the count is 99 or less), the 8080 does a JNC to COUNT. If the count goes from 99 to 100, the carry is set, and the result in register A is 000. Therefore, the JNC to COUNT is not executed. Instead, the memory address in register pair H is incremented, and the content of the carry is added to the content of this next sequential memory location. The JMP to CNTUP is executed so that the result of this addition is decimally adjusted and stored back in memory.

Now a subroutine must be written that "unpacks" the BCD data and prints the result on a crt or teletypewriter.

Example 6-26: A Subroutine That Unpacks Two-Digit, BCD Data Words

/THIS SUBROUTINE PRINTS THE PACKED BCD DIGITS
/THAT ARE STORED 2-PER-MEMORY LOCATION.

```
NMBOUT,   MVIC      /THERE ARE TWO MEMORY LOCATIONS IN USE
          002       /SO SET THE COUNT TO 002 (02).
          LXIH      /H&L POINT TO THE TWO MSBY'S,
          HUNTHO    /THE HUNDREDS AND THOUSANDS DIGITS.
          0
P2BCD,    MOVAM     /MOVE THE VALUE FROM MEMORY INTO A.
          RRC       /ROTATE THE THOUSANDS DIGIT INTO
          RRC       /THE 4 LSB'S OF THE A REGISTER.
          RRC
          RRC
          CALL      /MASK OUT ALL BUT THE 4 LSB'S,
          BCDOK     /AND THEN PRINT THE RESULT USING
          0         /THE BCDOUT SUBROUTINE.
          MOVAM     /GET THE VALUE IN MEMORY AGAIN
          CALL      /AND PRINT THE NUMBER IN THE FOUR
          BCDOK     /LSB'S.
          0
          DCXH      /DECREMENT THE MEMORY ADDRESS.
          DCRC      /DECREMENT THE MEMORY LOCATION COUNTER.
          JNZ
          P2BCD
          0
          RET
BCDOK,    ANI       /MASK OUT ALL BUT THE 4 LSB'S.
          017
          JMP
          BCDOUT
          0
```

As you can see, this subroutine is much longer than the NMBOUT subroutine (Example 6-24) used with the ASCII/BCD counter (28 versus 15). The subroutine is longer because two digits of the count are packed in one word. Therefore, rotate instructions must be executed to unpack the numbers. Also, the numbers must be converted from BCD to ASCII-based decimal characters. Even if you had to count events up to 20 digits (10^{20}), it would still require less memory to use the ASCII/BCD counter and printer software (Examples 6-23, 6-24) than the counter software that uses the DAA instruction (Examples 6-25, 6-26).

One of the problems that we have not discussed is what happens if a count larger than 9999 occurs in a subroutine that is programmed for a four-digit decimal count? In the ASCII/BCD subroutine (Example 6-23), the next memory location after THOU would be incremented by 1. Since this memory location was not initialized to 260 (B0), there is no way to know what the actual count in this memory location would be. Of course, it would be very easy to program the 8080 so that eight memory locations are initialized with 260 (B0) rather than four. This would mean that a count as large as 99,999,999 could be accommodated before unpredictable results occurred. There is little danger that this number of cars will pass through an intersection in one week. The NMBOUT subroutine (Example 6-24) would also have to be changed so that an eight-digit count would be printed rather than a four-digit count. As you have seen, it is very easy to make these changes.

LEADING-ZERO SUPPRESSION

Quite often, when numbers are printed on a teletypewriter or crt, the leading zeros in a number are not printed or are *suppressed*. This means that instead of printing the number 00302, the number 302 is printed. In the previous five-digit car-counting examples (Example 6-22, printer Example 6-20), a number such as 00302 or 01579 would be printed. A leading-zero suppression subroutine is not difficult to write.

In the subroutine, there has to be some type of a *flag* to indicate when the first nonzero character has been printed. After this flag is set by this nonzero character, any zeros that are encountered in the lesser-significant digit positions are then printed. If a number such as 0302 is to be printed, it would not be sufficient to ignore all ASCII zeros, since the number would be printed as 32. A subroutine that suppresses the printing of leading zeros by using a flag, as we have just discussed, is listed in Example 6-27.

This subroutine can be used to print the car count produced by the ASCII/BCD counter subroutine (Example 6-23). When the NMBOUT subroutine is called, register pair H is loaded with the address assigned to the symbolic address THOU. This is the memory location that contains the 1000s count. The C register is then loaded with the number of digits in the count, regardless of how many of them may be leading zeros. The D register is then loaded with 000 because it will be used as a flag to indicate when a nonzero character has been printed.

During the first pass through NXTOUT, the ASCII character stored in memory location THOU (1000s) is placed in the A register and compared to the ASCII value for the zero character (260, B0). Nonzero characters are printed through the execution of the JNZ to OKPRNT instruction. A zero character (260, B0) requires further checking. Has a nonzero character been previously printed? If so, the zero character just fetched from memory is printed. If a nonzero character has not been printed yet, a space is printed instead of the zero. In either case, the next character is fetched from

Example 6-27: A Subroutine That Suppresses Printing of Leading Zeros

```
/THIS SUBROUTINE IS A MODIFICATION OF THE PREVIOUS
/PRINTOUT SUBROUTINE. THE SUBROUTINE SUPPRESSES
/THE PRINTING OF LEADING ZEROS IN A FOUR-DIGIT
/NUMBER. THEREFORE, INSTEAD OF PRINTING 0302, A
/302 WILL BE PRINTED. INSTEAD OF THE SINGLE LEADING
/ZERO BEING PRINTED, A SPACE WOULD BE PRINTED.


NMBOUT,   LXIH      /LOAD REGISTER PAIR H WITH THE ADDRESS
          THOU      /FOR THE THOUSANDS DIGIT.
          0
          MVIC      /LOAD C WITH THE DIGIT COUNT.
          004
          MVID      /THE D REGISTER WILL BE USED AS A LEADING
          000       /ZERO FLAG.
NXTOUT,   MOVAM     /GET A CHARACTER FROM MEMORY.
          CPI       /IS IT AN ASCII 0 ?
          260
          JNZ       /NO, THEN PRINT THE CHARACTER.
          OKPRNT
          0
          MOVBA     /YES, SAVE THE ASCII 0 IN B.
          MOVAD     /WHAT IS THE STATE OF THE ASCII ZERO FLAG?
          ORAA      /SET THE FLAGS, BASED ON THE CONTENT OF A.
          MOVAB     /MOVE THE ASCII 0 BACK TO A.
          JNZ       /THE CHARACTER IS A 0, BUT A NONZERO
          OKPRNT    /CHARACTER HAS ALREADY BEEN PRINTED, SO
          0         /PRINT THIS ZERO (IT IS NOT A LEADING ZERO).
          MVIA      /IT WAS A LEADING ZERO, SO PRINT A
          240       /SPACE RATHER THAN A ZERO.
          JMP
          PRNTSP    /PRINT THE SPACE.
          0
OKPRNT,   MVID      /IT IS A NONZERO ASCII CHARACTER, SET
          377       /THE D REGISTER TO 377 (FF).
PRNTSP,   CALL      /PRINT THE CHARACTER.
          TTYOUT
          0
          DCXH      /DECREMENT THE MEMORY ADDRESS.
          DCRC      /DECREMENT THE DIGIT COUNTER.
          JNZ       /IS THE COUNT ZERO ? NO. PRINT
          NXTOUT    /ANOTHER CHARACTER.
          0
          RET       /ALL 4 WERE PRINTED, RETURN.


UNIT,     0         /THESE MEMORY LOCATIONS WERE LOADED
TEN,      0         /WITH ASCII NUMERIC VALUES BY EXAMPLE
HUN,      0         /6-23.
THOU,     0
```

memory and it, too, is tested. The content of the D register serves as a "flag." It is initially set to zero. When a zero character is encountered, the value of the D register is compared to zero. If the D register is zero, the zero character is not printed, but a "space" is.

This "flag" testing is performed whenever an ASCII value for the zero character is encountered. When the first nonzero character is encountered, the flag (the content of register D) is set to a nonzero value. This indicates to further zero characters that they *are* to be printed; i.e., the zero between 3 and 2 in 302. The flag is set by the MVID 377 instruction at the symbolic address OKPRNT.

CONCLUSION

Needless to say, we have strayed from the original goal of discussing number-base conversion programs. The ASCII/BCD counter subroutines were included so that a "different" solution to a counter/conversion problem could be examined and discussed. As you observed, the conversion programs that convert binary numbers to ASCII-based decimal numbers are long and at times difficult to understand. Also, they are very inflexible in terms of expandability. By attacking the same problem in a slightly different manner, the ASCII/BCD counter subroutine solved the counting problem with a minimum of software.

The leading-zero suppression subroutine was included because it is an interesting program. If the counting capabilities of the ASCII/BCD subroutine are increased to 99,999,999, it might be useful to incorporate the leading-zero-suppression subroutine in the 8080's car-counting software.

With all of the number-base conversion subroutines that we have presented in this chapter, you should be very comfortable programming the 8080 microcomputer to input octal, hexadecimal, or decimal numbers. After the numbers are "processed," the binary results can be readily converted to octal, hexadecimal, or decimal, and then printed on a teletypewriter or crt.

7

Microcomputer Input/Output (I/O)

In this chapter, we will explore the area of *interfacing* external (or peripheral) devices to the 8080 microcomputer. In previous chapters, it has been assumed that a teletypewriter or crt has been interfaced to the microcomputer. To read the eight-bit ASCII character that was transmitted by the teletypewriter keyboard or paper-tape reader, the 8080 waited for a *flag* signal to go to a logic 1, after which the ASCII character was input into the A register. How was the teletypewriter actually interfaced to the microcomputer? To answer this question, we will explore the design and development of software, as we have done in previous chapters, and we will also explore the design and implementation of some hardware. Hardware is a broad term that describes the electrical components, resistors, gates, drivers, and latches, that are used to electrically connect a peripheral device to the buses of the microcomputer. *This means that there will be actual electrical schematics of the electronic circuits used included in this chapter.* This may seem unusual for a book on assembly language programming, but we believe that assembly language programmers are not only interested in using software to communicate with peripheral devices, but that they are also interested in learning how peripheral devices are actually interfaced to the microcomputer.

There are some details of interfacing that we will not explore, such as the different methods of device address decoding and how to combine the decoded device address with the synchronization pulses generated by the microcomputer, such as $\overline{\text{IN}}$ and $\overline{\text{MEMW}}$. Many of these details are covered in *Introductory Experiments in*

Digital Electronics and 8080A Microcomputer Programming and Interfacing[1]. If you are not familiar with gates, decoders, or three-state integrated circuits, these books will provide you with excellent descriptions along with actual experiments that you can perform with these devices.

Why is microcomputer I/O so important? It is important because it is the only way that the 8080 can communicate or transfer data between external (or peripheral) devices and itself. If the 8080 cannot communicate with peripheral devices, it would be very difficult, if not impossible, for the 8080 to perform useful tasks. This means that it would be impossible to use teletypewriters, crts, paper-tape readers/punches, analog-to-digital converters, solid-state relays, keyboards, floppy disks, or any other peripheral devices.

The only method that has been discussed, which can be used to communicate with peripheral devices, is by using accumulator I/O by executing IN and OUT instructions. Both of these instructions are two-byte instructions in which the second byte of the instructions contains the *address* of the device that the 8080 is communicating with. For instance, when the OUT instruction is executed, the eight-bit content of register A is placed on the eight-bit bidirectional data bus, and the address of the device that is to receive this data is placed on the address lines A_0 through A_7 and also on lines A_8 through A_{15}. The IN instruction causes an eight-bit data value from a peripheral device to be placed on the bidirectional data bus and gated into the A register. During the execution of the IN instruction, the device address contained in the second byte of the IN instruction is placed on address lines A_0 through A_7 and on lines A_8 through A_{15}. When *any* accumulator I/O instruction is executed, one of two control signals is generated by the 8080 microcomputer. These control signals are used by the peripheral device electronics to synchronize the transfer of data between the 8080 and the peripheral device. These signals are often called $\overline{\text{IN}}$ and $\overline{\text{OUT}}$, or $\overline{\text{I/O READ}}$ and $\overline{\text{I/O WRITE}}$.

Another method of interfacing peripheral devices to an 8080 microcomputer is called *memory-mapped I/O*. This method can also be used to transfer data between the 8080 microcomputer and peripheral devices. When a peripheral device is interfaced to the microcomputer using memory-mapped I/O, the peripheral device "looks" like a memory location or a group of memory locations. This means that one 16-bit address is associated with each memory-mapped I/O device. What control signals are used to control the flow of eight-bit data words between the 8080 microprocessor integrated circuit and memory? The control signals memory-read ($\overline{\text{MEMR}}$) and memory-write ($\overline{\text{MEMW}}$) are used. These control signals, memory-read ($\overline{\text{MEMR}}$) and memory-write ($\overline{\text{MEMW}}$), are also used to synchronize the transfer of data between memory-mapped I/O devices and the 8080 microcomputer. This means that the 8080 cannot distinguish between reading an eight-bit data word from a memory-mapped I/O device or an actual memory location. They appear the same to the 8080. This is also true when the 8080 writes data to a memory-mapped I/O device or an R/W memory location. The microcomputer does not know what type of device it is writing data to. *It is the programmer's responsibility to distinguish between memory-mapped I/O devices and real memory locations in the microcomputer programs or software.*

Whenever the 8080 is programmed to transfer data between itself and memory, what signals must always be generated by the microcomputer? A 16-bit address and the proper control signals, which determine the direction of data flow on the bidirectional data bus, must be generated by the 8080 microcomputer. In many of our programming examples, either register pair B, D, or H provided a 16-bit address that was used as a memory address to transfer data between memory and the 8080 microcomputer. The content of these register pairs can also be used to provide an address so that the 8080 can communicate with a memory-mapped I/O device. For memory-mapped I/O devices, the control signals $\overline{\text{MEMW}}$ and $\overline{\text{MEMR}}$ rather than $\overline{\text{OUT}}$ and $\overline{\text{IN}}$, are used to provide the required synchonization for the transfer of data.

What instructions can be used so that an 8080 can transfer data to and from memory-mapped I/O devices? All of the 8080's memory-reference instructions can be used. This means that there are 33 *different* instructions that can be used to control memory-mapped I/O devices. The accumulator I/O technique can make use of only two data transfer instructions, IN and OUT. The variety of control instructions often makes the memory-mapped technique appear to be an attractive alternative. Some of the characteristics of each technique are shown in Tables 7-1 and 7-2.

Table 7-1. A Summary of Accumulator I/O Characteristics

8080 Instructions	IN and OUT (both two-byte instructions).
Control Signals	$\overline{\text{IN}}$ and $\overline{\text{OUT}}$.
Data Transfer	Between the accumulator and the I/O device.
Device Decoding	An eight-bit device address, on address lines A_0 through A_7, or A_8 through A_{15}, that is contained in the second byte of the IN or OUT instruction.
Terminology	The I/O processes are called **input** and **output.** The decoded device address, when combined with a synchronization pulse ($\overline{\text{IN}}$ or $\overline{\text{OUT}}$), is called a **device select pulse.** This signal is used to pulse the peripheral device.

There are some important points to keep in mind when you consider the use of memory-mapped and accumulator I/O. While the memory-mapped I/O technique makes more of the 8080's instruction set available, some of the instructions are not particularly useful. For example, the MOVMH and MOVML instructions do not make much sense unless we want to transfer a byte of the memory

Table 7-2. A Summary of Memory-Mapped I/O Characteristics

8080 Instructions					
MOVAM	MOVME	ANAM			
MOVBM	MOVMH	XRAM			
MOVCM	MOVML	ORAM			
MOVDM	STAXB	CMPM			
MOVEM	STAXD	INRM			
MOVHM	LDAXB	DCRM			
MOVLM	LDAXD	MVIM	$<B_2>$		
MOVMA	ADDM	STA	$<B_2>$	$<B_3>$	
MOVMB	ADCM	LDA	$<B_2>$	$<B_3>$	
MOVMC	SUBM	SHLD	$<B_2>$	$<B_3>$	
MOVMD	SBBM	LHLD	$<B_2>$	$<B_3>$	

Control Signals	$\overline{\text{MEMR}}$ and $\overline{\text{MEMW}}$.
Data Transfer	Between **any** of the 8080's general-purpose registers and the memory-mapped I/O device. An immediate data byte can also be written into memory.
Device Decoding	A 16-bit address, on address lines A_0 through A_{15}. This address may be in register pair B, D, or H, or may be contained in the second and third bytes of an LDA, STA, LHLD, or SHLD instruction.
Terminology	The memory-mapped I/O processes are called **read** and **write** rather than input and output. The decoded device address, when combined with a synchronization pulse ($\overline{\text{MEMR}}$ or $\overline{\text{MEMW}}$), is called an **address select pulse** rather than a device select pulse.

address to the memory-mapped I/O device. Also, the MOVLM and MOVHM instructions "write-over" portions of the address stored in register L or register H. The INRM and DCRM instructions could be quite useful, but only if the memory-mapped I/O device is wired as both an input port and an output port with the same 16-bit address.

All but four of the memory reference instructions, LDA, STA, LHLD, and SHLD, require that a 16-bit memory address be stored in register pair B, D, or H. This means that the address for the memory-mapped I/O device must be loaded into the required register pair. This means that for a simple I/O transfer, two instructions must be executed that require four memory locations for storage; i.e., an LXIH and an MOVBM instruction.

The memory-mapped I/O technique provides us with the capability of addressing more than 256 input and 256 output devices, but few of us will choose to use the memory-mapped I/O technique because of this feature alone. Actually, there is no overriding reason to choose one I/O technique over another from the software point of view. We have tended to favor accumulator I/O, and we have found very few problems that could not be solved by using it. The memory-mapped I/O users probably feel similarly about their technique.

It is important that you note that the techniques themselves are not fundamentally different from one another. Both require a device address and a synchronization pulse to generate the device select control signal for each I/O device. For further discussions and examples, we refer you to Units 20 and 21 in Book 2 of *Introductory Experiments in Digital Electronic and 8080A Microcomputer Programming and Interfacing*[1].

I/O DATA TRANSFERS—BUS CONTROL

When an output instruction is executed, how long does the content of the A register remain on the data bus? The eight-bit data word from register A is only on the data bus for about 1 μs. This is certainly not long enough for a teletypewriter to print a character or for us to see the number on a seven-segment, light-emitting-diode (LED) display. For this reason, the eight-bit content of the data bus is *latched* by the peripheral device interface electronics when an OUT instruction is executed. A device that *latches* the data is really a type of memory device. It generally has a control input and data inputs. When the control input is pulsed or clocked, the data on the inputs of the device are gated into the device and held, until the control line is again pulsed or clocked. In general, a gated combination of the $\overline{\text{OUT}}$ pulse and the eight-bit device address is used to pulse this control line. The same types of devices can also be used in the interface electronics for memory-mapped I/O peripheral devices. The number of transistor-transistor-logic (TTL) and metal-oxide-semiconductor (MOS) integrated-circuit devices that can latch data is almost unlimited.

When data values are read from memory or memory-mapped I/O devices, or when data values are input from accumulator I/O devices, how long is the data from these peripheral devices actually gated onto the data bus? The data from these devices is only on the data bus for about 1 μs, and the data from these devices is only on the data bus when these devices are properly addressed. This means that two memory locations or I/O devices cannot place data on the data bus at the same time. When a specific memory location or

I/O device is not selected, it must not place data on the data bus. For this reason, *three-state* integrated circuits are used to interface memory-mapped or accumulator input devices to the 8080's bidirectional data bus. There are also a tremendous number of three-state devices that can be used in microcomputer interfacing. If you are unfamiliar with three-state devices, latches, or some of the other concepts that we have mentioned, or if you would like to *experiment* with some of these integrated circuits, Books 1 and 2 of *Introductory Experiments in Digital Electronics and 8080A Microcomputer Programming and Interfacing*[1] provide a large number of experiments in which these devices are used.

THE 8080 AND SIMPLE I/O DEVICES

Perhaps the simplest output device that can be interfaced to the 8080 microcomputer is an eight-bit output port equipped with LEDs. The eight inputs to the two latches are wired to the eight-bit data bus, and the outputs of the latches are connected to the LEDs through current-limiting resistors. This interface is shown in Fig. 7-1.

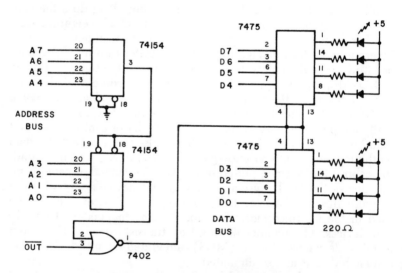

Fig. 7-1. An eight-bit output port with LEDs.

The SN7475 latches will only latch the content of the data bus when an OUT 050 instruction is executed. If register A contains 377 (FF) when this output instruction is executed, all eight of the LEDs will be turned on. If the A register contains 000 (00) when this instruction is executed, all of the LEDs will be turned off. A very simple program, which causes the 8080 to count in binary and display the count on the LEDs wired to output port 050, is listed in Example 7-1.

Example 7-1: A Binary Count With Display Program

```
/THIS PROGRAM COUNTS IN BINARY AND DISPLAYS
/THE COUNT ON AN LED-EQUIPPED OUTPUT PORT.

COUNT,   INRA    /INCREMENT THE CONTENT OF A.
         OUT     /OUTPUT THE COUNT TO THE
         050     /LATCHES AND LED'S (050 = HEX 28).
         JMP     /JUMP BACK AND INCREMENT THE COUNT
         COUNT   /AGAIN AND DISPLAY THE RESULT.
         0
```

If this program is executed, how fast does the 8080 increment the count? The loop in Example 7-1 requires 25 clock cycles or 12.5 μs (500 ns cycle time). This means that the counting frequency is 80 kHz. Of course, this is far too fast for anyone to actually see the counting take place. Therefore, a time-delay loop must be added to the program to slow down the 8080's counting rate.

Since the A register is used in the time-delay section of Example 7-2, the B register is used to store the count that is being displayed. Therefore, the INRB instruction increments the count. The count is

Example 7-2: A Slower Binary Count With Display

```
/THIS PROGRAM COUNTS IN BINARY AND DISPLAYS
/THE RESULT, BUT A TIME DELAY HAS BEEN ADDED TO THE
/PROGRAM SO THAT THE CHANGES IN THE COUNT
/CAN ACTUALLY BE SEEN.

COUNT,   INRB    /INCREMENT THE COUNT CONTAINED IN B.
         MOVAB   /MOVE THE COUNT TO A.
         OUT     /AND THEN OUTPUT IT TO THE LATCH
         050     /AND LEDS (050 = HEX 28).
         LXID    /LOAD REGISTER PAIR D WITH
         000     /000 000 = HEX 0000.
         000
WAIT,    DCXD    /DECREMENT REGISTER PAIR D.
         MOVAD   /MOVE THE MSBY OF THE COUNT TO A.
         ORAE    /OR IT WITH THE LSBY OF THE COUNT.
         JNZ     /IF THE RESULT IS NONZERO,
         WAIT    /JUMP AND EXECUTE THE DCXD
         0       /INSTRUCTION AGAIN.
         JMP     /WHEN THE CONTENT OF REGISTER PAIR D
         COUNT   /IS 000 000 OR 0000, INCREMENT AND
         0       /DISPLAY THE COUNT AGAIN.
```

then moved to register A and output to output port 050 (28), which is equipped with LEDs. Register pair D is then loaded with 000 000 (0000). The next four instructions will then be executed

65,536 times, as the content of register pair D is decremented to 377 377 (FFFF) and on down to 000 000 (0000). When the content of register pair D is finally 000 000 (0000), the JMP to COUNT is executed. At COUNT, the count in the B register is incremented and then displayed. Can this program be changed so that the 8080 counts down rather than up? By simply changing the INRB instruction to a DCRB instruction, the 8080 can be programmed to count down. In these examples (7-1 and 7-2), we do not care what the content of the A or B register is when the counting starts. We simply want the count to be incremented or decremented. If it is important that the count start at a specific value, we could easily program the 8080 to load an immediate data byte into either the A or B register.

Some additional circuitry can be added to the 8080 interface electronics so that the 8080 can input data into the A register (Fig. 7-2). An IN 050 instruction can be executed to input the logic 1 or logic 0 state of the eight switches into the A register. Only when an IN 050 instruction is executed will the state of the switches be gated onto the data bus. At all other times, the input port appears to be disconnected from the data bus. What does the program in Example 7-3 do?

The program in Example 7-3 simply inputs the state of the eight switches into the A register when the IN 050 instruction is executed. The output instruction then latches the content of the A register (the state of the switches) into the SN7475 latches. The LEDs then indicate the binary content of the A register. Therefore, the state of the switches is actually displayed on the output port. Since the 8080 is continuously inputting the state of the switches and outputting this data to the LEDs, any change in the state of the switches can be seen by observing the state of the LEDs.

Example 7-3: A Microcomputer Input/Output Program

/THIS PROGRAM INPUTS THE LOGIC LEVELS OF THE SWITCHES
/INTO THE A REGISTER AND THEN OUTPUTS THE CONTENT
/OF REGISTER A TO THE LATCHES AND LEDS.

```
QUESS,   IN      /INPUT THE LOGIC LEVELS OF
         050     /THE SWITCHES INTO A (050 = HEX 28)
         OUT     /AND THEN IMMEDIATELY OUTPUT THE SAME
         050     /DATA VALUES TO THE LATCHES AND LED'S.
         JMP     /JUMP BACK AND EXECUTE THE SAME
         QUESS   /SEQUENCE OF INSTRUCTIONS AGAIN.
         0
```

Of course, once these switches are interfaced to the 8080 microcomputer, they can also be used to input data. The program listed in Example 7-4 waits for the switch that is wired to bit D_7 of the

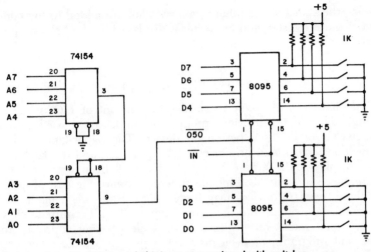

Fig. 7-2. An eight-bit input port equipped with switches.

data bus to be set to a logic 1. When this occurs, the states (logic levels) of the other switches are saved in the B register. The 8080 then waits for the same switch to go to the logic 0 state. When this

Example 7-4: A Simple Input, Addition, and Output Program

```
/THIS PROGRAM INPUTS TWO SEVEN-BIT BINARY NUMBERS FROM
/THE SWITCHES,  ADDS THE NUMBERS, AND DISPLAYS THE
/RESULT ON THE "LED" OUTPUT PORT.

INPUT,  IN       /INPUT THE DATA FROM THE SWITCHES.
        050      /050 = HEX 28.
        CPI      /IS THE MOST SIGNIFICANT SWITCH IN
        200      /THE LOGIC ONE STATE?
        JC       /NO, THEN DO NOT SAVE THE NUMBER.
        INPUT
        0
        ANI      /IT IS IN THE LOGIC ONE STATE, SAVE
        177      /THE SEVEN LSB'S. 177 = HEX 7F.
        MOVBA    /SAVE THE SEVEN-BIT NUMBER IN B.
IN1,    IN       /NOW WAIT FOR THE SWITCH TO RETURN
        050      /TO THE LOGIC ZERO STATE BEFORE
        CPI      /GETTING THE FINAL NUMBER.
        200
        JNC      /THE SWITCH IS STILL IN THE ONE STATE
        IN1      /SO KEEP WAITING.
        0
        ANI      /IT'S IN THE ZERO STATE, SO SAVE
        177      /THE SEVEN LSB'S.
        ADDB     /ADD THE OTHER SEVEN-BIT NUMBER.
        OUT      /THEN OUTPUT THE RESULT,
        050
        HLT      /AND HALT.
```

281

occurs, the states of the other seven switches are added to the content of the B register, and the result is displayed on the LED output port.

THE 8080 AND KEYBOARDS

You have already seen a considerable amount of I/O programming. Many of the previous program examples have used a teletypewriter or crt as a peripheral device. The paper-tape reader/punch, keyboard, and printer of a teletypewriter, and the keyboard and display logic (printer) of a crt have all been used in these examples. For some 8080 microcomputer systems, the cost of either of these two I/O devices may be too high. However, a method of entering data values into the microcomputer is still required. These data values might be entries in a data file, starting addresses for different programs, or even program steps (8080 binary, octal, or hexadecimal instruction op codes). For this reason, we will discuss two different methods that can be used to interface keyboards to 8080 microcomputers, and the software that is required to communicate with the keyboards.

THE SOFTWARE AND HARDWARE FOR A KEYBOARD USING A HARDWARE ENCODER

The schematic diagram for a 15-key keyboard, its hardware encoder, and its interface is shown in Fig. 7-3. The actual keyboard keys are on the right side of the diagram. The two SN7148 *priority encoder* integrated circuits encode the individual key closures into a binary code. The binary codes produced by these integrated circuits are combined by the four two-input NAND gates (SN7400) to produce a unique key code for each key. The outputs of the NAND gates go to the DM8095 (SN74365) integrated circuit, which is a *three-state buffer*. This integrated circuit is used to gate the binary key code and a keyboard *status bit* onto the 8080's bidirectional data bus and into the A register when an IN 000 instruction is executed.

Note that there are five wires going from the encoder to the DM8095 three-state device. Since the 15 keys can be represented by a four-bit binary code, why are there five wires? Four of the wires are used by the binary key code and the fifth wire is used to indicate that a key is pressed. Therefore, when an IN 000 is executed, the 8080 inputs a four-bit key code and the *status* of the keyboard. If you could examine the content of the A register after an IN 000 instruction is executed, you would see the values shown in Table 7-3.

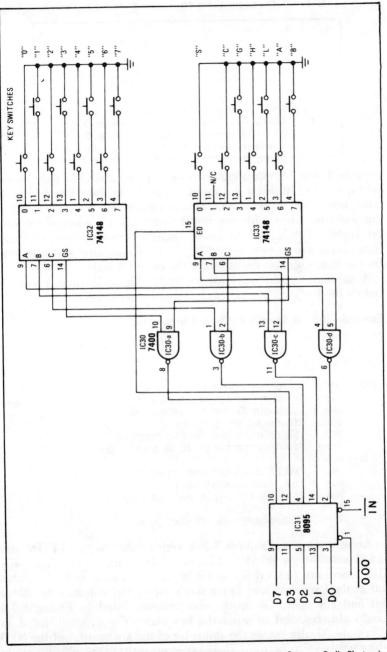

Courtesy Radio-Electronics

Fig. 7-3. The interface and encoding logic for a 15-key keyboard.

Table 7-3. The Content of A After Input From the Keyboard

D_7	D_6	D_5	D_4	D_3	D_2	D_1	D_0
S	X	X	X	C_3	C_2	C_1	C_0

S = Status of the keyboard.
If S = 1, a key is pressed.
If S = 0, no key is pressed.

C_3 = When a key is pressed, the MSB of the key code, D_3.
C_2 = When a key is pressed, the next key code bit, D_2.
C_1 = When a key is pressed, the next key code bit, D_1.
C_0 = When a key is pressed, the LSB of the key code, D_0.

From Table 7-3, you should realize that the code bits only represent a valid code when the status bit of the keyboard is a logic 1. Also, note that the key code and status bit are contained within one eight-bit word. This was not the case when a teletypewriter or crt keyboard was used to input ASCII characters. Two different input ports had to be accessed by the microcomputer software, one for the status bit and the other for the eight-bit code.

A subroutine that waits for the status bit to become a logic 1, before the key code is input, is listed in Example 7-5.

Example 7-5: A Simple Keyboard Input Program

```
/THIS SUBROUTINE WAITS FOR BIT D7
/TO BE A LOGIC ONE AND THEN THE FOUR-BIT
/KEY CODE IS INPUT.

KEYIN,  IN      /INPUT THE EIGHT-BIT WORD THAT CON-
        000     /TAINS THE STATUS AND DATA BITS.
        ANI     /MASK-OUT ALL THE BITS EXCEPT THE
        200     /STATUS BIT (D7). 200=HEX 80.
        JZ      /BIT D7 IS A LOGIC ZERO SO CONTINUE
        KEYIN   /WAITING FOR THE BIT TO BE A LOGIC ONE.
        0
        IN      /BIT D7 IS A LOGIC ONE, SO INPUT
        000     /THE EIGHT-BIT WORD AGAIN
        ANI     /AND THEN MASK-OUT THE FOUR MSB'S.
        017     /(017 = HEX 0F).
        RET     /RETURN WITH THE KEY CODE IN A.
```

As you can see, Example 7-5 is very similar to the TTYIN and TTYI subroutines listed in Chapter 3 (Example 3-20). The only differences are (1) a different bit in register A represents the status bit of the keyboard, and (2) a single input port contains the status bit and key code. Of course, the program listed in Example 7-6 could also be used to input the key code. The program listed in Example 7-7 also senses the status bit of the keyboard, but the 8080 does not have to perform a second input instruction or temporarily save the key code in another register.

Example 7-6: Another Simple Keyboard Input Program

/THIS SUBROUTINE WAITS FOR BIT D7 TO BE
/A LOGIC ONE. WHEN IT IS, THE KEY CODE
/WHICH IS STORED IN B IS MOVED TO A.

```
KEYIN,  IN       /INPUT THE EIGHT-BIT WORD THAT CON-
        000      /TAINS THE STATUS AND DATA BITS.
        MOVBA    /SAVE THE WORD IN B.
        ANI      /MASK-OUT ALL THE BITS EXCEPT THE
        200      /STATUS BIT (D7). 200=HEX 80.
        JZ       /BIT D7 IS A LOGIC ZERO SO CONTINUE
        KEYIN    /WAITING FOR THE BIT TO BE A LOGIC ONE.
        0
        MOVAB    /GET THE EIGHT-BIT WORD FROM B TO A.
        ANI      /MASK-OUT THE FOUR MSB'S.
        017      /(017 = HEX 0F).
        RET      /RETURN WITH IT IN A.
```

Example 7-7: The Simplest Keyboard Input Program

/THIS SUBROUTINE WAITS FOR BIT D7 TO BECOME A
/LOGIC ONE. THIS IS SENSED BY ADDING 200
/(HEX 80) TO THE INPUT PORT DATA. WHEN THE STATUS
/BIT IS A ONE, THE CARRY IS A ONE AND THE FOUR-
/BIT KEY CODE REMAINS IN A!

```
KEYIN,  IN       /INPUT AN EIGHT-BIT WORD THAT CON-
        000      /TAINS THE STATUS AND DATA BITS.
        ADI      /ADD 200 (HEX 80) TO THIS. IF THE
        200      /CARRY IS 0, THE FLAG IS 0 !
        JNC      /THE CARRY IS ZERO, SO THE FLAG IS
        KEYIN    /ZERO. THEREFORE CONTINUE WAITING FOR
        0        /THE FLAG TO BE A ONE.
        ANI      /MASK-OUT THE FOUR MSB'S WITH 017
        017      /(HEX 0F) AND RETURN WITH THE KEY
        RET      /CODE IN THE A REGISTER.
```

The subroutine in Example 7-7 uses an interesting trick. By adding 200 (80) to the content of register A after the keyboard's status bit and key code are input, the carry is set or cleared depending on the state of the status bit of the keyboard. If the status bit (D_7) is a logic 0 (no keys pressed), the carry flag will be a logic 0 as a result of the addition. However, if the status bit is a logic 1, the carry will be a logic 1 after the addition. Therefore, it is easy to see how the microcomputer senses whether or not a key is pressed. Once a key is pressed, the 8080 executes the ANI instruction, so that bits D_7 through D_4 are masked-out.

Suppose that you want to be able to enter key codes into the 8080 microcomputer and save them in memory. The program in Example 7-8 can be executed to do just this. What will happen when this program is executed? The first instruction loads the stack pointer with a 16-bit address for R/W memory. The LXIH instruction loads register pair H with the R/W memory address where the key codes will be stored. The keyboard input subroutine (KEYIN) is then called. In the KEYIN subroutine, the 8080 waits for a key to be pressed. When a key is pressed, the 8080 returns from the subroutine with the key code for the key that is pressed, in the A register. The content of the A register is then saved in memory, the memory address incremented, and the JMP to GETIT executed.

Example 7-8: Entering Key Codes Into the Microcomputer and Saving Them in Memory

```
START,   LXISP    /LOAD THE STACK POINTER WITH A
         100      /16-BIT ADDRESS FOR R/W MEMORY.
         100      /100 100=HEX 4040.
         LXIH     /LOAD REGISTER PAIR H WITH A 16-BIT R/W
         200      /MEMORY ADDRESS FOR STORING KEY CODES.
         100      /100 200 = HEX 4080.
GETIT,   CALL     /WAIT FOR THE KEYBOARD FLAG TO BE
         KEYIN,   /A LOGIC ONE BEFORE RETURNING
         0        /WITH THE KEY CODE IN A.
         MOVMA    /SAVE THE CODE IN MEMORY.
         INXH     /INCREMENT THE R/W MEMORY ADDRESS.
         JMP      /THEN GET ANOTHER KEY CODE AND
         GETIT    /SAVE IT IN R/W MEMORY.
         0
KEYIN,   IN       /INPUT AN EIGHT-BIT WORD THAT CON-
         000      /TAINS THE STATUS AND DATA BITS.
         ADI      /ADD 200 (HEX 80) TO THIS. IF THE
         200      /CARRY IS 0, THE FLAG IS 0 !
         JNC      /THE CARRY IS ZERO, SO THE FLAG IS
         KEYIN    /ZERO. THEREFORE CONTINUE WAITING FOR
         0        /THE FLAG TO BE A ONE.
         ANI      /MASK-OUT THE FOUR MSB'S WITH 017
         017      /(HEX 0F) AND RETURN WITH THE KEY
         RET      /CODE IN THE A REGISTER.
```

How quickly can you press and release a key on a keyboard? Can you do it in 50 or 100 ms? In Example 7-8, the 8080 needs only 42 μs (500 ns cycle time) to sense the key, input the key code, exit from the subroutine, save the key code in memory, increment the memory address, jump back to GETIT, and call the KEYIN subroutine again. Since a key may be pressed for 50 or 100 ms, the same key will be sensed and saved in 1000 to 2000 memory locations.

Why didn't we have the same problem when ASCII characters were input from the UART that was wired to the teletypewriter or crt, as described in previous chapters? In the interface between the UART and the microcomputer, *there was additional interface logic that was used to clear the status bit, or flag, whenever a key code was input by the 8080.* A typical teletypewriter keyboard input subroutine is listed in Example 7-9.

Example 7-9: A Typical Teletypewriter or CRT Input Subroutine

```
TTYI,   IN      /INPUT THE UART'S STATUS.
        001
        ANI     /SAVE ONLY THE RECEIVER'S STATUS.
        001
        JZ      /IF A=001, A KEY IS PRESSED.
        TTYI    /IF A=000, NO KEY IS PRESSED.
        0       /IF NO KEY IS PRESSED, KEEP WAITING.
        IN      /A KEY IS PRESSED, SO INPUT THE
        000     /CHARACTER'S ASCII CODE
        RET     /AND RETURN WITH IT IN THE A REGISTER.
```

When the IN 000 is executed, to input the key code, the device select pulse that is generated by the 8080 microcomputer is used to clear the flag that indicates that a key has been pressed. In this manner, a key code is only input twice if the key is actually pressed twice. *Remember, this clearing function is performed by hardware.* Finally, no matter how fast the 8080 can call the TTYI subroutine, it will not *exist* from the subroutine until the key that is currently pressed is released, and another key is pressed or the same key is pressed again.

Unfortunately, the interface hardware for the 15-key keyboard is not this sophisticated, so additional software instructions will have to be added to the KEYIN subroutine such that the 8080 will only

Example 7-10: Waiting for the Key to be Released Before Returning

```
/THIS SUBROUTINE WAITS FOR BIT D7, THE STATUS BIT,
/TO BE A LOGIC ONE. THE KEY CODE IS THEN SAVED IN
/B. THE 8080 THEN WAITS FOR THE KEY TO BE
/RELEASED BEFORE RETURNING FROM THE SUBROUTINE
/WITH THE KEY CODE IN THE A REGISTER.

KEYIN,    IN      /INPUT THE EIGHT-BIT WORD THAT CON-
          000     /TAINS THE STATUS AND DATA BITS.
          ADI     /ADD 200 (HEX 80) TO THE WORD SO
          200     /THAT A CARRY IS GENERATED IF
          JNC     /THE STATUS (FLAG) BIT IS A LOGIC ONE.
          KEYIN   /THIS JNC IS EXECUTED IF THE FLAG
          0       /IS A LOGIC ZERO.
          ANI     /MASK-OUT THE FOUR MSB'S.
          017     /(017 = HEX 0F).
          MOVBA   /SAVE THE FOUR-BIT KEY CODE IN B.
RELESE,   IN      /INPUT THE SAME WORD AGAIN
          000     /AND WAIT FOR THE KEY TO BE RELEASED.
          ADI     /ADD 200 (HEX 80) TO THE WORD SO
          200     /THAT A CARRY MAY OR MAY NOT BE
          JC      /GENERATED. EXECUTE THE JC WHEN
          RELESE  /THE KEY IS PRESSED AND THE STATUS
          0       /(FLAG) BIT IS A LOGIC ONE.
          MOVAB   /THE KEY IS NO LONGER PRESSED.
          RET     /RETURN WITH THE KEY CODE IN A.
```

save one key code in memory, regardless of how long a key is actually pressed. This is another example of a *hardware/software tradeoff*, in which we have asked ourselves, "Is it easier to perform the task with additional hardware devices or software instructions?" In this case, we will solve the problem by using additional software. The program listed in Example 7-10 solves part of this problem.

The first three instructions in this version of the KEYIN (Example 7-10) subroutine cause the 8080 to wait for the keyboard status bit or flag to become a logic 1. If the flag is a logic 0, the carry is cleared by the ADI instruction so that the JNC to KEYIN is executed. When a key is pressed, the flag goes to a logic 1, and the carry will be a logic 1 as a result of the addition. Therefore, the JNC to KEYIN is not executed. Instead, the content of the A register is ANDed with 017 (0F), and the result is saved in B. The key is still pressed, so the 8080 executes instructions that detect when the key is released. Only when the key is released will the 8080 return from the subroutine. Therefore, the key will only be sensed once, no matter how long it is pressed.

When we executed this program on one of our 8080 microcomputers, only 10 to 20 of the same key codes were saved in memory each time a key was pressed, rather than the 1000 to 2000 that were saved in memory when the program in Example 7-8 was executed. This is certainly better, but why isn't only one key code saved in memory each time a key is pressed? The problem is due to *key bounce*, which is a characteristic of many of the keys used in keyboards that are commercially available. When a key is pressed, you might expect the following output from the key:

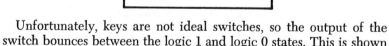

Unfortunately, keys are not ideal switches, so the output of the switch bounces between the logic 1 and logic 0 states. This is shown in the following sketch:

As you can see, the key bounces between the two logic levels, both when it is pressed and when it is released. As you might guess, the number of bounces, and the duration of the bouncing, is not fixed. We will assume that even if a key does bounce, it will probably not bounce for more than 10 ms. This is a realistic assumption. How can we modify the KEYIN subroutine so that the 8080 senses only one key closure, rather than the nine key closures that occurred in the previous sketch? The simplest solution is to program the 8080 so that a short time-delay subroutine is executed when the 8080 first detects that a key is pressed, and also when it first detects that a key is released.

Example 7-11. Debouncing a Key Closure With a Time-Delay Subroutine

```
/THIS SUBROUTINE PROVIDES THE DEBOUNCING SOFTWARE
/REQUIRED SO THAT ONE KEY CLOSURE DOES NOT LOOK
/LIKE MULTIPLE KEY CLOSURES TO THE MICROCOMPUTER.
/NOTE THAT THE DEBOUNCE SOFTWARE IS CALLED WHEN THE
/KEY IS FIRST PRESSED AND WHEN IT IS ALSO RELEASED.
/THE 8080 WILL RETURN WITH THE KEY CODE IN REGISTER A.

KEYIN,   IN        /INPUT THE EIGHT-BIT WORD THAT CON-
         000       /TAINS THE STATUS AND DATA BITS.
         ANI       /MASK-OUT ALL BUT THE FLAG BIT (D7).
         200       /200 = HEX 80.
         JZ        /THE FLAG BIT IS A ZERO, SO WAIT FOR IT
         KEYIN     /TO BE A LOGIC ONE.
         0
         CALL      /THEN CALL THE 10 MILLISECOND DELAY
         DELAY     /SUBROUTINE TO LET THE KEY DEBOUNCE
         0         /BEFORE THE KEY CODE IS INPUT.
         IN        /AFTER 10 MS, INPUT THE CODE.
         000
         ANI       /REMOVE ALL BUT THE DATA BITS.
         017       /017 = HEX 0F.
         MOVBA     /AND SAVE THE KEY CODE IN B.
RELESE,  IN        /INPUT THE STATUS AND DATA BITS AGAIN.
         000
         ANI       /SAVE ONLY THE STATUS OR FLAG
         200       /BIT, WHICH IS D7 (200 = HEX 80).
         JNZ       /THE KEY IS STILL PRESSED, SO
         RELESE    /CONTINUE TO WAIT UNTIL IT IS
         0         /RELEASED.
         CALL      /THEN CALL THE 10 MS DELAY SUBROUTINE
         DELAY     /SO THAT THE SWITCH BOUNCE IS IGNORED.
         0
         MOVAB     /MOVE THE KEY CODE FROM B TO A
         RET       /AND THEN RETURN.
DELAY,   PUSHPSW   /SAVE THE PSW ON THE STACK.
         PUSHD     /THEN SAVE REGISTER PAIR D ON THE STACK.
         LXID      /LOAD REGISTER PAIR D WITH
         101       /003 101 = HEX 0341.
         003
WAIT,    DCXD      /DECREMENT THE COUNT.
         MOVAD     /MOVE THE MSBY TO A.
         ORAE      /OR IT WITH THE LSBY.
         JNZ       /IF THE RESULT IS NONZERO, JUMP
         WAIT      /TO THE DCXD INSTRUCTION.
         0
         POPD      /THE RESULT IS ZERO, POP D,
         POPPSW    /AND THEN POP THE PSW.
         RET       /THEN RETURN (NO REGISTERS CHANGED).
```

The subroutine listed in Example 7-11 is straightforward. When it is called, the 8080 executes the three-instruction loop at the beginning of the subroutine until a key is pressed. When the status bit (flag) of the keyboard is a logic 1, bit D_7 of the A register is also a 1, so the JZ instruction is no longer executed. Instead, the 8080 calls the DELAY subroutine. The DELAY subroutine saves the PSW and register pair D on the stack, loads register pair D with a count, and then executes the loop within the DELAY subroutine until the count is decremented to zero. When the count is zero, register pair D and the PSW are popped off of the stack, and the 8080 returns from the DELAY subroutine. This process requires about 10 ms to be performed, assuming that the 8080 has a 500-ns cycle time.

When the 8080 returns from the DELAY subroutine, the key code is input into the A register, the four MSBs of the A register are set to zero, and then the four-bit key code is saved in register B. The 8080 then starts to execute the instructions at RELESE. At RELESE, the 8080 waits for the key that is pressed to be released. When the key is released, bit D_7 of the A register will no longer be a logic 1, and the DELAY subroutine is called again, so the 8080 executes the MOVAB instruction 10 ms after the key is released. After the key code is moved to the A register, the 8080 returns from the subroutine. Using this subroutine, only one key code will be entered into the microcomputer, no matter how long a key is pressed, as long as the key bounces no more than 10 ms.

Suppose you want to interface a keyboard to the 8080 microcomputer, but the keys bounce up to 20 ms. Can you still use the subroutine listed in Example 7-11? Yes, the same subroutine can be used, but you would have to change the time delay produced by the DELAY subroutine. How is this done? By simply changing the two data bytes for the LXID instruction in the DELAY subroutine, a delay of 20 ms can be produced.

If required, you can save a few memory locations by incorporating the DELAY subroutine in the KEYIN subroutine. This is shown in Example 7-12. By combining the two subroutines, a CALL and RET instruction are saved. Note that the MOVAB instruction is still near the end of the KEYIN subroutine. This means that if any other section of the program calls the DELAY subroutine, the content of the B register will always be moved to register A just before the 8080 returns from the DELAY subroutine.

Now that we have developed the KEYIN subroutine, the keyboard can be used to enter data values, instruction op codes, or even an address that the 8080 can jump to. One limitation of this keyboard interface is that it requires a number of integrated circuits. If 2000 8080 microcomputer systems were to be manufactured

Example 7-12: Shortening the Key Input and Debouncing Subroutine

```
                /THIS SUBROUTINE PROVIDES THE DEBOUNCING SOFTWARE
                /REQUIRED SO THAT ONE KEY CLOSURE DOES NOT LOOK
                /LIKE MULTIPLE KEY CLOSURES TO THE MICROCOMPUTER.
                /NOTE THAT THE DEBOUNCE SOFTWARE IS CALLED WHEN THE
                /KEY IS FIRST PRESSED AND WHEN IT IS ALSO RELEASED.
                /THE 8080 WILL RETURN WITH THE KEY CODE IN REGISTER A.


KEYIN,   IN       /INPUT THE EIGHT-BIT WORD THAT CON-
         000      /TAINS THE STATUS AND DATA BITS.
         ANI      /MASK-OUT ALL BUT THE FLAG BIT (D7).
         200      /200 = HEX 80.
         JZ       /THE FLAG BIT IS A ZERO, SO WAIT FOR IT
         KEYIN    /TO BE A LOGIC ONE.
         0
         CALL     /THEN CALL THE 10 MILLISECOND DELAY
         DELAY    /SUBROUTINE TO LET THE KEY DEBOUNCE
         0        /BEFORE THE KEY CODE IS INPUT.
         IN       /AFTER 10 MS, INPUT THE CODE.
         000
         ANI      /REMOVE ALL BUT THE DATA BITS.
         017      /017 = HEX 0F.
         MOVBA    /AND SAVE THE KEY CODE IN B.
RELESE,  IN       /INPUT THE STATUS AND DATA BITS AGAIN.
         000
         ANI      /ONLY SAVE THE STATUS OR FLAG
         200      /BIT, WHICH IS D7 (200 = HEX 80).
         JNZ      /THE KEY IS STILL PRESSED, SO
         RELESE   /CONTINUE TO WAIT UNTIL IT IS
         0        /RELEASED.
DELAY,   PUSHD    /SAVE REGISTER PAIR D ON THE STACK.
         LXID     /LOAD REGISTER PAIR D WITH
         101      /003 001 = HEX 0341.
         003
WAIT,    DCXD     /DECREMENT THE COUNT.
         MOVAD    /MOVE THE MSBY TO A.
         ORAE     /OR IT WITH THE LSBY.
         JNZ      /IF THE RESULT IS NONZERO, JUMP
         WAIT     /TO THE DCXD INSTRUCTION.
         0
         POPD     /THE RESULT IS ZERO, POP D.
         MOVAB    /MOVE THE FOUR-BIT KEY CODE FROM B
         RET      /TO A AND THEN RETURN.
```

using this keyboard interface, it might be more profitable to investigate other methods of interfacing a keyboard to the microcomputer. This is particularly important if the SN74148 priority encoder integrated circuits and the SN7400 NAND integrated circuit can be eliminated from the interface design. In the next section of this chapter, we will discuss multiplexed, or scanned, keyboards. The interface for this type of keyboard is simpler than the design that we have used in many of our previous keyboard examples. However, a multiplexed keyboard requires more complex software.

A SOFTWARE-DRIVEN, MULTIPLEXED (SCANNED) KEYBOARD

In the previous KEYIN subroutines, the interface electronics produced a different binary code for each key on the keyboard. Since we are eliminating the priority encoder integrated circuits from the interface, the actual production of the unique key codes must be done by software. This is another example of a hardware/software tradeoff. To start with, we will use a 16-key keyboard, with the keys arranged in a 4 × 4 matrix, as shown in Fig. 7-4.

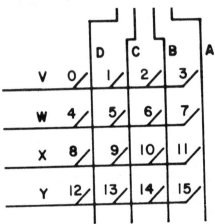

Fig. 7-4. Schematic diagram for a 4 × 4 key matrix.

Note that this keyboard is completely different from the keyboard that was used in the previous examples. How does this new keyboard operate? Suppose the A line is held at ground (logic 0) and the B, C, and D lines are held at +5 volts. The 8080 can then input and test the logic levels on the V, W, X, and Y lines. If all four of these outputs from the keyboard (V, W, X, and Y) are at the logic 1 level, then neither the 3, 7, 11, or 15 key is pressed. If this occurs, the A line is brought to the logic 1 level, and then the 8080 brings the B line to the logic 0 level. By testing the four output lines of the keyboard now, the 8080 can determine if the 2, 6, 10, or 14 key is pressed. By successively taking the C and then the D line of the keyboard to the logic 0 level, the 8080 can determine if the 1, 5, 9, or 13, or the 0, 4, 8, or 12 key is pressed. If none of the 16 keys is pressed, all of the outputs will be a logic 1, regardless of the input that is at a logic 0. Only when a logic 0 output is detected is a key pressed.

As you can see, there is no longer an individual status or flag bit that can be monitored to determine whether or not a key is pressed. Only by changing the logic levels at the four inputs of the keyboard, and monitoring the logic levels output by the keyboard, can the microcomputer determine whether or not a key is pressed. The interface electronics that give the 8080 microcomputer control of the keyboard are shown in Fig. 7-5.

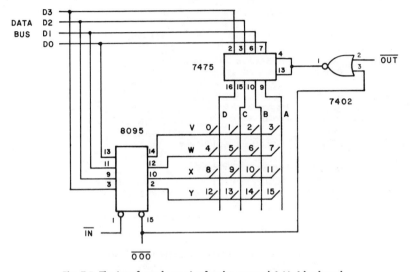

Fig. 7-5. The interface electronics for the scanned 4 × 4 keyboard.

How does the 8080 actually determine which key is pressed, and then produce a binary code corresponding to that key? To start with, the 8080 has to load register A with XXXX1110 (X = don't care), and then output this value to the SN7475 latch that drives the A, B, C, and D input lines of the keyboard. The 0 logic level will go to the A line of the keyboard or to the 3, 7, 11, and 15 keys. By inputting the logic levels of the V, W, X, and Y lines of the keyboard, via the DM8095 intergrated circuit, the 8080 can determine if the 3, 7, 11, or 15 key is pressed. If one of these keys is pressed, one of the inputs to the microcomputer from input port 000 will be zero. If neither the 3, 7, 11, or 15 key is pressed, the four LSBs of register A will be a logic 1. No part of input port 000 is wired to lines D_4 through D_7 of the data bus, so bits D_4 through D_7 of the A register will be a logic 1 when the IN 000 instruction is executed. However, the 8080 only has to examine the four LSBs to determine whether or not a key is pressed. The program listed in Example 7-13 performs the operations that we have just discussed.

Example 7-13: A 4 × 4 Matrix Keyboard Scan Subroutine

```
/THIS SUBROUTINE SCANS A MATRIX KEYBOARD
/THAT IS ARRANGED AS FOUR ROWS OF FOUR KEYS,
/A 4×4 KEY MATRIX.

KEYSCN,   MVID      /LOAD D WITH THE CODE FOR THE
          003       /FIRST KEY THAT CAN BE SENSED.
          MVIB      /LOAD B WITH THE WORD THAT IS USED TO
          376       /ACTIVATE ONE ROW OF KEYS AT A TIME.
NXTGRP,   MOVAB     /GET THE TEST WORD
          OUT       /AND OUTPUT IT TO THE KEYBOARD.
          000
          RLC       /ROTATE THE TEST WORD LEFT ONE BIT
          MOVBA     /AND THEN SAVE IT IN B.
          IN        /INPUT THE DATA FROM THE FOUR
          000       /ROWS OF KEYS.
          ANI       /SAVE ONLY THE FOUR LSB'S, WHICH CON-
          017       /TAIN THE ROW DATA.
          CPI       /SEE IF ANY KEYS ARE PRESSED BY
          017       /COMPARING 017 (0F) TO THE INPUT WORD.
          JNZ       /A KEY IS PRESSED IN THIS ROW, SO
          NXTKEY    /DETERMINE WHICH KEY IT IS.
          0
          DCRD      /NO KEYS ARE PRESSED IN THE TESTED ROW
          MOVAD     /SO DECREMENT THE KEY CODE BY ONE AND
          CPI       /SEE IF ALL FOUR ROWS HAVE BEEN TESTED,
          377       /377 = HEX FF.
          JNZ       /NOT ALL FOUR ROWS HAVE BEEN TESTED,
          NXTGRP    /SO TEST ANOTHER ROW.
          0
          JMP       /ALL THE ROWS HAVE BEEN TESTED AND
          KEYSCN    /NO KEYS ARE PRESSED, SO KEEP LOOKING.
          0
NXTKEY,   RRC       /ROTATE THE ROW DATA INTO THE CARRY.
          RNC       /RETURN WHEN THE CARRY IS ZERO.
          PUSHPSW   /OTHERWISE, SAVE THE PSW ON THE STACK
          MOVAD     /AND INCREASE THE KEY CODE IN D BY 4.
          ADI
          004
          MOVDA     /SAVE THE NEW KEY CODE IN D.
          POPPSW    /POP THE PSW OFF THE STACK
          JMP       /AND THEN TRY FOR A ZERO CARRY
          NXTKEY    /AGAIN.
          0
```

At the start of the subroutine (Example 7-13), register D is loaded with 003 (03), and B is loaded with 376 (FE). The D register is used to hold the key code for the first key that can be detected as being pressed, and the B register contains the word (test pattern) that will be output to the keyboard. At NXTGRP, the content of register B is output to the keyboard. Which input lines of the keyboard are now at a logic 1 or logic 0? The content of register A is 11111110, so the A line of the keyboard is the only line at logic 0. The B, C, and D lines are all at logic 1. After the output instruction is executed, the content of the A register is rotated to the left by one bit so that register A now contains 11111101. This value, which is the next test pattern that will be output to the keyboard, is then saved in register B.

After the first test pattern is output to the keyboard, the state of the four output lines, V, W, X, and Y, are input and tested. The ANI instruction masks-out the four MSBs of register A. The CPI instruction then sets or clears the flags based on whether or not one of the 3, 7, 11, or 15 keys is pressed. If no keys in the "A" column are pressed, the 8080 should scan the keyboard's B line. If none of the keys in the 3, 7, 11, and 15 column is pressed, the key code in register D is decremented by 1 and then checked to see if it has been decremented to 377 (FF). This would indicate that all four columns of the keyboard had been scanned. If register D is not equal to this value, the next column of the keyboard matrix must be tested. If register D does contain a 377 (FF), the JMP to KEYSCN is executed. At KEYSCN, the 8080 starts scanning the keyboard again.

If one of the keys is pressed, the 8080 jumps to NXTKEY, where it rotates the four outputs of the keyboard (V, W, X, and Y), which have already been input, into the carry. When a logic 0 is rotated into the carry, the 8080 returns from the KEYSCN subroutine with the binary key code for the key that is pressed, in the D register. If a logic 1 is rotated into the carry instead, a 004 (04) is added to the content of register D to create the key code for the next key within the same column. The 8080 continues to execute the instructions within the NXTKEY section of the subroutine until a 0 is rotated into the carry.

Suppose that the KEYSCN subroutine has just been called, and that the "7" key is pressed. The test pattern, 1110, is output to the latch so that the keys in the 3, 7, 11, and 15 column can be tested. Remember that the program rotates and stores the test pattern so that it will be set up for the next column test. The four keyboard output lines are input and tested to determine if one of the keys within the tested column is pressed. In this case, the pattern, 1101, has been input, since the "7" key is pressed. The NXTKEY portion of the subroutine rotates the input pattern into the carry. If the carry is equal to 0, the 8080 returns to the program that called KEYSCN. If a 1 is rotated into the carry instead, 004 (04) is added to the initial key code to generate the key code for the next key in the column that can be tested; in this example, the "7" key. The pattern is again rotated. After this second rotation, the 0 is detected in the carry and the 8080 returns from the subroutine with the key code for the key that is pressed, in the D register. If a column is tested and no key is found to be pressed, the starting key code in the D register is decremented by 1 to correspond to the starting code for the next column.

Suppose that two keys are pressed simultaneously, such as the "9" and "12" keys. What key code will the 8080 contain in register D after it returns from the KEYSCN subroutine? The 8080 will return with the key code 011 (09) in register D. This is because the combination of the C and X lines is tested before the combination of the D and Y lines. Can you determine the priority of all the keys; that is, can you create a list that shows what key code will be contained in the D register, if two or more keys are pressed at the same time? We obtained the following priority:

$$3 > 7 > 11 > 15 > 2 > 6 > 10 > 14 > 1$$
$$> 5 > 9 > 13 > 0 > 4 > 8 > 12$$

What changes have to be made to the hardware and software so that a 25-key keyboard, arranged as a 5×5 key matrix, can be interfaced and used with the 8080 microcomputer? An additional output port bit and an additional input port bit have to be incorporated into the interface electronics. The schematic for the keyboard interface appears in Fig. 7-6.

As you can see, another four-bit latch integrated circuit (SN7475) is required, so that one additional bit of the data bus, bit D_4, can be latched when the proper output instruction is executed. Another

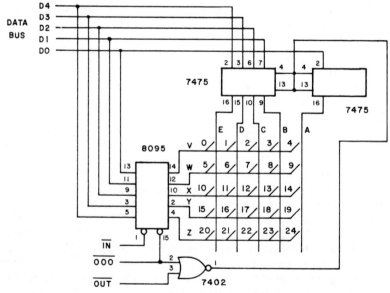

Fig. 7-6. The interface schematic for a 5 × 5 matrix keyboard.

DM8095 is not required, because each DM8095 integrated circuit contains six individual three-state buffers. Therefore, the additional row of the keyboard simply has to be connected to one of these previously unused three-state buffers, and its corresponding output connected to bit D_4 of the data bus.

Surprisingly enough, no additional software instructions need to be added to the previous KEYSCN subroutine (Example 7-13) that we used! However, some changes must be made to the subroutine. The data byte for the MVID instruction must be changed from 003 (03) to 004 (04), since the "4" key is the first key that can be detected. Likewise, the data byte for the ANI instruction must be changed from 017 (0F) to 037 (1F), because the keyboard now has five data output lines: V, W, X, Y, and Z. The data byte for the CPI instruction must also be changed from 017 (0F) to 037 (1F). Finally, the data byte for the ADI instruction in the NXTKEY section of the subroutine must be changed from 004 (04) to 005 (05). These changes have been incorporated in the KEYSCN subroutine listed in Example 7-14.

Regardless of whether a 5×5 or a 4×4 keyboard is used, there is still a serious problem with both of these subroutines (Examples 7-13 and 7-14). *No provision has been made in the software for debouncing the key closures.* Using the 4×4 matrix keyboard scan subroutine as an example, the 10-ms delay subroutine that we used in Example 7-11 will be used to debounce the key closures.

The subroutine in Example 7-15 senses a key closure in the same manner that the previous subroutine examples did. The only changes in the subroutine occur beginning at NXTKEY. When the 8080 senses that a key is pressed, it jumps to NXTKEY to determine exactly which key is pressed. However, the 8080 first calls the DELAY subroutine so that the key opening is debounced. When the 8080 returns from the DELAY subroutine, it executes the RRC instruction at AGAIN. If this instruction rotates a logic 0 into the carry, the JNC to RELESE is executed, rather than an RNC instruction, which was used in the previous subroutines.

When the 8080 executes the instructions at RELESE, it is waiting for the key that is pressed to be released. When the key is released, the four keyboard output lines, and thus the four input lines to the 8080, will be at a logic 1. Therefore, the 8080 will continue to execute the instructions in the RELESE loop until all of these lines are sensed as logic 1s. When the key is released, the 8080 calls the DELAY subroutine a second time, so that the key bounce, due to the releasing of the key, is ignored by the microcomputer.

As you can see in Table 7-4, there are a number of advantages and disadvantages in replacing hardware devices (integrated circuits and wires) with software instructions.

Example 7-14: A 5 × 5 Matrix Keyboard Scan Subroutine

```
/THIS SUBROUTINE SCANS A MATRIX KEYBOARD
/THAT IS ARRANGED AS FIVE ROWS OF FIVE KEYS,
/A 5×5 KEY MATRIX.

KEYSCN,   MVID      /LOAD D WITH THE CODE FOR THE
          004       /FIRST KEY THAT CAN BE SENSED.
          MVIB      /LOAD B WITH THE WORD THAT IS USED TO
          376       /ACTIVATE ONE ROW OF KEYS AT A TIME.
NXTGRP,   MOVAB     /GET THE TEST WORD
          OUT       /AND OUTPUT IT TO THE KEYBOARD.
          000
          RLC       /ROTATE THE TEST WORD LEFT ONE BIT,
          MOVBA     /AND THEN SAVE IT IN B.
          IN        /INPUT THE DATA FROM THE FIVE
          000       /ROWS OF KEYS.
          ANI       /SAVE ONLY THE FIVE LSB'S, WHICH CON-
          037       /TAIN THE ROW DATA.
          CPI       /SEE IF ANY KEYS ARE PRESSED BY
          037       /COMPARING 037 (1F) TO THE INPUT WORD.
          JNZ       /A KEY IS PRESSED IN THIS ROW, SO
          NXTKEY    /DETERMINE WHICH KEY IT IS.
          0
          DCRD      /NO KEYS ARE PRESSED IN THE TESTED ROW,
          MOVAD     /SO DECREMENT THE KEY CODE BY ONE AND
          CPI       /SEE IF ALL FIVE ROWS HAVE BEEN TESTED.
          377       /377 = HEX FF.
          JNZ       /NOT ALL FIVE ROWS HAVE BEEN TESTED,
          NXTGRP    /SO TEST ANOTHER ROW.
          0
          JMP       /ALL THE ROWS HAVE BEEN TESTED AND
          KEYSCN    /NO KEYS ARE PRESSED, SO KEEP LOOKING.
          0
NXTKEY,   RRC       /ROTATE THE ROW DATA INTO THE CARRY.
          RNC       /RETURN WHEN THE CARRY IS ZERO.
          PUSHPSW   /OTHERWISE SAVE THE PSW ON THE STACK
          MOVAD     /AND INCREASE THE KEY CODE IN D BY 5.
          ADI
          005
          MOVDA     /SAVE THE KEY CODE IN D.
          POPPSW    /POP THE PSW OFF THE STACK
          JMP       /AND THEN TRY FOR A ZERO CARRY
          NXTKEY    /AGAIN.
          0
```

INTERFACING ASCII-BASED KEYBOARDS TO THE 8080

Many keyboards are commercially available that contain 50 or more keys. Encoding logic is provided on these keyboards so that when a key is pressed, a specific code for the key is generated. In general, these keyboards produce seven- or eight-bit ASCII characters. How are these types of keyboards interfaced to the 8080?

Example 7-15: A 4 × 4 Keyboard Scan Subroutine With Debounce Instructions

```
/THIS SUBROUTINE SCANS A MATRIX KEYBOARD
/THAT IS ARRANGED AS FOUR ROWS OF FOUR KEYS,
/A 4×4 KEY MATRIX. IN ADDITION, INSTRUCTIONS
/HAVE BEEN ADDED TO THE SUBROUTINE TO DEBOUNCE
/THE KEYS.

KEYSCN,   MVID      /LOAD D WITH THE CODE FOR THE
          003       /FIRST KEY THAT CAN BE SENSED.
          MVIB      /LOAD B WITH THE WORD THAT IS USED TO
          376       /ACTIVATE ONE ROW OF KEYS AT A TIME.
NXTGRP,   MOVAB     /GET THE TEST WORD
          OUT       /AND OUTPUT IT TO THE KEYBOARD.
          000
          RLC       /ROTATE THE TEST WORD LEFT ONE BIT,
          MOVBA     /AND THEN SAVE IT IN B.
          IN        /INPUT THE DATA FROM THE FOUR
          000       /ROWS OF KEYS.
          ANI       /SAVE ONLY THE FOUR LSB'S, WHICH CON-
          017       /TAIN THE ROW DATA.
          CPI       /SEE IF ANY KEYS ARE PRESSED BY
          017       /COMPARING 017 (0F) TO THE INPUT WORD.
          JNZ       /A KEY IS PRESSED IN THIS ROW, SO
          NXTKEY    /DETERMINE WHICH KEY IT IS.
          0
          DCRD      /NO KEYS ARE PRESSED IN THE TESTED ROW,
          MOVAD     /SO DECREMENT THE KEY WORD BY ONE AND
          CPI       /SEE IF ALL FOUR ROWS HAVE BEEN TESTED.
          377       /377 = HEX FF.
          JNZ       /NOT ALL FOUR ROWS HAVE BEEN TESTED,
          NXTGRP    /SO TEST ANOTHER ROW.
          0
          JMP       /ALL THE ROWS HAVE BEEN TESTED AND
          KEYSCN    /NO KEYS ARE PRESSED, SO KEEP LOOKING.
          0
NXTKEY,   CALL      /A KEY IS PRESSED, SO EXECUTE THE
          DELAY     /DELAY SUBROUTINE FOR 10 MS.
          0
AGAIN,    RRC       /ROTATE THE ROW DATA INTO THE CARRY.
          JNC       /FOUND THE KEY, SO WAIT FOR IT TO
          RELESE    /BE RELEASED BEFORE RETURNING FROM
          0         /THE SUBROUTINE.
          PUSHPSW   /OTHERWISE, SAVE THE PSW ON THE STACK
          MOVAD     /AND INCREASE THE KEY CODE IN D BY 4.
          ADI
          004
          MOVDA     /SAVE THE NEW KEY CODE IN D.
          POPPSW    /POP THE PSW OFF OF THE STACK,
          JMP       /AND THEN TRY FOR A ZERO CARRY
          AGAIN     /AGAIN.
          0
RELESE,   IN        /INPUT THE DATA WORD AGAIN.
          000
```

```
          ANI          /SAVE ONLY THE FOUR DATA BITS THAT
          017          /REPRESENT FOUR ROWS OF KEYS.
          CPI          /COMPARE THIS VALUE TO THE VALUE OBTAINED
          017          /WHEN NO KEYS ARE PRESSED (017, HEX 0F).
          JNZ          /JUMP IF A KEY IS STILL PRESSED,
          RELESE       /AND WAIT FOR IT TO BE RELEASED.
          0
DELAY,    PUSHPSW      /SAVE THE PSW ON THE STACK.
          PUSHD        /THEN SAVE REGISTER PAIR D ON THE STACK.
          LXID         /LOAD REGISTER PAIR D WITH A COUNT
          101          /OF 003 101 (HEX 0341).
          003
WAIT,     DCXD         /DECREMENT THE COUNT.
          MOVAD        /MOVE THE MSBY TO A.
          ORAE         /OR IT WITH THE LSBY.
          JNZ          /IF THE RESULT IS NONZERO, JUMP
          WAIT         /TO THE DCXD INSTRUCTION.
          0
          POPD         /WHEN IT IS ZERO, POP D&E OFF OF THE STACK,
          POPPSW       /AND THEN POP THE PSW OFF OF THE STACK
          RET          /AND RETURN WITH THE KEY CODE IN D.
```

**Table 7-4. The Advantages and Disadvantages of
Substituting Software for Hardware**

Advantages

1. Lower microcomputer production costs, because the amount of hardware is smaller.
2. Smaller printed-circuit boards, as long as a large amount of additional memory is not required by the additional software.
3. Hardware circuits are less complex, which means shorter debugging time during production.
4. It is easier to duplicate software than hardware. Someone can program the ROMs for you.
5. Flexibility. It is easier to update software in the field, simply by plugging in some additional memory integrated circuits. Hardware revisions in the field can be very simple or very complex.

Disadvantages

1. Slower execution speed. It takes longer to determine the proper key code when scanning a keyboard with software than if a hardware encoder is used.
2. The execution speed or cycle time of the CPU limits how fast I/O operations can be performed.
3. The initial development costs of the software can be many times greater than the initial development costs of the hardware. Most savings, due to the substitution of software for hardware, occur in the production of the microcomputer system.

Interfacing one of these keyboards is almost as easy as interfacing a 16-key keyboard that has hardware encoding logic, such as the first keyboard example in this chapter. As shown in previous keyboard examples, there has to be some way of notifying the microcomputer, either through hardware or software, that a key has been pressed. Most of the ASCII keyboards have a *status line* that indicates whether or not a key is pressed. Since this is a hardware status line or flag, it will have to be input into the microcomputer, and the state of the flag will have to be determined by executing a few software instructions.

Let us assume that the keyboard being interfaced to the 8080 produces eight-bit ASCII characters. Because of this, two input ports will be required in the interface. One input port is used to input the *status* of the keyboard, and the other input port is used to input the eight-bit ASCII characters produced by the keyboard encoder logic. This keyboard interface is shown in Fig. 7-7.

If an IN 001 instruction is executed, the *status of the keyboard* will be input into the A register as bit D_4. When an IN 000 instruction is executed, the eight-bit ASCII character for the key that is pressed will be input into the A register. The software required to sense a key closure, and then input the eight-bit ASCII char-

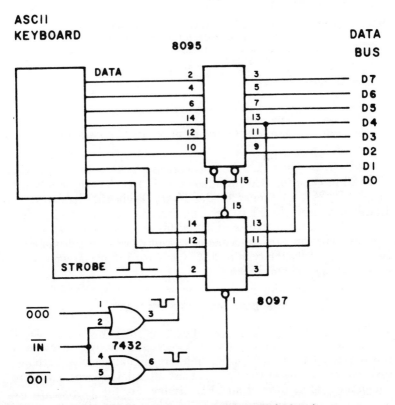

Fig. 7-7. The interface for an eight-bit ASCII keyboard.

acter, is very similar to the software that was used to read the key codes from a 16-key keyboard equipped with the hardware encoder.

By examining this software, you should be able to determine the state of the status line from the keyboard, both when a key is pressed and when no key is pressed. The flag or status line of the keyboard is a logic 0 when no keys are pressed, and it is a logic 1 when a key is pressed. Of course, there are ASCII keyboards where the *sense* of the status line is reversed. Example 7-16 could also be used with this type of keyboard, but the JZ to ASCKEY would have to be changed to a JNZ to ASCKEY. This change is probably easier than the addition of an inverter integrated circuit to the interface electronics.

Example 7-16: The Software to Sense and Input Key Codes From an ASCII Keyboard

```
/THIS SUBROUTINE SENSES A KEY CLOSURE ON AN
/ASCII KEYBOARD AND THEN INPUTS THE EIGHT-BIT
/PARALLEL ASCII KEY CODE.

ASCKEY,   IN      /INPUT THE DATA WORD THAT CONTAINS
          001     /THE STATUS BIT FOR THE ASCII KEYBOARD.
          ANI     /SAVE ONLY THE STATUS BIT FOR
          020     /THE KEYBOARD.
          JZ      /JUMP BACK TO ASCKEY IF THE STATUS BIT
          ASCKEY  /IS ZERO, BECAUSE NO KEY IS PRESSED.
          0
          IN      /A KEY IS PRESSED, SO INPUT THE
          000     /ASCII CODE INTO A,
          RET     /AND THEN RETURN TO THE CALLING PROGRAM.
```

We have assumed that the keyboard produces a strobe pulse of 15 or 20 µs duration. However, some ASCII keyboards simply produce a logic level similar to the 16-key keyboard that was previously discussed. If this is the case, then software instructions will have to be executed that sense a key being pressed and also being released. The software instructions that must be executed will really be determined by the type of ASCII keyboard that you want to interface to the 8080 microcomputer.

THE 8080 AND LED DISPLAYS

At some point in your programming you may want the 8080 to output data to a peripheral device. As we have discussed previously, this device could be a teletypewriter, crt, digital cassette, or floppy disk. However, one of the devices most often interfaced to a microcomputer is some form of an LED display. For this reason, we will interface some seven-segment LED displays to the 8080 microcomputer. These are the same type of displays used in hand-held calculators and digital clocks.

For a particular 8080 application, you want the 8080 to output a 10-digit, BCD number to seven-segment displays. One method of doing this is to use an SN7475 latch, an SN7447 or SN7448 decoder, seven resistors, and a seven-segment display for each digit. The schematic for wiring these devices together for a single digit is shown in Fig. 7-8.

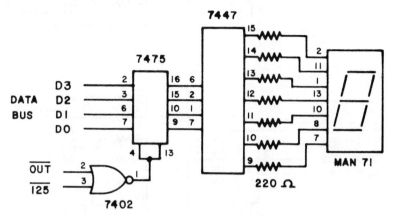

Fig. 7-8. A four-bit output port with a seven-segment display.

As you can see from this diagram, the input lines of the SN7475 latch are wired to the 8080's data bus. Only when an OUT 125 instruction is executed will the SN7475 latch the four LSBs of the data bus. This four-bit data value appears at the outputs of the latch that are used to drive the SN7447 decoder. The decoder determines which of the segments within the display are to be turned on, so that the value latched is actually displayed. Once a value is latched by the SN7475, it takes only about 50 ns for the decoder to decode the number and turn on the appropriate segments of the display. For more information about decoders and seven-segment displays, the reader should refer to *Logic & Memory Experiments Using TTL Integrated Circuits, Book 1* and *Book 2*[2]. Unit 5 of Book 1 deals entirely with decoders, and Unit 6 of Book 2 deals entirely with light-emitting diodes (LEDs). Both of these books provide experiments that you can perform with these devices.

By wiring an additional latch, decoder, and display (Fig. 7-9), with the inputs of the latch wired to bits D_4 through D_7 of the data bus, two BCD digits can be output by the 8080 at the same time, to the same output port. In this way, efficient use is made of an eight-bit data transfer for the two four-bit BCD digits.

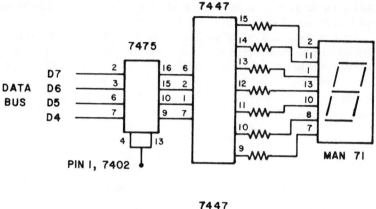

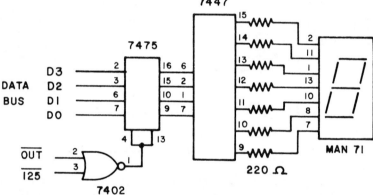

Fig. 7-9. A two-digit, seven-segment LED display interfaced to the 8080.

What software instructions have to be executed so that the number 39 is displayed on these displays? To display this number, the instructions in Example 7-17 can be executed. This program simply loads the A register with an immediate data byte, and then outputs the data to the displays. The 0011 is latched by the latch wired to bits D_4 through D_7 of the data bus, and the 1001 is latched by the latch wired to bits D_0 through D_3 of the data bus. This means that two BCD digits are packed into one eight-bit word.

What does the program listed in Example 7-18 do? Assume that the 8080 has a clock cycle time of 500 ns. This program will cause the displayed number to be incremented about once every 3/4 of a second. The count starts at 00 and reaches a maximum of 99. When 99 is reached, the count goes to 00 and the counting continues. The DELAY section of the program produces a delay of about 3/4 of a second each time the count is incremented. This delay has been added so that we can see the count change on the displays. To

Example 7-17: How to Output a 39 to the Seven-Segment LED Displays

```
/THIS SECTION OF A PROGRAM OUTPUTS THE
/BIT PATTERN 00111001 (OCTAL 071, HEX 39)
/TO AN OUTPUT PORT EQUIPPED WITH TWO
/SEVEN-SEGMENT DISPLAYS.
            •
            •
       MVIA   /LOAD A WITH THE FOLLOWING IMMEDIATE
       071    /DATA BYTE (HEX 39, BINARY 00111001).
       OUT    /OUTPUT IT TO THE SEVEN-SEGMENT
       125    /DISPLAYS EQUIPPED WITH LATCHES.
        •     /CONTINUE WITH THE REMAINDER OF THE
        •     /PROGRAM.
```

actually generate the count, a 001 (01) is added to the number stored in the B register, and the result is adjusted with the DAA instruction. This means that the content of register B is always a two-digit BCD number with a value between 00 and 99.

Example 7-18: Displaying a Count on Two, Seven-Segment Displays

```
START,  MVIB   /LOAD B, WHICH IS USED FOR TEMPORARY
        000    /STORAGE, WITH 000 (HEX 00).
DISPLY, MOVAB  /MOVE THE CONTENT OF B TO A.
        OUT    /OUTPUT A TO THE TWO SEVEN-SEGMENT
        125    /DISPLAYS EQUIPPED WITH LATCHES.
        ADI    /ADD ONE TO THE CONTENT OF A.
        001
        DAA    /DECIMAL ADJUST THE RESULT
        MOVBA  /AND SAVE THE RESULT IN B.
        CALL   /CALL A DELAY SUBROUTINE THAT RE-
        DELAY  /QUIRES APPROXIMATELY ¾ SECOND
        0      /TO BE EXECUTED.
        JMP    /THEN JUMP BACK TO THE DISPLAY
        DISPLY /SECTION OF THE PROGRAM.
        0
DELAY,  LXID   /LOAD REGISTER PAIR D WITH
        000    /000 000 (HEX 0000).
        000
WAIT,   DCXD   /DECREMENT THE CONTENT OF REGISTER PAIR D.
        MOVAD  /MOVE THE MSBY TO A.
        ORAE   /OR IT WITH THE LSBY.
        JNZ    /IF THE RESULT IS NONZERO,
        WAIT   /JUMP BACK TO WAIT.
        0
        RET    /OTHERWISE, RETURN.
```

To study a more complex problem, let's design the hardware and write the software to display a 10-digit BCD number that is stored in memory. To do this, five of the previous circuits (Fig. 7-9) will have to be constructed. Since each display has the capability of displaying two digits, five circuits can be used to display 10 digits. Of course, to display a 10-digit number, the five circuits will have to have different device addresses.

The number is stored in five consecutive memory locations as two-digit packed BCD numbers. The number 2,389,421,365 is stored as shown in Table 7-5. As you can see, one of the advantages of using the hexadecimal numbering system is that it is easy to work with BCD numbers. To display this number, we need 10 SN7475

Table 7-5. Storing the Number 2,389,421,365 in Memory

OCTAL		HEX	
Memory Location	Content	Content	Memory Location
004 120	145	65	0450
004 121	023	13	0451
004 122	102	42	0452
004 123	211	89	0453
004 124	043	23	0454

latches, 10 SN7447 decoders, 70 resistors, 10 seven-segment displays, and some additional gates to complete the interface. We will assume that the device addresses for the latches are 125, 126, 127, 130, and 131 (55, 56, 57, 58, and 59), where device address 131 (59) latches the packed BCD numbers contained in the A register into the two most-significant digits of the display. A program that fetches the data values stored in memory and outputs them to the displays appears in Example 7-19.

In this program (Example 7-19), the 8080 simply fetches a value from memory into register A, outputs the eight-bit value to an output port, increments the memory address by 1, and then outputs the content of the next memory location to another output port. Once all five data words (two BCD digits per word) have been output, the 8080 returns from the DISPLY subroutine. The 10-digit number that is displayed will remain displayed until the DISPLY subroutine is called again. This could happen in a minute, an hour, or a day from now.

Perhaps the largest problem associated with this method of displaying the content of memory is that many integrated circuits are required in the display interface. The cost of 10 latches, 10 decoders, and 70 resistors is over 20 dollars, in production quantities. This does not include the cost of the displays, device address decoders, or the miscellaneous integrated circuits required to complete the interface. As you can see, this type of display is relatively expensive.

A much less expensive method that can be used to display the same amount of information is to *multiplex* the display. This means

Example 7-19: The Software for a 10-Digit LED Display

```
/THIS SUBROUTINE DISPLAYS THE CONTENT
/OF FIVE CONSECUTIVE MEMORY LOCATIONS, WHICH
/EACH CONTAIN TWO PACKED BCD DIGITS.

DISPLY,  LXIH     /LOAD REGISTER PAIR H WITH
         120      /THE MEMORY ADDRESS WHERE THE NUMBERS
         004      /TO BE DISPLAYED, ARE STORED.
         MOVAM    /GET A WORD FROM MEMORY.
         OUT      /OUTPUT IT TO TWO DISPLAYS.
         125
         INXH     /INCREMENT THE MEMORY ADDRESS.
         MOVAM    /GET A WORD FROM MEMORY.
         OUT      /OUTPUT IT TO TWO DISPLAYS.
         126
         INXH     /INCREMENT THE MEMORY ADDRESS.
         MOVAM    /GET A WORD FROM MEMORY.
         OUT      /OUTPUT IT TO TWO DISPLAYS.
         127
         INXH     /INCREMENT THE MEMORY ADDRESS.
         MOVAM    /GET A WORD FROM MEMORY.
         OUT      /OUTPUT IT TO TWO DISPLAYS.
         130
         INXH     /INCREMENT THE MEMORY ADDRESS.
         MOVAM    /GET A WORD FROM MEMORY.
         OUT      /OUTPUT IT TO TWO DISPLAYS.
         131
         RET      /RETURN FROM THIS SUBROUTINE.
```

that only one digit in the multidigit display is turned on at a time. However, the digits are turned on and off so fast that the eye sees the display as being "on" all the time. By turning only a single digit on at a time, only two latches and two decoders are required to drive the display. The two decoders are required so that the data bus is not only decoded to turn on the required segment within the display, but to permit current to flow through only one display at any instant in time. This may seem like a complex method of displaying data, but electronically, it is reasonably simple. For this reason, *electronic calculators* and *digital watches* have *multiplexed displays*. In fact, unless you are reading this by candlelight or flashlight, the light that you are using is really flashing on and off, 60 times a second! This rate is just fast enough so that your eye cannot detect it. The same is true for the pictures that appear on your television set.

The schematic for a 10-digit multiplexed LED display is shown in Fig. 7-10. As you can see by examining the schematic diagram, only a single eight-bit output port is used in the interface. This requires only two SN7475 latches, an SN7442 decoder, and a National Semiconductor DM8857 seven-segment driver. The National Semi-

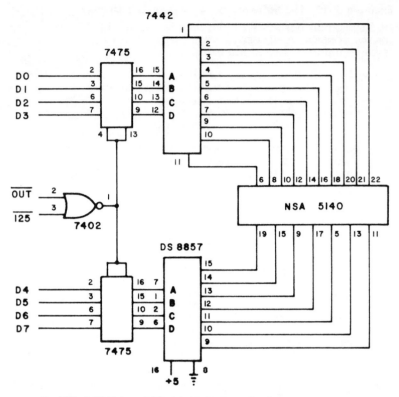

Fig. 7-10. A 10-digit, multiplexed LED display under microcomputer control.

conductor NSA-5140 display is specifically designed to display multiplexed seven-segment data words. Although this display can display 14 digits, we will use only 10 digits.

To display data on this display, we have to load bits D_0 through D_3 of register A with a *digit enable code* (the digit that we want to turn on), and bits D_4 through D_7 with the BCD data that we want displayed. To display the number "5" on the third digit, we would load register A with 01010010, and then output this to the interface. Since there are 10 digits in the display that we will use, the digit enable codes range from 0000 to 1001, which means that the third digit has a digit enable code of 0010. When an OUT 125 instruction is executed, the 0101 is latched by the SN7475 connected to the DM8857 integrated circuit, and the 0010 is latched by the SN7475 that is connected to the SN7442 decoder that is used as the digit enable decoder.

Based on how we have wired these integrated circuits to the microcomputer, the digit with the 0000 enable code is on the far right (the LSD), and the digit with the digit enable code of 1001 is on the far left (the MSD). To display the number 2,389,421,365, which is still stored in memory, the program listed in Example 7-20 can be executed. At the beginning of this program, register pair H is loaded with the memory address where the two least-significant digits (LSDs) are stored. Only five memory locations are required to store the 10-digit number, because the 10-digit number is stored in a packed BCD format. The D register, which is used to store the digit enable code, is then set to zero. The content of register D, which will eventually be latched by the interface hardware, is used to turn on one and only one digit at a time. If the software does this quickly enough, all of the digits in the display will appear to be "on" at the same time. At DISPL1, the DIGIT subroutine is called. At DIGIT, the content of memory addressed by register pair H is moved to register A. Since the data values are stored in memory as packed BCD digits, this subroutine will have to unpack them. The digit in the four LSBs of register A must be displayed first. Therefore, the content of register A is rotated to the left four times. The digit that is to be displayed is now in bits D_4 through D_7 of the A register. The OUTIT subroutine is then called.

At OUTIT, the four LBSs of register A are masked-out by the ANI instruction. Only the digit to be displayed is now contained in the A register, bits D_4 through D_7. The digit-enable code, contained in the D register, is then added to register A, and the result of this addition is then output to output port 125 (55). When this word is output, the four LSBs are used to determine which digit is to be enabled, and the four MSBs represent the value that is to be displayed on the enabled digit. If the memory location addressed by register pair H contains the packed BCD word 37 (octal 67, hexadecimal 37, binary 00110111), what is contained in register A when the output instruction in the OUTIT subroutine is executed? The A register contains 01110000 (octal 160, hexadecimal 70). This means that a "7" will be displayed on digit 0. This is the digit on the far right-hand side of the display, the LSD.

At the end of the OUTIT subroutine, the content of register D is incremented by 1 from 000 (00) to 001 (01). This means that the next digit to be enabled will be just to the left of the display that is currently on. Remember, the digit will stay on until the 8080 executes another output instruction that enables a different digit within the display. When the 8080 returns from the OUTIT subroutine, it will return to the MOVAM instruction just before OUTIT.

This instruction moves the same two-digit packed BCD word in memory to register A, but this time the most-significant BCD digit in the word has to be displayed. For this reason, no rotate instructions are executed. Therefore, at OUTIT, the ANI instruction sets

Example 7-20: The Software for a Multiplexed, 10-Digit, Seven-Segment Display

/THIS PROGRAM DRIVES A 10-DIGIT, MULTIPLEXED,
/LIGHT-EMITTING DIODE (LED), SEVEN-SEGMENT DISPLAY.

```
DISPLA,  LXIH    /LOAD REGISTER PAIR H WITH THE MEMORY
         120     /ADDRESS WHERE THE BCD DIGITS ARE STORED.
         004     /004 120 = HEX 0450.
         MVID    /LOAD D WITH THE FIRST DIGIT
         000     /POSITION THAT WILL BE ENABLED.
DISPL1,  CALL    /DISPLAY THE FIRST TWO PACKED
         DIGIT   /BCD DIGITS.
         0
         INXH    /INCREMENT THE MEMORY ADDRESS.
         MOVAD   /GET THE DIGIT ENABLE WORD INTO A.
         CPI     /COMPARE IT TO THE
         012     /ELEVENTH DIGIT ENABLE COUNT.
         JNZ     /HAVEN'T DISPLAYED ALL TEN
         DISPL1  /DIGITS YET, SO DO TWO MORE.
         0
         JMP     /HAVE DISPLAYED ALL TEN DIGITS,
         DISPLA  /SO DISPLAY THEM ALL AGAIN.
         0
DIGIT,   MOVAM   /GET THE PACKED BCD WORD INTO A.
         RLC     /ROTATE THE FOUR LSB BITS INTO THE
         RLC     /FOUR MSB BITS.
         RLC
         RLC
         CALL    /THEN DISPLAY THIS DIGIT.
         OUTIT
         0
         MOVAM   /GET THE SAME WORD AGAIN.
OUTIT,   ANI     /SAVE ONLY THE FOUR MSB'S.
         360     /(360 = HEX F0).
         ADDD    /ADD THE DIGIT ENABLE.
         OUT     /OUTPUT THE EIGHT-BIT VALUE.
         125
         INRD    /INCREMENT THE DIGIT ENABLE.
         RET
```

bits D_0 through D_3 of register A to zero while retaining the second digit that is to be displayed in bits D_4 through D_7. The digit-enable code in register D is then added to register A, and the result is output to the display interface electronics. This time, the digit enable code is 001 (01), so the second digit in the display is enabled. Only when this occurs is the first digit turned off. The INRD instruction then increments the content of register D to 002 (02) and the RET instruction returns program control to the INXH instruction.

This instruction increments the memory address contained in register pair H, so that it addresses the next packed BCD word stored in memory. The 8080 then checks to see if the digit-enable code stored in register D is equal to 012 (0A). This value is one more than the digit-enable code required to turn on the tenth or most-significant digit in the display. If all 10 digits have not been displayed yet, the JNZ to DISPL1 is executed, so that the next two BCD digits stored in a single memory location are displayed. If all 10 digits have been displayed, the 8080 jumps back to DISPLA. At DISPLA, the digit-enable code and memory address are re-initialized, and the display process is repeated. This means that the 8080 is *continually* executing these instructions, so that all 10 digits of information are displayed.

When we executed this program on one of our 8080 microcomputers, we found that the second, fourth, sixth, eighth, and tenth digits in the display were brighter than the other five digits. Can you account for this difference in display intensity? The reason that some digits are brighter than others is due to the difference in time it takes the 8080 to display one digit as opposed to another. Does it take the 8080 longer to fetch and display the least-significant BCD digit or the most-significant BCD digit contained in the same eight-bit word? It takes the 8080 a slightly longer time to fetch and display the least-significant digit of the two that are "packed" in a single eight-bit word. Do you know why? The reason is that it takes the 8080 longer to get a least-significant BCD digit from memory, rotate it into bits D_4 through D_7 of the A register, and display it. Also, after the most-significant BCD digit in a word is displayed, the 8080 has to return from the DIGIT subroutine. The memory address is then incremented, and the digit-enable code checked to see if it is equal to 012 (0A). If it is not, the 8080 calls the DIGIT subroutine again, so that the least-significant BCD digit in the next eight-bit word can be displayed. Therefore, the 8080 takes more time to "process" the least-significant BCD digits, so the most-significant BCD digits are displayed for a longer period of time.

To solve this problem, a delay subroutine can be incorporated into the display program. The delay program must produce a delay that is many times greater than the difference in time that it takes to display the two digits contained in an eight-bit word. Therefore, even though the most-significant BCD digits are on for a greater length of time than the least-significant digits, the actual difference in the times is very small. A DISPLA program that has this delay software incorporated in it is listed in Example 7-21.

Is there any reason why the most-significant digit, on the left-hand side of the display, cannot be displayed first? Absolutely not. The program listed in Example 7-22 does just that. This means that the digit-enable will start at 011 (09) and the decremented to 000 (00) and then to 377 (FF). It also means that when a word is read

Example 7-21: A 10-Digit Multiplexed Display Program With Intensification Instructions

```
/THIS PROGRAM DRIVES A TEN-DIGIT, MULTIPLEXED
/LIGHT-EMITTING DIODE (LED), SEVEN-SEGMENT DISPLAY.
/IN ADDITION, INSTRUCTIONS HAVE BEEN ADDED SO THAT
/THE INTENSITY OF EACH DISPLAY IS EQUAL.


DISPLA,   LXIH      /LOAD REGISTER PAIR H WITH THE MEMORY
          120       /ADDRESS WHERE THE BCD DIGITS ARE STORED.
          004       /004 120 = HEX 0450.
          MVID      /LOAD D WITH THE FIRST DIGIT
          000       /THAT WILL BE ENABLED.
DISPL1,   CALL      /DISPLAY THE FIRST TWO PACKED
          DIGIT     /BCD DIGITS.
          0
          INXH      /INCREMENT THE MEMORY ADDRESS.
          MOVAD     /GET THE DIGIT ENABLE WORD INTO A.
          CPI       /COMPARE IT TO THE
          012       /ELEVENTH DIGIT ENABLE COUNT.
          JNZ       /HAVEN'T DISPLAYED ALL TEN
          DISPL1    /DIGITS YET, SO DO TWO MORE.
          0
          JMP       /HAVE DISPLAYED ALL TEN DIGITS,
          DISPLA    /SO DISPLAY THEM ALL AGAIN.
          0
DIGIT,    MOVAM     /GET THE PACKED BCD WORD INTO A.
          RLC       /ROTATE THE FOUR LSB BITS INTO THE
          RLC       /FOUR MSB BITS.
          RLC
          RLC
          CALL      /THEN DISPLAY THIS DIGIT.
          OUTIT
          0
          MOVAM     /SAVE ONLY THE FOUR MSB'S.
OUTIT,    ANI       /SAVE ONLY THE FOUR MSBS.
          360       /(360 = HEX F0).
          ADDD      /ADD THE DIGIT ENABLE.
          OUT       /OUTPUT THE EIGHT-BIT VALUE.
          125
          INRD      /INCREMENT THE DIGIT ENABLE.
INTENS,   MVIE      /LOAD E WITH A NUMBER.
          100       /100 = HEX 40.
INTEN1,   DCRE      /DECREMENT THE NUMBER.
          JNZ       /IF IT IS NONZERO, EXECUTE THE
          INTEN1    /JNZ INSTRUCTION BACK TO INTEN1.
          0
          RET       /WHEN E = 0, RETURN.
```

from memory, the most-significant BCD digit is displayed first and then the least-significant BCD digit is displayed.

The program listed in Example 7-22 is exactly the same length as the program in Example 7-21 that displays the least-significant BCD digit first. However, a number of changes had to be made to

Example 7-22: A Program to Display the Most-Significant Digit First

```
/THIS PROGRAM DRIVES A TEN-DIGIT, MULTIPLEXED,
/LIGHT-EMITTING DIODE (LED), SEVEN-SEGMENT DISPLAY.
/IN ADDITION, INSTRUCTIONS HAVE BEEN ADDED SO THAT
/THE INTENSITY OF EACH DISPLAY IS EQUAL.
/THIS PROGRAM DISPLAYS THE MOST-SIGNIFICANT
/DIGIT FIRST.
```

```
DISPLA,   LXIH      /LOAD REGISTER PAIR H WITH THE MEMORY
          124       /ADDRESS WHERE THE MSB BCD DIGITS ARE
          004       /STORED. 004 124 = HEX 0454.
          MVID      /LOAD D WITH THE FIRST DIGIT
          011       /THAT WILL BE ENABLED.
DISPL1,   CALL      /DISPLAY THE FIRST TWO PACKED
          DIGIT     /BCD DIGITS.
          0
          DCXH      /DECREMENT THE MEMORY ADDRESS.
          MOVAD     /GET THE DIGIT ENABLE WORD INTO A.
          CPI       /COMPARE IT TO THE
          377       /ELEVENTH DIGIT ENABLE.
          JNZ       /HAVEN'T DISPLAYED ALL TEN
          DISPL1    /DIGITS YET, SO DO TWO MORE.
          0
          JMP       /HAVE DISPLAYED ALL TEN DIGITS,
          DISPLA    /SO DISPLAY THEM AGAIN.
          0
DIGIT,    MOVAM     /GET THE PACKED BCD WORD INTO A.
          CALL      /DISPLAY THE MOST SIGNIFICANT
          OUTIT     /DIGIT IN THIS WORD FIRST.
          0
          MOVAM     /GET THE SAME WORD FROM MEMORY INTO A.
          RLC       /ROTATE THE FOUR LSB BITS INTO THE
          RLC       /FOUR MSB BITS.
          RLC
          RLC
OUTIT,    ANI       /SAVE ONLY THE FOUR MSB'S.
          360       /(360 = HEX F0).
          ADDD      /ADD THE DIGIT ENABLE.
          OUT       /OUTPUT THE EIGHT-BIT VALUE.
          125
          DCRD      /DECREMENT THE DIGIT ENABLE.
INTENS,   MVIE      /LOAD E WITH A NUMBER.
          100       /100 = HEX 40.
INTEN1,   DCRE      /DECREMENT THE NUMBER.
          JNZ       /IF IT IS NONZERO, EXECUTE THE
          INTEN1    /JNZ INSTRUCTION BACK TO INTEN1.
          0
          RET       /WHEN E = 0, RETURN.
```

the program so that the most-significant BCD digit is displayed first.
The address bytes for the LXIH instruction at the beginning of the
program had to be changed, so that the address where the two most-
significant digits are stored is loaded into register pair H. These are
the first two digits that are displayed. The data byte for the MVID

instruction is also changed, so that the most-significant digit of the display is enabled first. Since the most-significant digit is displayed first, DCXH and DCRD instructions have to be executed rather than INXH and INRD instructions. Therefore, after the DIGIT subroutine is called, the memory address in register pair H is decremented. After decrementing the address, the 8080 compares the content of register D to 377 (FF). This is because the last digit-enable code that is used is 000 (00), which is the digit-enable code for the digit on the right-hand side of the display.

What is the major difference between the hardware and software for the 10-digit multiplexed display, and the displays that required 10 latches and decoders? When the 8080 outputs the 10-digit number to the 10 latches used in the previous display interface (no schematic was shown for the entire 10-digit display; see Fig. 7-9), it only has to output the information once, because ten latches are used, one for each digit. Once this is done, the 8080 can perform other tasks, because the 10-digit display continues to display the latched number. Only when the 8080 executes the display subroutine a second time can the display change.

When the 8080 executes the multiplexed display software, the displayed data must be *constantly updated*. This means that the 8080 must constantly change the digit-enable code and data word. This must be done, because if the 8080 leaves any one digit enabled for too long a period of time, five or 10 seconds, the LED display will burn out, because of the high amount of current that is used to drive the display. Since each digit of the display is only on for one-tenth of the time, 10 times more current must be supplied to the display for equivalent brightness. If the 8080 must perform some other operation for 20 or 30 seconds, the display cannot be "driven" continuously by the software, the display should be turned off by the 8080 before this long sequence of instructions is executed. Only when the 8080 has the opportunity to reenter the display section of the program, should the display be turned on again. Rather than worry about turning the display on and off whenever the 8080 has to perform some other task, a simple addition to the interface electronics in Fig. 7-10 can be made to accomplish this same task.

The circuit in Fig. 7-11 uses an SN74123 retriggerable one-shot (monostable). Note that the same pulse that causes the SN7475 latches to latch the eight bits of data from the data bus (Fig. 7-10) is also used to trigger this integrated circuit. Whenever this occurs, the output of the one-shot remains in the logic 1 state (pin 13) for about 10 ms. This output goes to the enable input (pin 5) of the seven-segment decoder (DM8857). If this input to the decoder is ever taken to a logic 0, the outputs of the decoder will not supply any current to any of the segments within the display. How does

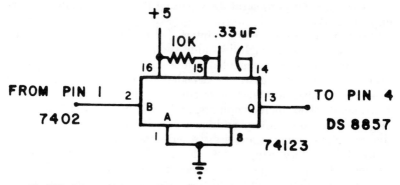

Fig. 7-11. An automatic power-off addition to the multiplexed display electronics.

this prevent a digit within the display from staying on too long? If OUT 125 instructions are not executed every 10 ms or so, the Q output of the one-shot will go back to a logic 0, causing the display to *blank* or turn off. If the OUT 125 instruction is executed at least this often, the display will display the data values that are latched out to it. If the 8080 ever has to execute another sequence of instructions for longer than 10 ms, the display will turn off. Only when the 8080 executes the instructions in the DISPLA program will the display be turned on.

You have now seen a number of different hardware and software examples that can be used with keyboards and displays. Some methods require more hardware than others, and some require more software than others. The choice of one method over another will be determined by (1) the amount of hardware you want to design and build, (2) your ability to write programs for the particular interfaces that you have constructed or purchased, or (3) your ability to apply the software examples that we have presented, to your particular interface. Last, and certainly not least, your choice of a hardware-intensive or software-intensive design should be determined by whether or not it is the best way of accomplishing your particular interfacing task.

MEMORY-MAPPED I/O

By now, you should be very familiar with accumulator I/O. When accumulator I/O is performed, IN and OUT instructions are used to transfer data between the A register in the 8080 and peripheral devices. If a peripheral device is wired to the 8080 microcomputer's address and data buses in the same manner as a memory device, and the control signals $\overline{\text{MEMR}}$ and $\overline{\text{MEMW}}$ are used to gate data onto and off of the data bus, then data can be transferred between the 8080 and the peripheral device using the 8080's memory reference instructions.

When peripheral devices are interfaced to the microcomputer for accumulator I/O, an eight-bit address has to be decoded so that only one I/O device is enabled at one time. For memory-mapped I/O, a 16-bit address has to be decoded. To do this requires a considerable number of integrated circuits. For this reason, some manufacturers of 8080 microcomputers, and some users, often allocate a large number of memory addresses just for memory-mapped I/O devices. For instance, some users reserve the upper 32K of memory space, for memory-mapped I/O devices. This means that memory address bit A_{15} is a logic 1 whenever the 8080 addresses a memory-mapped I/O device, and a logic 0 whenever the 8080 addresses memory. A simple decoder that can be used with up to 16 memory-mapped write, and 16 memory-mapped read devices, is shown in Fig. 7-12.

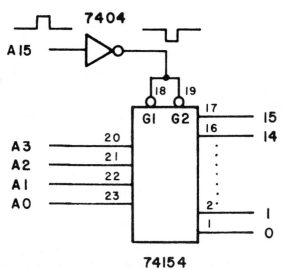

Fig. 7-12. A nonabsolute, memory-mapped I/O device address decoder.

The logic 0 outputs of this decoder still have to be gated with either $\overline{\text{MEMW}}$ or $\overline{\text{MEMR}}$, as required by the particular memory-mapped I/O device. When will the outputs of the decoder in Fig. 7-12 go to a logic 0? The outputs will go to a logic 0 when one of the memory locations between,

10000000   00000000

and

10000000   00001111

is addressed. These addresses correspond to 200 000 through 200 017 (8000 through 800F). Of course, since this is a *nonabsolute decoder*, which means that not all 16 address bits have been decoded, there are 2^{12} addresses that will cause the outputs of the decoder to go to a logic 0. For instance, the decoder cannot distinguish between the addresses listed in Table 7-6. All will generate a logic 0 at output 0, pin 1.

Table 7-6. Addresses That Cannot Be Distinguished by the Decoder in Fig. 7-12

10000000	00000000
10000001	00000000
10000000	11000000
10010001	10000000
11111111	11110000
11111111	00000000

As you can see in the schematic diagram of the decoder (Fig. 7-12), address bits A_{14} through A_4 are not decoded. Therefore, they can assume any value and the decoder will still decode address bits A_0 through A_3 when A_{15} is a logic 1.

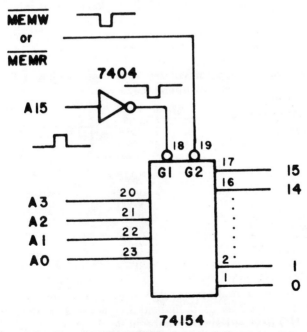

Fig. 7-13. Using $\overline{\text{MEMW}}$ or $\overline{\text{MEMR}}$ to enable the SN74154 decoder.

The decoder section of a memory-mapped I/O interface can be simplified by using either the $\overline{\text{MEMW}}$ or $\overline{\text{MEMR}}$ signal to enable the decoder (Fig. 7-13). In most 8080 microcomputer systems, two of these decoders would be required, one to enable devices that the 8080 can read data from, and one to enable devices that the 8080 can write data to. The $\overline{\text{MEMW}}$ signal is wired to the decoder used with devices that are written to, and $\overline{\text{MEMR}}$ is wired to the decoder used with devices that can be read from by the 8080. The signals from these decoders cannot only be used to transfer data between the 8080 and the memory-mapped I/O devices, but they can also be used for control. Ordinarily, only the outputs of the decoder enabled by $\overline{\text{MEMW}}$ would be used for this purpose. For software examples of how the 8080 communicates with memory-mapped I/O devices, some of the same examples used in the beginning of this chapter will be used.

A MEMORY-MAPPED I/O KEYBOARD WITH HARDWARE ENCODER

As you will remember, bit D_7 of the interface (Table 7-3) is the status bit of the keyboard. When it is a logic 1, the four LSBs of the word contain the key code for the key that is pressed. If bit D_7 is a logic 0, then no key is pressed. If the keyboard is interfaced to the 8080 as a memory-mapped I/O device, any of the subroutines listed in Example 7-23 can be used to wait for a key closure and read the key code.

Example 7-23: Methods of Waiting, and Then Reading a Key Code (Memory-Mapped I/O)

KEYIN,	PUSHH	KEYIN,	PUSHB	KEYIN,	PUSHD
	LXIH		LXIB		LXID
	000		000		000
	200		200		200
KEY1,	MOVAM	KEY1,	LDAXB	KEY1,	LDAXD
	ADI		ADI		ADI
	200		200		200
	JNC		JNC		JNC
	KEY1		KEY1		KEY1
	0		0		0
	ANI		ANI		ANI
	017		017		017
	POPH		POPB		POPD
	RET		RET		RET

Really, these subroutines are very similar. The only difference is which register pair is used to hold the address of the memory-mapped I/O device. Using the subroutine that uses register pair H as an example, the 8080 first saves register pair H on the stack when the KEYIN subroutine is called. After this is done, register pair H is loaded with the 16-bit address of the I/O device. What is this address? The address for the keyboard is 200 000 (8000). After this address is loaded into register pair H, the 8080 reads the eight-bit word from the keyboard into the A register. When the MOVAM instruction is executed, the address contained in register pair H is placed on the address bus, and the $\overline{\text{MEMR}}$ line is pulsed. Since this is the address of the keyboard, the data from the keyboard is placed on the data bus and gated into the A register. Just as there were no two accumulator I/O devices that placed data on the data bus at the same time, there cannot be two memory-mapped I/O devices that place data on the data bus at the same time. *Therefore, no memory (R/W or read-only) can have the same address as a memory-mapped I/O device.*

When the data from the keyboard is in register A, a 200 (80) is added to the content of register A. If the carry is a logic 0 as a result of this addition, then bit D_7 was a logic 1, which means that a key is pressed. If the carry is a logic 0 as a result of the addition, then bit D_7 was a logic 0 and no keys are pressed. Therefore, if no keys are pressed, the JNC to KEY1 is executed. If a key is pressed, the ANI instruction is then executed to mask-out the four MSBs. Register pair H is then popped off of the stack, and the 8080 returns from the subroutine with the four-bit key code in the A register.

As you can see, the software for this memory-mapped I/O keyboard is longer than the subroutine that performs the same functions using accumulator I/O. Example 7-24 contains two equivalent subroutines, one using memory-mapped I/O and the other using accumulator I/O. None of the other hardware encoder keyboard examples will be converted to memory-mapped I/O and discussed.

A MEMORY-MAPPED I/O, MULTIPLEXED (SCANNED) KEYBOARD

Few changes are required to convert the multiplexed (scanned) keyboard (Example 7-13) from accumulator I/O to memory-mapped I/O.

In this subroutine (Example 7-25), register pair H is pushed onto the stack and then loaded with the 16-bit address for the keyboard. Register pair B is then loaded with the first test pattern to be written out to the keyboard (376, FE), and the key code for the first key that can be detected (003, 03). The B register holds the test pattern and the C register holds the key code. In the previous scanned keyboard examples, registers B and D were used, so an LXIB instruction could not be used.

The first instruction at NXTGRP writes the test pattern contained in register B out to the keyboard interface electronics. This instruc-

Example 7-24: A Comparison of Accumulator and Memory-Mapped I/O Subroutines

Memory-Mapped I/O

```
/THIS SUBROUTINE WAITS FOR BIT D7 TO BE A
/LOGIC ONE. THIS IS SENSED BY ADDING 200
/(HEX 80) TO THE INPUT PORT DATA. WHEN THE
/FLAG IS A ONE, THE CARRY IS A ONE AND THE FOUR-
/BIT KEY CODE REMAINS IN A! THE KEYBOARD IS
/INTERFACED TO THE 8080 AS A MEMORY-MAPPED
/I/O DEVICE.

KEYIN,  PUSHH   /SAVE REGISTER PAIR H ON THE STACK.
        LXIH    /LOAD REGISTER PAIR H WITH THE
        000     /16-BIT ADDRESS FOR THE I/O
        200     /DEVICE.
KEY1,   MOVAM   /READ A CHARACTER FROM THE KEYBOARD INTO A.
        ADI     /ADD TO THIS, 200 (HEX 80). IF THE
        200     /CARRY IS 0, THE FLAG IS 0 !
        JNC     /THE CARRY IS ZERO, SO THE FLAG IS
        KEY1    /ZERO. THEREFORE CONTINUE WAITING FOR
        0       /THE FLAG TO BE A ONE.
        ANI     /MASK OUT THE FOUR MSB'S WITH
        017     /017(HEX 0F)
        POPH    /POP REGISTER PAIR H OFF OF THE STACK.
        RET     /RETURN WITH THE KEY CODE IN A.
```

Accumulator I/O

```
/THIS SUBROUTINE WAITS FOR BIT D7 TO BECOME A
/LOGIC ONE. THIS IS SENSED BY ADDING 200
/(HEX 80) TO THE INPUT PORT DATA. WHEN THE STATUS
/BIT IS A ONE, THE CARRY IS A ONE AND THE FOUR-
/BIT KEY CODE REMAINS IN A!

KEYIN,  IN      /INPUT AN EIGHT-BIT WORD THAT CON-
        000     /TAINS THE STATUS AND DATA BITS.
        ADI     /ADD 200 (HEX 80) TO THIS. IF THE
        200     /CARRY IS 0, THE FLAG IS 0 !
        JNC     /THE CARRY IS ZERO, SO THE FLAG IS
        KEYIN   /ZERO. THEREFORE CONTINUE WAITING FOR
        0       /THE FLAG TO BE A ONE.
        ANI     /MASK OUT THE FOUR MSB'S WITH 017
        017     /(HEX 0F) AND RETURN WITH THE KEY
        RET     /CODE IN THE A REGISTER.
```

tion can only be executed because the 16-bit address for the keyboard is in register pair H. The content of register B is then moved to register A, rotated once to the left, and then saved back in the B register. This simply creates the next test pattern that will be written out to the keyboard, if it is required. The 8080 then reads the four-bit data word from the keyboard into register A by executing a MOVAM instruction. The four MSBs of register A are then masked-out, and the result compared to 017 (0F). If no keys are pressed within the column of keys being tested, register A will con-

tain 017 (0F). If a key within the column is pressed, the 8080 will
have to determine which key is pressed.

Example 7-25: A Memory-Mapped I/O, 4 × 4 Matrix, Keyboard Scan Subroutine

```
/THIS SUBROUTINE SCANS A MATRIX KEYBOARD
/THAT IS ARRANGED AS FOUR ROWS OF FOUR KEYS,
/A 4×4 KEY MATRIX. THE KEYBOARD IS INTERFACED TO THE
/8080 USING MEMORY-MAPPED I/O TECHNIQUES.

KEYSCN,  PUSHH       /SAVE REGISTER PAIR H ON THE STACK.
         LXIH        /LOAD REGISTER PAIR H WITH THE
         005         /16-BIT ADDRESS ASSIGNED TO THE
         200         /KEYBOARD.
         LXIB        /LOAD REGISTER PAIR B WITH 376 003
         003         /(FE03). B=TEST PATTERN AND
         376         /C CONTAINS THE CODE FOR THE FIRST KEY.
NXTGRP,  MOVMB       /WRITE THE TEST PATTERN TO THE KEYBOARD.
         MOVAB       /THEN MOVE THE TEST PATTERN INTO A.
         RLC         /ROTATE THE TEST PATTERN LEFT ONE BIT,
         MOVBA       /AND THEN SAVE IT IN B.
         MOVAM       /READ THE KEYBOARD'S OUTPUT INTO A.
         ANI         /SAVE ONLY THE FOUR LSB'S, WHICH CON-
         017         /TAIN THE ROW DATA.
         CPI         /SEE IF ANY KEYS ARE PRESSED BY
         017         /COMPARING 017 (0F) TO THE INPUT WORD.
         JNZ         /A KEY IS PRESSED IN THIS ROW, SO
         NXTKEY      /DETERMINE WHICH KEY IT IS.
         0
         DCRC        /NO KEYS ARE PRESSED IN THE TESTED ROW,
         MOVAC       /SO DECREMENT THE KEY CODE BY ONE.
         CPI         /SEE IF ALL FOUR ROWS HAVE BEEN TESTED.
         377         /377 = HEX FF.
         JNZ         /NOT ALL FOUR ROWS HAVE BEEN TESTED,
         NXTGRP      /SO TEST ANOTHER ROW.
         0
         JMP         /ALL THE ROWS HAVE BEEN TESTED AND
         KEYSCN      /NO KEYS ARE PRESSED, SO KEEP LOOKING.
         0
NXTKEY,  RRC         /ROTATE THE ROW DATA INTO THE CARRY.
         JC          /THE CARRY IS A ONE, SO TRY
         ADDIT       /ANOTHER KEY POSITION.
         0
         POPH        /THE CARRY IS A ZERO, POP REGISTER
         RET         /PAIR H OFF OF THE STACK, THEN RETURN.
ADDIT,   PUSHPSW     /OTHERWISE, SAVE THE PSW ON THE STACK
         MOVAC       /AND INCREASE THE KEY CODE IN C BY 4.
         ADI
         004
         MOVCA       /SAVE THE NEW KEY CODE IN C.
         POPPSW      /POP THE PSW OFF OF THE STACK
         JMP         /AND THEN TRY FOR A ZERO CARRY
         NXTKEY      /AGAIN.
         0
```

Most of the remaining instructions in Example 7-25 are the same as those used in Example 7-13. However, not that since register pair H was pushed on the stack at the beginning of the subroutine, the 8080 cannot execute an RNC instruction just after NXTKEY. Instead, a JC to ADDIT is executed if the logic 0 for the key that is pressed is not rotated into the carry. When a logic 0 is rotated into the carry, register pair H is popped off of the stack, and the 8080 returns from the subroutine with the key code for the key that is pressed in register C. In the previous accumulator I/O, scanned keyboard subroutines, register D was used to store the key code for the key that was pressed. The subroutine that scans the memory-mapped I/O keyboard is five memory locations longer than the subroutine that scans the accumulator I/O keyboard.

MEMORY-MAPPED I/O LED DISPLAYS

One of the first programs that output data to a pair of seven-segment displays, caused the displayed count to be incremented by one, every 3/4 of a second. Once the interface electronics are changed from accumulator I/O to memory-mapped I/O, memory reference instructions can be used to transfer the changing count to the displays.

The program listed in Example 7-26 loads the 16-bit memory address for the two-digit, memory-mapped I/O LED display into register pair H. The B register is then cleared because it will be used to store the count being displayed. At DISPLY, the content of register B is written out to the LED displays, and then moved to register A. One is added to the content of the A register, and the result adjusted by the DAA instruction. The result is then saved back in the B register. The DELAY subroutine is then called. The 8080 returns from the DELAY subroutine approximately 3/4 of a second later. The 8080 then jumps back to DISPLY, where the incremented count is written out to the displays.

In one of the other display examples, the 8080 output the packed BCD content of five consecutive memory locations to 10 seven-segment displays. Each display was equipped with an SN7475 latch and an SN7447 decoder. If this same data must be written out to a memory-mapped I/O display, the 8080 will have to have two memory pointers, one for the data values stored in memory, and one for the different seven-segment displays.

The subroutine listed in Example 7-27 first loads the I/O address for the LED displays into register pair B. The address for the data values stored in memory is then loaded into register pair H. The 8080 then moves an eight-bit value from memory to register A, using the content of register pair H as the memory address. The content

Example 7-26: A Counter Program for Memory-Mapped I/O LED Displays

```
COUNT,   LXIH    /LOAD REGISTER PAIR H WITH THE 16-BIT
         125     /MEMORY ADDRESS ASSIGNED TO THE TWO
         200     /DIGIT DISPLAY (8055).
         MVIB    /LOAD B, WHICH IS USED FOR TEMPORARY
         000     /STORAGE, WITH 000 (HEX 00).
DISPLY,  MOVMB   /WRITE THE CONTENT OF B TO THE DISPLAYS.
         MOVAB   /MOVE THE DATA WORD TO A.
         ADI     /ADD ONE TO THE CONTENT OF A.
         001
         DAA     /DECIMAL ADJUST THE RESULT
         MOVBA   /AND SAVE THE RESULT IN B.
         CALL    /CALL A DELAY SUBROUTINE THAT RE-
         DELAY   /QUIRES APPROXIMATELY ¾ SECOND
         0       /TO BE EXECUTED.
         JMP     /THEN JUMP BACK TO THE DISPLAY
         DISPLY  /SECTION OF THE PROGRAM.
         0
DELAY,   LXID    /LOAD REGISTER PAIR D WITH
         000     /000 000 (HEX 0000).
         000
WAIT,    DCXD    /DECREMENT THE CONTENT OF REGISTER PAIR D.
         MOVAD   /MOVE THE MSBY TO A.
         ORAE    /OR IT WITH THE LSBY.
         JNZ     /IF THE RESULT IS NONZERO,
         WAIT    /JUMP BACK TO WAIT.
         0
         RET     /OTHERWISE, RETURN.
```

of register A is then written out to the memory-mapped I/O LED displays by the STAXB instruction. The two memory addresses are then incremented by 1, and then the next data word is moved from memory to the displays. As you might guess, this subroutine can be greatly simplified through the use of a loop.

In Example 7-28, register pair B is loaded with the memory-mapped I/O address, and register pair H is loaded with the memory address where the data values are stored. The D register is then loaded with 005 (05), because five memory locations are used for data storage, and there are five pairs of LED displays. At DLOOP, a data word is read from memory into the A register and then written out to the displays. The memory addresses are then incremented (INXH, INXB) by 1, and the word count in register D is decremented by 1. If this count is nonzero, the JNZ to DLOOP is executed, so that another word is transferred from memory to the displays. When all five words have been written out to the displays, the 8080 returns from the DISPLY subroutine.

This subroutine demonstrates another advantage of memory-mapped I/O. *A loop can be used to write data to, or read data from,*

Example 7-27: The Software for a Memory-Mapped I/O, 10-Digit LED Display

```
/THIS SUBROUTINE DISPLAYS THE CONTENT
/OF FIVE CONSECUTIVE MEMORY LOCATIONS, WHICH
/EACH CONTAIN TWO PACKED BCD DIGITS. THE DISPLAYS
/ARE INTERFACED TO THE 8080 AS MEMORY-MAPPED
/I/O DEVICES.

DISPLY, LXIB    /LOAD REGISTER PAIR B WITH THE FIRST
        125     /ADDRESS ASSIGNED TO THE DISPLAY
        200     /(8055).
        LXIH    /LOAD REGISTER PAIR H WITH
        120     /THE MEMORY ADDRESS WHERE THE NUMBERS
        004     /TO BE DISPLAYED ARE STORED.
        MOVAM   /GET A WORD FROM MEMORY.
        STAXB   /WRITE IT OUT TO THE DISPLAYS.
        INXB    /INCREMENT THE I/O DEVICE ADDRESS.
        INXH    /INCREMENT THE MEMORY ADDRESS.
        MOVAM   /GET A WORD FROM MEMORY.
        STAXB   /WRITE IT OUT TO THE DISPLAYS.
        INXB    /INCREMENT THE I/O DEVICE ADDRESS.
        INXH    /INCREMENT THE MEMORY ADDRESS.
        MOVAM   /GET A WORD FROM MEMORY.
        STAXB   /WRITE IT OUT TO THE DISPLAYS.
        INXB    /INCREMENT THE I/O DEVICE ADDRESS.
        INXH    /INCREMENT THE MEMORY ADDRESS.
        MOVAM   /GET A WORD FROM MEMORY.
        STAXB   /WRITE IT OUT TO THE DISPLAYS.
        INXB    /INCREMENT THE I/O DEVICE ADDRESS.
        INXH    /INCREMENT THE MEMORY ADDRESS.
        MOVAM   /GET A WORD FROM MEMORY.
        STAXB   /WRITE IT OUT TO THE DISPLAYS.
        RET     /RETURN FROM THIS SUBROUTINE.
```

Example 7-28: A Loop for a Memory-Mapped I/O, 10-Digit LED Display

```
/THIS PROGRAM USES A LOOP TO WRITE THE CONTENT
/OF MEMORY OUT TO THE TEN-DIGIT DISPLAY. THE
/DISPLAY IS INTERFACED TO THE 8080 AS A
/MEMORY-MAPPED I/O DEVICE.

DISPLY, LXIB    /LOAD REGISTER PAIR B WITH THE ADDRESS
        125     /ASSIGNED TO THE FIRST DISPLAY
        200     /(8055).
        LXIH    /THEN LOAD REGISTER PAIR H WITH THE
        120     /MEMORY ADDRESS WHERE THE NUMBERS TO
        004     /BE DISPLAYED ARE STORED (0450).
        MVID    /LOAD D WITH THE NUMBER OF WORDS.
        005     /005 = 05.
DLOOP,  MOVAM   /MOVE THE NUMBERS TO A FROM MEMORY.
        STAXB   /THEN WRITE THE NUMBER TO THE DISPLAY.
        INXH    /INCREMENT THE MEMORY ADDRESS.
        INXB    /INCREMENT THE I/O ADDRESS.
        DCRD    /DECREMENT THE WORD COUNT.
        JNZ     /IF THE COUNT IS NONZERO, THEN
        DLOOP   /JNZ TO DLOOP SO THAT ANOTHER WORD
        0       /IS WRITTEN OUT TO THE DISPLAY.
        RET     /WHEN THE COUNT IS ZERO, RETURN.
```

memory-mapped I/O devices that have consecutive addresses. This is not possible if the I/O devices are accumulator I/O devices, because the device addresses are actually part of an instruction. Therefore, loops cannot be used to access accumulator I/O devices that have consecutive addresses. However, most 8080 microcomputer systems do not have a large number of I/O devices that need to be accessed in this manner. Therefore, this advantage is often of little importance.

A MEMORY-MAPPED I/O, 10-DIGIT MULTIPLEXED DISPLAY

As you know from previous multiplexed display examples, most of the instructions in the programs deal with the manipulation of data words as they are read from memory. In fact, there was only one OUT instruction in the entire DISPLA program (Examples 7-20, 7-21, and 7-22). This OUT instruction was in the OUTIT section of the program. This means that very few modifications to the program are required, so that the data words are written out to a memory-mapped I/O, 10-digit multiplexed display.

Only one change is required to the previous display program (Example 7-21), so that a memory reference instruction can be used to write the data/digit-enable word out to the display interface. This change involves the substitution of an STA instruction for the OUT instruction, in the OUTIT section of the program. The remainder of the program is the same. Note that this example displays the digits from right to left (LSD to MSD), with intensification of the digits.

CONCLUSION

As you have seen, there are many more software instructions that can be used to communicate with a memory-mapped I/O device than can be used to communicate with an accumulator I/O device. In fact, two memory reference instructions can be used to transfer 16-bit words between the 8080 and memory, and memory-mapped I/O devices. What are these instructions? The SHLD and LHLD instructions. However, the interface electronics for memory-mapped I/O devices can be more complex, particularly in the area of device address decoders. The choice of one method over the other is really determined by which method will best accomplish the interfacing task. The cost of the interface, the speed at which data can be transferred over the interface, and the cost of the software required to "drive" the interface must all be considered. To date, most microcomputer manufacturers supply I/O devices for the 8080 that operate as accumulator I/O devices. Some manufacturers also

Example 7-29: A Program for a Memory-Mapped I/O, Multiplexed, 10-Digit, Seven-Segment Display, With Intensification

```
/THIS PROGRAM DRIVES A TEN-DIGIT, MULTIPLEXED,
/LIGHT-EMITTING DIODE (LED), SEVEN-SEGMENT DISPLAY.
/IN ADDITION, INSTRUCTIONS HAVE BEEN ADDED SO THAT
/THE INTENSITY OF EACH DISPLAY IS EQUAL. THE DISPLAY
/IS INTERFACED TO THE 8080 AS A MEMORY-MAPPED
/I/O DEVICE.


DISPLA,   LXIH      /LOAD REGISTER PAIR H WITH THE MEMORY
          120       /ADDRESS WHERE THE BCD DIGITS ARE STORED.
          004       /004 120 = HEX 0450.
          MVID      /LOAD D WITH THE FIRST DIGIT
          000       /THAT WILL BE ENABLED.
DISPL1,   CALL      /DISPLAY THE FIRST TWO PACKED
          DIGIT     /BCD DIGITS.
          0
          INXH      /INCREMENT THE MEMORY ADDRESS.
          MOVAD     /GET THE DIGIT ENABLE WORD INTO A.
          CPI       /COMPARE IT TO THE
          012       /ELEVENTH DIGIT ENABLE COUNT.
          JNZ       /HAVEN'T DISPLAYED ALL TEN
          DISPL1    /DIGITS YET, SO DO TWO MORE.
          0
          JMP       /HAVE DISPLAYED ALL TEN DIGITS,
          DISPLA    /SO DO IT AGAIN.
          0
DIGIT,    MOVAM     /GET THE PACKED BCD WORD INTO A.
          RLC       /ROTATE THE FOUR LSB WORDS INTO THE
          RLC       /FOUR MSB BITS.
          RLC
          RLC
          CALL      /THEN DISPLAY THE DIGIT.
          OUTIT
          0
          MOVAM     /GET THE SAME WORD AGAIN.
OUTIT,    ANI       /SAVE ONLY THE FOUR MSB'S.
          360       /(360 = HEX F0).
          ADDD      /ADD THE DIGIT ENABLE.
          STA       /WRITE THE DIGIT-ENABLE CODE
          125       /AND THE BCD DATA OUT TO THE MUL-
          200       /TIPLEXED DISPLAY (200 125 = HEX 8055).
          INRD      /INCREMENT THE DIGIT ENABLE.
INTENS,   MVIE      /LOAD E WITH THE NUMBER.
          100       /100 = HEX 40.
INTEN1,   DCRE      /DECREMENT THE NUMBER.
          JNZ       /IF IT IS NONZERO, EXECUTE THE
          INTEN1    /JNZ INSTRUCTION BACK TO INTEN1.
          0
          RET       /E = 0, SO RETURN.
```

supply I/O devices that can be interfaced to the 8080 as either an accumulator I/O device or a memory-mapped I/O device. It is our opinion that you will find accumulator I/O to be simple and effective in interfacing most devices to 8080-based microcomputers. In some microcomputers, you do not have a choice. In 6800-based and 6502-based systems, for example, memory-mapped I/O is the only type available.

REFERENCES

1. Larsen, D. G., Rony, P. R., and Titus, J. A. *Introductory Experiments in Digital Electronics and 8080A Microcomputer Programming and Interfacing, Book 1* and *Book 2*. Howard W. Sams & Co., Inc., Indianapolis, IN, 1978.
2. Larsen, D. G., and Rony, P. R. *Logic & Memory Experiments Using TTL Integrated Circuits, Book 1* and *Book 2*. Howard W. Sams & Co., Inc., Indianapolis, IN, 1978.

Index

S

T

TO THE READER

This book is one of an expanding series of books that will cover the field of basic electronics and digital electronics from basic gates and flip-flops through microcomputers and digital telecommunications. We are attempting to develop a mailing list of individuals who would like to receive information on the series. We would be delighted to add your name to it if you would fill in the information below and mail this sheet to us. Thanks.

1. I have the following books:

_____

_____

_____

_____

_____

_____

_____

_____

_____

_____

_____

2. My occupation is: ☐ student   ☐ teacher, instructor   ☐ hobbyist

☐ housewife   ☐ scientist, engineer, doctor, etc.   ☐ businessman

☐ Other: _____

Name (print): _____

Address _____

City _____   State _____

Zip Code _____

Mail to:

Books
P.O. Box 715
Blacksburg, Virginia 24060